PENGUIN BOOKS

LOVE BLOCKS

Mary Ellen Donovan is coauthor of *Women and Self-Esteem,* the Penguin bestseller that touched the lives of hundreds of thousands of readers, and has been praised for "combining intelligent analysis with a no-nonsense guide for individual growth" (*Working Woman*). She has written about psychology and women's issues for many national magazines, and has appeared on numerous television and radio programs nationwide. She lives with her husband in New York City.

William P. Ryan, Ph.D., is a psychologist who has worked as a college teacher and clinical consultant in many settings. For the past fifteen years he has been a psychotherapist in private practice in Huntington, New York. Although this is his first book, Dr. Ryan has written a number of papers for academic journals. He makes his home in Huntington with his wife and two sons.

Love
Blocks

BREAKING
THE PATTERNS
THAT UNDERMINE
RELATIONSHIPS

Mary Ellen Donovan and
William P. Ryan, Ph.D.

PENGUIN BOOKS

PENGUIN BOOKS
Published by the Penguin Group
Viking Penguin, a division of Penguin Books USA Inc.,
375 Hudson Street, New York, New York 10014, U.S.A.
Penguin Books Ltd, 27 Wrights Lane, London W8 5TZ, England
Penguin Books Australia Ltd, Ringwood, Victoria, Australia
Penguin Books Canada Ltd, 2801 John Street,
Markham, Ontario, Canada L3R 1B4
Penguin Books (N.Z.) Ltd, 182–190 Wairau Road,
Auckland 10, New Zealand

Penguin Books Ltd, Registered Offices:
Harmondsworth, Middlesex, England

First published in the United States of America by
Viking Penguin, a division of Penguin Books USA Inc., 1989
Published in Penguin Books 1991

10 9 8 7 6 5 4 3 2 1

THE LIBRARY OF CONGRESS HAS CATALOGUED THE HARDCOVER AS FOLLOWS:
Donovan, Mary Ellen.
Love blocks / Mary Ellen Donovan and William P. Ryan.
p.   cm.
ISBN 0–670–81625–6 (hc.)
ISBN 0 14 00.9964 6 (pbk.)
1. Intimacy (Psychology)   2. Love.   3. Interpersonal relations.
4. Intimacy (Psychology) — Problems, exercises, etc.   5. Love —
Problems, exercises, etc.   6. Interpersonal relations — Problems,
exercises, etc.   I. Ryan, William P.   II. Title.
BF575.I5D66   1988
152.4′1 — dc20   87-40654

Printed in the United States of America

Contents

Preface

Are you completely satisfied with the quality of all your personal relationships?

Do you go to bed each night feeling truly valued, appreciated, and understood?

Do you wake up each morning and say to yourself, "Gee, there's so much love and joy in my life, I couldn't possibly want more"?

Are loneliness, alienation from others, and a sense of not really belonging all feelings you've never experienced?

Isn't there someone in your life—a relative, friend, lover, spouse, potential partner, or child—you'd like to feel closer to, more comfortable with, more loved by?

Chances are good you found these questions easy to answer, and that you responded to only the last one with yes. In this you're not alone. Today we're living in the midst of what has been aptly called "the intimacy crisis."[1] It's a crisis that touches nearly everyone in one way or another, and it's causing countless people considerable pain. We all have hopes for relationships that will bring us happiness, fulfillment, growth, and an end to loneliness, but most of the time the reality falls far short of the dream. For some, the problem is not being able to find someone with whom to have an intimate relationship. Others have no trouble establishing relationships but can't sustain or deepen them over time. Still others have stable, long-term relationships with friends, romantic partners, and family members but don't obtain from them much real joy or a sense of genuine connection and inner peace. For nearly all of us, though, there is *some* problem that causes us to feel less fulfilled by our personal lives than we would like to be. The tragic result is that although we all long to be valued and loved, many people end up going through life feeling lonely, misunderstood, unappreciated, uncared for, estranged, or in some other way vaguely dissatisfied.

This book is the joint effort of two people—Bill, a psychologist practicing for nearly two decades, and Mary Ellen, a writer specializing in psychology—who came together because of a shared interest in seeing an end to the intimacy crisis and in alleviating the pain it has created. We identify and explain fifteen common psychological patterns that prevent people from finding happiness and fulfillment in relationships. We call these patterns "love blocks," because, put simply, they act as inner obstacles that inhibit a person's ability both to receive and to give love.

Some people are affected by love blocks to the extent that they are incapable of forming intimate bonds, even if they say intimacy is something they very much want. Others are able to establish intimate relationships, but their love blocks prevent them from really connecting with their loved ones in the way they would like. Regardless of how severely we are affected, though, nearly all of us have a love block; most people, in fact, have more than one.

Some people will balk at this idea, claiming that the problems dealt with in this book are of no concern to them. But even if they don't have any love blocks themselves—and we seriously doubt any such people exist—it's a sure bet that they know many people who do. And since it takes two people to have a relationship, when one has a love block it inevitably causes problems for the other as well.

The original idea for this book grew out of Bill's experience with the numerous men and women who have come to him for psychotherapy over the years. As he listened to them, certain themes came up again and again, and definite patterns—which he later labeled "love blocks"—began to emerge. Meanwhile, Mary Ellen had become aware of many of these patterns, as well as some additional ones, in the course of research conducted for a previous book, *Women and Self-Esteem* (Penguin Books, 1985). Believing in the old adage about two heads being better than one, we decided to pool our resources and collaborate. The end result is something of a rarity in publishing—a book about love relationships written by a man and a woman, rather than by two men or two women, who are professional colleagues rather than a married couple.

To illustrate the love blocks detailed in the following pages, we use case histories culled both from Bill's practice and from additional interviews. Names and certain details have been changed to protect the identity of the people who generously granted us permission to tell their stories, and in a few instances we have drawn from several different sources to present composite accounts. But all the stories are those of real people, and all are presented in a way that is true to actual experience.

Some of the people whose stories are told here grew up in stable, economically sound, basically healthy families and had childhoods that would be commonly characterized as happy. Others, however, are children of alcoholics, or incest survivors, or victims of egregious abuse and neglect. Some lost parents early in life, through death or abandonment. Others had parents who were chronically depressed or otherwise mentally ill, while still others grew up under economic hardship. To readers who grew up in more fortunate circumstances, some of these stories might seem unusual, extreme, or even a bit exotic. But they are stories of ordinary people from ordinary homes with ordinary problems that affect millions. According to the latest statistics, for example, twenty-eight million adults are children of alcoholics, and one in four suffered some form of sexual abuse as children. If there seem to be "too many" people with unhappy childhoods among the case histories in these pages, it's not because we went out of our way to find such people—it's because there are "too many" unhappy childhoods in real life.

Love blocks get in the way of all kinds of relationships, and we've made an effort to present case histories that demonstrate this important fact. Most people become aware of their love blocks in sexual or romantic relationships and will be drawn to this book because of problems with a spouse or lover. But when people have a love block that's interfering with their romantic relationships, chances are also good that the same block is also affecting—although perhaps in less obvious ways—their relationships with friends, co-workers, parents, siblings, and their own children. Moreover, as other case histories demonstrate, love blocks can have a spiritual dimension. Some find their blocks prevent them not only from feeling as truly connected to other people as they would like, but also from achieving the sense of connection with the universe that they seek.

Just as love blocks can get in the way of all kinds of relationships, they also affect all kinds of people from all walks of life, as we hope our case material reflects. Many books about relationships presume that everyone is heterosexual, and thus overlook the experience of gay men and lesbians. The experience of those whose chosen paths in life preclude sexual relationships is usually ignored as well. But homosexuals suffer from love blocks just as much as heterosexuals do, and love blocks create just as many problems for celibates as for the sexually active.

Although love blocks affect all kinds of people and all kinds of relationships, many readers will be most concerned with the ways that love blocks interfere with relationships between men and women, and we give the problems of heterosexual couples considerable attention as a result. In so doing, we've made an effort to show that in heterosexual relationships, love blocks are just as much a problem for men as for women, and it's frequently the case that the love blocks a man and a woman bring to a relationship dovetail and exacerbate each other. Many recent books about love and relationship problems have been written expressly for women, focusing almost exclusively on the problems they encounter in their intimate relationships with men. But our belief is that focusing on women's problems alone implicitly blames women. This approach also illuminates only half the story. As a result, women readers may increase their understanding of their own problems while learning little about what is going on with the men in their lives. Moreover, a one-sided approach ignores the fact that if there's any hope for improving heterosexual relations, men as well as women must take responsibility for the ways they contribute to the problems that divide them.

Love Blocks should also have special appeal to people whose primary interest is in good parenting. Many people say it doesn't matter if they're dissatisfied with their own lives as long as their children grow up to be happy. But parents who don't make an effort to understand and overcome their own love blocks will almost certainly pass them on to their children. As adults, then, these children will have just as much trouble finding happiness in relationships as their parents did.

At this point some readers might be asking whether it is really possible for individuals to overcome their inner love blocks—and if so, how does one go about it? Simply stating that change is possible is not enough; it's also necessary to provide evidence. As a result, in presenting the various case studies we try to give as much attention to how the individuals changed as to how their love blocks developed. Since our cases include a few people who dropped out of therapy prematurely, and a couple of interviewees who were not actively trying to overcome their blocks, there are some instances in which we don't know if or how the individuals eventually changed. In those instances, we discuss ways in which a person with the same block *could* change. Moreover, in an effort to provide a larger context for the individual cases, in Chapter 3 we give a general explanation of what the change process involves and how it usually occurs.

In a concluding section, "Letting Go of Love Blocks: A Step-by-Step Guide," we also provide readers with specific tools that can be used to bring about change. Here we offer concrete, easy-to-follow exercises and suggestions that have been used successfully by psychotherapy clients. While we can't promise that these methods will magically whisk your love blocks away, we do think they can be extremely effective in helping you understand how your own love blocks originated, how they affect you, and how you can begin to break free of them. For those who want even more help, we also provide guidance on finding a psychotherapist and suggest other books for further reading.

As a final note, we should add that although we have tried to be comprehensive in our approach, this book is about *inner* obstacles. We're well aware that in today's world there are also many *external* obstacles that can make it hard to build and sustain deep, meaningful connections with others. People today move around more than ever in the past, and economic pressures force most of us to spend too many hours working and commuting. Moreover, work environments tend to require suppression of a wide range of emotions; consequently, many find that even when they're not at work it's difficult to switch these feelings back on. The day-to-day chores of life—doing the laundry, taking the kids to the doctor, paying the bills—also leave people with too little time and energy to devote to personal relationships. For gay people, the homophobia and discrimination that straight society subjects them to can create further obstacles to building and sustaining relationships. And such factors as racism, anti-Semitism, prejudice against foreigners, discrimination against people with disabilities, and economic competitiveness—all of which are sadly rife in American society today—also limit the possibilities for meaningful and loving connections. Although we touch on some of these external obstacles, exploring them in any depth is beyond the scope of this one book. It is our hope, however, that as people begin to understand and overcome the inner obstacles to fulfilling relationships, we'll all then be in a better position to do something about the external ones.

Acknowledgments

This book would never have come into being without the help of many other individuals. Barbara Lang Stern brought us together, beginning what has been an extremely happy and fruitful collaboration, and an experience that has taught both of us invaluable lessons about the nature and necessity of human interdependence. From the very early stages of this project, Felecia Abbadessa has not only done an excellent job as our agent, she's also provided invaluable moral support—which at times we sorely needed. Pat Mulcahy, our original editor, enthusiastically backed us as we began writing. Nan Graham, our later editor, and her assistant, Kathryn Harrison, offered useful criticisms. And Mark Jaskowiak and Malcolm Nolen provided financial help that made it possible to bring the project to completion. To all, we express our heartfelt thanks.

We'd also like to thank the numerous individuals who generously gave us permission to tell their life stories. Those stories are the backbone of this book, and they will no doubt be the source of great inspiration for many readers.

In addition, each of us has a list of people to whom we're individually indebted. Bill would like to thank:

—My psychotherapist, Don Millman, who encouraged me to write this book.

—One of my former supervisors, Nick Dellis, who helped me find a collaborator.

—My friends, particularly the "Greenhill Gang," who have provided unflagging interest and encouragement in the course of writing, and who stepped in to cheerlead at critical times.

—My clients, who continue to be my greatest teachers, and who graciously consented to allow their own individual therapy processes to feed the creative process of writing this book.

—My spiritual mentors, from whom I've derived much of the insight and creative energy that has gone into this process.

—My wife, Chris, and my sons, Mark and Scott, who have patiently endured and loved me as I've struggled to work out my own love blocks; and who have supported me throughout the emotional roller-coaster ride of writing this book.

Mary Ellen would like to thank:

—The many friends who offered support and helped in various ways during the several years it took to complete this project: Linsey Abrams, Robin Barnett, Bill Bercow, Larry Bercow, Bettina Blohm, Elizabeth Bradburn, Donna Cohen, Anne S. Frey, Drew Giblen, Roberta Grant, Charlie Griffith, Ann Grobe, Linden Gross, Jamey Hampton, Mary Haviland, Helen Hertzog, Liz Hettich, Mary Honey, Mark Jaskowiak, John Keenen, Leslie and N.P. Kannan, Martha Koen, Mary Koen, Christine Loomis, Marie LaPré-Grabon, Diane Mack, Linda Markin, Steve Markowitz, Janet Maughan, Becky Messenger, Rob Mitchell, Anna Monardo, Valerie Mullen, Andy Murr, Joshua Neustein, Sara Purcell, Florence Ribola, Terry Riley, Bruce Shenitz, Tina Sheppard, Hope Silver, Harriet Surovell, Tucker Viemiester, Ann Volkes, and Nancy Wasserman. I'd also like to mention some new friends met in the course of writing this book who've been particularly enthusiastic and encouraging: Kim Lake and Al Puchala.

—The members of my Monday night writers group, who have been a constant source of support, inspiration, perspective, and humor: Leslie Dormen, Shelley Levitt, and Julia Lieblich, along with former member Dottie Enrico, itinerant member Corrine LaBalme, and newer members Jennifer Hull and Judith Stone.

—The Writers Room in Greenwich Village, where I found the quiet and sense of belonging that I needed to work, and where I met and felt supported by many other writers, including Jim Ellison, Signe Hammer, Nancy Milford, Carole Miller, Bernice Selden, and Daniel Quinn.

—My former supervisors at *Newsweek,* Madeleine Edmondson and Barbara Griffiths, who taught me a great deal about writing and offered invaluable guidance and support; my *Newsweek* colleagues,

Alden Cohen, Pat Glossup, Vibhuti Patel, and Marie Whiteside, who were very enthusiastic about this project; and two other *Newsweek* staffers, Michele Daly and Rose Marolda, who always let me know they were behind me.

—My colleagues at the New York Association for New Americans, especially Ira Goetz, Masha Gologor, and Barbara Miller; and all the ESL teachers with whom I was fortunate to work.

—Devon McCormick, who lent several books and consistently cheered me on during the time when we were both working at the Cooper Union in 1986 and '87.

—My psychotherapist, Rosemary Poulos, who has been a companionable, compassionate, intelligent guide as I've worked on identifying and overcoming my own love blocks; and Stuart Rauch, who also played an important role in the process.

—Patrick Pace and the staff at St. Vincent's Hospital, who caringly saw me through a time of illness in the middle of writing this book.

—My father, Daniel Donovan; stepmother, Kay Dunfey; brother, Patrick Donovan; sisters, Meg Donovan and Paula Sherwood; and in-laws, Jennifer Donovan, Steve Dunfey, and Ross Sherwood: for providing me with a sense of family.

—My mother, Arline, and sister, Elizabeth, whose spirits live on in these pages.

—Grace and Ralph Bean: whose positive impact on my own childhood I've grown more aware and appreciative of as I've sifted through the numerous stories that have gone into this book.

—The members of the new family that I've been lucky to become part of while writing this book: Eliot and Wilson Nolen, Christian and Anson Nolen, Eliot Nolen, and Tim Bradley, whose company during nonworking times fortified me for the long stints at my desk.

—Malcolm Nolen, who has given me more love than I thought possible, and was there to steady me when the going got a bit rough.

Part One

Laying
the Groundwork

Chapter 1
The Loss of the Receptive Childhood Self: An Overview

It hardly needs to be pointed out that the world would be a much better place—and its inhabitants much happier—if there were more love to go around. One doesn't have to be a keen observer of human behavior to notice that alienation, apathy, and animosity abound. Nor does one have to be especially perceptive to see that most people have less fulfilling personal lives than they would like. Whether they are suffering the loneliness of wanting but not finding a partner, the misery of being in a dull or destructive marriage or relationship, the frustration of not getting along very well with their parents or siblings, the desolation of not having friends they can really open up to and confide in, or the sadness of feeling worlds apart from their children, most people can point to some area of their personal lives that's causing them unhappiness. Although we live in a society with no shortage of material goods, there just doesn't seem to be enough love to go around.

But how can we increase the amount of love in the world? How can individuals become more loving? Most writers on the subject base their answers to these questions on the assumption that if people learn to become better at giving love, they'll eventually receive more love in return.[1] This book rests on a very different premise. We believe that the question that needs to be tackled first is not "How can people become more loving?" but "How can people become more receptive to love?" This is because the root cause for the lack of love in the world today lies with people's inability to take in love. Put simply, most people today are unable to feel genuinely loved, and therefore encounter great difficulty being loving. When people learn to increase their capacity for taking in love, their capacity for giving love will increase.

How We Thwart Love

Some will protest that this sounds backwards. But one of the most salient features of love is its expansive quality. The fact is, when we feel ourselves to be genuinely loved, we experience an inner warmth and expansiveness, and there is a natural tendency to be kinder, gentler, more caring, and more accepting of others as a result. It's as if people who feel loved radiate an inner glow that can't help but touch those around them. When one person feels loved, the love spills over to others, and this in turn enhances their feelings of being loved, which then causes them to be more loving to the people they encounter. Taking a wide-angle view, it becomes clear that the ripple effect that results from one person feeling genuinely loved creates the potential for the amount of love in the world to be geometrically expanded—and to keep on expanding to the point where there is plenty to go around.

Unfortunately, though, this potential has yet to be realized because even when we are in the presence of someone who is radiating love, most of us can't take it in. We block it instead. We say, in essence, "The love stops here," thereby thwarting its potential ripple effect.

As a simple example, let's look at what happens between Martha, a thirty-year-old secretary and Jack, a thirty-one-year-old salesman, the first time they sleep together. Martha and Jack have been dating for about six weeks, and they like each other a lot. After they make love, Jack tells Martha she has a very nice body. Jack means this sincerely; although Martha is not beautiful by fashion-magazine standards, to him at this particular moment she is lovely. If Martha were able to accept the compliment, it would help her to feel valued and appreciated; then she would experience an inner warmth that she would naturally want to share, perhaps by reaching out and saying something nice to Jack in return. Jack would then have the opportunity to experience a greater inner warmth himself, with the likely result that he would then express further tenderness toward Martha, which in turn would further enhance her sense of being loved . . . and on and on it could go, with each person feeling more loved and loving.

What actually happens, though, is quite different. As soon as Jack tells Martha she has a nice body, she feels not warmth but an inner tightness. Because the compliment doesn't correspond with what Martha already believes to be true—she thinks she's too fat—she can't take it in. So instead of saying "thank you" and telling Jack that he, too, has a nice body, Martha responds by questioning Jack's sincerity and judgment. "You don't have to try to flatter me," she says in a sarcastic tone that is far from friendly. "I know I've got a fat ass." By deflecting Jack's attempt at being loving in this way, Martha deprives herself of the pleasure of experiencing Jack's positive regard. Jack, in turn, feels hurt and annoyed, and he resolves not to compliment Martha again.

The next morning, a similar exchange takes place, only this time it's Jack who rebuffs Martha's attempt at being loving. Aware that something had gone wrong between them the night before, Martha tries to break down the wall between her and Jack by telling him what a great lover he is and how much fun she had with him last night. However, Jack responds not by feeling reassured, but by feeling threatened. He has deep fears about not being able to satisfy a woman sexually, and his fears now cause him mistakenly to read into Martha's words a demand that he make love to her again, right now, with the same energy and expertise that he showed last night. So rather than tell Martha that he, too, had a great time last night, Jack quickly kisses her on the cheek, then jumps out of bed and starts getting dressed. "Is something wrong?" Martha asks. "No, I've just got to get going," Jack says, and within minutes he's out the door. Needless to say, Jack's quick getaway leaves Martha feeling unappreciated and unloved. What's less obvious, but just as true, is that Jack leaves feeling equally unappreciated and unloved, for his fears have rendered him incapable of seeing Martha's behavior for what it was—a sincere attempt to show him affection.

Matthew, a forty-one-year-old advertising executive with two failed marriages behind him, also has trouble accepting the love and affection that is offered to him. Recently, Matthew has been having difficulties at work, and he's been getting increasingly depressed and despondent as a result. His third wife, Frances, a teacher he married last year, is understandably concerned. Night after night, she prods Matthew to open up and fill her in on what's bothering him, to tell her what she can do to help. Matthew's response is to say, "If you really loved me, I wouldn't have to explain! You'd just know." On one occasion, he shouts at her, "If I have to tell you what I need from you, what good is it?" In Matthew's view, people who love you should be able to read your mind, and love that has to be asked for isn't love at all. As a result, the more Frances expresses her concern for Matthew, the more unloved by her he feels. Frances, meanwhile, is beginning to understand why Matthew's other marriages didn't work out.

Joan, a sixty-seven-year-old retiree now living in Florida, habitually rejects the love and affection of her adult children. Joan's children visit and call as often as they can, but somehow whatever they do is never good enough for her. As soon as one of her children arrives for a visit, the first thing out of her mouth is, "So how come I never see you?" When they telephone, she immediately says, "So you couldn't call yesterday?" Joan rarely visits her children, but when she does she selects the dates without checking with them first. Then if they tell her that the time she has chosen isn't particularly convenient and recommend another date, she ignores their suggestions. Instead, she says, "So this is the thanks a mother gets? What if I had been too busy the day you were born?"

Frank, a twenty-seven-year-old stockbroker, also finds it difficult to allow himself the experience of being loved. He has been going out with Diane, a twenty-five-year-old attorney, for over two months, and last weekend they went away together for the first time. They had an idyllic weekend, during which Frank confided some of his deepest feelings and told Diane things about his childhood he's never told anyone before. By the time they got back to the city on Monday, Diane and Frank had achieved a new level of closeness, and Diane finally felt confident that their relationship had a long future. "I'll call you tomorrow," Frank said as they parted, and Diane had no reason to doubt him. But Frank didn't call—not on Tuesday, or on Wednesday, or on Thursday. When Diane finally phoned him at work Friday, his voice was cold and distant. "There's been no letup at work," he said, "and it looks like I'm going to be tied up with this deal all weekend. Why don't I call you next week?" Frank knows he's hurting Diane, but he hangs up the phone feeling more relieved than ashamed. Although he cares for Diane and wants to feel loved, his deep terror of intimacy causes him to push people away whenever they start getting too close.

Sara, a thirty-four-year-old journalist, recently received a promotion she had been working years to obtain. Her friends threw her a big party and honored her with an elaborate and very funny skit representing her climb to the top. The party and the skit were clearly labors of great love, but Sara went home that night feeling unloved. Why? Because Sara doesn't have a boyfriend, and she feels that romantic love is the only type of love that really counts. Although by objective standards there is considerable love in her life, she discounts it because the people giving her love are, after all, "just friends."

Love Blocks Defined

These are all examples of people with love blocks. A love block is a deeply ingrained psychological pattern that prevents us from being able to experience ourselves as loved and valued. While these patterns can cause us to behave in ways that minimize our chances of being loved, the most significant feature of love blocks is that they prevent us from experiencing ourselves as loved even when love does come our way. When we have love blocks, we simply cannot take in the love that others offer and allow it to fill us with a sense of warmth and joy. Instead, we deflect it, reject it, dismiss it, or distort it in our minds so that we see it as something other than real love. And because we can't take in love, it's difficult for us to give love back. After all, how can we return something we haven't received?

Love blocks fall into three main categories. Some primarily affect our inner view of ourselves. Common self-perceptions such as "I don't deserve love" or "I don't need anyone—I'm strong," for example, can seriously impair a person's receptivity to love.

Other love blocks primarily affect our view of the world in general and reflect our general philosophy and expectations of life. Many people, for example, were raised to view the world as a cold and depriving place, and thus believe "love just isn't in the cards for me." Others were raised to view the world as a place where opportunities for love expire early, and so they believe "it's too late for me; my time has run out."

The third type of love block primarily affects our views of other people and our expectations of how they should treat us. Many people, for example, believe "love has to be a certain way"; if love is offered to them in another way, they reject it on the grounds that it's not real love. Others take the view that if love has to be asked for, then it isn't really love; thus they approach their relationships implicitly demanding, "Why can't you read my mind?"

Most people have more than one love block, frequently from different categories. Often, in fact, people have love blocks of all three types working at once. Their perceptions of both themselves and the world are distorted, and they have unrealistic expectations of others as well.

Obviously, love blocks can express themselves in our conscious thinking, often in ways of which we're already aware. But usually love blocks are rooted in our unconscious, and they serve purposes and have effects of which we're not fully aware. This is why love blocks affect us so powerfully and tend to be so tenacious.

People are affected by love blocks in different ways and to different degrees. As the examples just given show, some people are in relationships that offer them the potential for feeling loved and valued, and for achieving true intimacy. But their love blocks prevent them from realizing the potential these relationships offer. Indeed, they behave in ways that are bound to create problems—perhaps even to destroy the relationships entirely.

Other people are more severely affected. Their love blocks cause them to get into relationships in which there is little or no chance that they'll feel valued and loved and find the intimacy they seek. They get involved with people who are withholding, distant, cruel, immature, self-centered, or in some other way decidedly poor choices—or they get involved with people who appear to have the potential of giving them love but for external reasons can't.

Beth is an example of someone affected in this way. Since graduating from high school ten years ago, Beth has had three boyfriends. The first, Christopher, was an alcoholic who verbally and physically abused her. The second, Chuck, wasn't cruel but wasn't particularly nice either. After sex, he would always become cool and leave or ask her to. He also would frequently "forget" to call her, sometimes for as long as a week. By contrast, Beth's third and current boyfriend, Ted, is kind, warm, and giving. He calls her nearly every day and constantly tells her he is crazy about her. There's one hitch, though: Ted is married, and despite his professed love for Beth, he's made it clear that he will never leave his wife and children.

Others with love blocks won't permit themselves to risk getting closely involved at all. Dorothy, a thirty-six-year-old office manager, has worked in the same place since graduating from college, and during that time the only friendships she has formed are with people at work. These friendships appear to be fairly close; in fact, however, when someone leaves the office for another job Dorothy does little to keep the relationship going, and soon it fades away. Dorothy takes the same passive stance regarding romantic relationships. She rarely expresses interest in dating, and when someone invites her to a party or tries to set her up, she always finds an excuse not to go.

Clearly, not everyone is affected by love blocks to such a great extent. But whatever our love blocks are, they inevitably have some effect both on our willingness to risk intimate involvement and on the kinds of people we choose to get involved with. Moreover, our love blocks definitely have an enormous influence on the way we treat others and the way they treat us in all our relationships. And they surely affect our chances of finding happiness and fulfillment in life. Even if we are lucky enough to have people in our lives who offer us ample love, our love blocks virtually guarantee that we'll never be completely satisfied—that we'll never quite shake the deep-seated feeling that something's missing or not quite right.

The Childhood Origins of Love Blocks

Everyone wants to be loved, so clearly no one develops a love block by conscious choice. We developed our love blocks unconsciously, and probably for good reason—as a way of protecting ourselves against some earlier experience that was frightening, confusing, or in some other way so painful and stressful that our fragile psyches could not handle it. From an intellectual adult perspective, our love blocks might not seem to make much sense. But if we explore our earlier experiences, we'll inevitably find that they make plenty of emotional sense.

Love blocks can be developed at any point in life. When a person develops a love block in adulthood, however, it almost always rests atop another love block developed in childhood or adolescence. Typically a person develops one or two love blocks in the early years of life, and these blocks serve as the foundation for future blocks. Thus, to understand the origins of our love blocks, we need to look at our earliest experiences.

No matter how strong and self-reliant we are as adults, each of us came into the world as a tiny and fragile bundle of needs—needs we were entirely incapable of satisfying on our own. When we were hungry, we couldn't go to the store or refrigerator and get ourselves some food, nor could we ask someone else to do this for us; we needed someone else to recognize that we were hungry and then to feed us. When we were cold, we needed someone else to see that we were cold and to cover us. When we soiled ourselves, we needed someone to see that we were dirty, to understand our discomfort and to clean and change us. When we wanted to turn over in bed because we were uncomfortable, we needed someone else to lift and turn us over.

Nature decreed that we also would remain in this helpless and dependent state for an unusually prolonged period. Most other animals mature within a relatively short space of time following birth, but the human infant is born when the brain and body are still years away from full development. For each of us individually, this meant that for the prolonged period of childhood and adolescence we were in an extremely vulnerable position. Chances were good that some of our needs would not be met, and we'd be powerless to do anything about it.

One of the greatest needs that each of us entered the world with was the need for love. Poets and philosophers have long struggled to define love, but in vain. It is known, however, that to be loved is a joyful, soothing experience: when we feel loved, we feel significant and peaceful; we're also filled with a warm inner sense that all is right with the world and that we belong in it. While we never outgrow the need for love, the need is felt most urgently early in life. Indeed, for an infant, to be nourished by love is as crucial to survival as being given milk to drink or air to breathe.

Sadly, though, it's very likely that our enormous childhood need for love was not always met. Even if we grew up in the most loving of homes, there were probably times when our cries went unheeded, our requests for a hug were ignored or rebuffed, or our clamoring for affection was met with annoyance. As well intentioned as our parents may have been, there inevitably were occasions when they were too tired, too preoccupied, too upset, or too overwhelmed by problems to give us the love and attention we needed. In many cases, our parents probably weren't even around when we needed them. And the chances are good that even when they were around, they simply didn't understand how much we needed their love, or how to give it to us.

When children's need for love is insufficiently satisfied, something tragic happens: they begin to lose their natural receptivity for love. Children come into the world with an unbounded capacity to take in love. Ideally, this natural receptivity to love will expand as their needs for love are met, just as their bodies will grow as their nutritional needs are satisfied. And as children's ability to receive love grows, so will their capacity to give love. But when a child does not get enough love, his or her natural receptivity for love shrinks in much the same way that a stomach shrinks in response to not being fed. If a child's need for love is consistently not satisfied over a long period of time, or if the child suffers a traumatic experience in which the reaching out for love was met with abuse or total rejection, the part of the child that came into the world open to receiving love may wither completely. It will be as if the child's naturally receptive self had died.

Nancy

Nancy, a former secretary and housewife who would later become a college admissions officer, is an example of someone who during childhood lost a great deal of her ability to take in love. An attractive woman, Nancy has a mane of flowing red hair and a very feminine build that suggests softness, solidity, and sensuousness. She started therapy in her early thirties, at roughly the same time that she had gone back to college after having spent the previous eight years at home raising her two daughters. In her first session, she explained that she had decided to seek help because she was unhappy in her marriage, and with her relationship with her daughters as well. Internally Nancy didn't feel that her husband and children loved her, but she wasn't sure whether this was actually the case or only her perception.

As Nancy elaborated on what was happening in her home life, it became clear that she was suffering from a number of love blocks, particularly "I Don't Deserve Love," the block elaborated on in Chapter 5. Although good-looking and very evidently bright and "on top of things," when Nancy was asked to describe herself, she didn't hesitate for even a second before blurting out "fat, ugly, stupid, and repulsive." Asked if she saw herself as worthy of love, Nancy responded as if the question were so ridiculous as to be absurd. "Love this?" she said, pointing to herself. "How can anyone love *this?*"

When Nancy was asked how she thought her sense of unlovability originated, she seemed perplexed. This feeling had been with her for so long that she had never thought to question where it came from. "I've always felt this way," she explained. "I was probably born feeling this way. It's how I'm supposed to feel."

As she eventually discovered, Nancy was *not* born feeling unlovable. At the time she started therapy, Nancy was reluctant to discuss her childhood home life in any detail or depth. There was no need to "poke around in the distant past," as she put it, because her childhood had been "fine." In fact, although Nancy had blotted them out of her consciousness for years, there had been problems at home when she was a child. These problems continued to affect her even as she maintained that they did not.

Nancy was the youngest of four children in a middle-class family that lived in a comfortable city townhouse with a large rear garden. The two oldest children, a boy and a girl, were healthy; however, the third, a girl born two years before Nancy, had been severely brain injured at birth. Nancy's parents were traumatized by their child's illness, and her mother in particular was overcome with grief and guilt. By the time she became pregnant with Nancy, Nancy's mother was already deep into a depression and completely depleted by the task of trying to take care of the three older children. Although Nancy's brain-injured sister, Marina, was institutionalized right before Nancy was born, their mother remained so preoccupied with Marina that she had little energy left for the newborn Nancy. Sadly, the passage of time only seemed to make Nancy's mother more distracted and exhausted. Routinely throughout Nancy's childhood, her mother would have "spells" in which she would pass out cold and collapse onto the floor, leaving Nancy and her older siblings frightened, bewildered, and forced to fend for themselves. When Nancy's mother was up and about, she spent most of her time furiously cleaning the house, an activity that increasingly obsessed her over the years. Occasionally she would have moods in which she tried to be loving to her children, but just as often she had "bad days" in which her principal way of relating to them was through screaming and yelling. Sometimes she also struck out at them physically, with enough rage and force that Nancy and her siblings "were afraid that one of us was literally going to die."

Nancy's mother did not ever tell Nancy she was unwanted, but this is the message that Nancy inferred from the way her mother often treated her. In one particularly important therapy session, Nancy had a vivid memory of an incident that occurred when she was about four. Her mother was cleaning the kitchen stove when Nancy approached her in hopes of getting a hug. As Nancy came closer, her mother looked at her, then turned back to furiously scrubbing a grimy spot on the stove. In a plaintive voice, Nancy asked,

"Mommy, do you love me?" When her mother didn't answer, Nancy asked again, at which point her mother, never taking her eyes from the stove, said, "Stop bothering me! Can't you see I'm busy?" As Nancy recalled this scene three decades later, tears streamed down her cheeks. Gulping for air in between sobs, she said, "I was totally devastated. I remember standing there and thinking, 'How important can I be if my mother pays less attention to me than to dirt?' "

The return of this early memory marked Nancy's first major step in understanding how she had lost her natural receptivity to love. Until this point, Nancy had avoided going into details about her childhood, maintaining that everything at home had been "normal and fine." But once this memory returned, the complete story of her growing-up years started to spill out, and her true feelings about what had happened started to surface, too. She began to realize that she once had been a little girl who was naturally receptive to love, but because of the many rejections she experienced in the course of her childhood, that little girl had withdrawn and she had become emotionally closed off. The tears Nancy's memory triggered were tears of grief over the loss of a part of herself that until then she was unaware had ever existed. She was not born feeling unlovable as she had thought; her ability to allow herself to be loved had atrophied as a result of what happened to her as a child.

Some readers might scoff at the significance of what happened to Nancy that day in the kitchen. "Are we really supposed to believe," they might ask, "that this one experience was enough to screw Nancy up for life? Come on. That's ridiculous." But as is usually the case with strong memories of childhood, Nancy's memory wasn't just a recollection of one particular event; it was an encapsulation of many similar experiences. It was a shorthand summary of what Nancy's home life, particularly her relationship with her mother, was like *in general* during her childhood. This is why it became imbedded in her unconscious and came back to her years later with so much emotional force and resonance.[2]

Fortunately, during her childhood Nancy was able to turn to her father. For many years, he was a dependable and overflowing source of warmth, consolation, and physical affection. When Nancy was a child, he would readily hug her, put her in his lap, and kiss her; he also spent time having lengthy conversations with her. The drawback was that Nancy's father wasn't around as much as she needed him to be. Because her parents had a then-conventional marriage in which the husband went off to work, Nancy's primary parent was not the parent best suited for the job of child rearing.

Moreover, when she was about eleven years old, Nancy began to mature sexually, and her father abruptly stopped showing her any physical affection. Although he continued to converse with her, he would no longer hug her, kiss her, or even touch her hand. He never acknowledged that his behavior toward her had changed at all; but Nancy, crushed by what she perceived as a sudden rejection, longed for an explanation. When she looked in the mirror and saw her budding breasts and the weight she was starting to put on in her hips and thighs, she thought she had found the answer. "He doesn't love me anymore because of the way I look," she concluded. "He must be repulsed because I've become fat and ugly." In this way, Nancy, who already saw herself as unlovable and "worth less than dirt," began to see herself as "fat, ugly, and repulsive," too.

It's important to note that although Nancy's father never told his adolescent daughter that she had become repulsive, she did not arrive at this idea solely on her own or just pull it out of the blue. Nancy grew up in a culture in which she was constantly bombarded with the message that any girl or woman with a normal female build is fat, and that being fat is bad and shameful. She also grew up in a culture in which girls and women are taught to see their "too fat" and otherwise "defective" bodies as the source of all their problems—and to believe that "if only I lost weight, everything in my life would be okay." Understood in context, Nancy's conclusion makes a lot of sense.

Unintentional and Unconscious

The purpose of telling Nancy's story is not to assign blame. When parents cause their children pain, as in Nancy's case, it is usually not intentional. Nancy's mother was not a villain or a bad woman. She was emotionally crippled by her own problems, overwhelmed by her role as primary caretaker of four children, and simply inadequate to the formidable task of giving Nancy what she needed. Nancy's father was not a mean-spirited man, either. He was restricted by his own role as breadwinner; the evidence is good that he had conflicted, unresolved feelings about his daughter's sexuality and his own; and he probably thought that backing off when she entered puberty was the right thing to do. Neither parent intentionally set out to cause their daughter to see herself as ugly, repulsive, unlovable, and worth less than dirt. This was the inadvertant result of their actions, not the result they desired or decided on ahead of time. If Nancy had been born to different parents, or born to her own parents at a healthier point in their own development, it's very likely that she would have developed a very different view of herself.

Just as Nancy's parents didn't consciously intend to hurt their daughter, Nancy didn't consciously decide to develop love blocks. The primary function of the unconscious is to minimize the experience of emotional pain so that our lives will not seem so intolerable that we can't go on. When Nancy's repeated reaching out for maternal love met with repeated rejections, she suffered pain so intense that she had to find a way to protect herself from it. The small child obviously did not say to herself, "Hmmm, I'm in pain. Let me see what I can do about it." Instead, Nancy's unconscious automatically took over and activated an emotional shut-off valve that stopped her from feeling pain. But like most shut-off valves, this one couldn't discriminate: eventually it blocked off many other emotions, even those she yearned to feel.

One of the most striking aspects of Nancy's story is how well she seemed to have turned out. Meeting her, others would never guess that she'd had a difficult childhood. She has always struck other people as easygoing, and because of her friendly, open manner people warm up to her quickly. People also admire Nancy because of her energetic involvement in a variety of community activities, from scouting to local political campaigns. Nancy, in fact, is the kind of person often pointed to as proof that a difficult childhood "builds character." But like many other seemingly stoic survivors of troubled childhoods, Nancy went through most of her life with a lot of hurt and unhappiness hidden inside—hurt and unhappiness only those really close to her were able to see.

Of course, not everyone with love blocks grew up under such difficult conditions as Nancy did. Many people come from homes that, for the most part, were very loving—yet they ended up with love blocks anyway. This is because no matter how wonderful parents try to be, there is no such thing as perfect parenting. Children come into the world with so many needs, and such enormous ones, that it's virtually guaranteed that some of their needs will go unmet some of the time. Certainly, someone from a generally loving home will have a far smaller chance of being severely troubled by love blocks than someone who grew up in an atmosphere of neglect or hostility. But there are very few people on earth who went through childhood without ever feeling unappreciated, insufficiently paid attention to, unfairly treated, or in some other way unloved. Thus, even someone from an essentially happy home probably won't escape love blocks entirely.

At the same time, not everyone who had a troubled childhood will have love blocks to the same extent as Nancy. Some children do seem to be far more resilient than others, although why this is so is not entirely clear. However, it's important to point out that the number of people who have survived difficult childhoods without being scarred has been greatly exaggerated. Many people only *appear* to have gone through difficult childhoods with no ill effects: it's not that they feel less pain than someone who is obviously troubled, it's that they're better at hiding it. Although they may go through their early adult years giving everyone (including themselves) the impression that nothing inside is amiss, eventually the buried pain of the past catches up with them. Hence the often-seen phenomenon wherein high-functioning and ostensibly well-adjusted people get to midlife and start suffering debilitating emotional problems. Although their emotional troubles may seem to have suddenly developed for no apparent reason, in fact unresolved traumas from childhood are finally surfacing in much the same way that the wounds of war show up only many years later through "delayed-stress syndrome."

While not everyone who experienced emotional deprivation in childhood reacted in the same way, it's a rare person indeed who grew up without developing psychological defenses and thus losing some of the natural capacity to take in love. In childhood and adolescence, this was necessary for psychological survival. Nancy, for example, had no way to stop her parents from hurting her, nor did she have the option of leaving to find a more loving home. The only way she could protect herself was by shutting down emotionally and telling herself "this is the treatment I deserve." Since it did enable her to survive, this tactic clearly worked for her. As Nancy was later to discover, though, the survival mechanisms that aided us in childhood often work against us in adulthood as love blocks, ultimately doing us more harm than good.

This is not to say that all the inner barriers we erect to protect ourselves from feeling pain are necessarily unhealthy or serve as love blocks. Since there are plenty of invasive, exploitative, manipulative, and cruel people in the world, we all need the kind of protective inner mechanisms that allow us to detect these types of people and to defend ourselves against them. And since a lot of invasive, exploitative, manipulative, and cruel behavior is presented in the name of love, we also need to be able to make distinctions between what's really love and what's only being passed off as love.

But love blocks don't keep out only those who are in fact threatening to our well-being; they make it difficult to let *anyone* in. And they don't just prevent us from being "taken in" by people who claim to love us but in reality don't; they prevent us from taking in genuine love when it's offered as well. In short, love blocks are protective mechanisms that have outlived their usefulness and gone haywire. Although we may have needed them to survive childhood and adolescence, in adulthood we need to free ourselves of them to experience the love and growth we seek.

Chapter 2
The Importance of
Dealing with
the Past

Carole, a market analyst for a large investment firm, has strawberry-blond hair and a pretty, rounded face with freckled and unlined skin that makes it hard to believe she's thirty-seven. Short and *zaftig*, she has an effusive manner and punctuates her speech with dramatic facial expressions. Her husband, Stan, a forty-year-old architect, is also blond, with deep blue eyes and a lean, athletic build. Although quieter and less outgoing than Carole, he has an equally expressive face and also speaks with his hands, which are often holding a cigarette or fidgeting with a lighter. When Carole and Stan speak, both laugh easily and often.

As they explained during a series of interview sessions, Carole and Stan began couples' counseling in an attempt to save their seven-year marriage. Both had just come out of divorces when they met and fell in love, and both entered the new relationship with the hope that they could begin, "with a clean slate," as Carole put it. But despite their good intentions, as their relationship progressed they found themselves repeating many of the same patterns that had caused them so much unhappiness in their first marriages. Although Carole in many respects seemed very different from Stan's first wife, he often felt she was behaving in similar ways. And although Stan had struck Carole as very different from her first husband, she, too, found herself responding to him in similar ways. "Carole and I would keep getting into awful fights that had this weird *déjà vu* quality about them," Stan explained. "We'd say the same things that we had said to our other partners, then we'd slam doors and feel really awful, then we'd kiss and make up, but without really solving anything. A couple of weeks later, we'd have another fight, and go through the whole routine once more. It was like we were trapped in something that was bigger than both of us, and although we knew we had been in the same place before we had no clue of how to find our way out."

After a few sessions in couples' therapy, the therapist said she thought the problems Carole and Stan were encountering in their marriage had their source in their separate backgrounds, and she advised each to seek individual therapy as well. But both reacted to this suggestion with strong resistance. "I was willing to work on my marriage, but I didn't want to look very closely at myself," Stan later explained. "I wanted to be able to blame Carole for all our problems, and I think she wanted to do the same to me. The therapist we had seen said she thought a lot of our problems stemmed from our separate childhoods, but I've always had trouble with all that business of dredging up the past. I've always felt what's done is done, and you should let bygones be bygones. I went to counseling so that we could move ahead. I had no desire to waste a lot of time going back."

Carole's response echoed Stan's: "I wanted to keep the focus on me and Stan—preferably on Stan," she recalled. "I hated the idea of going into my own stuff, and I particularly hated the idea of having to look at my childhood. Everyone I knew who'd been in therapy always seemed to be talking about their mothers and what their parents did to them when they were kids, and I had always found that so boring and beside the point. I mean, when you're thirty-seven and have kids, as I do, isn't it time to stop complaining about what your mother did to you when you were three? The idea that what my parents did when I was three could still be affecting me at age thirty-seven was something I just didn't want to deal with. I still don't really want to deal with it now."

Stan and Carole were not unusual in adhering to such views. They wanted to improve their relationship, but at the same time were unwilling to accept that the problems in their marriage had their roots in their individual pasts and separate family histories. They took the attitude that "dwelling on the past," as each often put it, was a waste of time that only diverted them from dealing with the problems they were going through in the here and now.

Legions of others agree that dredging up the past is a fool's enterprise. One obvious reason is that, for many people, the past was painful. Not wanting to acknowledge this, they stoically look only to the future, saying "let's put the past behind us." Or perhaps they allow themselves to remember the past, but only a fantasy version that supports the claim "I had a very happy childhood."

Shutting the door on the past is a psychological reaction that people everywhere in the world practice. But the extent to which individuals do it and the nature of their rationalizations are influenced by where they happen to live, and at what point in history as well. For those of us who live in twentieth-century America, cultural factors often dovetail with psychological factors to reinforce a disinterest in the past. In Europe, for example, reminders of the past are everywhere; the buildings, the streets, the monuments, the traditions all add to an awareness of the past—and how the present arises from it. By contrast, the United States is a very young country, and the culture that has developed here is one that is forward-looking, progress oriented, and inclined to value the new far more than the old. Perhaps as a result, many Americans have only a vague sense of history, particularly world history, and schools don't do much to remedy this situation. Many children grow up with such a scant grasp of history that they do not even consider this a deficiency. "Who cares?" their attitude is. "The latest fads (movies, records, fashions, TV shows, etc.) are all that matter . . ."

Many Americans have little sense of their own family history as well. They never learned who their ancestors were, when they came to this country, what kinds of lives they lived, what kinds of hopes and dreams they harbored, and what disappointments and hurts they endured. Many people know little about their own parents, in fact. This is true of many in the general populace, not just those whose parents have special reasons not to want to talk about the past (such as Holocaust survivors or Americans of Japanese descent who were interned by the U.S. government during World War II).

American attitudes toward the past probably have a lot to do with the fact that the United States has been settled by people seeking to break free of constraining Old World traditions and to put the past behind them. But the breakdown of the extended family has contributed, too. In previous times, children often had direct, frequent contact with grandparents and great-aunts and -uncles. These relatives not only gave children a sense of family history that went back three generations, they also served as a conduit through which the children obtained information about *their* parents. In today's highly mobile society, many children live so far from their grandparents and other relatives that they miss out on this kind of experience.

In some families, the past is either overtly lied about or hushed up. If the children ask questions that probe into the past, they are silenced with lines such as "It's none of your business," "That had nothing to do with you, you were only a baby then," or "That was before you were born, it didn't affect you." Perhaps they're simply told "That's over and done with now. It doesn't really matter."

In fact, the past matters greatly. Just as genes are passed on from one generation to the next, so are psychological patterns and problems, including love blocks. The more ignorant of his psychological heritage a person is, the more likely he is to get mired in repeating his family's past patterns and dramas again and again. Moreover, without an understanding of why and how a love block developed, any effort to overcome the block will be superficial and doomed to failure. Many people take an attitude of "I don't care where my blocks came from, just tell me how to get rid of them." But overcoming a block begins with understanding its origins, and that is possible only when a person is willing to examine her family history and her own earlier experiences.

Time and the Unconscious

As a way of buttressing their argument that exploring the past is a pointless waste of time, at first Stan and Carole repeatedly insisted that "what was then was then, what's now is now," and there's really no connection between the two. This is a common enough belief, but one that rests on a deeply flawed premise: that the human psyche operates according to linear time and can make clear distinctions between past, present, and future. In fact, only the conscious mind is able to distinguish among past, present, and future; the unconscious mind does not make such neat distinctions. The unconscious has no sense of linear time at all, in fact.[1] Perhaps the best way to illustrate this is to envision the unconscious as a huge, automatic memory bank. Whenever we have a strong emotional reaction to an event in our lives, our memory of that event and our accompanying feelings are automatically deposited and stored in our unconscious. As we proceed with our lives, we have other experiences that trigger unconscious memories of our past experiences, and as those unconscious memories resurface, the feelings we had in reaction to our past experiences resurface as well. But when the feelings from the past come rushing back to us, we don't experience them as old feelings, we experience them in the here and now, often as intensely as we felt them the first time—even if that was thirty or forty or seventy years ago.

As an example of how the unconscious mind works, imagine for a moment that you're listening to some "golden oldies" on the radio. Over the air comes a song that was a favorite of yours when you were a teenager. As you listen to the song, your mind is flooded with vivid memories of things you did, places you went, and people you knew as a teen, and you suddenly feel the way you did then, too. It may have been so long since you consciously thought of these things that you believed you had forgotten all about them, but now the past comes rushing back. Perhaps you feel sad, or anxious, or excited, or happy—just as you had felt then. If the song is one you associated with your first romantic relationship, you may feel yourself suddenly in love again, or once more hurting over the loss of that relationship. Although in your head you know these feelings come from the past, you nonetheless are feeling them *now*—as if the time that had elapsed between then and now were really no time at all.

As another example of the unconscious mind's obliviousness of linear time, consider for a moment something we'll call the "back in diapers" phenomenon. No matter how adult, accomplished, and responsible they are now, many people find that when they get together with their parents and siblings for, say, holidays, they suddenly begin to feel like little kids again. If their parents make a critical comment, they may find themselves not mildly irritated but completely enraged, as if the remark had been an all-out attack. Just as being around their families is sure to trigger memories of childhood, it's equally certain to bring forth many of the feelings associated with childhood as well. It's as if their adult identities have been suddenly stripped away, and they feel like powerless children once again. Though they may be dressed in grown-up clothes, inside they feel as if they were back in diapers again.

Most people have also had the experience of feeling a certain way for no apparent reason. It's common to hear people talk about waking up one morning feeling inexplicably sad, or of going about their daily business when suddenly an intense feeling—anxiety, sadness, fear, guilt, joy, or remorse—wells up, seemingly "out of the blue." In these instances, feelings from the past are resurfacing while the memory of the actual event that occasioned those feelings remains buried. Sometimes the specific details of the past experiences appear to get lost in the unconscious; no matter how hard some individuals may try to remember, they can't recall exactly what happened to them. Nevertheless, while the unconscious may sometimes seem to slip up when it comes to storing the details of past events, it always does store away the feelings. Although it may seem that certain feelings occur "out of the blue," in fact they are surfacing from the unconscious. And although buried feelings may return to conscious awareness "for no apparent reason," in fact there's usually been some-thing to trigger them, albeit something very subtle—a smell or a sound, for example, or the carriage or look of a person seen for a fleeting instant walking down the street.

If a person has suffered an extremely traumatic experience, the memory may never be retrieved, either because it's so deeply buried in the unconscious or because at the time when it happened the psyche was unable to integrate it. A person in this situation may go through life without ever having any conscious recollection of what the traumatic experience was; he may become convinced that because he remembers nothing, then nothing happened. Very likely, though, he will suffer emotional troubles—depression, anxiety, fear of inti-macy, eating disorders, for example—the very existence of which indicates that at some point in his past something traumatic did indeed occur. Even if the memory of a painful experience seems to have been obliterated, the emotional consequences of that experience live on.

Judy

People who suffered sexual abuse in childhood often have no recollection of what happened, but they experience emotional problems that signal past trauma. Judy, a forty-five-year-old housewife who is discussed at greater length in Chapter 5, entered therapy feeling very unhappy with her marriage of twenty-five years. Her sexual relationship with her husband, Art, was particularly unsatisfying. He equated sex with intercourse, Judy complained, and spent very little time on foreplay or afterplay. This not only left Judy unsatisfied, it caused her to feel "used."

Her husband's reported selfishness in bed, however, did not account for all Judy's unhappiness with their sex life. As Judy revealed more of her feelings, she divulged that she was unable to look at or touch her husband's penis, or anywhere near it. The sight or thought of "that disgusting thing" filled her with panic and caused her to feel sick to her stomach, she explained. Judy believed the revulsion she felt was a direct consequence of her husband's focus on his penis during sex, and the situation was simply a matter of "the more he tries to force himself on me, the more rejecting I feel." Asked gently if anything else had happened in her life to cause her to feel so repulsed, Judy said no. She thought she was responding to her husband's behavior and nothing else.

As Judy's therapy progressed and she began probing her past and paying special attention to her dreams, she began to remember events that for years and years she had forgotten about so completely that "I didn't remember them ever having happened at all." One particularly painful experience that had "slipped" her mind all this time was the experience of being sexually molested by her brother Steve, who was older by four years. Beginning when Judy was about eleven, there were repeated episodes in which Steve coerced her into fondling his penis, bringing him to ejaculation with her hands. This went on at least once a week for several years, until Steve finally went away to college. As some memories of precisely what had happened resurfaced, Judy expressed shock at "how much I blocked out," and for how long.

Yet Judy still did not make any connection between her past trauma and present sexual difficulties. It was only gradually that she came to see that her revulsion toward her husband's penis had its roots in the shame and pain her brother's molestations had caused her, and in her never-vented anger toward him as well. When she finally saw the connection between her feelings then and her feelings now—a connection so deep as to make it impossible ultimately to differentiate between the two—she felt overcome with sadness. As Judy later explained, the only way she had finally allowed herself to look at what had happened to her as a child was to tell herself that it hadn't really affected her. It was very painful to admit that the sexual abuse not only affected her, but was still affecting her decades later.

Judy's inability to touch or even look at her husband's penis obviously put limits on what kinds of sexual activity they engaged in, and how much pleasure they experienced. Although Judy could see very clearly how her aversion made it impossible for her to give love to her husband through sexuality and touch, at first she was unaware that it blocked her from receiving love from him as well. But because her experiences with her brother left her with guilt, shame over her sexuality, and a sense that her body was "ugly" and "bad," she automatically rejected any comments her husband made about how pretty or sexy she was. It wasn't simply that she didn't believe the compliments; she responded with anxiety and anger, as if they were lies that objectified her and were intended to "sweet talk" her into sex. She also could not accept her husband's attempts to show his love through nonsexual touch. Whenever he caressed her in a loving but nonsexual way, she would angrily pull away, saying "All you care about is sex!" or "Take your hands off me and stop acting like an animal!" Because they stirred up her unresolved feelings about her brother, Judy was put off by any physical demonstration of affection from her husband, in fact. Instead of feeling warmed and comforted by a hug or a squeeze on the arm or knee, Judy felt threatened, angered, and "used."

Of course, it's not necessary to have gone through the same experiences that Judy went through to have similar feelings. Other heterosexual women share Judy's revulsion toward male genitalia and her general discomfiture with sexual intimacy, even though they did not suffer any noticeably traumatizing experience. Their antipathy often stems from a variety of sources—the way sexuality is depicted in the pornography they saw as youngsters; the unfortunate but nearly universal female experience of having men "expose themselves" to them in public; the equally common experience of being sexually harassed on the street; the boorish and humiliating treatment they may have received from the males they had their earliest sexual encounters with, and so on. Just growing up in a culture where there's so much sexual inequality, male violence against women, and patronization of women and their sexuality can be enough to make a woman feel as thoroughly "turned off" to sex with men as Judy was.

In the course of her therapy, and the counseling she and her husband received together, Judy was able to pinpoint just what particular love blocks she was suffering from. "I Don't Deserve Love," "I Feel Threatened When Another Person Gets Close," and "Anger Keeps Getting in the Way" were her predominant ones, along with "I Don't Want to Deal with My Feelings." But the first step in overcoming these blocks was to recognize that they originated in the past, and to make herself open to exploring her own history, her family's history, and the cultural climate that shaped her formative years. The more she understood where she came from and what she had gone through in the past, the more successful she was in breaking free of the self-punishing behavior, thought patterns, and feelings that the past had left her with.

Carole and Stan

For Carole and Stan as well, recognizing the ways in which their past experiences were impinging on their present relationship was the first step. One of the major issues they repeatedly fought about was the amount of time they spent together. As Stan and Carole discovered, the specific nature of their complaints—and the way they carried out their arguments—had a lot to do with things that had happened to them long before they ever met.

When they first became involved, Carole and Stan spent a lot of time together. They went to movies and museums, took long bike rides, and spent hours just "lying around talking and laughing," Stan recalled. As both became increasingly involved in their careers, the time they spent together gradually diminished, and in the fourth year of their marriage, when their son, Evan, was born, it all but disappeared. Carole was sad about no longer having much time with Stan, but she accepted it as the price they'd have to pay for being working parents, and she also saw it as temporary. Once Evan was in school and she and Stan had reached the peak of their earning power, she felt they'd have more leisure time to spend with each other. She also hoped they'd be able to do some of the things they'd dreamed about when they first fell in love, such as traveling to Asia and New Zealand.

Stan felt differently. Although one of the reasons he initially had been attracted to Carole was that she was independent and committed to her work, as their marriage progressed, and especially after Evan's birth, Stan found himself feeling angry and resentful that Carole wasn't spending much time with him. He began to subtly pressure her to quit her job, which she adamantly refused to do. When they would fight, he would tell her she was "selfish"—to which she would retort, "Selfish? You think I'm selfish? You're the one who's selfish! You never talk about quitting your job, so why should I quit mine?" He would also insinuate that Carole wasn't serious enough about being a mother, to which Carole would respond by calling him a "sexist pig," screaming "I don't know why I ever married you," then slamming the bedroom door and refusing to speak to him or even acknowledge his presence, sometimes for days at a time.

Stan's Child-in-Waiting

Was Stan really just "a neanderthal," as Carole complained? Actually, no. At the bottom of Stan's behavior were unresolved feelings toward his mother. Stan's mother was an intelligent, energetic woman whom Stan remembers as very loving when she was with him. The problem was, he felt she wasn't with him enough. During Stan's childhood, there were many demands on his mother. Her own mother was slowly dying of cancer and she was the primary caretaker; Stan's older brother was discovered to have a serious hearing problem that necessitated several operations and a lot of extra care; and Stan's father, who owned a very successful women's clothing store, needed and expected his wife to help run the business. As a result, it always seemed to Stan that his mother was "either running to or from some other activity, and I was squeezed in somewhere in between." Although Stan admired his mother's stamina, and came to really admire her when she ended up spearheading several new strategies that turned the family business into an even bigger success, as a little boy his greatest wish was that she would have only one focal point in her life: him. "I remember how she would come into my room to tuck me in," Stan recalls. "She'd sit next to me and stroke my forehead and tell me stories, and I was in heaven. But then she'd have to go tuck my brother or sister in. I remember lying there wanting more from her. My whole childhood, I wanted more."

Stan's early experiences with his mother left him with a lot of ambivalent feelings about women, feelings that resurfaced in his first marriage, and later came up again in his relationship with Carole. Stan was attracted to women who were like his mother in that they were energetic, intelligent, involved and competent in the work world. But he also experienced the loss of time with Carole as an abandonment akin to that by his mother. He was afraid that he would never again be able to enjoy as much time as he wanted with his wife; despite her assurances that they would have more time together once Evan was older, Stan felt "it's already over, I'll never have her back the way it was."

It wasn't coincidental that Stan's feelings became particularly strong around the time when his own son was born. Although forty, Stan still had within him a child-in-waiting who hungered for time and affection from his mother and who felt unexpressed rage toward her for not giving him enough. When he was first with Carole, he thought he had finally found what he had been seeking all his life— a smart, independent woman who was nonetheless willing and able to devote a good portion of her time to just being with him. To Stan, the early stages of his relationship with Carole were utter bliss.

Then the baby came along and everything changed. While he did feel enormous fatherly love for Evan, he also experienced Evan as a mirror of his own needy inner child and as a competitor for Carole's time and affection.

It is very common—more common than not—for an adult to have a child-in-waiting within. In most cases, this inner child is waiting for mother love or father love, or perhaps both. Although a person might have no conscious awareness that she has a child-in-waiting within, the child nonetheless exerts enormous influence over the kind of adult relationships she enters into and how she behaves and feels within them. It is not an exaggeration, in fact, to say that through their central adult relationships most people are trying to obtain at last the father or mother love that they didn't get enough of as children. To the unconscious, each important adult relationship a person has is an opportunity to "do over" the parental relationship (or relationships) that left the inner child feeling wounded, uncared for, or otherwise incomplete.

Carole's Child-in-Waiting

If Stan was seeking mother love from Carole, she, too, was seeking from him something that had been missing in her childhood, and it's because she was deprived *once again* that she reacted to Stan's behavior with so much frustration and anger. Granted, many of the things Stan said were out of line, but someone else might have been able to say, "This is your problem, don't put it on me." Carole reacted so angrily because for her entire life she had wanted and needed emotional support for her career aspirations, but she had never received it until she met Stan—and now he seemed to be pulling his support out from under her.

Carole was the oldest of four children, two girls and two boys. Although she and her sister invariably did much better than their brothers in school, the boys were always treated as "the ones who were going to be something," Carole recalled, "while me and my sister were treated like we didn't count. The best we could hope for was to marry somebody who was something." When Carole wanted to go to college, she had to do it on her own because the money her parents had put aside for college was already earmarked for the boys. The girls were just going to get married anyway, Carole's father explained.

In her late teens and early twenties, Carole had a boyfriend who really wanted to marry her. Although she cared for him very much, she wanted to find out who she was and establish herself in the work world before settling down. When she broke off the relationship with her boyfriend and announced that she was planning to go on in school and get an M.B.A., her family—who had really liked him— was very upset. They called her stupid and selfish, and warned, "You'll be sorry one day."

Throughout grad school, Carole's parents could not bring themselves to support her choice, and they continued to pressure her to marry. When she was twenty-six Carole did get married, to a man she had met in her last year of business school. Her family was delighted. What they didn't know was that the main reason Carole married was that she was pregnant. Carole's plan was to wait until after the wedding to let the family know, and then to pretend the birth was premature. Instead, she had a miscarriage, and once there was no longer the baby to hold them together, Carole and her husband realized their marriage had little basis. He wanted a child very much and nagged Carole to become pregnant, but she wanted to focus on her work for a few more years. He, too, told her she was being selfish, and after many months of arguing and making up and arguing again, they divorced. Carole's parents, who had always made it clear that they didn't "believe in" divorce, were horrified. Telling her that "you made your bed and you can lie in it," they showed their disapproval by treating her coldly for months.

By the time she met Stan, Carole was carrying around a good deal of unexpressed anger at her family. She felt they would love her only if she molded her life to fit their preconceived notions of how it should be, and she was hurt and saddened by their unfairness. Carole also had seen enough discrimination in graduate school and the work world, and had heard enough women speak of the lack of emotional support they got for their endeavors, to have reason to feel women in general "got a raw deal, got gypped." At the same time, though, Carole didn't feel 100 percent certain that her anger was legitimate.

Maybe what others told her was right; maybe she was really selfish, after all. Moreover, she didn't want to come across to others as "a militant type," as "one of those hard-as-nails women with an axe to grind."

With all these unexpressed feelings building up within her, Carole was an explosion waiting to go off. And the things Stan said and did after Evan's birth served as the perfect detonators. When she called him names, slammed doors, refused to speak to him, and reviewed his shortcomings in her mind again and again so that she could hardly stand to look at him, Carole was venting rage that she had never expressed at her family, at her first husband, and at the world. While she had reason to be angry with Stan, the level and ferocity of her anger were totally disproportionate to the present situation. Although Carole experienced it as "now" anger, much of it was anger from the past that she had never let out.

Stan and Carole are good examples of people who came from essentially loving homes, yet developed love blocks all the same. Given their life circumstances, Stan's parents were as loving as they could be. But tiny Stan, coming into the world with the enormous needs that we all were born with, still needed and wanted more. By contemporary standards, Carole's parents were unfair and unkind in the way they treated her as she struggled to make a way for herself in the work world, but by the standards with which they themselves were raised, they were only doing what was best for their daughter. Just as Stan and Carole caused each other pain despite the best intentions with which they entered their marriage, Carole's parents certainly never meant to hurt one of their children. On the contrary, they raised her in as loving a home as they knew how to provide.

As much as Stan and Carole's story illustrates the power of the past, it also illustrates how liberating knowledge of the past can be. Prior to counseling, when Stan and Carole found themselves feeling angry, resentful, and annoyed with each other, they each took it for granted at first that this was because "he/she made me feel that way." As most people do, they tried to locate the source of their own feelings in the other person's behavior when, in fact, this was only part of the story. True, both Carole and Stan needed to take responsibility for how they treated each other. But they both also had to take responsibility to look within themselves and acknowledge that their reactions to each other had as much—perhaps more—to do with what had gone on in their separate pasts as with their present situation. Their feelings no longer seemed so baffling, and the particular love blocks they were beginning to identify and understand no longer seemed so insurmountable.

Chapter 3
Understanding How People Change

It's one thing to come to an understanding of how the past has affected us, but it's another to overcome the patterns that the past has etched in our psyches. Just how does a person with love blocks go about surmounting them? When an individual commits himself to the process of psychological change and growth, what exactly happens? While there's no one route that everyone follows, a general understanding of what the change process entails for most people can be obtained by looking at the experience of Nancy, the redheaded former secretary and housewife discussed in Chapter 1.

Nancy seems so warm and at ease with herself that it's hard to believe she spent most of her life lugging around a heavy burden of self-loathing. She has come a long way indeed. But as a child, Nancy suffered maternal rejection that caused her to feel that she was "worth less than dirt." Later when she entered puberty, her once affectionate, demonstrative father suddenly cooled toward her, leading her to conclude that she must be "ugly and repulsive." For many years, these beliefs were the dominant elements in Nancy's life. They not only caused her great inner pain, they also shaped whom she married, the kind of work she did, how she conducted her relationships, how she acted, and what she expected from life.

In the hope of proving that she had some worth, Nancy had always applied herself in school and gotten excellent grades. Her father, renowned in his synagogue as an extremely learned man, had always encouraged Nancy's intellectual development, and even after he cooled toward her in other ways he remained interested in her academic progress, albeit less so as she approached what he considered the marrying age. She won a full scholarship to college, and although she had doubts about whether she really deserved it, she nonetheless accepted and went off to college when she was eighteen. For the first two years, she kept mostly to herself and concentrated on her studies, afraid that if she slacked off for even a week, she would fail and everyone would discover she wasn't really very smart after all.

At the end of her sophomore year, Nancy met an upperclassman named Josh. Soon they began dating, and shortly after he graduated the next year, they married. At that time, Nancy dropped out of school and started working as a secretary in order to support Josh's pursuit of a graduate degree in economics. She continued secretarial work for several years, while he went on to become a professor at a community college.

To a casual observer, Nancy and Josh had a happy marriage—at least according to the standards of the era, the mid-1960s. In fact, Nancy experienced very little happiness in the marriage. Although she had fantasized that Josh would be her "prince charming," he turned out to be the kind of man with whom she would reexperience her early feelings of rejection. While not physically abusive to Nancy, Josh was extremely egocentric and bullied her emotionally. A hypercritical man, he routinely downgraded her abilities and worth as her mother had. He also told her she was "fat," "gross," and "disgusting," as Nancy felt her father had.

Although Nancy had actually been a far better student than Josh, one of the central tenets of their marriage was that Josh was brilliant while Nancy was a dummy. As time wore on, this myth became increasingly entrenched. According to their unwritten pact, Josh's genius was proved by his being a college professor, and her stupidity by her being a college dropout who had once worked as a secretary and was now a housewife. Nancy had so little self-esteem to begin with that it didn't take her long to forget her own accomplishments (which she considered flukes, anyway) and embrace the idea that she was a "mental defective" who was lucky that such a brilliant guy had deigned to marry her.

Another woman in a different era or with a different history might have been able to see that Josh's need to always put her down grew out of his own pathetic insecurity and immaturity. But Nancy and Josh were married at a time when it was widely taken for granted that a woman's duty was to boost her husband's "fragile male ego," even if this meant sacrificing her own self-worth entirely. Moreover, since the way Josh treated Nancy resembled the way her parents had treated her, it triggered in her the same sort of emotional responses; as a result, she felt in the relationship that Josh was a powerful parent figure and she was a helpless little girl. This made leaving the marriage—or standing up in any way to her husband—seem utterly impossible.

Early in her marriage Nancy gave birth to two daughters. She enjoyed being a mother and thought she was good at it, too. In fact, at the time she entered therapy, motherhood was the one area of her life in which she felt genuine self-esteem. She made a point of giving her daughters the time, attention, affection, and praise that she had not been able to get from her own mother. Periodically, though, Nancy would lose her temper and lash out at her daughters, telling them that their rooms were "pigstys" and that they were getting "disgustingly fat." The older her daughters got, the more frequent the critical outbursts became, and the more hurtful the nature of her comments. In turn, Nancy's daughters became increasingly critical of their mother. This only heightened Nancy's inner sense of being unlovable, which in turn fueled her inner anger, which in turn led to more critical outbursts against her daughters.

The Change Process: Nancy's Way

Nancy has been in psychotherapy at two different times in her life. The first time was for a period of about a year and a half when she was in her early thirties. After several years of staying at home being a full-time mother, she had recently returned to college to finish the degree interrupted by her having taken a secretarial job to support her husband. This took a lot of courage, and was evidence that she was becoming ready to make concrete changes in both her self-perceptions and her life.

It was evident from the start that Nancy's primary problem was the "I Don't Deserve Love" block (discussed at greater length in

Chapter 5). Her belief that she was unworthy of love kept her in a loveless marriage that reinforced her negative feelings about herself. It also kept her from being able to take in fully the love of her daughters, whom she alternated between seeing as "too wonderful to be mine" and as mirror images of her own unworthy self. Her relationships with other people outside her family were affected by her lack of self-esteem, too. Friends and acquaintances she knew through community and political activities were very admiring of Nancy's intelligence and competence, but she was never able to take in their high regard because it didn't jibe with her low opinion of herself.

During Nancy's first time in treatment, she was dimly aware of the developing problems with her daughters. But the main focus was on two things: her relationship with her husband, and whether to get a divorce; and her relationship with her mother, which she increasingly realized she was reenacting in her marriage.

As mentioned in Chapter 2, in important adult relationships, particularly sexual ones, people are often unconsciously trying to obtain the mother or father love they did not receive in childhood. It does occasionally happen that someone whose parents were cold, withholding, or rejecting is emotionally rescued by someone who is warm, giving, and accepting—and they live happily ever after. The problem is, it doesn't happen enough. It doesn't happen very often at all, in fact. What more typically happens is that people find adult partners who embody their parents' traits and proceed to build relationships that entail essentially the same psychodynamics as their early relationships with their parents. So instead of taking refuge from the pain of the past in the new relationships, they relive that pain all over again, precisely as Nancy was doing in her marriage to Josh.

To be in the best position possible to deal with her relationship with Josh, Nancy first had to come to terms with the primal relationship her marriage replicated, her relationship with her mother. This was a long and complicated process, and it would be misleading to suggest that it can be easily broken down into discrete linear steps. For the sake of illustrating at least some of what was involved in Nancy's process of change, however, it could be said that this involved five principal tasks.

The first task was for Nancy to acknowledge what had really happened as a child. Although she would occasionally make passing references to the difficulties of her childhood, for the most part Nancy had convinced herself that her childhood home life had been "fine," and that what problems had existed were of little import or consequence. Yet the reality was that in Nancy's childhood home the norm was for her mother to be incapacitated and depressed, preoccupied with cleaning or with Nancy's brain-injured sister, or full of rage. When in the latter state, the same woman who at moments could be quite gentle could be very violent, "bashing me around like a human punching bag," as Nancy recalled. To begin coming to terms with her relationship with her mother, Nancy had to give up the fiction that her childhood had been "fine" and acknowledge the harsh, heartbreaking reality.

The second task Nancy had to undertake was to acknowledge how she really felt about what had happened in her childhood. Even as she began to recall more vividly what her childhood had actually been like, Nancy maintained that it didn't really affect her. But an indisputable fact of life is that whatever happens to children does indeed have an impact. As a child, Nancy felt an overwhelming amount of pain, loss, sadness, confusion, despair, and anger, feelings she eventually numbed herself against. Decades later, she would find that after she finally acknowledged, experienced, and released those feelings she felt cleansed and lightened. When she began to let those long-buried feelings surface, however, it was extremely frightening, disorienting, and painful.

Nancy's third task in coming to terms with her relationship with her mother was to understand why she had the mother she had. Like many people with low self-esteem, Nancy grew up believing that the reason she was born into a problem-ridden family was that this was what she deserved. It came as news—and disturbing news at first— when Nancy learned that she and everyone else on earth ended up in their particular families because of luck. There was no logic to it at all.

Fourth, Nancy had to reach an understanding of why things had happened in her family as they did. As it turned out, Nancy had very little concrete information about how her parents had been raised and what their families had been like. She began to ask some discreet questions of her mother, her mother's relatives, and some of her father's relatives (he died when she was in her twenties). She began to ask her older brother and sister what they remembered of certain childhood events, and what their interpretation was. In the past, this sort of reminiscing had always led to fights, with each sibling trying to prove that the way he or she remembered things was the way it had really happened. But now Nancy and her siblings traded memories and insights with the shared realization that there is no one right way to remember—each child in a family will remember things differently, but each way of remembering has validity.

Nancy learned many things that helped explain what had happened in her childhood home and why. She found out that several members of her mother's family suffered from chronic depression, that her mother's own father had left his wife and family several times, and that her mother had had another pregnancy when Nancy was very young but had miscarried. She also learned that her father had been believed to be having an affair with his secretary for much of her childhood, information that shed a different light on his behavior toward her mother and toward Nancy's developing sexuality.

For Nancy, there will always be unanswered questions about why her parents were the way they were. But by exploring the variety of possible reasons her parents acted as they did, she was able to view her childhood with more realism and less self-loathing. Nancy had always assumed that if her parents behaved rejectingly toward her, it must have been because she was a worthless, repulsive nothing who deserved rejection. Now she realized that if they were rejecting, it was probably for a complex variety of reasons that went back many years before her birth, and that may even have had very little or nothing at all to do with her.

Nancy's fifth and final major task in coming to terms with her mother was to give up her illusion of control. People who grew up without getting the love and security they needed tend to believe that if only they had been better children, they would have received better parenting. In fact, Nancy's parents would probably have treated her in much the same way even if she had been a very different child. Their ability to be parents was determined by their own upbringings and other factors—their physical and mental health, economic resources, level of personal fulfillment—that had nothing to do with what kind of children they had. Even if Nancy had been a perfect child, this wouldn't have transformed the human, complicated people who raised her into perfect parents.

Although Nancy had to take on these five tasks in order to come to terms with her relationship with her mother, she did not take them on in neat, linear, sequential order as this listing might suggest. She worked on them simultaneously and somewhat haphazardly, making progress on each without entirely finishing any. Such tasks tend to be ongoing, and as long as Nancy is alive, she'll probably find that even in the areas where she has made the most headway, there'll still be work to be done.

After she had begun to come to terms with her relationship with her mother, Nancy was in a position to better understand her relationship with her husband, Josh. The "hook" of this relationship, she came to realize, was that it caused her to feel the same sort of pain, self-loathing, and powerlessness she had felt when at the mercy of a troubled and rejecting mother. The difference was, this time Nancy had a choice. She now had the power to try to change the relationship. She could also leave it. She wasn't a helpless little girl in relation to her husband; she only felt that way.

It can be suicidal for a small child to stand up to a violent parent. But as Nancy was increasingly able to separate her relationship with her mother from that with her husband, she saw that in her marriage there was no need to continue taking abuse. As an adult she had power and access to resources that opened up other options.

Nancy had always taken her husband's abuse because her inner view of herself was that she was so flawed, ugly, and worthless that she deserved to be treated badly. Now, with repeated encouragement, she began overhauling her self-image. She gradually came to accept that she wasn't born flawed and deserving of punishment but had been taught to see herself that way. Gradually she came to see that she had learned this primarily through the influence of her depressed and disturbed mother. And gradually she came to see that she really wasn't so terribly ugly, repulsive, dumb, and worthless after all.

When speaking of the change process that Nancy went through, the aptness of the word *gradually* cannot be overemphasized. Nancy had to be told many, many times that she was not bad and deserving of abusive treatment before it began to sink in. And when it did start sinking in, it sank in intellectually—in her head—at first. It took much longer for this new knowledge to sink in emotionally, in her gut, heart, and soul. Crucial as intellectual understanding is, change can only be carried out and completed once what is understood intellectually is "gotten" emotionally and begins to penetrate deeper and deeper into the psyche. Even when Nancy had begun intellectually to believe that she wasn't so bad after all, it was still awhile before she felt ready to begin actually changing her behavior.

Finally but, again, gradually Nancy did begin standing up to her husband. In the past, it had been Josh's habit to put her down when out in public. Now when he did that, Nancy told him on the way home, "I don't want you to talk to me that way. I deserve better treatment. If you have an issue with me, bring it up privately." When Josh persisted, Nancy decided to stop waiting until the ride home. On the spot, in front of everyone, she said, "You can't talk to me that way. I might have put up with it before, but no more. I deserve better, and from now on I expect it."

Although it was in her capacity as a mother that Nancy felt best about herself, for years she had permitted Josh to call her "incompetent," "unfit to be a mother," and "too easy on the kids." But now she began to respond with, "You're wrong. If there's one thing in the world I know I am, it's a good mother. No matter what you say, you can't take that away from me."

Nancy's transformation from someone who accepted abuse as a fact of life to someone who stood up against it did not happen overnight. She went through many periods when she reverted to her old ways of behavior. Each time she seemed to take a step forward, inevitably she'd have another experience in which she felt she was taking a step back. Over the long run she was making progress, but her day-to-day sense of things was often that "I'm not getting very far."

Nancy also felt great trepidation. Intellectually she knew Josh was not her mother and she was not a helpless little girl, but she still felt that in challenging him she was "like a little baby waving a tiny fist at my mother." Not standing up to her mother had enabled her to survive her childhood, and she understandably felt that if she gave up that behavior now, it just might kill her. It took Nancy a tremendous amount of courage to face that fear and then go ahead and change her behavior anyway.

In many marriages, the husband would have responded to his wife's newfound self-respect and assertiveness with increased regard for her, and the relationship would have evolved accordingly. But the stronger Nancy grew, the more critical and enraged Josh became. One night after she challenged him, he beat her up. She called the police and filed charges and the next day announced, "This can't go on anymore. I want a divorce." She remained in treatment for the next six months, focusing primarily on emotionally disengaging from the marriage and continuing to build self-esteem.

The Change Process: Nancy Continues

Two years later, Nancy initiated treatment for a second time. "I have no doubts that I made the right decision about the divorce," she said. "I spent the first thirty years of my life living with someone who was always putting me down, and in therapy I learned that I didn't have to do that anymore. I had been waiting until my husband changed and stopped being abusive, but I realized that no matter what I did, I couldn't change him—I could only change me. That was a big step, and it's made a big difference in my life."

But improved as Nancy's life was, she felt there was still room for considerable change. "I've been dating a lot of men and they find me attractive sexually and as a person," she explained on first returning to treatment. "But there's something inside me that says, 'They don't know me.' When I look at myself, I still feel 'How can anyone love *this*?' I hate the way I look." Also, Nancy later confided, "I'm eating too much. I go on binges. I hate myself for it. Most of the time I can't look in the mirror without wanting to throw up."

Nancy's other main concern when she entered therapy for the second time was her relationship with her daughters. Although she felt warm and loving toward them the bulk of the time, the moments when she felt overly critical were becoming more common. Now that they had become sexually maturing teenagers, she found herself more and more often feeling that they were "fat," "ugly," "too sexual." Nancy knew that there had to be a link between these negative feelings toward her daughters and her feelings toward her own physical self. She hoped that therapy would shed more light on the connections.

During the second time in treatment, much attention has been on Nancy's relationship with her father, which previously had not been explored in any depth. Nancy's father influenced her in two major ways. His most obvious legacy to her was her negative body image. At the time she began treatment again, Nancy still saw herself as repulsive, disgusting, monstrous-looking. These feelings had been with Nancy for so long that she could not remember ever being without them; consequently, she assumed that she had always had them, and would have them the rest of her life, too.

As she explored her past more, however, Nancy realized that there once had been a time when "I didn't go around filled with thoughts of how disgusting and ugly I am." As a little girl, in fact, there had been times when she either felt pretty or was totally unaware of her physical self. All this changed, she realized, at puberty, when she started filling out, becoming what by society's standards would be considered a little on the plump side. In a healthier family, Nancy's parents would have helped their pubescent daughter deal with her bodily changes, reassuring her that girls who fill out in puberty very often slim down later naturally, and letting her know that her appearance was not the most important thing about her anyway. But in Nancy's family, her mother remained unreliable as a source of love, and her father suddenly started treating her coldly and distantly, without any explanation or even acknowledgment. As discussed in Chapter 1, this was a traumatic blow. Desperate to make sense of the change, and then perhaps reverse it, she looked in the mirror and concluded that her father had stopped loving her because she had become "fat, ugly, and repulsive." It was then that she started to become preoccupied with her weight.

As Nancy began to explore her relationship with her father, it soon became apparent that she had a lot of unresolved grief to work through. He had died when she was in her mid-twenties, and although she had mourned him openly for several years, her mourning was unfinished. This was because she had never actually mourned her first loss of him, at puberty. Although from that point Nancy and her father had continued to have a relationship that was in many ways helpful and supportive, in an emotional sense, this was when Nancy really experienced his death. Nancy spent many sessions talking about how heartbroken she had been because of her father's rejection, how much she missed him and wished she could return to the idyllic days of their early relationship. In the process, she shed many tears, which were a natural part of the mourning process she needed to go through.

Like many people who grew up emotionally undernourished and who have body-image problems, Nancy had some problems relating to food. At night, feeling sad and alone, she would go into the kitchen and binge, mostly on cookies, cakes, and pastries. This made her feel less emotionally empty for a brief while, but it also made her feel more loathing toward her body. While this is a common pattern, in Nancy's case it turned out to have a curious twist. During her childhood, Nancy's father had been a partner in a number of different businesses, among them a bakery. Nancy remembered several incidents when her father took her to the bakery and would let her take whatever she wanted. Nancy's mother had been strict about sweets, so Nancy and her father had a pact not to tell her about their bakery visits. The secrecy further cemented the bond between father and daughter, but it led as well to some feelings of shame. Nancy's sense of shame was carried over to her later binges, also conducted in secrecy. Unable to have her father with her in actuality, it was as if Nancy were seeking closeness with him by symbolically re-enacting their secret visits to his bakery.

Psychotherapy is often discouraging for client and therapist alike, because issues are discussed at length and great insights are obtained, yet no change seems to occur. This was what happened with Nancy. She talked about her relationship with her father at great length, exploring it from many different angles. She mourned her loss of him, both through his rejection of her and his later death. She came to understand much more about her negative body image, where it came from, and how she perpetuated it through her eating binges. She came to realize what psychological purposes her bingeing served, and why baked goods in particular had such an added appeal to her. But nothing seemed to change. Nancy still hated her body. And she still got up in the night and stuffed herself with cookies, cake, and pastries.

After many months of seeming stuck in the same place, Nancy arrived at therapy one day and announced that something important had happened. A few nights before, feeling lonely, anxious, and unable to sleep, she had gone into the kitchen and opened a bakery box. As she put a cheese Danish into her mouth, "a strange feeling came over me," she explained. "I suddenly thought, 'I don't want this' and took the Danish out of my mouth. I stood there looking at it, and it had no appeal to me. It didn't look gross or anything, it looked good, but it just didn't appeal to me. I realized that what I really wanted was love, and that that wasn't something that a Danish was going to give me. I put it back in the box, and went back to bed. I stayed up all night thinking that if I really wanted love, what were some ways that I could go about getting it."

All Nancy's painstaking therapy during the preceding months had only *appeared* to be going nowhere. In fact, Nancy had been laying the internal groundwork that made possible a breakthrough experience, and finally enabled her to make concrete changes in her feelings and behavior.

When Nancy realized that what she really wanted was love, she saw it was time to begin seriously dating again. In the two years since her divorce, she had gone out with several men. None was interested in a serious relationship, which was fine with Nancy. But after several years of being single again, this began to change. Increasingly, she felt that there was "a piece missing" from her life, that she and her daughters formed an "incomplete picture," and that she wanted "a full family." These feelings become more and more predominant until one day she had a rather amusing epiphany. "It suddenly hit me," she explained, "that I really liked being married. I just didn't like who I was married to."

When the men she had dated since her divorce complimented her appearance, Nancy had always discounted their comments, writing them off as evidence of insincerity or poor judgment. As long as it was a barrier against men whose affection she didn't want, there was something safe and insulating about her negative body image. But when Nancy started to date men she was more interested in getting seriously involved with, it began to function as a love block, keeping out positive regard she wanted to receive. Nancy realized that if she were serious about finding someone who would love her, she'd better get serious about learning to accept her lovableness.

One of the ways Nancy did this was to join a health spa. At first she hated the exercise, but as she kept up with it, she experienced a sense of bodily well-being of the sort she had not felt for decades. "I feel like a young girl again," she reported. She did not lose much weight, but she became much more fit, thereby recapturing some of the early positive feelings she had had toward her body before puberty. For the first time in her adult life, she was treating her body with love. Of course, she had periods of backsliding—old feelings and patterns don't disappear that easily—but eventually she would return to exercising and watching her diet.

As a result, Nancy began to find it easier to take in positive attention from men. She doesn't believe she is Christie Brinkley, but Nancy has been increasingly able to look at herself in the mirror and say, "Not bad, kid, not bad at all. Not great, but not bad either."

However, Nancy needed to be cautioned against taking concern with her appearance too far. In today's overly body-conscious culture, many people, especially women, think, "My problem is my body; therefore, if only I had a better body, I'd feel better about myself." But the body is often less the source of low self-esteem than its repository. For many people, poor body image is a manifestation of vague, nebulous feelings of self-dislike, and a way of making those feelings concrete and understandable to themselves and others. Because of this, improving the body through exercise and diet programs does not necessarily yield higher self-esteem. Although many people who lose weight and get in better shape *do* feel better about themselves as a result, many others continue to hold on to a negative body image; witness all the anorectics who continue to perceive themselves as fat. In other cases, people feel better about their bodies, but their underlying low self-esteem is then manifested in other ways. In both sets of circumstances, it's crucial to determine whether the root problem is really with the body or whether a negative body image is serving as a cover for deeper, less easily identifiable self-esteem problems. If so, improving the body may actually make the problems worse.

Moreover, even when improving the body does lead to improved self-esteem, this can perpetuate an excessive preoccupation with the body that works against the development and maintenance of high self-esteem over the long run. The fact is, nature has decreed that human beauty and strength are by definition fleeting. Too many people, particularly women, derive too much of their self-esteem from having a particular kind of body, which then erodes along with youthful beauty and firmness. To build self-esteem that lasts, it's wise to pay more attention to developing other aspects of one's self and not be so concerned with looks.

In Nancy's case, it was helpful to get in better shape but even more helpful to pay attention to another area she had long neglected—the work and intellectual spheres. As mentioned earlier, Nancy's poor body image was one of two legacies left to her by her father. The other legacy was her lack of faith in her own intellectual capabilities. When Nancy was a child and adolescent, her father spent a good deal of time discussing intellectual topics with her, and he encouraged her to strive for high standards in school. As Nancy explored her relationship with her father in greater detail, however, it became apparent that he was really giving her messages that were much more mixed. One message Nancy got was "Yes, you're smart—for a girl, that is." As a conservative Jew, Nancy's father saw learning as an essentially male privilege; as much as he encouraged Nancy to do well in school, he made it clear to her that the highest, most sacred form of learning was the study of the Torah—strictly off-limits to females. So another message Nancy received was "You're capable of doing well as far as you can go, but because you are an inferior female, you can't go very far." Finally, Nancy's father believed his daughter had one appropriate role in life—that of wife and mother—and he feared that if she were too obvious about being smart, she wouldn't land a suitable husband. So yet another message Nancy got was "Your intelligence is a liability that reduces your sexual attractiveness and hurts your chances in the marriage market." These mixed messages gave Nancy the notion that there was something wrong and "flukey" about her intelligence, that if she did well in school, either it had to be an accident, or it meant she was unfeminine.

Nancy had started to reevaluate her long-standing low opinion of her intellectual capabilities even before she started therapy and decided to divorce Josh, as evidenced by her courageous decision to return to college. Once back in school, though, she felt intimidated by the professors and also by the other students, who struck her as "so much smarter and younger and quicker" than she. Although she did extremely well—getting all A's and winning several awards—she felt all the while that "it's all a fluke and I'm really an impostor." She even had fantasies that one day the college authorities would find out "what a dummy I really am and revoke my diploma."

After finishing her degree, Nancy got a job as a high school guidance counselor. Apparently, she was a great success at it. Students sought her out to talk to her. Her colleagues often asked for her advice about how to deal with problem kids, telling her "you really know how to reach them." The head of the guidance office, the principal, and the assistant principal all gave her consistently excellent evaluations. Yet because of her inner view of herself, Nancy wasn't able to take in all this positive feedback. She dismissed it, without allowing it to penetrate within.

Eventually Nancy realized the praise and affirmation were always "drowned out by an old voice" or an "old tape." Her mother, it turned out, never asked about her work success. And whenever Nancy brought up the subject, her mother would listen impatiently, then quickly interrupt with "have you met any nice men yet?" This would be annoying to anyone, but it had extra power and resonance for Nancy because it echoed Old World values that had been deeply instilled in her. Nancy's parents were Eastern European immigrants who believed a woman's only valid role in life was that of wife and mother, and although intellectually Nancy rejected this notion, unconsciously she felt that her parents were correct: since she was divorced and no "nice marriageable man" had appeared on the horizon, whatever else she did was of no consequence. As Nancy became more aware of the extent to which she had internalized her parents' voice, she gradually came to replace it with her own inner voice, which said, "I am not my parents. In my world a woman has value in other ways beyond being a wife and mother." The more she said this to herself, the more able she was to take in the praise and affirmation she received at work.

After several years of work as a guidance counselor, Nancy was feeling ready to take on some new challenges. She heard about an opening as a counselor in the dean of students' office at a local college, but she had barely considered the possibility before she decided not to apply. She was afraid of not getting the job, and the feelings of rejection, self-doubt, and disappointment that would ensue. But more than that, she was afraid of getting the job. "The people there are so smart," she explained. "I felt I hardly belonged at college as a student, so how could I ever *work* at a college? I'd feel so small and inadequate surrounded by all those intellectual giants. I just don't belong there." As Nancy looked at these feelings more closely, she realized that symbolically the college represented the intellectual world of men; it represented the world of higher learning which her father had told her God had declared off-limits to girls. As she became aware of the source of her fears, she saw that in fact she would not be betraying her father; if he were alive he probably would have offered her at least some words of encouragement. Although terrified, Nancy managed to apply for the job, and got it. She has been so successful that she now heads up the college's admissions office. In the process, she discovered that college administrators and professors "aren't as big or smart as I thought. They're mostly regular people. I fit in well."

Shortly after starting work at the college, Nancy began dating the college attorney, a divorced man named Peter. He treated her well, her daughters liked him, and Nancy enjoyed his companionship and was especially happy with their sex life. After about six months of serious dating, Peter began talking about marriage. Nancy became very anxious and ambivalent. Part of this reaction had to do with the normal doubts that anyone contemplating a lifetime commitment would feel, compounded by the anxiety that many divorced people have about not wanting to make the same mistakes all over again. But there was something deeper going on, too. Nancy felt Peter was too gruff, opinionated, and argumentative. She wanted him to be "soft and gentle and soothing, a motherly best friend who will calm me down and quiet all my worries." But that was not his nature. She would often ask for his opinion or advice, then be upset because the advice he gave wasn't the advice she wanted to hear, or wasn't expressed in the way she wanted. A frustrated Peter would then respond, "If you didn't want my advice, then why the hell did you ask for it?" A fight would usually follow.

It was obvious that Nancy had made great headway in overcoming her main love block, "I Don't Deserve Love." But when a person overcomes one love block, he often finds that behind it stand other love blocks. As Nancy developed more self-esteem, she became aware of other love blocks, including "I Want Love, But Only If It's a Certain Way" (examined in Chapter 16). Looking for the source of her doubts about marrying Peter, she realized that since she was a little girl she had been carrying an unconscious fantasy about "the Bigby family," the ideal family of the sort she secretly dreamed of. The Mr. Bigby of her fantasy was a gentle, reassuring, motherly man who never raised his voice or displeased his wife in any way. Because Peter did not fit this image, she was blocked from taking in the kind of love he did offer. Unconsciously, she was taking a stand characteristic of this block, a stand that says, "I want a particular kind of love in a particular kind of way, and if anyone tries to give me a different kind of love in a different way, forget it. I'd rather do without."

After several months of considering marriage, Nancy made a decision. "I've dated a lot of men, and no one has loved me more or treated me better than Peter has," she explained. "I could go the rest of my life looking for my Mr. Bigby. Maybe I'd never find him. Or maybe I would, but he'd fail to fit my fantasy in some other way. Maybe it's time to give up the fantasy." She and Peter married, and after three years things seem to be working out. She still wishes he were the "soft, gentle, consoling" type, but she has developed several close friendships with women and men who have more of those qualities. They provide her with some of the kinds of love that Peter can't, and this has enabled her to have greater appreciation for, and receptivity to, the sort of love he does give her.

As Nancy has overcome her love blocks, her relationships with her daughters have continued to deepen. As she has become more accepting of her body, she has become more accepting of theirs. She no longer criticizes them for being "fat and ugly." As she has increased her self-esteem through work, intellectual pursuits, community activities, and a variety of relationships outside the home, she has also become more appreciative of her daughters as whole and complex human beings. If they let their rooms become pigstys, or don't take care of their appearance as she would like, or don't show a willingness to do what she wants them to do, Nancy doesn't get agitated and angry. "For the first time in my life, I feel I'm okay, and that allows me to trust that my daughters are going to turn out okay, too," she explained. Plus, she added, "even though Peter isn't the motherly kind of husband I always wanted, I know I can lean on him in very basic ways. I know that he will try to be there for me. This makes me feel like a loved person and that makes me feel more loving toward others."

The more loved and appreciated she feels, the less frequently Nancy is given to feelings of free-floating anger. "I think I used to have a lot of anger about my childhood and first marriage and life in general, and I would take that out on my daughters," she explained. "I still get pissed off and can scream and yell, but I'm much less liable to explode than I used to be." This, combined with her less critical attitude, has made Nancy seem much more approachable and thus has allowed her daughters to reach out to her in loving ways more often and more easily. "We have our rough times, and I'm sure we always will," Nancy explained. "But basically, I feel good about my relationship with my daughters. I love them, and I know they love me. I used to wonder, 'how could these adorable girls have come from me?' I felt I didn't deserve them. Now I look at them and can see that it's not just my more negative qualities they inherited. Some of the good things about them come from me as well."

The Principles of Change

Nancy's story is the story of a particular woman, but it's also illustrative of something larger: how people with love blocks can overcome them. Many self-help books give the change process short shrift, or skip over it entirely. The reason is obvious: the change process is so subtle and complex that it is virtually impossible to describe accurately in words. In presenting Nancy's case, for example, no effort was made to recount her progress in psychotherapy session by session, or to describe the nature of the interaction between client and therapist. Nevertheless, Nancy's case illustrates the general principles of the change process that most people who make a commitment to overcoming their love blocks will go through.

In Part Two, the stories of many different people with different love blocks will be told. But first, here are the thirteen basic principles of the change process, outlined one by one and discussed in a bit more detail. These principles of change will enable you to place individual cases into a larger, constructive framework:

1. *Change begins with a desire to change, along with the realization that change is possible.* Many people go through life as if they were sleepwalking, with little or no awareness that there are any problems in their relationships with others or themselves. Other people are aware that something is amiss, as expressed in a variety of ways: "I'm in a lot of pain," "I need to grow more as a person," "I want more out of my life and relationships," "My relationships never seem to work out the way I want," "I'm in a rut," "Something's missing," and so on. These same people may also feel "I am the way I am, there's nothing that can be done to change that." But after seeing people around them change, it eventually dawns on them that "Maybe I don't have to be the way I am now forever. Maybe I can change, too." That is the point at which change can begin.

2. *Change occurs most easily with the help of a guide.* When embarking on a journey into unfamiliar territory, it's always a good idea to consult someone who has been there before. A guide can suggest which roads to take, alert you to pitfalls and high points, tell you what to expect on your journey, rekindle your interest and enthusiasm if they flag, and tell you about the experiences of others who have already traveled the same route.

In the realm of psychological change, many different kinds of guides can be of help. Self-help books are one kind of guide. Spiritual teachings and practices can serve as other kinds of guides, as can support groups such as Alcoholics Anonymous. And then there are individual guides. In much of the world for much of history, a personal guide would probably be a spiritual teacher, a "guru" or mentor. In American culture at this point in history, however, a personal guide usually means a psychotherapist.

A caveat should be added here: Although most of the people in the forthcoming pages relied on the guidance of a psychotherapist during the change process, therapy is not the only way to overcome love blocks. Psychotherapy is definitely in order for those whose love blocks severely hinder their ability to have relationships, but those who are mildly affected might find other types of guides sufficient.

3. *Even the best guide is only a guide; it is the client or student who does the changing.* Many books written in recent years give the impression that the only way anyone ever makes any substantial changes in his inner life and outward behavior is through long-term, one-on-one psychotherapy. What's more, a spate of recent self-help books by psychotherapists depict the change process by placing the therapist in the starring role and making him or her out to be an all-knowing sage who always says the right thing at the right time. According to these formulaic accounts, the client arrives at the therapist's office, her life a total shambles but reluctant to go into details, so the therapist skillfully pries her story out of her with a series of sleuthlike questions. Hardly has the client recounted her story when suddenly the therapist reaches a complete understanding of the client's problems and how to resolve them. Even more startling, the therapist is instantly able to communicate all this to the client in a speech that is compassionate, eloquent, and succinct. Within a short time, the client returns to the therapist's office and gratefully reports that her life is dramatically changed.

Therapy clients who read these types of depictions get discouraged because they have not experienced such enormous changes, and conclude that something must be wrong with them or their therapists, who aren't nearly as quick or infallible as those in the books. This is not the case. There's something wrong with the way the therapist and the therapy process are being presented. Therapists are not gods; even the wisest, most insightful and brilliant therapist is only a guide. Moreover, in therapy it is the client who does the bulk of the work and all of the changing. The therapist is involved for a few hours a week at most, but for the client the change process goes on twenty-four hours a day, seven days a week. And a therapist can have insights and dream interpretations that are truly brilliant, but they will not help the client one iota unless the client has reached the same conclusions herself.

4. *Conscious awareness is a key ingredient in the change process.* Much of the time, people conduct their relationships unaware of what they're doing, and unaware of why they behave the way they do. Obviously, as long as a person remains unaware of his behavior patterns, changing them is going to be very difficult. So conscious awareness is crucial.

Conscious awareness of *why* these patterns are occurring is crucial as well. Many people who have not seriously endeavored to understand and change their pyschological and behavioral patterns scoff at the notion that conscious awareness is important. They hold fast to a stance that says, "Assuming I did discover that my problems in adulthood have to do with what happened when I was a child, what difference would it make?" This sort of question is usually asked rhetorically, but there is an answer: When a person discovers the root reasons for why he feels and behaves as he does, it makes an enormous difference. It is like a powerful light going on in a dark tunnel. The tunnel remains dim and filled with shadows, and long as well. But when the inside walls are illuminated, revealing the tunnel's shape, size, and texture, it is much easier to see the way out. With awareness, the previously jumbled pieces of the puzzle of an individual's life start coming together in a semblance of order, and many things that always seemed mysterious, unfathomable, and baffling start to make sense.

5. *For significant change to occur, conscious awareness must be followed by integration.* For some people in some situations, a conscious understanding of what they are doing and why is sufficient to enable them to start changing their feelings and behavior. For most people, however, it's only the first step. Real changes in how a person feels inside and acts toward others require integration. Each of us has many different layers of consciousness, and the capacity for different ways of knowing. There's intellectual or rational knowing, or knowing that occurs in the head. Then there's emotional or visceral know-

ing, knowing that occurs in the heart, gut, and soul. For most people in cognitive-oriented cultures such as ours, insights are known or "gotten" in the head first. But "getting" or knowing that same insight at gut level takes more time, and it is then that the most profound changes take place.

6. *Different kinds of changes occur at different rates, but the deepest changes occur very slowly.* Sometimes the most effective tack is for a person to change his behavior first, with the hope that the way he feels inside will then change accordingly. When Nancy was contemplating applying for her first job after college, for example, she was terrified to the point of not being able to write up her résumé or make the necessary phone calls. She could have worked on overcoming her fears first, then have made her moves toward getting a job afterwards. But she decided to accept her fears for the moment, and take action despite them. Once she got a job and began working, she found that many of her fears had to do with her sense that she wouldn't fit in or would screw up on the job, and she also found that they automatically began to dissipate. This was a case when it made sense to change behavior first.

But often this approach is not effective. When dealing with deep, characterological patterns like love blocks, there usually must be some change in the way a person feels inside before he is ready to begin behaving differently. Nancy is a good example. She made a number of positive steps in her life, yet her underlying feelings of self-loathing remained fairly well entrenched. Only after exploring, analyzing, and discussing these feelings again and again did she reach increasing levels of understanding, and only after she began to "get" in her gut how these feelings originated did they begin to leave her. This took years, and even now the last of these feelings has not left her.

Unfortunately, the fact that significant change takes place slowly does not sit well with most Americans. In other parts of the world, people take it for granted that change and growth take time. In technologically advanced, result-oriented, hurried American culture, however, people expect things to happen fast. When an American discovers he has a love block, the typical response is some variation of "Okay, I understand that this is my problem. Now tell me what to do about it so I can fix it quickly, then get on with my life." But when it comes to deeply entrenched patterns like love blocks, patience is called for. The process of change is usually lifelong. It should not be viewed as a preamble to life, but as a way of life.[1]

7. Often when nothing seems to be happening, profound changes are actually occurring. The slowness of the change process is alone sufficient cause for frustration. To add to the frustration, most of the deep changes that occur do not occur in dramatic ways. Some people do sometimes have epiphany-like experiences that make them want to shout "Eureka!" More often, though, the changes that occur are experienced very subtly. Sometimes they are so subtle that nothing seems to be happening at all. The person seems to be completely stuck.

In fact, though, it's often precisely then that the most profound changes are in the making. The change process is a lot like gardening or farming. Imagine a long-neglected plot of land that's overgrown with weeds, strewn with rocks, and laden with soil that's depleted of vital nutrients. If a gardener plants seeds here, there's no way they'll germinate, take root, and grow. Before the gardener plants, she needs to remove the rocks and weeds, turn over the soil, and apply fertilizer. This takes a lot of time, and it's not particularly exciting. Many people would consider it excruciatingly boring. But when the gardener finally finishes preparing the plot and then plants the seeds, growth appears suddenly and dramatically. Almost overnight, it seems, the plot becomes a lush garden alive with growth. But the process could not have occurred without all that tedious preparation. When a person is engaged in the change process, he often feels that "I'm going over the same ground again and again but getting nowhere." But this is precisely what enables noticeable change to finally occur.

8. Change does not occur in a smooth, linear fashion; there are fallbacks and bumps along the way. Sometimes a lull *is* just what it seems—a time when nothing is really happening. Lulls like this are inevitable. As nice as it would be for change to occur in a never-wavering onward, upward pattern, there are times when the rate of change will slow down, or come to a temporary halt.

Inevitably, there are also times when a person actually seems to be going backward. As Nancy worked to overcome her binge eating, for example, there were times when she fell back on her old ways. Regressions like this are never pleasant, but they are also not cause for despair. The change process is a forgiving one; people can slip up, falling off the wagon, so to speak, then can climb back on again. There is no penalty. The person is not sent "back to square one" but can take up the journey again at the points where he left it.

Just as it's not always onward and upward, the change process isn't always great fun. In fact, as it triggers memories long suppressed, it often brings up dormant feelings of pain, loss, sadness, anger, and yearning that can be very difficult to bear. In some cases, there is a danger that the person engaged in the change process will feel so flooded by painful feelings that she will have trouble functioning or will become seriously depressed. Any time the change process gets into such rocky territory, professional help should be sought out immediately. There is no reason in the world that a person in intolerable pain or depression should have to go on in that state. A physician working with a psychotherapist, or a therapist working in tandem with a medical doctor, should be able to recommend treatment, perhaps including medication, to help an individual get through the rough period and continue on in the process of change.

9. Many of the answers are already inside you. As mentioned before, many people respond to the discovery that they have a love block by saying, in essence, "Okay, I understand that I have a problem. Now tell me what I can do about it." Being open to receiving help and advice is a healthy trait, but many carry it too far. They want their chosen guides not just to simply point to the possible routes, but to choose for them which one to take. Not trusting their inner selves, they do not realize that within their unconscious they may already have a very good idea of exactly what it is they need to know.

For the process of change to progress, there needs to be an increasing awareness of, and reliance on, one's own inner sources of wisdom. Each of us has an unconscious inner voice that knows what's best for us. This voice tries to communicate with our conscious selves in a variety of ways—through dreams, through images or memories that seem to hit us "out of the blue," through physical maladies that seem difficult to explain or remedy. There are a variety of ways to become more attuned to one's inner voice. These include: meditation;

visualization exercises; writing in a journal; getting into the habit of recalling, recording, and analyzing dreams; praying, chanting, fasting, and participating in religious rituals; and dancing, singing, playing musical instruments, painting, and other creative arts. When a person becomes more in touch with her own inner sources of wisdom, she'll be in a much better position to decide which advice that others offer she should follow.

10. The change process can be tiresome and can make you feel stupid. It's not just the slowness that can make the change process tiresome, it's also all the talking about the self that is involved. No matter how much some people might initially love self-exploration and analysis, eventually even they may reach a point where they feel "I've had it. I am so sick and tired of talking about my own life and problems. I hate all this looking under the surface and analyzing everything. I'm bored by my own neuroses. I just want to shut up about them and ignore them for a while." During any long journey, sometimes feeling sick and tired of traveling and bored by the scenery is inevitable. These feelings need to be accepted and waited out. They are part of the change process, not reason to abandon it.

The same can be said for the feelings of stupidity that usually arise. When people begin making connections between what happened in their childhoods and what's happening in their lives now, often it strikes them that many of these connections are "so obvious that anyone could see them." When they get an insight, they don't think "Eureka! Isn't it great that I've realized this." Instead, they respond with some version of "What's wrong with me that I didn't see this before? It's so obvious only a moron could have missed it" or "I must have been blind! What an idiot I am." But the fact is, many of the things that are most obvious about ourselves and our lives in other people's eyes are precisely the things that are hardest for us to see. This needs to be kept in mind when working toward change.

11. Change is scary. Deeply ingrained patterns like love blocks originated for one reason: to help us survive. As a result, when a person is in the process of giving them up, he may feel that his survival is at stake, that he is literally going to die. There is no way to get around the fact that it is scary, often terrifying, to change lifelong patterns of feeling and behavior and to take new and unfamiliar approaches to life.

Looking back on childhood, most people can find a metaphor that illuminates this terror and makes it easier to cope with. Nancy, for example, used the metaphor of crossing the street. She grew up in New York City, where crossing the street meant literally "taking my life in my hands." When as a young girl she finally learned to cross the street with some confidence of safety, she was glad to find whole new worlds of experience on the other side. Now Nancy used this metaphor to help cope with the inevitable fear that arose each time she made changes in her ways of seeing herself and behaving in the world. She imagined herself standing on one side of the street, knowing the other side would turn out to be a much better place for her to be. Looking across the wide avenue with all its unpredictable traffic, she was terrified of stepping off the curb. But visualizing her guide (in her case a psychologist, Bill) as a "uniformed crossing guard holding my hand," she was always able to muster up the courage to make her move. And always, she found life was better on the other side.

12. *It's never too late to change*. This is one of the principles of change that meets with the stiffest resistance. Many people with love blocks and other psychological problems reach a point in life where they think, "I've missed my chance to change. I've been this way as long as I can remember, and I guess I'm bound to stay this way until I die." In our youth-obsessed culture, it's widely taken for granted that once people get beyond a certain age, they lose their capacity to change. This is patently false. The people whose stories are told in the following pages embarked on their efforts to change at all ages, some in their late twenties, most in their thirties or forties. Several were in their fifties. For none was age a barrier, and most found that their greater experience gave them wisdom, perspective, and humor which actually aided their efforts.

13. *Change is lifelong work*. This final principle is often strongly resisted, too. Nancy hasn't finished the change process, nor have many of the other people whose stories appear in upcoming pages. After making significant progress, a person may get to a point where he feels "that's it, I'm all better, there's no more work to do." Then, two days or two months or two years later, he'll realize that there is more work to do, perhaps at a deeper level, or on completely different issues he hadn't been aware of earlier. It can be very discouraging

to realize that "Oh no, I'm not all better as I'd thought. I have more work to do." It's helpful to keep in mind that there are two ways to look at the situation. A person can groan and say, "Oh no. I thought I was all better, and now I find out that I'm still really screwed up! How discouraging." Or she can say, "Oh wow. I thought I had already gone as far as I could, and now I find out that there's still room for improvement. I can feel even better!"

Part Two

Love Blocks

Chapter 4
"I Don't Want to Deal with My Feelings"

Love is an emotion, a feeling. In order to feel loved and loving, then, a person must first have the capacity to experience emotions. This sounds simple, so obvious that some might say it's ludicrous to point it out. Yet the fact is, many people want to be able to feel loved and loving while at the same time remaining generally unemotional. Although they may look upon passionately "falling in love" as a desirable experience, they believe that as a rule emotions should be kept in check, held tightly under control, not given in to, and not allowed to "get the better of you." In their view, getting carried away by feelings is a sign of weakness, poor character and/or bad breeding, although being swept away by the specific feeling of love, particularly romantic or parental love, may be permissible, even desirable.[1]

Those who are most severely affected by the "I Don't Want to Deal with My Feelings" block tend to fall into two broad categories. First, there are those who can't tolerate emotional intensity. Strong feelings of any kind make them uncomfortable, even the "nice" ones like love. They strive to keep their own feelings under control, maintaining an air of unflappable calm, and usually try to control other people's feelings as well, using such stock lines as "don't feel that way," "you can't let that upset you," "stop overreacting," and so on. They may want very much to feel loved, but when they finally do get the chance they become upset and anxious to find that the experience stirs up everything inside them, perhaps even leaving them lightheaded, overwhelmed, confused, and ungrounded. To them, the prospect of going through life without getting much in the way of love may be less frightening than going through the unsettling experience of being loved.

For the second group of people with the "I Don't Want to Deal with My Feelings" block, the issue isn't how intensely they feel but *what* they feel. They want to feel selectively, experiencing only those feelings they consider "good," "nice," and "positive." They don't mind feeling these "good" feelings intensely, so long as they never feel any "bad" feelings, such as anger, envy, or resentment.

These two different manifestations are equally effective in blocking receptivity to love. People in the first group block themselves from taking in love because in so doing they would run the risk of feeling shaken up and "knocked off their feet." Such intensity is literally too much for them to handle. People in the second group block themselves from taking in love because they mistakenly believe they can close themselves only to "bad" feelings. They don't realize that since all feelings are inextricably connected, a person can't suppress a few select "bad" feelings without eventually losing the capacity to experience all other feelings as well, including the "good" ones.

Not everyone with the "I Don't Want to Deal with My Feelings" block is severely affected, nor does everyone fit neatly into one or the other of these two groups. For many, the block manifests itself subtly: they don't spend every waking moment tensely on guard against strong feelings, but they're not totally comfortable with their feelings either. They might agree that in theory it's natural, healthy, and wonderful to have feelings, but in reality they're always trying not to feel certain "bad" feelings—and they're really not fully at ease feeling any emotion with genuine intensity. If they find themselves experiencing a feeling they consider "bad"—resentment toward a loved one, say, or sexual desire toward someone other than their partner, or envy toward a friend—they are quick to censor and repress this feeling, telling themselves "I shouldn't feel this way." And if they experience an emotion with great intensity, whether it be rage or euphoria, it fills them with the fear that if they don't keep it in check, the feeling could overwhelm them and cause them to behave in reckless, foolish ways they'll later regret. For them, this block results in a muting rather than a deadening of the emotions. They experience fear as "uncomfortable," joy as "nice," and anger as "unpleasant." Although they can feel fondness and love for others, they hold back from loving in a no-holds-barred way because that would mean losing control. And although intellectually they may know that others love them deeply, they can't experience the expansive inner warmth that comes from permitting themselves to really open up and let another person's love penetrate their deepest selves.

Cultural Influences

Certainly our early family experiences determine to a large extent our style of dealing with our feelings. But one reason so many people are uncomfortable with their feelings is that we're all products of a culture characterized by a strong anti-emotion bias. In American culture, "manly" rationality is the trait we're taught to admire and aspire to, while emotionalism is put down as being both womanish and childish. Popular culture has lionized the strong, silent type who never "gives in" to his feelings, depicting him as noble, heroic, and even sexy. By contrast, open expression of feelings is seen as unseemly, embarrassing, and undignified, and those who are "in touch with" and vocal about their feelings are frequently perceived as weak and foolish.

Of course different ethnic groups have different attitudes toward emotions and different rules about expressing them. Generally speaking, German, Scandinavian, English, Scottish, and Irish cultures tend to be much more emotionally repressed than Latin and Mediterranean ones. And among the various Asian cultures, as well as among Arab and African ones, there are different beliefs about which feelings are acceptable, and what are permissible ways to express them. When we speak of a general anti-emotion bias running through American culture, we're speaking of a trend among the dominant mainstream culture, which so far remains most heavily influenced by the cultures of northern Europe.

It's true that this anti-emotion bias does serve some good purposes. Since commerce and social relations would crumble if everyone went around emoting all the time, a certain amount of emotional suppression on the part of everyone is necessary if we're to live in a somewhat orderly, efficient, civilized world. But it's equally true that this also makes it very difficult for many people to achieve the healthy acceptance of their emotions that is so crucial to psychological well-being and satisfying relationships.

Along with the general bias against feelings, there's a pervasive belief in our culture that certain feelings are especially bad. Grief and sadness, for example, strike many as unseemly, unhealthy, and in poor taste. As children, many people learned that it was wrong, silly or impolite to have these feelings, or that they were not entitled to them. Their parents may have admonished them that "big boys/girls don't cry," tried to convince them that "you don't really feel that way," teased them with such expressions as "bet you can't smile," or told them "you have no right to feel sorry for yourself. In China [or wherever] children are starving." Even if a child was allowed to experience grief and sadness, chances are good he was taught that he shouldn't let these feelings go on too long, lest he'd end up "wallowing" in them. As a result, when they have these feelings in adulthood, many people become angry and impatient with themselves, telling themselves it's wrong to have these feelings and to "hurry up and snap out of it."

Anger is another feeling many learned it would be best to hide— or not to feel in the first place. As children, many people were punished for feeling anger. The punishment might have been overt, as in the case of children who were hit for throwing a tantrum or sulking. Or the punishment might have been subtle, as in the case of those whose parents withheld love, approval, or food until the children began smiling the way the parents believed little children should.

Gender has a big impact on what feelings we learned to consider unacceptable. Women, for example, are generally given more license than men to have feelings and to be open about them. But the rub is that this freedom applies only to that relatively small group of human emotions considered "feminine," such as compassion, tenderness, humility, and maternal and romantic love. Other human feelings, such as anger, lust, ambition, aggression, hatred, and self-pride have been branded "unfeminine."

Men, too, learn that only certain feelings are acceptable. Ambition, pride, jealousy, lust, and competitiveness may be permissable, but not the softer, "feminine" emotions. And although members of both sexes often learn in childhood that anger is wrong, as adults men are given more freedom to feel it. The "angry young man," represented by such figures as James Dean and Marlon Brando, is a standard fixture in pop folklore, but there are no corresponding images of attractive angry young women. As Philip Slater has observed, in a society that prohibits anger in women but accepts and even encourages it in men, "women often dissolve into tears instead of raging in anger, while men get angry when their feelings are hurt and they feel like crying."[2]

The most troubling feelings to some people are sexual ones. For people who are uncomfortable with sexual feelings, sex may be less of a means to intimacy than a barrier against it. For example, Judy, the woman in Chapter 2 who was repulsed by her husband's genitalia, could relax with friends and let their love in because she felt it was understood that there were clear limits on how much physical contact was permitted. But her relationship with her husband, which by definition was supposed to entail sex, felt threatening and exploitative because it triggered repressed memories of being sexually abused as a child.

In a reverse of Judy's situation, some people are able to experience intimacy with sexual partners, but not with friends. This is because they associate the warm feeling of being loved with the "tingling all over" sensation of sexual arousal and are terrified that the warmth of close friendship will ignite sexual feelings they consider unacceptable and inappropriate. For heterosexuals the fear may be particularly intense when the friendship is with someone of the same sex, while for homosexuals it may be the reverse.

When a person fears feeling sexual stirrings in a friendship, physical contact with the friend will be either avoided or restricted. Many men, for example, are horrified by the prospect of kissing their male friends, even if all that's involved is a quick peck on the cheek. Then there is the rarely discussed issue of how long a hug should last— an issue that affects all kinds of friendships. Many people freely hug their friends, meanwhile subconsciously counting how many seconds the hug lasts. They feel comfortable hugging "only for so long"; if the hug lasts longer, they immediately start to tense up and either freeze in the embrace, or start to pull away.

Another feeling many people have a difficult time accepting in themselves is ambivalence.[3] Many people grew up believing that one day they would reach a magical point when they would know exactly who they are and what they want, and from that day on they'd be free of self-doubt and mixed feelings. But ambivalence is an inevitable fact of life. Even if a person feels sure that a particular relationship— or career choice, childbearing decision, geographical move, etc.—is the right one for her, she's also bound to have conflicting feelings about it. Such feelings are entirely normal in sentient, multidimensional, complicated beings. But because many people mistakenly believe ambivalence is a sign that "something's wrong," they get upset and anxious when they feel it.

The High Costs of Emotional Suppression

Although most people have learned to consider certain feelings—be they anger, sexual arousal, envy, resentment, jealousy, or fear—bad, wrong, silly, or stupid, such labels are, in fact, inappropriate. Feelings have no IQ, and it's self-punishing to subject them to moral judgments. What we do with our feelings—our behavior—can be characterized as right or wrong, good or bad, but there's nothing that's wrong or bad to feel. In her book *For Your Own Good,* the renowned Swiss psychoanalyst Alice Miller makes this point in discussing anger and hatred. As Miller explains, anger and hatred are often appropriate responses to the cruelties and injustice that many people suffer in the world; both are normal human feelings, and "a feeling has never killed anyone."[4]

Whether they are talked out, physically worked out, or acted out through behavior, feelings need to be let out in some way. But, instead of learning healthy ways to release their feelings, many people have been taught to practice denial ("I don't really feel this way"), to be judgmental and self-censoring ("I shouldn't feel this way"), and to try to make their feelings conform to externally imposed expectations ("It's the holidays—I'm supposed to feel happy"). These are common defenses against emotions, and they can be effective at keeping troubling feelings at bay, for a while at least.

But over the long term, it's damaging to deal with feelings in these ways. First, defenses work against self-esteem. To have a genuine sense of self-worth, an individual needs to be able to say, "I am a feeling being with a capacity for the whole range of human emotions—and that's okay." Put another way, respecting yourself means respecting your feelings—all of them.

When people censor and suppress their feelings, they also deprive themselves of an important source of information and guidance. Fear, for example, may be alerting a person to the fact that she's in danger, that it might be in her best interest to exercise caution or flee. Sadness that comes seemingly "out of the blue" might be telling a person that he didn't sufficiently mourn a loss and had better take the time now. If someone consistently feels angry or put-upon in her relationships, it may be a sign that she needs to place some limits on what others can ask of her. But if a person is too busy censoring her feelings, she won't be able to "hear" what they're trying to tell her.

Physical health is also often affected. Depending on how much someone tries to keep his feelings in check, his susceptibility to a variety of psychosomatic problems increases. These can run the gamut from back-, neck- and headaches to mild digestive-tract disorders to more serious problems like asthma, ulcers, and colitis. People who deny and suppress their feelings also run a high risk of developing drinking and drug problems, for as recovering alcoholics and drug addicts know, booze and drugs are often used to keep one's true feelings buried.

Recent studies also suggest that when people fall physically ill, their chances of recovery can be affected by the way they deal with their emotions. A study at the University of California at San Francisco, for example, found that among patients with melanoma—a serious form of skin cancer—those who freely expressed feelings such as distress and anger had more positive immune responses to the disease than did those who suppressed their feelings.[5]

Many people believe that if they pretend they don't have a certain feeling, such as anger or resentment, it will simply go away. In fact, though, we human beings can't make our feelings disappear. We can push them down into our unconscious where it may seem they've disappeared, but it takes a tremendous amount of energy to do so, and as time goes on more and more energy will be required to keep them suppressed. This inevitably leads to bouts of exhaustion, or to a chronic fatigue that seems to be without cause. And since everyone has a fixed amount of psychic energy, the more a person puts into suppressing her feelings, the less she'll have left over for other life pursuits.

The Toll on Relationships

Another problem with suppressing feelings is that ultimately it always turns out to be an exercise in futility. Eventually buried feelings will resurface. This can wreak havoc in relationships because buried feelings often resurface when they're completely unexpected and with a surprising amount of force. Everyone who has ever suddenly blown up at a loved one for reasons that have nothing to do with the matter at hand knows this full well.

The "I Don't Want to Deal with My Feelings" block interferes with relationships in a number of different ways, in fact. Since the principal way in which people connect and build intimacy is through the shared experience and expression of emotions, often intense ones, people who endeavor not to show their feelings—or not to have feelings in the first place—are bound to feel lonely, estranged, and unloved even when in ostensibly close relationships. Their sense of alienation from others mirrors their inner alienation from their natural emotional selves.

When people are intolerant, dismissive, and frightened of their own feelings, they often display the same attitudes toward other people's feelings. Thus, they also may give the mistaken impression that they are insensitive. Although they may tell themselves that by suppressing their own "negative" feelings they are protecting others, in fact their lack of warmth, tolerance, and emotional ease often hurts others and drives them away.

Projection is another consequence of not directly dealing with one's own feelings. This occurs when a person mentally places his feelings inside another person, imagining her to be the "feeler" or carrier of emotions that in truth are his own. Projection occurs especially often with feelings that make a person uncomfortable. For example, a woman who is angry at her husband but can't permit herself to acknowledge this will get it into her head that *he* is angry at her. Or a man who is feeling insecure in a relationship might project his feelings of vulnerability onto his lover, in whom they seem far less threatening. "We moved in together because she wanted the close-ness," he'll say, never acknowledging that he needed it just as much as she. Projection goes on all the time in all kinds of relationships, and accounts for a major portion of misunderstandings between people.

Rosa

Rosa, a political activist and writer, suffered the high costs of sup-pressing her true emotions for years. Short, with a muscular build and intense dark eyes, Rosa talks very fast and has a frenetic air that makes it seem as though she were always in motion—*fast-forward* motion. When she started psychotherapy, she was in her late thirties and in the midst of a major depression. Habitually, she would arrive at the office with her head bowed and turned to the side, as if expecting a physical blow. "I know I shouldn't feel this way," she would say as soon as she began to acknowledge her depressed state. "It's stupid and self-pitying. I'm sorry, I'm really sorry."

Born and raised in Puerto Rico, Rosa moved with her family to Florida, then to New York in her teens. The Roman Catholic nuns who taught her had such a great and positive impact on her that when she finished high school she decided to enter the sisterhood herself. A member of a liberal Roman Catholic order, she spent several years doing missionary work in Central America, then re-turned to the United States, where she works with the poor and on social-justice issues. Most recently, she has been active in the move-ment to give sanctuary to Central American refugees.

Rosa started psychotherapy because she became depressed to the point of immobilization in response to difficulties in her relationship with her stepsister, Maria. Rosa's mother, a widow, married Maria's father, also widowed, when Rosa was in her late twenties and Maria was in her early twenties. The two young women, neither of whom had a sister, became devoted to each other. Rosa was especially attached; she would do anything to be with Maria. When Maria was in her early thirties, she started psychotherapy, and one of the results was that she attempted to become more separate from Rosa, whom she felt was often overbearing and possessive. Rosa's consequent depression led Maria to suggest that Rosa pursue psychotherapy on her own.

In therapy, Rosa revealed that she had gone through bouts of depression throughout her entire life. It soon became clear that she had ample reason: she had experienced a number of painful losses in her life that she had never permitted herself to mourn. But rather than feel any sympathy for herself and accept that she had both the right and ample reason to feel depressed, Rosa would react to her depressive periods by getting angry and impatient with herself. With her inner voice she would call herself "stupid" and "weak," and would relentlessly beat herself up, saying "How can you let yourself get this way?," "Stop feeling sorry for yourself," "Get a hold of yourself," "Cut the pity party," and "Snap out of it."

Rosa's inability to accept her own sad feelings was the direct outgrowth of her experience as a child. When she was six, her father died, leaving her mother to support Rosa; her eleven-year-old brother, Raoul; and her three-year-old brother, Julio. When their mother was at work, which was most of the time, Rosa and Julio were left under the care of Raoul. Overwhelmed by such responsibility at such a young age, Raoul became a pint-sized tyrant who ruled his younger siblings with constant verbal abuse, beatings, and angry threats of the punishments he would inflict if they told their mother what was going on. Whenever Rosa would cry about their father's death or anything else that saddened her, Raoul would become especially enraged, and would attack her with both fists and words, calling her "stupid," "weak," "babyish," "self-pitying," and so forth.

Unfortunately, Rosa was not able to get any solace from her mother. Prior to her father's death, Rosa remembers her mother being made of "velvet and steel," but afterwards the soft, tender, warm, and loving part disappeared, leaving only the steel, the hardness, and coldness of an embittered survivor who hid her pain behind a mask of stoicism. Thus, when Rosa's father died, she in effect lost her mother, too.

In retrospect, Rosa could see that her brother's reaction to her grief, sadness, and tears was a form of self-protection. Her sad feelings were too vivid a reminder of his own unbearable feelings, so he had to stop her from having them. At the time, however, Rosa took what her brother said as the "gospel truth": she *was* just feeling sorry for herself, and she had no right to. Consequently, Rosa never was to go through the natural grieving process that people need to go through in the wake of major losses.

As Rosa grew up and then lived an adult life, each new loss she experienced (such as the loss of the close relationship with Maria) inevitably brought up her feelings about her earlier losses. But she could never allow herself to really feel and release the sadness, despair, anger, hopelessness, and depression she had been carrying around for years. Instead, each time these "weak" and "babyish" feelings came up Rosa would berate herself for "wallowing in self-pity" and "dwelling on the negative." Once again, then, Rosa would suppress her deepest feelings, valid though they were. The long-term result was that Rosa became chronically depressed, and her depression had two components. She was not only depressed because she had experienced losses that she had never sufficiently mourned she was also depressed about being depressed. Her anger at herself for feeling depressed about her losses did not make the depression go away, as she had hoped; it made her depression deeper and even more impossible to simply talk herself out of or to will away.

Until she finally got help, Rosa went through life assuming that everyone else in the world would react to her sadness and depressions in the harsh, critical, condemning way her brother had. As a result, when she felt down and blue she would hide her feelings under a mask of false cheer, and spend as much time as she could alone. She thereby blocked herself from receiving the consolation, support, and general kindness that friends and colleagues could have provided.

Rosa's inability to accept her own feelings served as the foundation for other love blocks as well. For example, one of her other major blocks was "I Don't Deserve Love" (discussed in the next chapter). A principal reason she felt she did not deserve love was that she had so many "bad" and "negative" feelings. If she were a "sunnier" person, she believed, she'd be more deserving of love.

Bernice

Readers who had happier childhoods might find Rosa's story difficult to relate to. But the "I Don't Want to Deal with My Feelings" block is common even among those who grew up in homes where there were no obvious problems. Bernice, a woman in her early forties who works as a bookkeeper, is a case in point.

Tall and stately-looking, Bernice has a pleasant face framed by a fluff of pretty brown hair. But what stands out most about her is the way she carries herself. When she walks into a room, she looks as if she had just stepped out of posture class. As she sits down and begins to talk, her back stays rigidly erect and she keeps looking at her hands. If she makes eye contact for even a second, her face immediately reddens and she abruptly looks away.

At the time Bernice initiated treatment, she had been married for seventeen years to Will, an electrical engineer, and had two teenaged daughters. Bernice and Will spent a lot of time together with their children in various school, athletic, community, and church activities, but hardly any time together as a couple. They had no real intimacy and for years hadn't had much of a sex life, either. If he didn't have a meeting or outside activity, Will would come home from work in the evening and go directly to bed. "Unless he has something structured to do, he goes straight to sleep," Bernice said. "Ninety-nine percent of the time we have free time to spend together, he's in bed sound asleep."

By the time Bernice began therapy, things were so bad between her and Will that they were seriously considering divorce. As her treatment progressed and she and Will started counseling together as well, it became clear that many of their problems stemmed from the fact that both of them were already divorced—from their own feelings. Bernice and Will were both very emotionally constrained and uncomfortable with their own and other people's feelings. Although having this in common helped them become a couple in the first place, the long-term consequence was that both felt lonely and detached in their marriage.

When Bernice began treatment, she described herself as "just like my mother, not emotional." As time progressed, it became apparent that the direct opposite is true: she is a highly emotional person who experiences a wide range of feelings with great intensity. This is her basic nature. But instead of being taught to trust and love her natural self, she had been taught to be suspicious and condemning of it, and spent years denying it.

An only child, Bernice grew up in an upper-middle-class home she recalls as quiet, calm, and secure. There were no money problems, her parents' marriage seemed solid, and Bernice grew up feeling safe, protected, and "more or less content." Yet there was always an undercurrent of subtle tension in the air, for the same environment that felt so safe and calm to Bernice was one that did not allow much room for emotional expression. Both Bernice's parents, but especially her mother, were vigilant in keeping their own emotions tightly contained, and expected their small daughter to do the same. Whenever Bernice showed any strong feelings, her parents scolded her with such comments as "Don't get so emotional," "Control yourself," and "You're being hysterical, stop that." Although Bernice was discouraged from displaying any emotion—even excitement, joy, and love—too intensely, her parents' reaction was particularly harsh when Bernice became angry, afraid, or tearful. Rather than comfort Bernice at these times, they would often give her "the silent treatment" and refuse to be in the same room with her until she could "behave properly." If they spoke to her about her sad, angry, or frightened feelings at all, it was only to tell her to "stop that childish nonsense."

The only strong emotion Bernice saw expressed during her childhood was her father's anger. Periodically, he would have violent temper tantrums, after which he would be irascible and depressed. Although Bernice's mother was devoted to her husband, she could not abide his outbursts, and when he "got that way," as she euphemistically put it, she would give him disdainful looks, punish him with "the silent treatment," or belittle him in a cruel but constrained way. Bernice herself was frightened of her father because of the unpredictability and violence of his temper. He always maintained an emotional distance from his daughter, which she took as a sign that "there must be something bad about me."

Bernice did not have an unhappy childhood. Her parents were responsible, for the most part kind, and they did their best to give her what they believed was best for her. She was not subjected to what most people would characterize as abuse. Nevertheless, Bernice's home environment made it impossible for her to grow up with a healthy regard for her emotional self. If her father's frightening, violent outbursts were any indication of what happens when people let their feelings out, Bernice couldn't help but conclude that it was best to keep her feelings as tightly reined in as her mother did. Eventually emotional constraint became second nature to her, so much so that when she began therapy, she could not recall any times in childhood when her natural emotional self had still been vibrant and alive.

Bernice was especially uncomfortable with anger. Given her family environment together with her experience of growing up female in a world where anger in women is considered taboo, this was probably inevitable. And to reinforce what she was already well on her way to learning, Bernice had only to look at the women she saw on TV. As an introverted child, she spent a good deal of time home alone, watching TV. Her favorite shows were "The Donna Reed Show" and "Father Knows Best," and since she had no other significant women in her life besides her mother, these TV mothers became her models. These TV women never seemed to get moody or angry, which Bernice took as further proof that emotional intensity, and anger in particular, are unladylike and generally bad.

Although neither of Bernice's parents was an alcoholic, her father's periodic temper tantrums created an atmosphere of unpredictability similar to that found in alcoholic homes. As a result, Bernice developed several characteristics that are common among the nearly thirty million American adults who are children of alcoholics. Her tense, rigid body posture and her tendency to keep her emotions tightly in check are both hallmarks of children of alcoholics, in fact. Most children of alcoholics grew up on guard against doing anything to "set off" the drinking parent, having learned through painful experience that no matter what they felt—whether sorrow or joy—it was enough to "get him [or her] started" or "make things worse." This pattern of not showing emotions soon enough turns into a pattern of not feeling them in the first place. In adulthood, the inability to express and experience emotions continues, leaving the now-grown children blocked from feeling emotions they want to feel (such as love).

The Change Process: Bernice's Way

Bernice's first main task in therapy was to give herself permission to feel. She had a number of strict beliefs about what she should and should not feel. To get a clearer picture of exactly where these beliefs came from, she made a list of all her "shoulds" and "should nots" and was asked what particular persons and/or particular incidents were associated with them. At first, Bernice felt foolish doing this, and no images came to mind. Eventually, however, she found herself recalling many specific incidents. Having always felt guilty and ashamed for feeling sexually attractive, she recalled a number of episodes when as a teenager her mother would caution her "not to walk so proudly and brazenly" and "not to smile so much" because "men will get the wrong idea about you." For "I shouldn't feel sad," she remembered one of her elementary school teachers telling the class that it takes more muscles to frown than to smile, which means "smiling is natural, what God intended you to do," whereas frowning is unnatural, an aberration that runs counter to God's plan.

Once Bernice had a clearer idea of where her beliefs about feelings came from, her next major task was to begin to be more precise about identifying what she felt. Until this point, Bernice had gone through life thinking only in terms of "I feel bad" and "I feel good." This made it difficult for her to describe her feelings more precisely. To facilitate the process, she made a list of words describing different emotional states. Each day, she took a few minutes to go over the list, selecting the words that most accurately completed the statement "Today, I felt . . ." Soon she became aware that when she felt "bad," she could in fact be feeling any number of distinctly different things, such as disappointed, sad, frustrated, anxious, guilty, afraid, or resentful. Similarly, when she felt "good," she was really feeling happy, satisfied, calm, proud, optimistic, confident, and so forth.

As Bernice became more attuned to what specific emotions she was experiencing, she also began to be less afraid and censoring of them. In the past when she had labeled an emotion "bad," she meant not just that it was unpleasant or painful, but also that it was morally wrong. She had always believed a whole range of emotions—anger, jealousy, hate, resentment, for example—were not permissable to feel. Only very gradually did Bernice begin to see that these are all normal, natural human feelings, and that having them did not make her an evil person.

Bernice had a particularly hard time permitting herself to feel tired. She had always believed that feeling tired meant she was lazy, depressed, "not strong enough." It eventually emerged that her mother and several of her friends are the type of people who can and do get by on only four or five hours of sleep a night. Bernice had always compared herself to these literally tireless dynamos, convinced they represented the normal, correct way to be. She had never been able to accept that she is the kind of person who needs a lot of sleep. Only after talking about the issue in therapy a number of different times did Bernice gradually begin to let herself admit and experience how truly tired she was. Eventually, she made a dramatic change, and decided to start taking afternoon naps. She was particularly pleased one afternoon when she woke herself up by loudly snoring, "something women aren't supposed to do."

When Bernice was first becoming more emotionally open, she was afraid that her feelings would overwhelm her and turn her into a "feelings fanatic," someone in a constant state of emotional intensity. Many people with the "I Don't Want to Deal with My Feelings" block have this fear. In most cases, though, first there is a wave of emotional intensity that crests and then naturally breaks; afterwards, the intense feelings recede, giving way to a sense of being more emotionally balanced, and often to a sense of a deep calm. This was Bernice's experience. Although much more emotionally alive than in the past, she is also more at ease. She feels her feelings fully at the time they arise, and then the feelings pass. She is actually less "a slave to her emotions" now than when she was putting so much energy into suppressing them.

Once she began to know her own feelings better, Bernice then faced the task of learning to tell her friends and family what she felt. In the past, whenever anyone asked how she was or how things were going at home or at work, Bernice always answered "fine," a habit left over from her childhood. An unwritten but sacrosanct rule in Bernice's parents' home was that no matter how many problems there were at home, work, or school, the only polite and permissible thing to do was to pretend everything was "just fine."

When Bernice began to tell her friends what she was really feeling, she was surprised at how accepting and supportive they were, and how relieved and loved that made her feel. She had always assumed that "no one would want to know" how she really felt. But she found that when she was honest about her feelings, other women she knew admired her, warmed up to her, and often reciprocated by confiding that they sometimes felt that way, too. Although a few acquaintances were put off by Bernice's new frankness, most of the women she knew drew even closer, enabling Bernice to experience the female friendship for which she had always longed.

Bernice's new forthrightness had a positive impact on her relationship with her kids, too. Until now, she had tried to be "super mom," doing everything for her kids and then getting irritated and resentful when she inevitably ran out of energy. Now when her kids wanted her to do something for them, she began to tell them simply, "I can't. I'm too tired." She did not say, "You want too much," "You expect too much of me," or anything else along those lines. She simply stated the truth: "I'm tired. I can't." After some initial shock and grumbling, the kids gradually adjusted. They began to do more for themselves, and to be more helpful to Bernice. Bernice felt enormously relieved, as though "a big weight that had been on my shoulders was lifted," and as she expressed her appreciation of what the kids did with her and for her, they became more appreciative of her in turn. True, their house was not as neat and clean as it had been, and their dinners were not as carefully planned and prepared (Bernice had spent years trying to live up to the standards of her mother, who was a gourmet cook and impeccable housekeeper). But it was a home in which both mother and children felt more loved and loving than ever before.

Bernice's efforts were initially resisted and resented by her husband.

In the past, any time Bernice had started to show even a hint of emotionalism, Will would withdraw and go to sleep. His shutting her out in this way mirrored her own internal censorship of her feelings and reinforced her sense that there was something wrong with her. As Will began to work on his own love blocks, though, he discovered that his constant desire for sleep grew out of his own inner censorship. He had put so much energy into suppressing his own feelings for so many years that he was chronically exhausted. Gradually, he joined Bernice in trying to become more emotionally expressive, and his fatigue diminished accordingly.

One emotion Bernice and Will had special difficulty being forthright about was anger. Bernice took the lead in trying to bring their angry feelings to the surface for discussion. But each time she did Will reacted defensively, telling her he didn't know what she was talking about, then going to sleep. Only after a great deal of conflict and frustration did Will stop undermining Bernice's efforts and join her. Once they learned to express anger in an honest, direct, non-accusatory way, they both became less afraid of letting it out into the open. They noticed that after their "angry sessions," they felt warmer toward each other and entered a making-up phase characterized by its gentleness and eroticism. Often this led to "the best sex we've had in years." What Bernice and Will were discovering is that suppressed anger (as we discuss more fully in Chapter 18) tends to sit in the chest like a cement block, making it impossible to let love either in or out.

The Change Process: Rosa's Way

In neither Bernice's nor Rosa's case did change come easily or overnight. Bernice, however, was able to make noticeable progress from the very start of therapy. Because Rosa's block was so deeply entrenched and had its roots in a childhood that was extremely painful, her progress was slower and more difficult to achieve.

A key step for Rosa in overcoming this love block was to understand that, in her unconscious mind, she was still a helpless little girl bullied by her much bigger brother. It had been years since Rosa lived with Raoul, and he was no longer the towering bully he once had been. Yet Rosa had kept the young Raoul alive in her psyche, where he still towered over and tyrannized her. Like Bernice, Rosa had to go through her beliefs about her feelings one by one, look at where they came from, and dispense with those that caused her to wage war against her emotional self. This was the only way she could get herself out from under the shadow of her brother and begin feeling and expressing the sadness and pain she needed to release in order to move on in her life.

Rosa, too, was afraid of ending up overwhelmed by her long-buried emotions. But after a time of feeling flooded by her surfacing grief and sadness, Rosa then entered a state characterized by a sense that "something's given way inside me," a sense of having been "cleansed" and "released." She learned what others who have overcome the "I Don't Want to Deal With My Feelings" block have also learned—that the only way they'd ever begin to feel better would be to first permit themselves to feel more.

As Rosa became more accepting of her true feelings, she needed to test out her long-held assumption that everyone else in the world would react to her feelings in the hysterical, condemning way her brother once had. There was only one way to do this—by telling some other people what she truly felt and seeing how they responded. This was not easy for Rosa to do, nor was it something she did without preparation. In therapy, she rehearsed what she might say to someone else. She also was very careful in choosing whom she would open up to; wisely, she knew she'd be taking too big a risk if she poured her heart out to just anyone.

One of the first people Rosa decided to open up to was a political organizer she worked with. She admitted to him that she was depressed and, as a result, feeling overwhelmed and very tired. He reacted with kindness and concern, confiding that he had gone through a couple of major depressions in his life, too. Rosa began to realize the extent to which she had deprived herself of the consolation and understanding others could offer.

Rosa had a more difficult time expressing her feelings to the editor of a magazine she wrote for on a frequent basis. They had always gotten along well until he made her do several rewrites on a story he had assigned and, in the end, rejected it anyway. Rosa arrived at therapy furious at him. She felt he had misled her about what he wanted, and she was particularly stung by his criticisms, which she thought were unfair. But she hadn't even tried to confront the editor, she explained, because "inside I feel like a scared little mouse." With her voice growing tremulous, Rosa explained, "It's like I'm going up against my brother."

Rosa arrived at the next session smiling triumphantly. She had finally gotten up the courage to approach her editor. She told him that she disagreed with his comments and felt he had been unfair. She told him how discouraged she had been and expressed concern that this incident would spoil a working relationship that meant a lot to her. Rosa was shocked when the editor apologized. He thought his criticisms had been constructive, he explained; he had no idea that she had been so upset. He then told her some positive things about her work, admitting that perhaps he had failed to mention them before. Although there was still some tension between them for a few days, Rosa found that her openness enabled her to "hold my head up high" at the magazine, and that the wall between her and the editor had been broken down.

In addition to having to tackle the symbolic relationship with her brother that had dominated her psyche, Rosa had to do something about her relationship with the real Raoul. Over the years, Raoul had become a very successful businessman and mellowed quite a bit. As he became more and more successful he also became very giving materially. He often sent Rosa lavish gifts as well as plane tickets so that she could visit their mother in Florida and Raoul and his family, who had moved back to Puerto Rico. Rosa loved Raoul's wife and children, and after her mother's death she increasingly relied on such visits with them to provide her with a sense of family. Yet she never felt really at ease or at home at Raoul's. Although generally nicer, Raoul still had periodic temper tantrums, and several times each visit he would go into a tirade about Rosa's political views. Rosa was pretty sure her brother wouldn't go so far as to hit her but, nevertheless, would feel the same terror she had felt as a child—now expressed as a headache and a "sick feeling in my stomach."

Rosa talked about her past and present relationship with Raoul for session after session, never feeling she was making any progress.

But eventually she decided she was up to a confrontation. On a subsequent visit to Puerto Rico, she told Raoul she wanted to speak to him privately, at some length. She told him that she didn't like the way he sometimes spoke to her, that it hurt her feelings, and that she would appreciate it if he would treat her with more respect. She then began to talk about their childhood, focusing on how much pain she had felt rather than on his behavior. She told him that she had come to realize how painful and stressful it had been for him, too. Rosa and Raoul sat up talking "halfway through the night." As they were finally going off to bed, Raoul hugged his sister warmly and closely, and he said, "Please forgive me for all the hurt I've caused you." This was the first time in her life that Rosa had ever heard her brother say "forgive me" to anyone. "It was like a miracle," she reported in therapy later. "It was the last thing on earth I ever expected."

Rosa's relationship with Raoul is still not without problems; perhaps it never will be. But there has been much more openness, warmth, and ease between them since that night. There has also been more expression of love on both sides. As Rosa has become more open in expressing her true feelings to the people in her life, love is coming to her from a variety of sources—including the one source that for years she had "known" could only provide her with more pain.

Chapter 5
"I Don't Deserve Love"

Judy, the woman in Chapter 2 whose childhood sexual abuse caused her to find sex with her husband exploitative and repulsive, is strikingly attractive. She has luminous dark eyes and thick, long black hair that she wears swept back from her delicately featured face. Although very sensuous-looking, it is obvious from the way she walks and holds herself that she is not fully at home in her body.

Judy initiated treatment at age forty-seven because she had long been unhappy about her relationship with Art, a business executive to whom she had been married for twenty-five years. But as she began to open up in therapy, it soon became evident that Judy's major problem was that she was unhappy with her own self. Very unhappy. Judy had no trouble describing herself; she saw herself as an "ugly, stupid big-mouth." Other words she commonly used to describe herself included "gross," "screwed up," "idiot" and "a big mess." What's more, Judy casually mentioned one day that she avoided looking in mirrors, that she hadn't really looked at herself in one in years, in fact. Despite her good looks, Judy had never felt pride in her appearance, believing that her head-turning attractiveness and obvious sexuality marked her as "a slut, an easy lay."

Judy began therapy with several love blocks, but her primary one was the belief that "I Don't Deserve Love," or low self-esteem. This is one of the most common love blocks of all, causing countless

people great difficulties in establishing and maintaining healthy relationships. Low self-esteem also frequently serves as the foundation
for other love blocks that, in turn, reinforce a person's belief that "I
Don't Deserve Love."[1]

People with this block are convinced they are so flawed and imperfect that they are unworthy of love. When others offer them love,
they cannot allow it to penetrate to their inner selves. Instead, their
brains come up with all sorts of reasons to reject it. They may conclude that the person offering the love has a false impression of them,
telling themselves that "if s/he knew what I'm really like, s/he would
never be able to love me." They may decide that the other person
has horrible taste and judgment, or is insane, telling themselves "anyone who would love me must have something really wrong with
him." Or they might decide the other person is dishonest and un-
trustworthy; in this case, their inner logic would go like this: "Since
I am unlovable, there is no way anyone can love me; therefore, anyone
who claims to love me must be lying."

One of the most common symptoms of low self-esteem is an inability to accept a compliment.[2] Although this might seem like a
trivial thing, if a person cannot accept a compliment it's a surefire
sign that she'll have trouble taking in love. At the time Judy started
treatment, for example, it was her habit to respond to any attempt
at complimenting her by immediately pointing out one of her many
perceived flaws. She had been raised to believe that this was healthy
modesty and argued that it was good manners, too, unaware that
she was in effect depriving herself of an opportunity to feel valued
and appreciated—and was also rudely rejecting another person's gen-
erosity. She had never considered that the *really* polite thing to do
is to graciously utter a simple "thank you," to savor the compliment
for a moment, then let it go.

People with low self-esteem often seem set on intentionally blocking their receptivity to love. But this really isn't the case. It's not that
they don't want to take in love, it's that in order to take in love they
would have to reconsider and ultimately discard a belief that is central
to their way of looking at the world and on which their entire lives
are based. Most people with this block have believed in their unlovability so long and so deeply that it feels like an integral part of them;

they would no more question this "fact" than they would question whether the earth is round.

Self-Love Is Not Narcissism

One of the simple truths of life is that a person will not be able to accept love from others if she does not love herself first. Similarly, a person won't be able to feel love for others unless she also loves herself. Christ implied this, saying not "love thy neighbor *better* than thyself" or "love thy neighbor *instead of* thyself," but "love thy neighbor *as* thyself."

When a person has self-love, he values and cares about himself; he sees himself as a person deserving of compassion, kindness, and happiness. He is very much aware that he has flaws and makes mistakes, but rather than seeing his imperfections as evidence of his worthlessness and unlovability, he sees them as evidence of his humanity.

Nevertheless, many people balk at the notion of increasing their self-love because they're afraid that doing so will make them vain, narcissistic, selfish, and self-centered. However, the very fact that they have this concern indicates that they will not become that way. People who are genuinely self-centered don't have such worries.

Although the terms "self-love" and "narcissism" are often treated as synonymous, they are not. A narcissistic person is a demanding perfectionist who becomes angry when he and others don't live up to his high expectations. By contrast, as a person becomes more self-loving, he becomes more accepting of himself and others; he no longer judges himself or others according to impossible standards.

A narcissistic person also has a sense of entitlement and is impatient when others don't cater to him as he thinks they should. A person who is self-loving is confident that he deserves the best in life, but doesn't believe he is owed special treatment.

A narcissistic person has an inflated sense of himself and sees himself as superior to others. A person who has genuine self-love has a realistic view of himself as a complex being who is neither superior nor inferior to others. This view enables him to have high regard for others and to appreciate their complex humanity as well.

Finally, a narcissistic person wants to hoard the good feelings he has about himself. "I am special, and I want only me to have this feeling," he in essence believes. By contrast, a genuinely self-loving person wants others to feel good about themselves and will do whatever he can to foster their self-worth. "I like the person I am, and I want you to like the person you are, too" is his attitude. Unlike the narcissist, who believes that his own specialness will be diminished if others come to value themselves, the self-loving person knows that his own life can only be enriched as others become more self-loving.

The Learning Process

Many people are so accustomed to seeing themselves in a certain way that they never question where their ideas about themselves came from; they assume that if they don't like themselves, they were probably born that way, and it must be what they deserve. But no one came into the world seeing herself as ugly, bad, stupid, or unlovable— or as pretty, good, smart, or lovable either. As far as ideas about ourselves are concerned, each of us began life with a blank slate— we had no idea whatsoever whether we were smart or not so smart, significant or worthless, pretty or ugly, even whether we were male or female. All our knowledge about ourselves has been *learned*.

As we grow up and acquire definite ideas about who we actually are, we also acquired definite ideas about who we *should* be. Typically, we constantly compare the two, holding up our perceived self to our ideal self. If our perceived self falls far short, we'll disapprove of who we are and our self-esteem will be low.

Most of us developed our basic sense of who we are and who we should be in childhood, based primarily on how our parents treated us, what they told us about ourselves, and how we saw them behave. If, for example, a child was frequently hit or screamed at, she probably got the idea that she was bad. If her parents told her she was a certain way—whether stupid or smart, pretty or ugly—she most likely internalized these labels as the truth. Children lack the intellectual skills to question their parents' judgment, so they have no choice but to accept their parents' labels as facts. Even when children grow savvy enough to begin to question, doing so is just too threatening to their sense of security. Psychologically, children can not afford to see their parents as flawed and fallible because it's too terrifying. So a child tells herself that her parents must know best, even when they say things that hurt her deeply.

Those who grew up with a sense of being unlovable were generally raised in homes where they received a great deal of criticism and very little praise, or none at all. They were also typically expected to live up to standards of behavior and performance that were so high that the children couldn't possibly meet them. In instances when the children did meet them, their achievements were completely ignored, dismissed with comments like "we expected no less," or acknowledged with a faint word of praise immediately followed by a qualifying "but," as in the case of parents who responded to a child's bringing home a 99 on an exam by saying "Very good, but what about this one question you got wrong? What happened there?"

People who grew up feeling unlovable did not receive unconditional love as children. People who raise children to have high self-esteem will not withhold their love when their child misbehaves or fails to live up to their expectations. They will let him know that they might dislike his *behavior*, but they won't communicate the message that he is an irredeemably bad person for behaving badly or disappointing them. People who have low self-esteem, though, usually grew up in homes where love was withdrawn when they behaved in ways that displeased or disappointed their parents.

Many people with very low self-esteem also grew up in "shame-based" families, in which criticism and abuse constitute the principal ways of relating.[3] In these families, the dominant emotion inculcated in the children is personal shame—the sense that there is something inherently, irrevocably wrong with them, which makes them unlovable and unworthy. They grow up equating closeness with criticism, intimacy with humiliation, and being loved with being used as a scapegoat for someone else's problems.

Parents Aren't the Only Influence

Although our basic sense of self and self-worth was developed in childhood and our parents played the most influential role, they weren't the only sources of influence. In our early years, other people within the intimate sphere—siblings, grandparents, other relatives, family friends and, finally, friends of our own choosing—also helped shape our developing sense of who we are and whether we measure up. And typically as we grew older the role of chosen intimates—friends, lovers, spouses—and our own children began to have an increasing impact. Moreover, our sense of who we are and how we should be has probably also been shaped to some extent by people and institutions outside the intimate sphere, such as experiences in school, religious training, and the books, magazines, movies, TV shows, music, advertisements, and other cultural influences we've been exposed to.

Unfortunately, the impact of the larger world puts certain groups of people at a disadvantage when it comes to developing and maintaining high self-esteem. A child of color, for example, can come from the most loving of homes, but as he looks about and moves through the world he'll inevitably encounter racism, and this can limit his sense of worth and possibilities. A child whose native language is not English might get a great deal of unconditional love at home, but if she is taught at school that English is the only acceptable tongue, she might reasonably feel ashamed and out of place. Lesbians and gay men might take great pride in their sexual identity, but in a world where heterosexuality is seen as the norm and homophobia abounds, they will inevitably encounter taunts, discrimination, and unintended insults—and these can pose a threat to their feelings of self-worth. People with physical or mental disabilities might lovingly accept themselves as they are, but since the larger world makes it so difficult for them to fit in—or even get around—they suffer daily assaults on their sense of dignity, worth, and belonging that those without disabilities don't have to endure.

The fact that we live in a culture where men traditionally have been considered to have greater worth is relevant, too. A boy whose parents don't seem to love him enough can find some consolation in the fact that he is a male, and as such is supposedly more intelligent, more competent, more significant, and generally more worthy than his female counterparts. A girl whose parents fail to provide her with sufficient love cannot find similar consolation.

Instead of serving as a bulwark against the sexism of the larger culture, many families actively promulgate the idea that males are innately superior. And as males are raised to think they have more reason for high self-esteem than females do, they are also given greater license to have high opinions of themselves. According to an age-old double standard, high self-esteem is an exclusively male prerogative. Men are supposed to have positive opinions of themselves, while women are supposed to be self-deprecating and are taught to be very careful not to come off as conceited or too self-satisfied. As a result, parents who fail to equip their sons with sufficient self-esteem are seen as having committed a terrible crime, while raising a daughter with low self-esteem is seen as normal and acceptable. We hear a lot, for example, about the fragile male ego, and girls and women are brought up to regard bolstering men's sense of self-worth as one of their most important roles in life. But very little is ever said about the fragile female ego, and boys and men are not raised to see it as their duty to build women's self-esteem.

Judy

Judy, the self-described "ugly, stupid big-mouth" mentioned at the beginning of this chapter, is a classic example of someone whose sense of self-worth was severely damaged by what happened to her in childhood, and whose sense of lovability was further damaged by her experience of being female in a culture where femaleness is often equated with being flawed.

Judy initiated therapy because of longstanding dissatisfaction with her marriage, which was then in its twenty-fifth year. Her husband, Art, had always had a tendency to emotionally withdraw. Whenever he was upset, feeling overwhelmed by the pressures of having a high-powered job and a family, or just going through a blue period, he would never talk to Judy about what was bothering him. Instead, he would go on day after day in an increasingly severe bad mood characterized by sulky silence, irritability, wanting to be left alone, and constant nagging and criticism of Judy. As mentioned earlier, Judy also felt sexually used by her husband. It's because she had reached the point where she felt "I can't go on living like this any longer" that Judy finally sought help.

As it turned out, Judy had problems that long preceded her marriage. She was the youngest of two children in an upper-middle-class family. Judy's older brother, Steve, was "a fair-haired boy who could do no wrong" in their parents' eyes, and to whom Judy was constantly compared. Since Steve was an honor student, an athletic star, and very handsome, outgoing, and popular, it would have been difficult for anyone to fare well in comparison with him. But it was especially hard for Judy, who was shy, not very athletic, only borderline pretty, and an average student. Next to those of her brother, these traits—which another family might have accepted—appeared in her parents' eyes as gross deficiencies, so they labeled Judy unpopular, clumsy, ugly, and stupid. They also explicitly told her that they hadn't wanted to have her and frequently denigrated her for being a girl with comments like "if we had to have a second child, at least we could have been lucky enough to have gotten a boy." Judy's mother had two particularly cruel pet names for her daughter—"ugly duckling" and "the growth." Even when Judy turned into a "swan" years later, these labels lost neither their tenacity nor their sting.

Judy worshiped Steve, and her relationship with him was the sole close one of her childhood. The family lived in a sprawling split-level, with Steve and Judy in adjacent bedrooms located at the opposite end of the house from the main living area and their parents' room. At night, Steve was often left to take care of Judy while their parents went out to parties or to the movies. On one such night when Judy was ten or eleven, Steve, who was then about fourteen, approached her and very gently began stroking her hair. Then he fondled her breasts and took his penis out of his pants and had her masturbate him. Over the next several years, Steve molested Judy in this way every time their parents went out, and on increasing occasions at night when they were in the house as well.

Judy never told her parents about the incest. Since they saw Steve as a demigod who could do no wrong, Judy knew they'd never believe her, or that they'd blame her. Also, Judy, who looked to Steve as her only source of love, was afraid of betraying his trust and thus losing his affection. So she dealt with the trauma of being sexually abused by blocking it out of her consciousness, pretending "this isn't really happening" after all, and eventually repressing much of her memory of it and all of her feelings about it. When she finally brought the incest up in therapy nearly forty years later, it was the first time she had ever spoken of it.

During her childhood and adolescence, Judy had two dominant emotions: desperate loneliness and deep self-hatred. She longed to be a boy and was so ashamed and rejecting of her femaleness that she never attempted to become friends with other girls. When she sought out friendship at all it was only from boys, and when the boys she sought out proved uninterested, she invented imaginary friends who were all male as well. Her only source of the attention, affection, and physical contact she was starved for was Steve. Thus, it was through molestation that Judy had her only experience of being wanted.

Judy was married when she was in her early twenties, and from the start she and Art had problems. The central problem from which most of the others stemmed was simple lack of communication. They both had great trouble expressing their true feelings; indeed, they both suffered from the "I Don't Want to Deal with My Feelings" block and thus had difficulty knowing what they really felt. They also could not deal with conflict. Afraid to "bring things up," they never directly dealt with problems between them, instead passively hoping those problems would just go away. The result was that problems between them never got solved, and as year after year's worth of grievances, hurts, and anger piled up, a mounting tension and distance developed between them. This only heightened Art's tendency to emotionally withdraw and sulk. As time wore on, he was in a bad mood more and more often, and the moods had become worse and worse. Judy felt his criticisms of her at these times had become progressively crueler, too.

Another woman might have responded to Art's moodiness and criticalness with anger, or at least an awareness that these were *his* problems. But Judy felt she must have been at fault, and she became preoccupied with finding out what she had done wrong. In the course of her self-examination she would discover all sorts of things that she had probably done, which further diminished her already extremely low self-esteem. She felt like "a total screw-up who is always doing everything wrong."

Judy felt like a failure particularly as a wife and mother. One reason was that as a child she had developed a very idealized fantasy of how marriage and family life should be. Her marriage, she told herself, was going to be a perfect one, just like the ones on TV; and she would be the perfect wife and mother, again just like the actresses on TV. When the reality fell short, Judy didn't question whether there might be something wrong with the picture of perfection she felt compelled to live up to. Instead she assumed that "there must be something wrong with me." Judy thus concluded that if she wanted to fix her marriage, then all she would have to do is work on fixing herself. Since this strategy left Art entirely off the hook, it's not surprising that he was happy to go along with it. So off Judy went to therapy, with high hopes that if she could learn to be a better person, then her marriage and family life in general would get better, too.

The Change Process: Judy's Way

In fact, Judy's marriage did improve as Judy continued with therapy. But this wasn't because she learned to fashion herself into a mold labeled "better person." Instead, Judy learned to stop trying to be something she wasn't. She learned to start accepting herself as she was, and to see that there was plenty to love and value about herself even in "as is" condition. As she became more self-loving, she became more open to receiving other people's love; moreover, since she no longer spent almost every minute of every hour focused on what was wrong with her, she became much more pleasant to be around.

The therapy process for someone like Judy tends to be especially slow and plodding. When an attempt is made to describe it, it inevitably sounds tedious. Basically, what Judy needed to do in therapy was to dismantle her existing view of reality and construct an entirely new one. As is the case with virtually everyone with low self-esteem, it wasn't just Judy's perceptions of herself that were distorted. Her skewed sense of self had caused her to have a skewed sense of others, along with a very much skewed sense of the world, of how it works, and of how she and others fit into it. Thus, in order to build a new self-image, Judy had to turn virtually everything she ever believed on its head and examine and question it. Then she had to figure out which of those beliefs were accurate, and which were distorted. Next, she had to get rid of those she decided were distorted. Then, and only then, did she reach the point where she could start putting new, more accurate, beliefs in place of the distorted old ones she had done away with.

It's important to emphasize here that this was a process that occurred very slowly and with great difficulty. Therapy for Judy was not a matter of her therapist's saying, "Gee, Judy, you don't look like a stupid, ugly big-mouth to me!" and then having her respond, "Gosh, I must have gotten it wrong, then. If you say I'm smart, attractive, and worthy, I guess I am. Thanks for pointing this out, Doc. It changes everything." Therapy for Judy began with drawing out her beliefs and feelings, then prodding her to look at things in a different light. Sometimes she accepted new perspectives quickly and readily, but more often the new views were too alien, her old beliefs too entrenched. The same things had to be said over and over again, in session after session, and in a variety of different ways, before Judy finally began to make tangible changes in the way she thought and felt about herself.

While slow, Judy's progress was not unusually slow. Although a person can begin making some dents in his "I Don't Deserve Love" block by doing something as simple and quick as reading this chapter, in most cases overcoming this block is a process that takes months and years—indeed, a whole lifetime—of work. This is because a person's most basic beliefs about her worth, traits, and place in the world tend to be very deeply entrenched. Even when a person thinks she has reached the point where she's ready to take on a new, different view, she very often finds that a belief she thought she had rejected is still there in her psyche, often at a deeper level. Moreover, beliefs about the self tend to be especially tenacious, causing even the least stubborn kinds of people to be rather mulish about giving them up. For example, at the time Judy started treatment, she was thoroughly convinced that whenever there was a problem, it had to be because she had done something wrong. Judy thought virtually everything about herself was wrong, in fact. Yet when it was suggested to her that these perceptions might be a bit skewed, Judy balked. Although she'd jump at the chance to admit she did or said something wrong, when it came to her belief that she was a "stupid, ugly big-mouth who messes everything up," Judy was adamant that she was right.

One of the most significant steps Judy took in reconstructing her sense of reality was to stop taking all the blame for all the problems in her marriage. She came to see that Art's moodiness, emotional withdrawal, and tendency to be hypercritical were *his* problems, and he had to take responsibility for dealing with them. After pressure from Judy, Art eventually did take responsibility and entered marriage therapy with her. It's because both parties were willing to look at their own contributions to the problems between them that after twenty-five years they were finally able to start having a marriage in which they both feel cared for and appreciated.

As Judy began to question and revise her view of reality, she became aware of the extent of her own projections. When she began therapy, Judy had felt that Art was always criticizing her. In fact, Art *was* pretty critical. From their joint therapy sessions, however, it became clear that while Art did have a genuine problem with being overcritical, he wasn't nearly as critical as Judy had perceived him to be. *Judy* was the most critical of Judy, and it was because she assumed that everyone—especially her husband—must be as critical of her as she was of herself that she saw Art as so critical.

Judy realized that she saw the whole world as critical of her because running through her mind virtually every waking moment was a nonstop barrage of self-denigration. When she felt hungry, she told herself, "You pig." When felt tired, she told herself, "You slug." When she made a mistake, she told herself, "You jerk, you screw-up. You never do anything right." Although she could be relentless in criticizing herself, whenever she had a critical thought about something (the design of a new building, the wallpaper in someone's house) or someone else, she would tell herself, "That's a terrible thing to think. You're a horrible person for having such thoughts. Who are you to make such harsh judgments anyway? . . ."

An important task for Judy was to become fully conscious of what she said in her head to run herself down. Once on the alert for the start of these mental tapes, she would tell herself, "Stop!" and silently repeat a "self-esteem mantra" instead. The mantra she started with was "You're not a bad person. You're no great shakes, but you're okay." When she began to feel more positive about herself, she moved on to a new mantra: "You're okay. You've got flaws, but so does everyone. You're really pretty okay." Eventually she was able to move on to: "You're a good, kind, and decent person. You deserve to be treated well." And finally, she was able to move from the second person to the first, saying "*I'm* a good, kind and decent person. *I* deserve to be treated well."

Once Judy refused to allow herself to be harshly judged, she also found herself feeling that Art was criticizing her far less often. In some cases, this was because the reality of their relationship had changed: Art actually was being less critical. In other cases, it was because Judy's way of perceiving the relationship had changed: she was no longer reading criticism into Art's every word, look, and gesture. Obviously, this led to better feelings and less tension between the two, enabling Judy to feel more loved and respected by Art.

One very concrete step Judy took was to begin spending time in natural settings where she felt at home. Living in such a technologically advanced, urbanized world, many people today lose connection with nature. But one of the wonderful things about nature is that it doesn't criticize. It nourishes and calms. Communing with "Mother Nature" can thus feel similar to having an experience of positive mothering. Since Judy didn't have many such experiences with her real mother, it was helpful for her to think of nature in this way. She realized that she felt most connected to nature at the beach. She began spending time there, sometimes with Art and their children, sometimes with a friend, sometimes alone. Whenever she goes, she always leaves feeling calmed, refreshed, and revitalized. These feelings, in turn, enable her to be more loving and less critical toward herself.

Judy and Art's Problems with Sex

Of all their problems, Judy and Art's sexual problems struck them as most hopeless. Yet it's there that they made the fastest visible progress.

From the start of their marriage, Art's primary focus in bed was on sexual intercourse, and he rarely paid attention to activity that would be more pleasurable for Judy. It wasn't that he didn't care about her pleasure, it was that he was inexperienced and unskilled. Also, he had a tendency to ejaculate quickly, which only added to his insecurity and nervousness. Judy, however, did not know any of this. She interpreted Art's narrow focus and hurried manner as evidence of selfishness. On an unconscious level, her experience with Art stirred up memories of her earlier experiences with her brother, and with those memories came some of the anger, fear, and humiliation the sexual abuse had caused her. Not surprisingly, then, Judy responded to sex with Art by feeling objectified, humiliated, and "used." She also felt angry.

Unfortunately, Judy never told Art how unhappy she was with their sex life. She felt so worthless that she assumed she had no right to ask him to act differently. Besides, even if she could have mustered up the gumption, what would she have said? Like most people, Judy had never learned how to talk about sex. Sex, she believed, was supposed to just happen; certainly, two people who really loved each other weren't supposed to need to talk about it. So Judy kept her true feelings in, all the while becoming more and more convinced that "all I'm good for is to give him physical release. I'm just a piece of meat to him. I don't matter to him at all." As a result, each time Art and Judy made love, Judy actually felt *less* loved by her husband, not more.

Each time she and Art had sex, Judy experienced a diminishment of *self*-love, too. There were two main reasons for this. One was that each time Art approached Judy sexually, he was unwittingly entering what Judy unconsciously viewed as "brother territory"; for Judy, this was bound to bring up some of the shame, embarrassment, self-blame, and self-loathing that was left over from her earlier experiences. The other reason was that in twenty-five years of marriage, Judy had never once come out and openly refused to have intercourse with Art. Acting passively in a sexual situation was the only way she knew how to act; besides, she didn't feel she had the right to refuse Art because, after all, he was her husband. But Judy nevertheless felt angry at herself for never saying no to Art, and she felt even more angry at herself for "letting" Steve molest her, for it was her conviction that even at age eleven, she should have been able to stop him.

While Judy never actually told Art of her unhappiness with their sex life, he could see how tense, distant, and angry she seemed to become whenever they had sex. From her refusal to touch or even look at his genitals, he knew that she found his penis repulsive. But in the absence of any knowledge of Judy's history of sexual abuse, Art had no idea why she felt this way, and so he concluded that she was "just one of those women who can't stand sex." Figuring that Judy was "frigid," a problem he believed was beyond remedy, he did not try new techniques or activities that might have given her more pleasure. Instead, he got his own pleasure in the simplest and quickest way possible so as to be the least bother to her. Thus, Art's hurried manner and seeming preoccupation with intercourse and that alone were not evidence of selfishness as Judy had thought; on the contrary, he acted that way out of concern for her. Of course, what happened was that Judy's and Art's behavior was mutually reinforcing, and over time their misunderstanding of what was really going on with each other only grew. The more perfunctory Art would be in bed, the more "used" and angry Judy would feel; the more "used" and angry Judy felt, the more Art would sense her tension and try to get "it" over with as soon as possible. Judy, in turn, would feel "used" and angry . . . and on and on this went for years.

The Change Process: Judy and Art's Way

For Judy and Art, the key to overcoming their sexual problems—indeed, most of their problems—was in learning to talk to each other. This sounds simple, but as we discuss in Chapter 15, which is about the "Why Can't You Read My Mind?" block, it's not. Growing up, most people did not learn how to identify their own feelings or how to articulate them in a direct, honest, noninflammatory and non-hurtful way. Nor did most people learn how to listen.

In order to break their noncommunication patterns, Judy and Art started off by taking turns speaking. Judy would have twenty minutes to say what was on her mind, and in those twenty minutes Art had to give her his undivided attention and could not interrupt her. The next day, Art would have his turn to speak. The only other rule is that they could not spend the twenty minutes making accusations; the focus was to stay on "I feel . . . ," not on "you are . . . ," "you always . . . ," and so forth.

As Judy and Art began to get better at communicating their true feelings toward each other, they started to become aware of how much they both projected and misinterpreted. For the first time in their twenty-five years of marriage they also began to talk about sex— what their early experiences had been, what they liked and didn't like, what their fears and insecurities were. As often happens when two people who have tried to read each other's minds for years begin to really communicate, they were shocked at how little they actually knew each other.

For Judy, becoming more comfortable with sex as both a topic of conversation and as an activity further required making an effort to improve her body image. This entailed the same process that Nancy, in Chapter 3, went through. Even more fundamentally, Judy also had to begin facing up to and releasing some of the anger, hurt, and shame that remained from her brother's molestations. Understandably, being sexually abused by her brother left Judy with a form of "I Feel Threatened When Another Person Gets Close," the block discussed in Chapter 12.

Because of the amount of shame, degradation, and guilt Judy had about the molestations, they were very difficult for her to talk about. But once she was past the painful first hurdle of admitting that this was what had happened to her, she found that talking about it caused her finally to let out some of the pent-up tears and rage she had been carrying around for more than thirty years. Slowly but perceptibly, her burden began to lighten.

While talking was a step in the right direction, Judy and Art still needed tangible help in developing a sexual relationship that would cause each to feel valued and loved. When a couple's sex life has been in a rut, and such a deep one, for as long as Judy and Art's was, it's unrealistic to expect them to be able to jump suddenly into bed with each other and start making love without a hitch. In these situations, it's usually more effective to use guided exercises that allow them to begin anew and gradually approach sexual intimacy. Judy and Art, for example, started with some exercises devised by sex therapists Masters and Johnson.[4] In the first exercise they remained fully clothed and lay down on their bed together. For forty-five minutes Art very gently caressed Judy from head to toe, but without touching her breasts or pubic area. During this time, Art was to concentrate on being attentive to Judy's response and to ask her questions she could answer with a nod or a shake of her head, such as "Does this feel good? Should I go slower?" and so forth. Judy during this time was to try to stay relaxed through controlled breathing (see exercise on pages 346–47) and to try to just let herself take in the love and warmth Art was giving her through his touch. In later exercises, they gradually moved toward nudity, genital touching, and different sexual activities.

When Judy and Art came to therapy the week after having been assigned the first exercise, they reported that they had felt stupid and ridiculous when they began the exercise, but once they had gotten over the initial awkwardness, it had really worked. For Judy, "It was the most intense experience of being loved that I've ever had in my whole life. Actually, it was the first time I truly felt loved by anyone." Art, too, was astounded by what an impact such a simple exercise could have. "I can't believe the difference in her, and how easy it was to please her," he said. "In all these years, I never felt even half as close to her as I did that night."

Although this was a breakthrough experience for Judy and Art, it of course was not a magical solution. It gave a glimmer of what kind of progress was possible and illuminated one possible path, but it did not whisk their problems away. At the time this chapter was going through final revisions, Judy and Art were still working on their other love blocks, and they both felt they had a way to go.

Bob

Bob, a sociology professor in his mid-thirties, comes from a family of three children who grew up in an inner-city housing project. He has curly brown hair and eyes that change from gray to green to a greenish-blue in different kinds of light. Short and trim, he has the compact but well-muscled build that brings to mind images of high-school wrestling matches. Affable but serious, Bob chooses his words very carefully, sometimes pausing at length to find just the right ones.

Like Judy, Bob grew up with a deep-seated feeling of unlovability, but he expressed his sense that he doesn't deserve love in a very different way. Women are generally encouraged to wear their feelings of low self-worth on their sleeves, so to speak, while men who have those same feelings are taught to hide them. So at the time Bob began treatment he was in the habit of masking his feelings of low self-esteem under a veneer of smugness and superiority.

Bob's mask of superiority was a legacy from his father, who simply could not admit mistakes. Men in general have difficulty being honest about their mistakes and limitations both to themselves and to their friends and families. Their sons then grow up with no model for accepting, revealing, and taking responsibility for their own short-comings and failures. Instead they learn that the "manly" thing to do is to deny and hide their mistakes and limitations, or to project them onto others, particularly wives and children. At some level, however, they're aware that this "manly" method of coping with shortcomings and mistakes is, in fact, cowardly. This, in turn, gives them more reason for the feelings of inadequacy and shame they're taught to hide and deny.

In addition to being a model for Bob's feigned bravado, Bob's father was the primary source of his low self-esteem. His father was a perfectionist who instilled in his son a terror of "doing things the wrong way." No matter what Bob was doing—cleaning his room, learning to ride a bike, or trying to mend a broken toy—the older man made it clear that he had to do it exactly right. Inevitably, Bob would make an error, and then his father would angrily take over and show him how to do it "the right way" (the father's way), all the while shouting at Bob and berating him for being "such a screw-up" and "wimp." Bob would then feel humiliated and despairing about "never doing anything right."

Although Bob is very bright and did well in school all his life, when he looks back on his childhood what he remembers most vividly is being about eight years old and struggling with some arithmetic homework under his father's critical eye. His father forced him to go over the assignment again and again until he got everything exactly right. Bob sat there for hours being watched and criticized. From this type of experience, repeated over and over throughout his life, Bob internalized his father's criticalness and developed a deep-seated sense that he does not deserve love because he is not perfect.

Unfortunately, Bob's father's critical presence dominated the entire household. His mother rarely stood up for herself when her husband bullied and berated her, and rarely took a stand against him on behalf of the children, either. Although kind, gentle, and generally loving toward Bob and his brother and sister, she was an essentially timid, docile person who was obviously frightened of her husband. Her demeanor conveyed to Bob and his siblings the sense that the world is a scary place. And her weak and unsuccessful attempts to act as a buffer capable of protecting the children from the father taught them that in a world where bullies ruled, there was just no way to win.

What little praise Bob and his siblings received from their father was "*but* praise," as in "That was good, *but* . . ." Often the list of *buts* was so long that Bob wouldn't even hear the praise because he was so braced for the criticism that was sure to follow. In an atmosphere where criticism "seemed to permeate the air we breathed," Bob would try hard to be good so that his father would ease up on the criticism for a while. While other children might have sought more praise from their parents, Bob learned that "the best I could hope for was not to be criticized for a while," and he experienced any period when his father would let up as a profound relief. By the time he reached adolescence, Bob had internalized his father's judgments to the point where there was a critical presence within him operating "full tilt" all the time.

Bob's relationship with other boys in his working-class neighborhood only reinforced his feelings of worthlessness, and his need to hide them with a swaggering bravado. In therapy, Bob revealed that he frequently had dreams in which "there's a group of guys who are about thirteen or fourteen or so. They're all standing around making fun of one guy, and he's trying to hide how hurt and humiliated he feels, how much he wants to run away and cry." For Bob and many men, the adolescent peer group clearly exerted a large influence on how comfortable—or *un*comfortable—they are about revealing inner feelings. Among teenage boys and young men, to reveal inadequacies or "weak" feelings, such as fear or homesickness, is to set oneself up for almost certain ridicule. When boys (and, sadly, men too) get together in groups, they tend to form a hierarchy in which there is constant jockeying for status in a never-ending game of one-upmanship. In this hierarchy, there are three principal ways of obtaining status: by demonstrating physical, mechanical, mental, or sexual prowess; by pretending to or boasting of such prowess (even if that means lying); and by publicly claiming that another member of the group lacks such prowess, and then putting him down for his reported deficiencies. As Bob described it, to reveal an inadequacy or to admit to lack of self-confidence when among such a group is like "handing the other guys a weapon to clobber you with." Looking back on his own adolescence, Bob said he "lived each school day with the fear that I'd get found out for not being manly enough."

As an adolescent, Bob tended to remain quiet among his peers so they would not discover that he really felt inadequate in comparison with them; in this way, he appeared to be "one of the boys" but felt like an outsider who didn't belong. In his early adolescence he also lost a number of fights, which reinforced his inner feeling that he was a wimpy coward who was inferior to others of his gender. Later, in high school, college, and graduate school, Bob avoided close friendships with male peers because they might have discovered how undeserving and unmanly he really was, and humiliated him as result.

For years Bob steered clear of girls as well because they, too, might have found out "how I really was." He had only one date in high school, and "it was an utter disaster" because Bob was so overwhelmed by anxiety. His main focus in high school was on his academic work, and this remained the case throughout college. It was less painful for him to work so much that he had no time for a social life than to admit he was too scared to risk forming close relationships.

The Change Process: Bob's Way

It was through his training as a sociologist that Bob became acquainted with psychotherapy. He decided to try it because he thought it might make him a more effective academic and researcher. He was aware that he lacked the genuine confidence necessary for outstanding work, and also felt he lacked the interpersonal skills required of a college teacher and adviser.

Many people enter therapy to deal with one problem, then end up spending a great deal of their time working on other issues they weren't aware of at first. This is what happened to Bob. When he started therapy he had no idea how pervasive and deep his self-esteem problems were. But unlearning the lessons of the past and building self-esteem turned out to be his primary concern in therapy.

Bob had to go through the same painstaking process of revising his view of himself, others, and the world that Judy went through. He had always intellectually known how much he had been influenced by his father, but now, for the first time, he began to feel how much hurt and longing his relationship with his father had left him with. Bob spent many sessions alternately weeping over the father he loved and wanted to please and venting his anger at his father for being so demanding, critical, and impossible to satisfy.

As he became more viscerally aware of how much his father had influenced him, Bob realized that his father's powerful, critical voice lived on within him. Like Judy, Bob spent a good deal of his waking hours listening to tapes in his head that relentlessly ran him down. "Sissy," "wimp," "shit for brains," "moron," "asshole," "good for nothing," "coward," "fuck-up" and "dummy" were among the names he commonly called himself. Academic successes brought barely a moment of pride before the tape began spinning out "fake," "impostor," "know-it-all," and "goody-goody teacher's pet." Like Judy, Bob had to train himself gradually to replace these messages with more positive statements about himself.

Bob also changed the way he related to other men. Although he became increasingly aware of how thoroughly humiliated he had always felt among the gang of boys he grew up with, he still remained involved with them as an adult, going to sporting events and playing on a softball team with them. Part of the reason was guilt: Bob was one of the few boys from his neighborhood who had gone on to college, and now that he had a Ph.D. and taught in a college, he was very sensitive about not "leaving my roots behind and acting like I'm too good for them." There was an element of reverse snobbery involved, too: few academics he knew had working-class back-grounds, and Bob got a lot of mileage out of presenting himself as "more proletarian than thou."

In addition, Bob wasn't sure how to go about making new male friends. He knew how to get together with other guys to *do* things but had avoided getting to know any of his academic colleagues better because he knew it would entail talking, the way women did. He was afraid that if he had to sit down and talk about himself, he would "reveal how I'm really not that smart after all, and I'd be humiliated."

As Bob became more aware of how little he enjoyed "the old gang," he eventually decided to quit the softball team and stop hang-ing out with them. Not long afterward, he ran into another guy from his childhood neighborhood, someone who had been similarly alienated from the group because he was a good student (the gang called him "Einstein" and "Four Eyes") and no good at sports ("fairy" and "Blob Man"). Now an official in the city welfare department, this man and Bob eventually developed a deep friendship. Although Bob remained hesitant to open up, he was reassured that this friend knew what it was like to be mortified by other guys. This gave Bob confidence, making him feel less like "the guy who's always on the outs, the last guy that gets picked when they're choosing sides in gym class."

Bob made changes in the way he related to women, too. Growing up, Bob felt a lot of pressure to prove his manliness, and one of the surest ways to prove that in his neighborhood was to demean women and "show you didn't care about them and didn't need them." Bob and "the gang" took the position that "all women want is a good lay. They want you to take them home and fuck them." Yet even as Bob participated in this macho posturing, he had frequent fantasies of being gently kissed and caressed by a woman, tenderly kissing and caressing her in return. Although the fantasies themselves were plea-surable, they also humiliated Bob, who took them as a sign of how "unmanly" he was. He was sure that if a girl or woman discovered that he wanted tender kisses and caresses and not a "manly fuck," she'd scorn and reject him.

As Bob revised his view of reality and learned that a lot of what he believed about himself wasn't true, he also realized that he actually knew very little about women. In therapy, he was encouraged to date more and be himself with women. Gradually he started to tell the women he dated about himself, even though he often blushed and got tongue-tied as he did so. To his great surprise, he discovered that the gentle, warm, kind person that he had been hiding for years was not considered "wimpy" by women; on the contrary, many women found Bob's real self quite attractive. For years he had believed that because he failed to live up to his inner standards of perfection and his father's standards of masculinity, he was unlovable. Now he found out that it was precisely because he was not perfect and did not measure up to conventional standards of masculinity that women liked him.

Bob changed the way in which he related to women sexually, too. Rather than forcefully "take" a woman as he thought real men were supposed to and as he had done in the past, he let his more gentle side out. He would slowly and tentatively take a woman's hand, kiss her tenderly, and hold her without pushing on to "home base." He enjoyed kissing and caressing as pleasurable acts in themselves, not just preliminaries to be rushed through on the way to "getting a score." He was shocked and relieved to find that a lot of women actually *liked* to be treated this way.

As his self-acceptance and confidence grew in his relationships with women, Bob started revealing his inadequacies to his male acquaintances and colleagues, too. For example, in a discussion with some other guys about sports, he confessed that he had hated most sports as a kid because "I was uncoordinated and always on the verge of making a fool of myself." This sort of disclosure made Bob begin to feel more at ease with the men he knew, and many of them seemed to feel more at ease with him, too. They started to tease him in a good-natured way about his self-acknowledged limitations, mistakes, and "sore points." This teasing is a modified, adult version of the adolescent "ranking out" that he so feared as a teenager, and Bob now experiences it as a form of male camaraderie and bonding. Paradoxically, something he previously feared from his peers is now welcomed by him as a special kind of love.

But the most noticeable change in Bob is that he has shed his air of superiority. He is finally secure enough about his own worth not to have to constantly trumpet it. And he has discovered yet another truth that seems paradoxical: the more genuine self-love a person has, the less self-preoccupied he becomes. When a person feels confident of his worth, he is freed of the burden of always having to prove it.

Chapter 6
"I Don't Need Anyone—
I'm Strong"

Alan, a successful attorney with his own practice, is tall and handsome, with an athletic build and an aloof, formal manner. A Little League coach and school-board member, he has long been an admired member of his community. At age thirty-five, he reluctantly entered therapy at the insistence of his wife, Ann. He had suddenly started using cocaine, and Ann feared that he was heading down a road similar to that trod by her father, an alcoholic. Although in his first session Alan admitted that he had been snorting cocaine "on occasion," he felt this was a normal reaction to the enormous stress he had recently been under at work, and he complained that Ann was "pushing the panic button." "I'm only here to make Ann happy," he explained in a resentful tone. "I've always handled my problems on my own, and I can handle this on my own, too."

No one meeting Alan at the time would have guessed that he had problems in relationships or that he was seeing a psychologist. By society's standards, Alan was a "regular guy," and his apparently happy family had long been the envy of many of his neighbors and colleagues at work. Only if they had tried to live with him would they have found out what Alan's wife and children already knew— that Alan could not be intimate, that, as Ann put it, "there's something missing from him, something you notice only when you get up real close."

As Alan proceeded with therapy, it became clear that he had a number of different love blocks. But his major one was "I Don't Need Anyone—I'm Strong." Alan relied heavily on the support and help of his wife of twelve years, as well as that of his longtime secretary and the younger lawyers who worked for him; yet his inner view was that he was a loner who had little or no need for the love and assistance that others offered. Again and again in his early therapy sessions, Alan adamantly remarked, "I don't need to be here. I'm only doing it for Ann." When asked if he saw something wrong with needing help, Alan responded with an angry look and sullen silence. "Of course, there's something wrong," he finally explained. "If you need help, it means you can't make it on your own. It means you're weak—and if there's one thing I'm not, it's weak!"

The "I Don't Need Anyone—I'm Strong" block is nearly as pervasive as the "I Don't Deserve Love" block; often, in fact, these two love blocks go hand in hand. People like Alan believe that to need and depend on others is to be shamefully weak, so they strive to maintain an image of strength and emotional self-reliance. They take great pride in not being dependent or needy and appear to have very high self-esteem. In fact, though, theirs is a false sense of self-esteem, based on denial of a very important part of themselves—the part that needs love—rather than the genuine self-esteem that comes from full self-acceptance. Unable to accept that they need love and aid from others, they have tremendous difficulty taking it in when offered; to do so would be to acknowledge that there's a needy child within, which in turn would threaten the sense of self-reliance and strength that their self-worth is based upon.

In many cases, the "I Don't Need Anyone—I'm Strong" block also coexists with the "I Don't Want to Deal with My Feelings" block discussed in Chapter 4, and can be considered an extension or specific manifestation of it. People who are uncomfortable with their feelings in general are often especially uncomfortable with their feelings of neediness and dependency.

Many people who say, in essence, "I Don't Need Anyone—I'm Strong" are unaware that this stance serves as a love block. On the contrary, they believe that others love them because of their strength and self-reliance, and fear that if they weren't so strong others would love them less. They don't realize that there's a difference between love and admiration, and that while strength and self-reliance might be admirable, most people don't find them particularly lovable—or at least not as lovable as such traits as openness, softness, humor, and vulnerability. Nor do they realize that because many people have a need to be needed, a stance of total strength and self-reliance actually may put others off. Alan, for example, had built such a wall around his feelings of neediness and vulnerability that he struck many people as cold and superior, with the result that many actually disliked him. And although his wife, Ann, loved him very much, she had gotten so sick of trying to break through his facade that she was considering leaving him.

Many people with the "I Don't Need Anyone—I'm Strong" block probably wouldn't even read this book, and those who would probably reject our premise that everyone needs the love and help of others to get through life. Granted, individuals vary in the amount of love and nurturance they need, and in the ways it's shown. But everyone has some need for love, even those who appear the least needy. In fact, those are precisely the ones whose needs for love are often the greatest. It's because their needs are so large—and so unsatisfied—that they feel compelled to hide them, lest anyone else get wind of what's really inside.

Alan

Alan is a typical example of a person whose outward appearance of emotional self-reliance was developed as a way of trying to cover up the fact that he has deep and unsatisfied needs. Ideally, Alan's parents would have been able to provide the unconditional support and affection a young child needs. They would have allowed him to lean on them, aware that it's only after a child feels secure in the knowledge that he can depend on others to help and take care of him that he becomes ready to take the steps toward increasing independence. Unfortunately, though, Alan's parents had themselves been brought up on the premise that children, particularly boys, should be able to get along on their own at a very early age. They raised Alan and his three brothers to believe what they had been raised to believe—that there's something shameful about needing help, consolation, or reassurance.

Alan has many fond and happy memories of childhood. The ones that kept returning time and again in his therapy, however, were of the disappointment he felt over repeatedly striking out in his first Little League game; the fear he felt when older boys beat him up on his way home from school; and the grief he felt when, at age seven, he saw his dog get hit by a car and die. In each instance, he yearned for his parents to comfort him and validate his feelings through a tender touch or word of consolation. Instead, in each case they gave him a stern look of disapproval, told him he was acting like a sissy, and lectured him on the importance of learning that life is a series of trials that "you just have to tough out." Crying in particular was taboo, and whenever Alan or his brothers would actually shed tears their parents would respond by hitting them with a razor strop, saying "if you want to be such a baby, then we're going to give you something to cry about." Only when the tears stopped would the punishment also cease.

As would have happened with any child whose basic emotional needs were not met, Alan concluded that he was wrong to have needs—not that his parents were wrong in failing to meet them. His childhood experiences left him with a sense of shame about his "weak" emotions, and whenever he felt any stirring of neediness inside himself he'd immediately experience an awful, overwhelming feeling of humiliation. For Alan, there was only one way to survive this pain— and that was to deny the existence of his needs, to psychically kill off the part of himself that longed to be hugged, consoled, and taken care of.

In adulthood, this part of Alan remained buried and a source of shame. In any situation that might have caused others to feel fear, disappointment, or sadness and to reach out for loving help, Alan would so thoroughly repress his feelings that he not only couldn't ask for help—he also couldn't really feel his feelings at all. In therapy he gradually came to see that drugs were a way of keeping the needy, vulnerable, and deprived part of him dead and buried.

Cultural Influences

Even if his childhood had been different, Alan still might have developed shame and discomfort about being needy and dependent because of the the long-standing bias against emotional dependency that runs through mainstream American culture. In many other cultures, particularly Asian and African ones, there's great emphasis on community, and people grow up with a deep awareness of the ways in which they're connected to and dependent on others. The white settlers who founded the United States, however, had uprooted themselves from their families and pasts, and the culture they created in the new land placed a strong emphasis on self-reliance. The American penchant for individualism is reflected in our legal system's emphasis on the protection of individual rights, and it pervades American popular culture as well. Rugged individualism is one of the most admired traits in American culture, and among the most esteemed of American heroes are the self-made man and the pioneer brave enough to go it alone.

While the protection of individual rights is indeed a worthy political goal, the lionization of the idea of individualism in our culture is not without its drawbacks. For one, the focus on the individual's rights has blinded many people to their responsibilities to the larger community; in fact, it's blinded many people to the fact that they exist within a community at all. From a very early age, most of us were taught to focus on what sets us apart from others, not on what we have in common; and as we learned to be hyperaware of differences, we also learned to equate difference with inequality—to assume that if, say, two people have skin of a different color, then one must be superior, the other inferior.

The concern with differences and hierarchy not only creates tremendous antagonisms within our society, it often also leads to a painful sense of personal alienation. Oblivious of how much they have in common with others, many troubled people suffer from the tragic delusion that "I'm the only one who feels this way—no one else would understand." When and if they finally get into a situation where they can honestly discuss their feelings with others—be it an intimate one-on-one relationship, group therapy, or a self-help group like Alcoholics Anonymous or Adult Children of Alcoholics—they're usually shocked and relieved to discover that many others share their supposedly unique experiences, perceptions, and feelings.

Men's Denial of Their Emotional Neediness

In our culture, men in particular tend to have trouble recognizing the ways in which they're connected to and dependent on others. As explained in Nancy Chodorow's *The Reproduction of Mothering* and Carol Gilligan's *In A Different Voice,* boys and girls in our culture develop markedly different senses of themselves in relation to others.[1] This is because the primary responsibility for the care of infants is usually taken on by mothers. Being the same gender, girls do not develop a deep sense of differentness and separation from the mother, and this sense of being similar and connected to the person with whom they had their first intimate relationship shapes the way they approach and view their later relationships. Conversely, boys develop a strong sense of themselves as separate individuals very different from the person with whom they had their first intimate attachment, and this awareness colors their perception of their later attachments. These different ways of seeing the self are then reinforced via sex roles. A male in our culture traditionally has been encouraged to develop a strong identity as a separate individual, while a female is supposed to derive her identity by merging with a more highly valued male, and ideally bearing him sons. The end result is that men tend to see themselves as distinct selves somewhat detached or entirely cut off from others, while women view themselves as connected selves embedded in a complex web of relationships.

Within the same relationship, a man will often see himself as less dependent than he really is, and a woman will see herself as more so. For example, when Alan began therapy, he had been dependent on Ann to take care of his physical, sexual, and emotional needs for more than a dozen years. Without Ann's emotional support, Alan would have trouble facing the outside world; and without her practical services—such as doing his laundry and taking his car in for repairs—Alan probably wouldn't have been able to get dressed in the morning. Nevertheless, Alan persisted in seeing himself as a self-sufficient loner, like many men in similar situations.

By contrast, Ann was like many women in that she had an insufficient sense of her own capacity for self-reliance—and was blind to the ways that others leaned on her. For most of Alan and Ann's marriage, Ann had believed that she needed and depended on Alan far more than he needed and depended on her. She minimized the fact that she had worked double shifts as a nurse to help him through law school, saying "he didn't really need me. If I hadn't been there, he would have found some other way to do it." At the same time, she also minimized her own accomplishments, believing that being a nurse was easy, while becoming a lawyer "was really difficult. I couldn't have done it." It was only after ten years of marriage that Ann, who by then had entered group therapy, began to question these assumptions.

In many heterosexual relationships there is an unspoken agreement that the woman will act as the carrier of the neediness and dependency for both parties. The man is thus able to keep up the pretense that he is not needy, which soothes his ego and obscures the reality: that both man and woman depend on each other in various ways. A man might say, for example, that he got married to appease his wife's need for security, and as long as neither party challenges this the man doesn't have to acknowledge that his own need for security was a factor, too. Or a man might tell himself that he calls his lover several times a day because she needs to hear from him, reasoning that allows him to remain oblivious of the possibility that *he* needs the contact. Similarly, by saying he began therapy "only to make Ann happy," Alan was able to avoid dealing with the reality of his situation— which was that his cocaine use was out of control and that he would have been in need of help even if Ann hadn't been around to insist that he get it.

The Change Process: Alan's Way

Alan stayed in therapy for only about a year, far too little time to overcome such a major and deeply ingrained problem as his "I Don't Need Anyone—I'm Strong" block. His progress was additionally hindered by the humiliation people with this block tend to feel about even the most cursory discussion of their neediness. Nevertheless, even within a relatively short time frame, Alan was able to make some considerable dents in his block, which in turn enriched his emotional life considerably.

In talking to another man about his childhood, Alan eventually developed more compassion for the needy little boy he had once been. As this happened, he became more sensitive to other people's feelings, and to the way he treated them. One relationship that dramatically changed was with his secretary. For years he had communicated with her by wordlessly dropping work and cold, bossy memos on her desk or giving her orders as if she were a soldier under his command. Gradually he began to approach her with phrases like "Could you get me . . . ?" "I would appreciate it if you would . . ." and "I need your help with . . ." This made the atmosphere of the office much warmer and calmer. As a result, the secretary seemed to have more appreciation for Alan as a human being, and more respect for him as a boss, which pleased Alan.

The fundamental dynamics of Alan's relationship with his secretary were unchanged. But Alan's perception of it—and of himself—was dramatically different. When he realized that he had always been dependent on her but just had never consciously acknowledged the dependence, he began to see that being dependent on someone wasn't really so bad after all.

As Alan opened himself up to looking at his childhood, he became aware of an inner emptiness created by his lack of real companionship with other boys. He realized this was a lack that had carried over into his adult life. It also dawned on Alan that he wanted male friends. For a long time he had been in the habit of lunching at his desk, but now he started to make lunch dates with other men—establishing a rule that there be no discussion of business. He began inviting other men to sports events. On one occasion he called an acquaintance who was a school administrator and said, "I wonder if we could talk. I need some help with my son."

Proud of his ability to "take care of things on my own" and "keep my own counsel," Alan had never shared his inner thoughts or feelings with his wife, Ann. This made Alan feel isolated and made Ann feel like "an outsider, not part of his life." Although it went against everything he was raised with, Alan finally decided to begin to talk more openly to Ann, to begin to "let her in" on his fears, doubts, and insecurities. He confessed that, despite his success, he felt inadequate about his personal interactions with his staff and clients;

afterwards he felt much closer to Ann, and much more accepted and loved by her. An unexpected benefit was her insight on the subject, which was quite helpful to him personally and professionally.

Not long afterwards, Alan's mother became seriously ill, and he was glad he had begun to open up more. He now found it easier to tell Ann about his fears of his mother's dying, his feeling of powerlessness, and his horror at his impending loss. He even began to cry. Ann comforted Alan throughout this period, and since Alan had started speaking to her in the way in which he spoke to his secretary ("I need you to . . . ," "I'd really be grateful if you . . . ," etc.) she did not feel resentful or taken for granted as she had in the past. After more than thirteen years of marriage, Alan was finally beginning to take in his wife's love. She, in turn, was beginning to feel appreciated and valued by her husband, rather than as though she were being stepped on like a doormat.

While still in therapy, Alan's work pressures eased up and he stopped using cocaine. Although he did make tangible progress in improving his relationships and overcoming his "I Don't Need Anyone—I'm Strong" block, it would be misleading to give the impression that he left treatment "cured." On the contrary, Alan still had difficulty being needy and dependent. In fact, he used the same words to explain why he was ending therapy that he had used to explain why he was reluctant to start it in the first place: "I don't need it anymore," he said. "I really don't need it."

Joyce

Since many women have been raised to perceive themselves as dependent, it would seem logical to conclude that women are less likely to suffer from the "I Don't Need Anyone—I'm Strong" block. Yet many are affected by this block as deeply as men. Joyce is one such woman.

Joyce has been in psychotherapy twice, first for several years in her mid- to late twenties, and again for three years in her mid-thirties. When she started treatment for the first time, she had been working as a secretary since high school and had just started attending college at night. A soft-spoken woman whose braided hair and feminine appearance recall the "flower child" look of the early 1970s, Joyce at first glance seemed to approach the world with a tentative, scared-rabbit air. Very quickly, though, Joyce revealed that underneath her soft demeanor she was in fact "a rock," as she put it, capable of singlehandedly managing any problem that might come her way. She was, in fact, quite proud of how little she needed from others.

Joyce and her younger brother, Teddy, grew up in a medium-sized city in the Midwest, in a home where both financial and emotional resources were scant. Their father was a manual laborer whose income would have meant a struggle to make ends meet even under the best of circumstances; he was also an alcoholic and chronic gambler who was always deeply in debt. Although Joyce's mother was a kind woman, she never had much to give her children in the way of warmth, affection, and time because she was always depleted from the strain of working as a waitress and a seamstress, taking care of a household, and coping with the consequences of her husband's addictions. And even with the money that Joyce's mother earned working long hours, the family was never far from being, as Joyce put it, "tossed out onto the street." A cloud of instability always hung over them, coupled with the fear that "something really bad was going to happen any minute."

When Joyce was ten and Teddy eight, something really bad did happen: their father left for work one morning and did not return; he never contacted his family again. Joyce was crushed. Although in the past her father had been generally unreliable and often absent, he also had a boisterous, carefree aspect to his personality and he would sometimes take Joyce on outings, buy her extravagant presents (usually to celebrate his winning big at the track), and spend long afternoons regaling her with tall tales of his past feats—tales that the small Joyce was too naive to understand were untrue. These intermittent episodes constituted the most memorable happy occasions in Joyce's early life, for they were the only times that her needs for attention, approval, intimacy and affectionate doting began to get met. As a result, she experienced her father's abandonment as a devastating loss.

At the time, though, Joyce repressed her real feelings. Her mother was so enraged that she would not even permit her husband's name to be mentioned, let alone allow anyone to mourn him. Moreover, her father's disappearance lacked the finality of death, so Joyce was left in a sort of emotional limbo, seesawing back and forth between grief and hope, and wondering which was more valid. In the following years, Joyce held on to the hope that one day she would receive a letter or phone call from him and fantasized that he would make an unannounced appearance at the apartment door "dying to see me," then whisk her off for dinner at a fancy restaurant. In her early twenties, these hopes and dreams evaporated when an old friend of her father's called to say that he had died of a heart attack.

When Joyce's father walked out, he left a number of legitimate debts with virtually every business in their part of the city, and suddenly people began calling and coming to the apartment demanding their money. The meager savings Joyce's mother had squirreled away were quickly paid out, but people kept coming. Joyce and Teddy didn't want to answer the door or phone and they were afraid of running into people in the street. Frequently, they would be stopped by adults who would demand, "Where is your father?" Increasingly, "creepy-looking men" seeking payment of gambling debts hounded the family, too. Strangers would come to the apartment at all hours of the night. On several occasions, Joyce knew she was being followed when she went out. She and Teddy lived in constant shame and fear.

Joyce, Teddy, and their mother eventually moved to the home of one of Joyce's maternal aunts. This began a series of moves from one relative to another over the course of the next several years. While her mother worked double shifts so that they could save money to get their own apartment, Joyce and Teddy endured very harsh treatment. Their cousins and aunts belittled them, demanded that they do a lot of housework, and threatened to kick them out if they didn't obey. "I felt like Cinderella" is the way Joyce characterized that period of her life.

Joyce never told her mother about this treatment because she had an intuitive sense that "my mother didn't want to know," and believed "she couldn't have done anything about it, anyway." Also, in their case the natural order had reversed: Joyce had become mother to her mother. Joyce was her mother's moral support and confidante, the one who listened to her stories of how hard life was, both with and without her father. After they were finally able to move to their own apartment, Joyce would have the place cleaned and a meal waiting when her mother returned, exhausted, from work. It was her job to take care of Teddy, too. "As far back as I can remember, I had to take charge," Joyce later recalled. "Even as a little girl, I felt like an old lady."

As Joyce grew older, she grew more and more accustomed to playing the role of caretaker—and she received a good deal of positive reinforcement for doing so, too. Her mother and other adults would frequently marvel at how self-reliant Joyce was, how she could handle so much without assistance or complaint. Like many children who are forced into a caretaker role before their own needs to be taken care of have been satisfied, Joyce convinced herself that she was better off this way. She told herself that having to cope with so much so early had caused her to develop "character." Only years later did she realize that her strength had been acquired at great cost.

During adolescence Joyce had little time or energy to develop her own social life or interests. Although very pretty, she did not date. When she finished high school, she immediately got a secretarial job and focused her energy on saving enough money to move out of her mother's cramped apartment. Interestingly, she wanted to move out not to escape the caretaker role (she would remain closely involved with her mother and brother even after moving out), but to enhance her sense of self-reliance—to be *really* on her own.

While in her secretarial job, Joyce met a number of other women of different ages and began to develop personal friendships with them. No matter how old the other woman was, in each relationship Joyce took on a maternal role. She listened to other people's problems while never divulging her own. Because her needs for love and nurturance had been suppressed so long, however, Joyce did not have any conscious sense that there was something lacking in these relationships.

After getting her own apartment, Joyce began saving to pay for college. Always an excellent student, she hoped to major in child psychology. After several years as a secretary at a large insurance firm, she was promoted to executive secretary and started going to college part-time at night.

Joyce was twenty-three when she started college and began dating around that time, too. She had a number of unsettling experiences with a series of men who would ask her out a couple of times, then disappear, never calling back or offering her any explanation. When she was twenty-four, she started seeing two different men steadily and remained involved with them simultaneously over the next two years. One of the men was a student she had met in night school who was several years younger than she; the other was a salesman who did business with her company, in his forties and married. It was partly in order to figure out what to do about these two involvements that Joyce decided to start therapy for the first time.

With the younger man, Joyce played the role of caretaker. She would listen to his problems, cook meals for him, and frequently pick up the tab for the both of them. When they went out, they usually did what he wanted to do.

Her relationship with the older man was better in several respects. He was kind to her, brought her presents, took her out to fancy dinners, and was always attentive and affectionate. But he had made it clear from the start that he had no intentions of ever divorcing his wife.

What was most significant about these two affairs was that while Joyce was intellectually aware that they weren't fulfilling her, this did not anger or upset her. She was very blunt in calling the younger man self-centered, and she could freely admit she wasn't getting much out of the relationship. But this didn't bother her because she maintained that aside from an occasional sexual tryst, she didn't need anything from him—or from anyone, for that matter. Joyce viewed her relationship with the older, married man with similar equanimity. Very occasionally she had vague twinges of wanting more from him, but these feelings were fleeting and not very powerful. She was for the most part satisfied with these two unfulfilling relationships because, she explained, she did not need to be fulfilled. "I'm just not the kind of person who needs a relationship," she said. "I do fine on my own. The last thing I need to make my life complete is a man."

In therapy, however, Joyce revealed that she sometimes experienced a fleeting feeling of wanting more in her relationship with the older man. Joyce was initially reluctant to discuss this feeling, and the needy, dependent part of her psyche it arose from. Only after many sessions of circling around the subject did Joyce finally begin to examine this feeling, and to allow herself to start really experiencing it. When she did, she discovered that this vague and fleeting feeling was an expression of, and a way of tapping into, a veritable well of sadness, grief, and neediness that she had been carrying inside since she was a small girl—especially since her father's abandonment. In the wake of this terrible loss, she had needed to be consoled, comforted, reassured, and babied. Denied this, Joyce had one way to survive—get rid of her needs.

For Joyce, developing an outward stance of being "a rock everyone can rely on" was a way of covering up the fact that deep inside she felt, as she put it, "like a real marshmallow," who is "ready to cry at the drop of a hat." As long as Joyce could remember, she had felt unbearable fear and shame about being "so weak inside." "I'm afraid that if I broke down and started to cry, I'd never stop," she explained in one session. "And that would be so humiliating because I'd reveal myself as weak, and other people don't want to see that." But as she was to learn, the real problem for Joyce wasn't that others didn't want to see her neediness; it was that *she* didn't want to see it.

As Joyce continued with therapy, she also began to talk about her relationship to food. Joyce would periodically go on eating binges in which she would devour a lot of food, then force herself to throw up. This was another clue suggesting that Joyce was not actually as free of emotional needs as she initially believed herself to be. Inside there was an emptiness that needed to be filled up.

One day Joyce had a memory that illuminated the origin of her problem with food. She was in a room with her younger brother, who had just been born, which meant Joyce was about two at the time. Both she and her brother were crying, and their mother came into the room and picked him up, began cuddling him, then left the room with him in her arms. Joyce began crying even harder, and a few minutes later her mother returned, still holding her brother, and gave Joyce a bottle and a cookie. As she recounted this memory, Joyce cried again, and then sat up straight in her chair with a look of shock on her face. "It's never occurred to me, but that was the start of my overeating," she said. "Instead of getting hugged and held, I got something shoved in my mouth to shut me up." As cocaine had been for Alan, overeating for Joyce had become a way of trying to "shut up" the emotionally starved inner child.

Women's Shame About Being Needy

Although the details of Joyce's story are unique, her experience is in several respects emblematic of the experience of many women, even those who grew up in happy homes. Raised to be nurturers, many women began taking care of other people's needs at a very early age—long before their own needs were met. As a result, many women walk around with a hunger for the love and coddling they never got as children. Many try to cope with this hunger by overeating, drinking to excess, and/or devoting themselves to a life of self-sacrifice. Indeed, self-sacrifice is built in to the traditional female role. Although today it may seem obvious that Joyce was settling for too little in her relationships, until very recently it was taken for granted that a woman's only concern should be with her husband's and children's emotional fulfillment. And just as Joyce's constant giving to others distracted her from how much she longed to be given to, generations of women have found a certain solace in the traditional role because always attending to other people's needs prevented them from confronting their own.

Any child whose natural needs to be taken care of and to lean on others are not met in childhood will conclude that "my needs are bad, and there's something wrong with me for having them"—and a child will reach this conclusion regardless of gender. But women have special reasons for feeling shame about feeling needy and dependent, too. Although our culture gives women more license to appear needy and dependent than men, this license comes with strings attached. Girls are taught not that feelings of neediness and dependency are human but that they're *feminine* and, therefore, that such feelings are evidence of inferiority rather than humanity. At the same time that girls learn that "real" women are needy and dependent, they also learn that women are of less value than men—and that one of the reasons this is so is that men aren't needy and dependent the way women are. This circular logic puts girls and women in a no-win situation: they can either acknowledge their neediness and dependency and bear the shame of being inferior, or deny these feelings and bear the shame of failing the femininity test. Men, too, end up in a no-win situation: they either acknowledge their neediness and dependency and risk being labeled wimps and sissies, or they hide these supposedly shameful feelings and worry about the humiliation of being found out.

The notion that neediness and dependency are distinctly female emotions not only perpetuates the myth that men are not needy and dependent, it also allows men to escape responsibility for the problems they have in dealing with these feelings. After all, since men don't have these feelings, they can't have problems with them—or so the logic goes. Also, designating neediness and dependency as female emotions reinforces the idea that there's something wrong with these feelings in the first place. Although the conventional view is that these feelings are inherently problematic, it would be more accurate to say that we as a culture have a problem in dealing with them.

Unfortunately, in recent years some women have felt even greater shame over the fact that they have emotional needs, particularly the need for love. A truly liberated woman, some people mistakenly believe, is one who has outgrown or overcome her human need for love and needs only her work and self to be fulfilled. Many women believe that to admit a desire for love, particularly the love of men, means they have failed an important test of feminism.

Another reason some women feel shame over being needy and dependent is that admission of these feelings challenges their perception of themselves as nurturers. The fact is, although women are supposed to be the needy and dependent sex, they're also supposed to be the caretaking sex. Many women base a good deal of their self-esteem and sense of femininity on their ability to take care of other people's needs, and it can be threatening for such women to acknowledge that they, too, have needs. After all, how good a nurturer can a woman be if she's preoccupied with her own needs? Also, many women have been taught to equate being needy with being selfish, and they've also been taught to consider selfishness one of the worst traits a woman can have.

The Change Process: Joyce's Way

During her first time in therapy, Joyce realized that she had been brought up to believe that it was selfish of her to have needs, and doubly selfish to try to get those needs met. Slowly she began making steps toward a more fulfilling life. First, she ended both romantic relationships, deciding to put her energy into developing her own interests. Although she said she wasn't sure she wanted to get involved with anyone else, she at least expressed more openness to the idea of someday finding a more rewarding relationship. This was a step forward from her previous stance of "I don't need to be involved with anyone, least of all a man."

Joyce also finished college and began training to become a counselor for adolescents. Eventually she quit her job and joined the staff of a center for runaway youths. She excelled at her new job, and one day she mentioned that for the first time in her life she felt truly "fulfilled" by her work. She liked the word, she said, noting that it sounded like a combination of the words *full* and *fill*. She also realized she deserved credit for putting herself through night school and making such a big career move. So many people continue along in jobs that are devoid of challenges and opportunities for growth, trying to "fill" themselves "full" through excessive drinking, drug use, or eating. Especially since she was the child of an alcoholic and a compulsive gambler, and had already had some trouble with binge eating, she could easily have taken one of those routes. It was a testament to her capacity for growth that she did not.

As is often the case with people with shame-producing behaviors like binge eating, Joyce discovered that just the act of finally revealing her secret to someone else had brought a tremendous relief. Since her binge eating had always been sporadic, Joyce felt she didn't need much help to deal with it. At the same time, though, Joyce had started to become aware that whenever she heard the words "I don't need . . ." go through her head she should interpret them as warning bells. "Maybe when I'm most sure I don't need, I really need the most," she realized. So when a woman she knew from the insurance firm where she worked mentioned one day that she was attending meetings of Overeaters Anonymous, Joyce decided to tag along.

Through OA, a self-help group modeled after the highly successful Alcoholics Anonymous, Joyce met other people who had similar shame about being needy, and she developed friendships with several of them. Also through OA, Joyce was introduced to the literature and theories of the growing self-help movement of Adult Children of Alcoholics, or ACOAs. Since both OA and ACOA are based on the premise that everyone needs the help of other human beings and their "higher power" (meaning God or a God substitute), the programs have stood as constant reminders of something Joyce and others with the "I Don't Need Anyone—I'm Strong" block tend all too easily to forget—that the road to recovery is virtually impossible to go alone.

Although Joyce did make considerable progress her first time in treatment, when she left therapy her work was nowhere near finished. Several years later, Joyce resumed treatment. This time, more of her story unfolded, and it became evident that she was suffering from another major love block, one that hadn't been apparent before. The rest of Joyce's story, in the following pages, is testimony to the fact that psychological growth is a lifelong process.

Chapter 7
"Love Just Isn't in the Cards for Me"

"No one will ever love me." Most people have said this to themselves at one time or another—after the breakup of a romantic relationship, when they've been let down by someone they love, or during a bout of intense loneliness or despair. For some people, however, "no one will ever love me" isn't just a hackneyed phrase that comes to mind in fleeting moments of despair—it's a statement that sums up a sincere conviction they carry with them all the time. Such people see the world as a personally depriving place, one in which others have been destined to be loved and taken care of, but they've been fated to do without. When they say "no one will ever love me," they're not indulging in momentary self-pity. They're articulating what they've always taken for granted as an incontrovertible, unalterable fact of their existence—that "Love Just Isn't in the Cards for Me."

People with the "Love Just Isn't in the Cards for Me" block often have much in common with those who take the stance of "I Don't Need Anyone—I'm Strong," the block discussed in the preceding chapter. But there are important differences between these two love blocks. Those with the "Love Just Isn't in the Cards for Me" block don't necessarily deny that they have emotional needs, nor do they necessarily feel that there's something wrong or shameful about having such needs. On the contrary, some are quite willing to admit that they need love and affection and can accept that this is natural. But they also believe that there are two groups of people in the world: those who have been fated to get the love they need, and those who have been destined to go without. And because they view themselves as members of the second category, they take it on faith that their needs for love are bound to remain unsatisfied regardless of how hard they try to get those needs met. "No matter how much I might need, want, and seek love, I'm not going to get it anyway," they in essence say. "So why should I bother to try?"

For people who view the world as a depriving place for them personally, life has a grayness and blandness about it, and their inner lives are characterized by a feeling of profound emptiness. An overriding sense of resignation to their so-called "fate" tends to dominate. Many take little or no action to obtain love, either by making efforts to form new relationships or by trying to make their needs and wishes known in existing relationships. Typically, if they have close relationships at all, they tend to settle for ones that are not very deep and rewarding, or are even destructive. Although aware that others have more fulfilling relationships, they don't try to get more fulfillment for themselves, figuring that "this is more than I ever expected, and it's probably as good as it's going to get. I'd be tempting fate if I asked for more."

While they tend to be passive when it comes to seeking love, people with this block often actively reject love that others offer. Because they're convinced they are entirely right about no one ever loving them, when love comes their way it feels all wrong, so they can't let it in.

People who take emotional deprivation for granted frequently believe they're destined to live in a state of financial and material deprivation, too. Some come from homes where the lack of emotional resources went hand in hand with a lack of financial resources, and the two kinds of deprivation then became inextricably linked in their minds. Others who grew up with plenty of money still came to the same conclusions. The sense of emotional deprivation pervading the atmosphere in their childhood homes spilled over into the material realm, coloring the way money was viewed and handled, causing everyone to feel poor and the children to grow up with a "poverty mentality."

People who believe they've been destined to go through their lives in a state of emotional deprivation tend to fall into two groups. In the first group are people for whom the belief that "Love Just Isn't in the Cards for Me" is a conscious belief that they can usually express in words. They're fully aware that they see the world as a personally depriving place, and although they may be resigned to their so-called fate, they still think it's unfair that others get love while they're forced to do without. People in this group tend to display a "woe is me, nobody knows the trouble I've seen" type of attitude, and approach life in the grudging sort of way best described by the phrase "a chip on his shoulder." Typically, people who manifest this love block in their conscious thinking are very susceptible to three love blocks discussed in later chapters—"I Want Love, But Only If It's a Certain Way"; "Why Do I Always Have to Give So Much to Get So Little?"; and "Anger Keeps Getting in the Way."

Others with this love block are not consciously aware of their particular world view. They're so thoroughly accustomed to living in a state of emotional deprivation that they don't recognize that anything's missing. Their sense of emptiness is like air—it's just there, so basic a part of their experience that they wouldn't think to question or lament it.

A large number of people in this second group develop what could be called a "caretaker" or "earth mother" personality type, like that of Joyce in the preceding chapter. Although they unconsciously take it for granted that they will have to go through life without their own emotional needs being met, they devote a good deal of their time and energies to making sure that this same fate won't befall anyone else. Or, to put it another way, while they are resigned to accepting emotional (and perhaps material) deprivation for themselves, they are committed to creating emotional (and perhaps material) abundance for others. Caretakers often choose careers in the helping professions (nursing, social work), are actively involved with children through work (as teachers) or volunteer activities (the Big Brother program), and are attracted to such causes as helping impoverished children, protecting animal rights, ending hunger, stopping child abuse, and ensuring world peace. In their personal lives, caretakers often take on a mother role, and have a great need to be needed by those they love. They also often have a particularly strong urge to have children of their own.

Although this block is most apparent in people who believe love *in general* isn't in the cards for them, not everyone with this love block extends it to cover all kinds of love. Many believe it's only a certain kind of love that's not in the cards for them. A single heterosexual woman who has had a hard time finding suitable men to date, for example, might believe that "romantic love just isn't in the cards for me," while still believing in the possibility of love from friends and children. A man who was raised to relate to other men only on a superficial basis might believe "intimate love with other men just isn't in the cards for me," while still believing in the possibility of intimate love with a woman. And someone who has never had a very good relationship with his family might have come to believe "mother and father love just aren't in the cards for me" or "sibling love isn't in the cards for me," while still holding on to the possibility of love from other sources.

Joyce

Sometimes a person overcomes one love block only to find that behind it stands a bigger, more deeply entrenched block. This is what happened with Joyce, the woman discussed in the preceding chapter. Joyce's first time in therapy was when she was in her mid-twenties; then, her main focus was on overcoming her "I Don't Need Anyone—I'm Strong" block. It seemed at the time that the principal obstacle preventing Joyce from having fulfilling relationships was her inability to acknowledge and accept that she had emotional needs. But when Joyce returned to therapy several years later, it became evident that underlying her "I Don't Need Anyone—I'm Strong" block was the "Love Just Isn't in the Cards for Me" block.

Joyce initiated treatment for a second time because of problems with Daniel, a man she had been living with for three years and was considering marrying. Then in her mid-thirties, she still had the same distinctive soft voice and flower-child appearance. In many respects she was thriving. After leaving her secretarial job, she had become a counselor in a program for runaway youths and was now the program director. She had developed deeper friendships with several colleagues, continued her involvement with Overeaters Anonymous, and recently begun attending meetings for Children of Alcoholics as well. Although often working twelve-hour days, then rushing off to a meeting, Joyce started her first session back in therapy by saying that aside from her relationship with Daniel, everything in her life was great.

Daniel, a probation officer for juvenile offenders, and Joyce had been involved for more than four years. Daniel's teenage daughter from a previous marriage, Bonnie, was now living with them, which suited Joyce fine. She had always had a strong desire for children and looked upon Bonnie as her own daughter. However, Joyce was having doubts about Daniel. Although he could be "loving and gentle as a lamb," increasingly he was having angry outbursts during which he would become extremely critical and unreasonable. What's more, these "fits," as Joyce called them, were entirely unpredictable. Almost in passing, Joyce mentioned that Daniel seemed to drink and use pills a lot, but quickly dismissed the possibility of a connection between this and his behavior.

During her initial session back in therapy, Joyce kept the focus on her relationship with Daniel for nearly two thirds of an hour, during which she was a model of composure. Then, following an account of a recent incident that had upset her, she suddenly blurted out, almost as an afterthought, "And I'm so tired," and started to cry. Her shoulders heaving with sobs, she then confessed that everything else in her life was *not* great. "I feel drained to the point of not being able to go on," she said. Working all day (and sometimes nights) with emotionally troubled teenagers, taking care of her lover and his daughter, spending many extra hours being a special confidante and friend to the daughter, keeping her own mother company because "she is lonely and has no one else," going to often emotionally demanding self-help meetings, spending hours on the phone listening to her friends' problems and "being there" for them—these were the routine activities of Joyce's day-to-day life, and they were "all starting to get to me." Plus, she added, Daniel and she were in the middle of doing major renovations on Daniel's house, where they were living at the time, and since Daniel insisted that they do most of the work themselves this made for a particularly stressful home life.

Joyce had long presented herself to the world as an earth mother, as well as a supercompetent dynamo who could "get more done in a day than most people get done in a week." Her view of herself as a giving, compassionate "doer" was the source of most of her self-esteem. Yet as her treatment went on, she began to reveal that for several years, almost from the beginning of her relationship with Daniel, in fact, she had suffered from periodic bouts of exhaustion when she would "run out of steam" and feel so entirely depleted that "just getting out of bed seemed too much." During these times, she would often lash out at Daniel, engaging in lengthy and violent arguments with him. At other times, she would have a complete physical collapse, during which she would inevitably get sick and "feel like sleeping forever or shutting off from everyone and just being by myself."

Joyce had no idea why she was having these spells. They seemed to occur "out of the blue" and "for no reason," she said. As she talked about her life, though, it quickly became clear that although Joyce was more aware of her emotional needs than she used to be, she was still allowing the vast majority of those needs to go unmet. It eventually became clear that unconsciously she was convinced that her emotional needs would never get met, no matter how openly she acknowledged them or how much she tried to get them met.

One of the most unfortunate aspects of the "Love Just Isn't in the Cards for Me" block is that it can easily become a self-fulfilling prophecy. Although Joyce now had had a long-term lover and several friends she considered "close," she never asked them for help, and on those occasions when it was offered, she never took them up on it. Whenever Daniel or someone else reached out to her in a loving way—by giving her flowers or doing her a favor, for example—Joyce responded not by feeling loved, but with bewilderment. The whole experience of being given to was so alien to Joyce that she always felt "like they were speaking to me in a foreign language," she explained. "When someone tries to be really nice to me, I just don't know how to react. It's so strange, I don't know how to handle it."

Joyce eventually came to see that because being in the role of recipient felt so unaccustomed and made her uncomfortable, she actively made sure she'd be in that position as little as possible. Sometimes this meant rejecting other people's kindnesses and love outright. At Christmas, for example, she would remark that whatever gifts she received were too expensive and frivolous, or simply "too much." If a friend or work colleague did her a favor, she would protest with a litany of "you shouldn't haves" rather than simply showing appreciation and saying thanks.

Joyce was aware that her rejecting responses to others' loving gestures were hurtful to them, and she felt sorry and guilty about that. But it took her quite a while to see that she was also hurting herself by, in effect, re-creating her childhood experience of "emotional malnutrition" again and again. She was unwittingly making sure that her inner belief that "love's just not in the cards for me" would be proven true.

This inner conviction played a particularly great role in shaping Joyce's relationship with Daniel. Although they claimed to love each other, the emotional connection between Joyce and Daniel seemed rather weak, and the relationship didn't seem to fulfill either. When not fighting, they related only in the most superficial ways—"more as housemates than soulmates," as Joyce would say. They rarely talked about their deepest feelings, and it was not uncommon for them to go for weeks at a stretch without having much in the way of a real conversation at all. During a typical evening at home, Joyce would listen to her friends on the phone or spend time talking to Daniel's daughter, Bonnie, and Daniel would have a few beers and watch TV or spend hours alone working on some aspect of the household renovations. Usually, Daniel went to bed early, and Joyce would stay up for several more hours reading, watching TV herself, and catching up on household chores. They rarely had sex, and when they did it was only in the most perfunctory fashion.

Nevertheless, Joyce's dissatisfaction really didn't run very deep. In an early therapy session, she explained, "I'm not *that* unhappy with Daniel. He's got his faults, but so does everyone. He doesn't lie to me or run around, and he's really great with Bonnie, whom I love having with us. I could do a lot worse." When it was pointed out that other people might find the relationship lacking, and might think she deserved a man who could claim more to his credit than simply not lying nor running around, Joyce shrugged. Since she had never expected anything in the way of deep love and intimacy in her life, Joyce herself was not particularly bothered by the relationship's limits.

Joyce's feelings about having children were also shaped by her inner conviction that "Love Just Isn't in the Cards for Me." During her first time in treatment, her desire for children was the only strong desire she voiced, and she spoke about it often. When she returned to treatment several years later, however, she did not mention the subject for a number of sessions. Then one day she made a casual reference to "my hysterectomy." As it turned out, after stopping therapy for the first time she developed some serious gynecological problems that ultimately resulted in a the removal of her reproductive organs. Asked how she felt about this, she admitted to a great deal of sadness. Yet even as she began to let out some of her sadness and grief in later sessions, Joyce still felt no anger, despite evidence that her doctors might have jumped the gun and performed the hysterectomy unnecessarily.

Others in Joyce's situation would feel that they've been gypped, that life has been awfully unfair to them—and they'd be plenty angry about it, too. Joyce, however, accepted the loss of her ability to have children for the same reason that she never got angry with Daniel or her previous boyfriends for not giving her more: Joyce was accustomed to not getting what she wanted in life; she was accustomed to not getting much at all, in fact. Other people might respond to these kinds of deprivations and tragedies Joyce has experienced in life by saying, "Why me?" But to Joyce, the logical question was always, "Why *not* me?"

The Change Process: Joyce's Way

An intelligent woman with a degree in child psychology, Joyce didn't have much trouble reaching an intellectual understanding of her "Love Just Isn't in the Cards for Me" block. She knew enough about the human psyche to accept that while she consciously wasn't hungering for more love and deep connection than her relationships were providing, unconsciously she yearned for a great deal more. But as discussed in Chapter 3, in order for change to occur, intellectual understanding—while a crucial first step—is not enough. To be in a position to really make changes, a person not only has to "get" what his block is all about in a cognitive sense, he also has to "get it" in an emotional sense—he has to "get it" viscerally, in his gut. Searching for the metaphor, image, or memory that will trigger this kind of visceral connection is what a good deal of therapy with someone like Joyce is all about.

As it turned out, it was in her dreams that Joyce found the imagery she needed. Joyce frequently dreamed about cars, not a surprise since she really liked her car and saw it almost as an extension of herself. In one dream that she had again and again, a car was rapidly moving along a highway only to suddenly come to a full halt, either because it had run out of gas or broken down due to lack of maintenance. Other frequent dreams involved cars that had been abandoned by the highway, seemingly forgotten by their owners, or of cars that were stuck in muddy ditches that not even the most enormous tow truck could get them out of. The feeling Joyce associated with these dreams was one of utter hopelessness.

The car imagery in her dreams was the metaphor that finally enabled Joyce to make the connection between the state of emotional deprivation she took for granted as her lot in life and her periodic spells of exhaustion and collapse. As the driver of her own car, Joyce had routinely permitted herself to go along feeling emotionally empty or near-empty most of the time. Occasionally, the car would sputter and make noise, indicating that a breakdown was imminent and that she had better take the car to a gas station (her lover or one of her friends) for a fill-up (emotional nourishment and support). Yet Joyce would never take the car in because the idea of a fill-up was not in her frame of reference: she expected it simply to be able to drive on forever with the gas gauge on empty. As a result, Joyce would ignore the warning signals and the car would eventually break down, ending up stuck and abandoned by the roadside, and requiring a tow truck (enormous effort on her part) to get back on track.

For Joyce, therapy involved several major tasks. First, she had to come to the realization that her belief that "Love's Just Not in the Cards for Me" had no basis in objective reality. What happened to Joyce in childhood happened because of specific circumstances that could have been very different; fate did not decree that it had to be that way. Nor did it decree that because she was once emotionally deprived, she would always be. By letting go of these beliefs, Joyce was able to see that in fact the world is full of people who could provide the love she failed to receive in childhood.

Another task for Joyce in therapy was to realize that her "Love's Just Not in the Cards for Me" block put her very survival at risk. The increasing frequency and intensity of her breakdowns were a clear warning that she could not go on much longer in such a depleted inner state. For her the choice was clear: begin learning how to go to "gas stations" and "fill up," or end up forever conked out, literally in a ditch from which there's no way out.

In practical terms, Joyce began to identify which people in her life were "filling stations" and began making a conscious effort to spend more time with them. For years she had been in the habit of spending a great deal of time visiting her mother and talking to her on the phone. Although she felt guilty, she gradually cut back, which in itself freed up a great deal of energy. Joyce had never realized how thoroughly draining those calls and visits really were.

Joyce also started to realize that just as real filling stations offer different brands of gas and different repair services, her friends offered different forms of emotional nourishment. One friend, for example, was particularly playful and lighthearted. She would do things like go to an amusement park or fly a kite with Joyce, who always felt energized and buoyant after spending time with her. In the past, Joyce had thought she already had to be feeling "up" to spend time with this friend, but then she saw her one day when she was exhausted and overwhelmed, and her spirits immediately lifted. Joyce concluded from this that when she was in need, she did not necessarily know *what* she needed. Using the car metaphor again, it dawned on her that "sometimes when I think I need gas, I might really need an oil change—or a transmission overhaul."

Continuing with the car metaphor, Joyce also began doing some "body work." She had gone through life never really taking care of her physical self. She routinely skipped meals, missed sleep, worked extra hours without taking any compensation time, and rarely exercised, all of which contributed to her periodic collapses. Now she started taking comp time soon after she earned it. Sometimes she would sleep in and go to work late; other times she would take an extra few hours at lunch and do some pleasure reading or take a stroll in the park. Eventually, she started taking exercise classes once in a while, too. These might seem like trivial things to some people, but the fact is that people whose childhood deprivation forced them into prematurely taking on the role of caretaker usually have no idea how even to *begin* taking care of themselves.

Joyce's progress did not occur in a straight upward curve—nobody's journey toward greater emotional health ever does. Despite her own serious doubts and the advice she received, Joyce went ahead and married Daniel. Over time, his "fits" became more and more frequent, and his criticisms of Joyce grew more vitriolic, too, putting Joyce through a great deal of psychological abuse. Had she still adhered to the belief that "Love Just Isn't in the Cards for Me," Joyce might still be stuck in that destructive marriage now. But she did leave. When contacted about giving permission to use her story in this book, Joyce was happy to be on her own. She felt confident that someday she'd find a partner with whom to have a better relationship. In the meantime she was feeling more loved and fulfilled than she ever had, thanks to her work, her growing network of friends, and her own increasing openness to the good things life can bring.

Rich

Joyce's "Love Just Isn't in the Cards for Me" block covered all kinds of love. Rich, a forty-one-year-old fireman, had a more selective form of this block.

Tall, well-muscled, and lean, Rich has sandy-colored hair and a bushy mustache. Although he has a serious air, he is also very easygoing and warm, which makes it pleasant to be around him. Rich entered therapy because he wanted to retire from the fire department but could not decide on a second career, and had become depressed as a result. Happily married for more than twenty years and the doting father of four, Rich did not have any overt problems in his relationships. In fact, Rich and his wife, Dolores, have one of those rare marriages that seems the stuff of fairy tales. They fell in love in high school, and since then their ardor, devotion, and admiration for each other have grown.

In the process of dealing with his depression, Rich became aware that although there was considerable love in his life, one kind of love was missing—the love of other men. As a fireman, Rich was surrounded by men, but with none of his co-workers did he have a relationship that could be called close. He was friendly enough to fit in at work, and he participated in some of the joking and banter that went on there, but that's as far as his involvement went. He did not socialize with any of the other fireman, nor did he ever talk about his personal life. Although he was "friends with" men who were part of the group of couples that he and his wife socialized with, those relationships were rather superficial and involved getting together in pairs, never one-to-one.

Some men in Rich's situation might be aware of the lack of male love in their lives but not be bothered by it. Rich, however, was. One day in therapy he began talking about a minister he knew through some community work he was involved in. He really liked this man and wanted to get to know him better. As Rich explained this, his voice was wistful and he sighed deeply. Asked what the sigh was about, Rich realized it was a sigh of resignation. He knew other men got a great deal of love from the men in their lives, but Rich believed that "Male Love Just Isn't in the Cards for Me."

As Rich became aware of how deeply entrenched his block in the area of male love was, he also came to see how he had turned it into a self-fulfilling prophecy. He never sought out other men for companionship, and rejected overtures of men who sought him out. When other men invited him to sports events, he would reason, "I played enough sports as a kid, I don't want to waste time watching them now." With card games, his response was similar: "I'm a family man, not the kind to take a night out with the boys." These sounded like good, sensible reasons, so the other men in his life eventually stopped asking. But while Rich's excuses sounded good, they also functioned as rationalizations that masked his belief that "male love just isn't in the cards for me, so what's the point of pretending otherwise?"

In therapy, Rich realized the roots of this block were in his relationship with his father, a self-employed surveyor who had very little to say to anyone, including his son. When Rich was small, he and his father would spend time in the same room, but without any real interaction. Rich's father did not play with Rich, teach him things, ask him questions, tell him stories, or hold or touch him in any way.

He was not cruel; he was just distant, emotionally remote, not really *there*. When Rich was in his teens, his father would often take him along to help on surveying jobs; they would characteristically spend eight hours working alongside each other in almost total silence.

Fortunately, Rich's mother was very demonstrative with Rich and gave him a great deal of love, support, advice, and warm human contact. It's because of this strong relationship that Rich was able to have such solid ones with his wife and children.

The Change Process: Rich's Way

At the time this was being written, Rich had still not resolved the career dilemma he was grappling with when he started therapy. As he became more and more connected to his inner life and true feelings, however, his depression lifted, and he was no longer feeling overwhelmed and immobilized. At the same time, he made considerable headway in resolving his "Love Just Isn't in the Cards for Me" block.

Because Rich's love block did not color his entire world view the way Joyce's did, it was easier to remedy. Once he became aware of how much he longed for close male companionship, figuring out how to go about getting it was not difficult. Not long after he first identified what he wanted, he overheard some of the other firemen at work talking about getting tickets for some upcoming baseball games. "Hey, that sounds like fun," Rich said. "How about counting me in?" The other men were delighted; what Rich hadn't realized before was that by always turning down their invitations, he had given the impression that he considered himself too good for them—and this had hurt their feelings. Of course, at the ballpark with a bunch of guys Rich did not get the kind of intimacy he really wanted. But that kind of intimacy isn't something that develops overnight, Rich realized: he would have to spend quite a bit of time with a person, especially a man, before either one would be ready to do much opening up. Besides, the camaraderie of going to some games with some guys from work was something that Rich was learning to value in and of itself.

When Rich and Dolores got together with other couples, Rich

began experimenting with different ways of physically relating to the other men. In the past, he would just nod hello and good-bye to them, sometimes shaking their hands, sometimes not. Now he made a point of shaking their hands and letting his hand linger in theirs, placing his hand on their backs to make a point, or punching them lightly on the upper arm. These gestures seem trivial and corny when described, and at first Rich certainly felt awkward. But with time they came more naturally to him, and they made a small but significant difference in how close he felt to these friends. Eventually, Rich reported that at a party over the weekend he had approached a couple of guys he knew and tentatively hugged them. The other men put their arms around Rich and returned the embrace. Although these hugs lasted only a few seconds, Rich felt warmed by them and came away with the sense that "so this is what I've been missing all these years."

In therapy one day, Rich commented that "I've spent the last twenty years working for my family and putting them first, but now I think I'd like to do something just for me." He then let his mind "go" and talked about the images that popped into his head. The strongest image was of walking with someone else in the woods. He realized that "what I really want to do is spend some time in the woods, but not with my family and not by myself." As he talked further, he recalled that the minister he knew and wanted to get to know better once had mentioned a cabin in the mountains where he sometimes went. Once, in fact, the minister had actually invited Rich to go there with him, but since that was long before Rich became aware of his unconscious yearning for male love, he automatically turned the minister down. He decided to call the minister the next day. "If that offer of the trip to the mountains is still open, I'd like to do it sometime," he said. About six weeks later, they spent three relaxing days there "just getting to know each other better." Their relationship has continued to grow in following months, and they are developing a very deep friendship.

Rich did not enter treatment to work on his marriage, but when Dolores saw how much more her husband seemed to be getting from life, she decided to start therapy herself. She too became more emotionally alive, as well as more independent, more confident, and less fearful of separation. One obvious result was that they began to fight more, which some might interpret as evidence of a deteriorating marriage, but was actually a sign that their relationship was becoming more solid. Conflicts that used to be swept under the rug, where they smoldered, were now brought up and hashed out in the open, and the arguing showed that they both were much more comfortable with conflict and their "negative" feelings, and were developing more self-esteem. One of the reasons that they had rarely fought in the past was that Rich's low self-esteem caused him always to have to be right, while Dolores's caused her always to assume she was wrong. Now he was open to the risk of being proven wrong, while she wouldn't automatically take the blame. True, Rich and Dolores are a much noisier couple than they were several years ago. But they're much happier, too.

Michael

It's easy to see how Rich's relationship with his father could have left him convinced that "male love just isn't in the cards for me— never was, never will be." Many boys would have responded in the same way, by unconsciously but very effectively writing off half the human race as a potential source of love. What's interesting—if terribly confounding—is that some boys would have a very different response. Michael, an editor just past thirty who grew up in Texas and now lives in Manhattan, is a case in point.

Michael has angular features and slightly spiked short, dark hair. Of medium height and build, he has lively blue eyes and the sort of smile that can light up a room. Known for his sense of humor, he laughs often and easily as he talks.

Michael grew up in a well-to-do family. Like Rich, he had an emotionally remote father and a warm, attentive mother. The main difference was that Michael's father was more openly critical than Rich's: an articulate executive, he could skewer his son with harsh words.

Despite the similarities in their backgrounds, Michael has always had a very different attitude toward male love. Michael has many male friends with whom he feels quite close, and he feels very loved by them. He also has had several male lovers with whom he has had serious, steady relationships; in fact, at the time he was interviewed, he has been living with one man in a monogamous relationship for the past two years. Obviously, Michael believes that it's possible for him to have an abundance of male love in his life—and he also has faith that this will remain so in the future.

The reasons that some people turn out to be heterosexual and others turn out to be homosexual are complex, and it would serve no purpose to discuss the subject here. What's significant about Michael's and Rich's stories when seen side by side is how well they illustrate how different people develop love blocks. Rich felt his early experience with his father "closed the door" on the possibility of being close with a male, and "closed it for good." After having a similar experience with his father, Michael, however, responded with a stance of "since I didn't get enough from the first man in my life, I'd better make sure I get love from other men—it's my due!"

Unfortunately, though, Michael's openness to male love has not meant that he's free of love blocks altogether. He, too, has been blocked from a particular kind of love—familial love. Since high school, Michael has had very distant relationships with the other members of his family, who all still live in Texas. His father and mother are born-again Christians who have always been very conservative, and Michael's two sisters and one brother have followed suit. This makes Michael, with his left-wing politics and fast-track New York life, the "odd duck" in the family. Growing up, he was very close to his mother and one of his sisters, Sheryl, but as time went on they had drifted apart.

As if Michael's politics and general sensibility didn't set him apart enough, there's the matter of his homosexuality. Although Michael realized he was gay in his late teens, he believes that his parents would have nothing to do with him if he told them, and that his siblings would reject him, too. He hasn't lied outright, but he has let everyone believe he is straight. When the family gets together for holidays and family occasions, everyone else seems to come away with a feeling of connection and belonging while Michael feels estranged and that he doesn't fit in. He usually feels angry and resentful, too.

For many years, Michael was so caught up in his career and his friends and lovers that as he went through his day-to-day routine, he wasn't bothered by the lack of familial closeness. As he approached his thirtieth birthday, however, this began to change. Perhaps it was simply because he was growing older. Perhaps it was because several of his friends lost their parents, and he began to be aware of his own parents' mortality. Or perhaps it was because he had gone through the tragedy of losing several friends to AIDS. Whatever the reason, Michael began to feel a growing longing for a sense of connection with his family. He wanted to feel they cared about him. He wanted to feel secure that they would take care of him if he became sick. He wanted to feel they really loved him—the real him, not the Michael they thought they knew. Yet he was still afraid that if they really knew who he was, they would cut him out of their lives and hearts forever.

Michael was in a seemingly no-win situation. Hiding the truth about himself from his family made him feel bad about himself, as though he were shameful and sneaky; it diminished his self-love. But if he revealed the truth and his family rejected and reviled him, chances were good he would feel even worse. This is the painful dilemma millions of people who are homosexual, bisexual, or otherwise different from accepted norms have been forced to live with.

The Change Process: Michael's Way

It was hard to tell how much of Michael's problem was due to internal love blocks, and how much was due to external ones. Hostility toward homosexuality is rampant in our society, and some people are so plagued by homophobia that they actually *do* stop loving their own children and other blood relations who are gay. Clearly, much of Michael's apprehension was grounded in objective reality—the reality of a homophobic world. Yet was Michael's belief that familial love was not possible for him *entirely* based on objective facts? Could Michael really be certain, 100 percent sure, that if he came out to them, his family would reject him? For a long time, Michael was convinced that he had no choice but to remain in a situation wherein he could not feel genuinely loved by his family "because the me they love is not the real me, so their love for me can't be real either." But was this really Michael's only choice?

In order to answer these questions, Michael had to assess each member of his family and his relationship with them one by one. As is common with individuals who feel estranged from their families, Michael saw his situation in "me against them" terms. His sense of being apart from everyone else in his family caused him to lump his parents and siblings into one undifferentiated mass called "my family," a mass so forbidding as to be unapproachable. Now Michael began to see that his family was actually made up of individuals who disagreed with each other, had conflicts, and in many ways were far more different from one another than he thought. In the process Michael began to see that while it was probably unrealistic to expect that he could get the love he longed for from every member of his family, it might be possible to get it from some.

Michael decided to start making some overtures toward his sister Sheryl, with whom he had once been close but from whom he had drifted away over the years. Obviously, he did not call her up one day and say, "Hey, I know we haven't really spoken much for years, but guess what—I'm gay!" By blurting out the news without first getting a sense of how she might respond, Michael would have made himself unnecessarily vulnerable to being rejected and hurt. Instead, he started building a bridge to his sister, so to speak. He began by sending her interesting books and articles, along with friendly notes. They started talking on the phone, at first once in a while, then more frequently. Sheryl started sending Michael clippings from the Texas papers, and chatty letters, too. Once the bridge seemed solid, Michael was in a position to gauge more accurately whether it would stand under the weight of his disclosure.

Now Michael tried to feel out how tolerant of his homosexuality Sheryl might be. He sent her a critically acclaimed collection of short stories whose characters were mostly gay. He casually mentioned in a phone conversation that he had gone to a benefit for AIDS research. He spoke more and more often about his lover, Tim, referring to him now as "my friend" or "Tim" rather than as "my roommate." Each time, Sheryl seemed completely unfazed.

Once Michael finally told Sheryl, not only was she not upset, she was greatly relieved. For years, she had been pretty sure that Michael was gay but hadn't felt comfortable broaching the subject. She told him that she felt much more relaxed with him now that "I don't always have to be careful not to say something that will let on that I know what you don't want me to know." She also felt honored and happy that he trusted her enough to confide in her. Michael, too, felt much more relaxed and at home with his sister. She knew the real him and still loved him, which meant she loved the real him. For the first time since acknowledging his homosexuality, Michael experienced himself as being really loved by a member of his family.

Sheryl, in turn revealed that she had secrets, too. In college, she had had an abortion. Their parents don't know, and Sheryl is sure they would banish her from their house forever if they did. Sheryl revealed that other members of the family also have hidden aspects to their lives, a fact Michael had completely missed because of the distance he kept from them.

Something else that Sheryl was able to tell Michael was that a cousin of theirs named Charlie was gay, too, news she'd been dying to tell Michael for years. Sheryl had also heard that Charlie had moved to New York, and a few weeks later Sheryl confirmed this and gave Michael their cousin's phone number. Although Sheryl and Michael grew up hardly knowing Charlie, Michael gave him a call and invited him to lunch. In the past six months, the two men have spent hours comparing notes on their families and the relatives they have in common. With Charlie, Michael feels a familial bond that he's never felt with anyone before. Here is a blood relative who is a lot like him! By telling his sister the truth about himself, Michael not only gained a sense of being genuinely loved by her, he also stumbled on a completely unexpected source of familial love.

In opening up to the love of his sister and cousin, Michael has had to give up something, however. All the years that he felt so alienated and separate from his family, he also felt superior to them. Partly as a way to assuage his hurt feelings, and partly out of sheer grandiosity, Michael had looked upon himself as the special, so-phisticated member of the family, and the rest of them as ordinary, uninteresting, and provincial hicks. To let in familial love, Michael has had to realize that in many respects he isn't so different after all.

Michael still feels certain his parents are too homophobic to be told that he is gay. "They'd go berserk," he believes. Michael may well be correct. He might have to go through life never telling them, and thus never getting the authentic parental love he longs for. But at least now he has two family members to whom he can turn. He might never get *all* the familial love his heart yearns for, but he'll at least get *some* of it, which is substantially more than he ever expected.

Chapter 8
"God's Love Isn't in the Cards for Me"

Bob, the sociologist discussed in the "I Don't Deserve Love" chapter, did not always want to be an academic. Growing up, what he desired most of all was to become a minister, and after high school he went to a seminary to begin his training. After less than a year, however, he transferred to a secular college, where he gave up on theology and began studying history and sociology instead. Now whenever friends and acquaintances find out that Bob had once planned to be a minister, they comment that "you must have given it up because you wanted to make more money," or "you must've realized you wanted to get laid every once in a while instead of being a goody-goody all your life." When people make these comments, Bob half nods and says nothing. He is too ashamed to admit that the real reason he left the seminary is that he believed he wasn't holy or good enough to be a man of God; he didn't feel worthy enough of God's love to deserve the honor of divine service.

Rosa, the Puerto Rican-born political activist and writer discussed in the chapter on the "I Don't Want to Deal with My Feelings" block, did actually enter religious life; in her case, this meant becoming a Roman Catholic nun. Like Bob, however, Rosa has doubts about whether she's worthy of God's love. She sometimes fears, in fact, that she should not have joined a religious order because "I'm not good enough or holy enough to have the privilege of being called into His service."

There are many people who are not particularly concerned with the issue of whether God or some other "higher power" exists in the universe or with whether God loves them. They don't believe in God and they feel no lack in their lives because of it. Bob, Rosa, and countless others, however, feel a deep need for spiritual expression and spiritual union, and for them, these are questions of great importance and urgency. They long to believe that there is indeed a God or higher power in the universe, and that this higher power loves them. But many of them have trouble really believing it—either because they can't fully convince themselves that God exists, or because the image they have of God is not a particularly loving one. Although they want to feel themselves warmed by God's love, they instead believe that "God's Love Isn't in the Cards for Me." Whereas others may view God as a source of unlimited love that anyone can draw on at any time, those with the "God's Love Isn't in the Cards for Me" block see God's love as limited to certain people under certain conditions, and they view themselves as cut off from it.

If a person has a hunger for spiritual fulfillment but has not been able to find a way of satisfying it, he will always have a vague, perhaps sometimes acute, sense that something's not quite right, something's missing. Many people try to fill their inner void, or to divert their attention from it, by seeking success and worldly achievement. Others become excessively concerned with material and physical security, as if a solid investment portfolio or a warm, inviting home could add more weight, solidity, and permanence to their existence. Still others try to fill their inner emptiness, or at least dull their awareness of it, with alcohol and/or other drugs. Recovering addicts have a saying about the spiritual roots of addiction that is worth repeating: an addict is a person who received a spiritual calling but answered it by going to the wrong address.

The belief that "God's Love Isn't in the Cards for Me" can seriously affect a person's chances of finding satisfaction in *human* relationships, too. A person with unfulfilled spiritual needs may expect others to fill the void inside her, and when they can't, she becomes disappointed, frustrated, and angry. Even if there's a good deal of human love in her life, it inevitably is not enough to eliminate her spiritual longings and give her inner peace, so she can't fully appreciate it. As one person we interviewed explained, "It was only after I opened myself up to God's love that I really became open to letting in other people's love." And as others explained, once they felt secure in their knowledge that God loves them, they began to feel more relaxed, more accepting, and more giving in their relationships. "I used to always have a hunger for love that I looked to other people to meet," one said. "But a lot of that hunger was a spiritual hunger that was misdirected. Now that my spiritual needs are taken care of, I can turn to other people for the needs they can meet, and I'm not always angry and critical of them for not being able to give me inner peace."

We don't mean to suggest here that everyone who believes in a supreme being is necessarily more capable of receiving and giving human love as a result. There are many people who claim to have let God into their hearts, and who have become less tolerant, less open-minded, and less loving as a result. Throughout history, true believers by the millions have used their zealous religious convictions to treat other human beings in ways that are anything but loving—witness all the cruelty, injustice, and political persecution that have been carried out in the name of God over the centuries, and that is still being carried out in many parts of the globe from the Bible Belt to the Persian Gulf region today. At the same time, some of the greatest humanitarians in history have been either atheists or agnostics.

But for some people—and the word *some* should be emphasized—spirituality *can* be a path to feeling more loved, and behaving in more loving ways, too. If a person does not feel a spiritual hunger—or what Howard M. Halpern calls the hunger for "attachment to the timeless"[1]—there is no reason to bother with spiritual concerns; after all, why try to fill an empty space that doesn't exist? But for those who do feel this need achieving a sense of attachment is often the first step in being able to form more satisfactory human attachments. It's also what permits them to continue to feel loved when those human attachments prove painful, disappointing, or end altogether. People who feel a spiritual emptiness that they wish to fill can do so in a wide variety of ways, as Halpern explains:

> There are many avenues for feeling attachment to the timeless. For some, it may be in experiencing the wonder of breathtaking landscapes

or unending suns and vast spaces of the cosmos. For others it is their sense of *connection with all living things.* For others it is their sense of *kinship with mankind.* And for many it takes the form of communing with *their concept of a Supreme Being,* either through formal religious doctrine and ritual or through their own conceptualization of a higher power. When someone who has ended or lost a love relationship is able to feel "I am not alone because God loves me," he may be in touch with some of his earliest experiences of being loved and protected. When he feels "I am one of God's creatures" or "I am part of a greater plan," he re-experiences some of the earliest (positive) experiences of family, and he feels less alone.[2]

Sharon: In Search of God

Sharon, a documentary filmmaker in her early thirties, had to resolve some spiritual issues in order to become more capable of receiving and giving human love. Sharon looks a bit like the actress Kathleen Turner, only more petite. She has a highly animated manner and frequently pauses as she talks to point out something funny or make a self-deprecating comment.

Sharon had a childhood that was for the most part very happy. She grew up in a well-heeled and intellectual environment. Her father, a political scientist and well-respected professor at a renowned university, and her mother, a mathematics professor, did their best to provide Sharon and her two brothers with a stimulating, loving home life. They never hit the children, gave them all music, dance, and tennis lessons, and put great effort into nurturing each one's academic, athletic, and artistic potential. "Compared to most people's families, mine was really great," Sharon recalled. "My parents gave us just about everything, and I don't just mean in the material sense. They would really talk to us, and we knew they really were there for us and really loved us."

There was, however, one thing Sharon wanted but did not get from her parents—an outlet for spiritual expression. "My parents were very passionately involved with ethical and political issues, and we kids were raised with a lot of emphasis on examining questions of right and wrong, good and evil," Sharon explained. "We even formally studied comparative religions. As far as the moral component of religion and the history of religion goes, my upbringing was great. What was lacking was the spiritual component. We never as a family shared any religious rituals, and there was never any sense of mystery or mysticism. Believing in God or in some higher universal plan or cosmic force was considered insanity. I remember when I was about ten saying I believed in God, and my parents were horrified. 'How can you believe in God?' they said. In their view, only people with low levels of intelligence or without the courage to be independent thinkers believe in God."

While Sharon's parents were both Jewish, neither observed even the highest of high holidays, nor did they encourage any sense of Jewish identity among their children. On the contrary, Sharon explained, "there was always this undercurrent of anti-Semitism in the house, especially from my father. He's a Jew who believes Jews are vulgar. To this day, he still always makes disparaging, offensive comments about 'the brotherhood' and 'Yids.' "

As opposed to the people in the previous chapter who believe "Love Just Isn't in the Cards for Me," Sharon did not grow up seeing the world as a depriving place or herself as destined to do without much in the way of love. On the contrary, Sharon "always had a sense of the world as a place of endless possibilities," and she took it for granted that people could and would be loving to her. But while she grew up with the sense that the temporal world is a nourishing place, Sharon also grew up believing that the larger universe—the one she contemplated when she looked at the stars, as she frequently did in childhood—was characterized by coldness and nothingness. Although sure that human love was in the cards for her, she had no corresponding sense that God's love was as well. "All my life I wanted to believe that God loved me, and there was a part of me, I think, that was always a closet believer," Sharon recalled. "But at the same time, I had all these intellectual, rational arguments telling me that God didn't exist. So while I wanted God to love me, I never really felt secure in believing He did, because I was never fully convinced, never really sure that God really existed."

Many very well adjusted people don't believe in God and feel no lack in their lives because of it, just as many poorly adjusted people do believe in God and seem to be no more at peace because of it.

Sharon's parents could find no intellectual grounds on which to base a belief in God, and because they approached the world cognitively they had no trouble living without faith. Sharon, however, was different. From the time she was very small, she experienced a need to connect to God, and to relate to God not with her head, but with her heart and soul. What made Sharon have this need when her parents did not is a question that can never be satisfactorily answered. What *is* clear is that until Sharon satisfied her longing to believe in God, she was bound to suffer an inner emptiness that would have a damaging impact on both her general outlook on life and her interpersonal relationships.

Although Sharon's parents did not realize it at the time, by telling her it was ridiculous to believe in God they were saying that all her needs must be met by humans. The problem with this view is that all humans are limited in their ability to be giving, and all have shortcomings and flaws. As a result, human relationships alone often aren't sufficient to satisfy all a person's emotional needs. Moreover, most people have feelings, thoughts, and problems that they are unable to express and explain to other people, or are too ashamed of to share. When sharing with another human is impossible, many people derive great solace and strength from their faith in God's presence and willingness to lend an ear and a helping hand. Sharon needed that solace, even if her parents did not.

Sharon's unmet spiritual yearnings had a particularly pronounced impact on her relationships with men. She had a history of what she calls "making relationships with men serve as replacements for my own spirituality." Each time a man she was involved with would inevitably prove incapable of satisfying her longing for spiritual fulfillment, she would feel let down, frustrated, enraged, and thoroughly unloved.

Since her college years, Sharon has had three major romantic relationships. Each lasted for at least three years, and in each she and the man became formally engaged but broke up before actually marrying. "There were major problems in each relationship, and I knew that all along," Sharon said. "But at the time I was involved with these guys, I was blind to how bad they were for me, even though I was in a lot of pain and I knew my needs weren't getting met. One of the problems was that I grew up believing that whatever's lacking in my life, a man could fill. I was hungering for a sense of God, but I hadn't yet found a way to feed this hunger, so what I did was to get into all-consuming relationships with men and make the man into God."

Sharon's first serious relationship was with someone she described as "ultra-Waspy," and who in the course of their relationship became a deacon in the Episcopal Church. As he became more involved in actively practicing Christianity, Sharon for the first time started going to synagogue and observing some of the practices of Judaism. This did not satisfy her spiritual hunger, however. "I remember in the last few months of that relationship having such a spiritual yearning," Sharon recalled. "I held on to the relationship a lot longer than was healthy for me because of that yearning. I felt I had no inner core, no solid center, and so losing the relationship meant losing everything."

Sharon's next relationship was with "a guy who was as ultra-Jewish as the first boyfriend was ultra-Wasp," she said. "From the moment we met, I was sure we were soulmates. He was going to save me. He was going to be the link to my spiritual core. He was going to give me quick entrée into Judaism, be my ticket to salvation and inner peace. I made him God." As it turned out, Sharon's new "God" had a drug problem, was chronically depressed, and had serious self-esteem problems, particularly about his career. Shaking her head in mock disbelief and quietly laughing, Sharon said, "This guy couldn't write his résumé, yet I had it in my head that he was going to rescue me. He couldn't even give me the basics of love and affection, and I wanted him to give me what no man can give me—a sense of spiritual connection."

Sharon's next relationship was with a man named Matthew who was on a spiritual quest much like her own. His parents were also intellectuals who scoffed at the idea of believing in God. Matthew and Sharon "tried on" a variety of different religions together; they studied Buddhism, Hinduism, Taoism and met some people involved in charismatic Roman Catholicism and liberation theology as well. During this time, Sharon began meditating daily, a practice that she has kept up.

While Sharon's relationship with Matthew was "good in a number of respects," it was also quite stormy. Matthew "could be very loving, but he hated it when I got at all dependent or showed any neediness and he'd become distant," Sharon explained. Eventually, he began using his spiritual beliefs as a means of distancing himself from her. "He became very superior, sort of taking a 'more enlightened than thou' stance," Sharon recalled. "He convinced me all our problems had to do with my not being spiritually evolved enough, while he acted like he was approaching spiritual perfection. He really began to treat me like shit, and when I called him on it, he made it out like everything was my problem."

The Change Process: Sharon's Way

At the time she was interviewed, Sharon had been in therapy for more than two years, and during that time she had identified and worked on a number of different love blocks. These included "I Don't Deserve Love," her primary block, and "I'll Inevitably Get Hurt," the block discussed in Chapter 11. Here, we'll keep the focus on how she dealt with "God's Love Isn't in the Cards for Me" in particular.

After many stormy months, Sharon and Matthew finally ended their on-again, off-again relationship for good. That night, Sharon stuffed as many of her belongings into a suitcase as she could, slammed the door on the apartment she and Matthew had shared, and checked herself into a hotel room. The breakup left Sharon in such immense and unbearable pain that she could think of only one way to lessen it—by killing herself. She thought of calling friends, her therapist, and Matthew, but none of them, she felt sure, would be able to help her. She bought a bottle of bourbon and began lining up the assortment of pills she had been collecting for months. She figured she had enough to do herself in.

As Sharon was just about to begin downing the lethal mix she had assembled, an image of a woman she had once met came to mind. She was a former Catholic nun named Therese whom Sharon had met while researching an educational film on the changing roles of women in modern society. Sharon had liked Therese very much, and been impressed with her peaceful, gentle, almost otherworldly air.

But Sharon had not seen her nor really thought about her since. Now suddenly, here was an image of Therese so vivid and strong in Sharon's mind that she could not shake it. What did this mean? Sharon wondered, and she felt herself edging back from the brink of killing herself. She called a friend, who came over to the hotel room and swore she would not leave Sharon alone until her despair had begun to lift. When Sharon told her friend about how this virtual stranger's picture had come into her mind the friend suggested she call Therese.

The next morning, Sharon dug Therese's number out of her address book and called her. As it turned out, Therese had telephoned Sharon the night before, but Matthew hadn't known where to reach her. Therese had called on a work-related matter, but once Sharon told her of her uncanny experience the night before, Therese began to speak intimately and consolingly. She told Sharon she had gone through several "dark nights of the soul" herself and that she, too, had considered suicide. She had gotten through these experiences, she added, by going on retreat to an old monastery in the country, about four hours away. "That sounds wonderful, like a hospital for the soul," Sharon said. "I wish there was a place like that I could go to." But there is, Therese answered. The monastery was still run by a religious order of priests and nuns, but it was now open to lay people of any religion. "If you want," Therese added, "I can call up there right now and see if they'd be willing to have you come stay with them." The next day, a friend of Sharon's drove her to the monastery, where Sharon stayed for more than a week.

At the monastery, Sharon rested, ate, read, and poured out her heart to the young nun who had been assigned to look after her. She also spent many hours praying. "I had never really prayed before, but when I got to the monastery I prayed and prayed for strength," Sharon recalled. "I felt God was testing me, but that He hadn't given me the strength to pass the test. I felt that was very unfair. I felt that He was the one who had put the yearning for Him inside me, so why was He making it so difficult to find Him?"

The nun who spent time with Sharon listened to her for hours, and told of some of her own spiritual doubts and the difficulties and crises these had given rise to. During one particularly important conversation together, the nun said to Sharon, "It sounds to me like you're pretty angry at God." Sharon looked away, her head down. Although she was indeed very angry at God, Sharon felt very guilty about it, believing it just proved how undeserving of God's love she was; "If I were really a good person like this nun obviously is," Sharon figured, "then I wouldn't be angry at God." So it came as a surprise when the nun patted Sharon's hand and said, "It's perfectly okay to be angry with God. He's used to it, you know. You think He can't take it? Do you really think He hasn't heard it before?" Both women laughed for several minutes, and then Sharon began to cry. "I cried and cried my heart out for hours," she recalled. "It was like something in me that had been building up pressure my whole life suddenly gave way and released a flood."

For Sharon, coming to the realization that being angry at God was normal, permissible even, was a breakthrough experience that enabled her to make the "leap of faith" she needed to make in order to experience herself as someone who is loved by God. She was first interviewed ten months after "the dark night of the soul" that took her to the monastery, and again a year after that. Since reaching her decision that God exists and God loves her, she had meditated and prayed every day, "but quietly, without announcing it to the world or even letting most people know." Although she said she still had "a lot of things to work out spiritually and in other respects," she now felt "a kind of serenity and peace I've never felt before. I've found some sort of center that I never had before. People always told me that I had to grapple with the big existential questions, to confront the human condition and find some way to make peace with it *on my own*. But I could never bear that. I couldn't face the void, so I would make a man or my work the center of my world. I always knew drugs and alcohol were not the answer, but it took a long time to realize those other things weren't either. It took me a long time to learn that the only thing that will relieve the pain and the longing is to find a center within me and from that core find a link between me and the universe, me and God, that's direct, one on one."

Sharon's newfound belief that God loves her did not eliminate her need for human connections. However, it enabled her to approach human relationships with less desperation and more appreciation for what they can and cannot provide. Commenting that the two years since her breakup with Matthew marked the first time in her life she had gone for any extended period without a boyfriend, Sharon said, "I used to be a real mess when I was between relationships, but this is different. I would like to get involved again, but for the first time in my entire life, I don't feel there's this big chunk that's supposed to be there but is missing. I really feel the love of my friends more than I've ever felt it. And I really feel like I belong. Like when I go outside and look at the sky and breathe the air I feel I'm part of it all, that I'm connected. It sounds corny and stupid, but I feel for the first time in my life that God is with me and loves me, and just as this was something no one else could give me, it's something no one can take from me either."

Troubling Perceptions of God

For many others, the problematic question isn't whether God *exists,* it's *what God is like.* Bob and Rosa, for example, have always taken it on faith that there is a God. But according to the image of God they were raised with, God is so demanding that He doubtless would find them unworthy of His love. They were suffering from the "God's Love Isn't in the Cards for Me" block, but in a different way.

This form of the block is very common. Although some people become more open to receiving both human and divine love once they have embraced a belief in God, for many others belief in God actually results in diminished feelings of being worthy, valued, and connected and a shrinking of the capacity to take in love. This is because the vast majority of people who were raised to believe in God were also raised to believe in a certain kind of God—a God who is not a friendly, merciful, patient, tolerant, and all-loving God, but a God having the opposite qualities. Here are just a few of the images of God common among Americans today:

—*God the creator who has rigged the game:* In this view, God has stacked the deck from the start by giving people a number of different natural urges and tendencies, then saying they're sinful.

For example, God gave people the desire for and capacity to enjoy sex, but many religions teach that except in certain narrow circumstances God views sex as wrong. As another example, God gave people the brains to doubt God's existence, but many religions teach that God gets angry when people question His existence and He views such questioning as a sinful lack of faith.

—*God as a judge who misses nothing:* In this view, God spends every moment of every day watching every move of each person on the planet. God not only sees every little sin and imperfection, He then also marks them all down in a big ledger, keeping a running tab. Some people further believe that God monitors every person's inner thoughts and feelings, too, judging "bad" thoughts and feelings just as harshly as "bad" acts.

—*God as punisher:* In this view, God's constant surveillance is accompanied by constant doling out of punishments meant to make people pay for how much they have hurt and offended Him. This God has a tendency to be quite capricious—and often very cruel—in handing out sentences, punishing masturbation or having unkind thoughts about an obnoxious neighbor, for example, as severely as an act of intentional physical harm. Although God is supposed to be all-powerful and all-knowing, this view makes Him out to be neither concerned with, nor capable of, making fine distinctions.

—*God as demanding perfection:* In this view, God makes human beings flawed on purpose, so that everyone can then go through the challenging experience of forever striving to be a better person. This view holds that if a person is not constantly struggling to overcome his limitations, God will justly withhold His love.[3]

These sorts of images create problems not only for those who openly believe in God, but also for many who adamantly reject a belief in a personal God. Many atheists were raised according to a religion and rejected it because of the way God was depicted; their early exposure in effect vaccinated them against religion for life. But while they might be able to reject religion, it usually turns out to be much more difficult to erase their image of God: hence, many atheists find that in their hearts and minds they are still carrying around a clear, strong image of the God they no longer believe in. What's more, this internalized image of the God they don't believe in continues to shape their view of themselves and the world. As a result, it's possible even for atheists or agnostics to have the "God's Love Isn't in the Cards for Me" block.

God the Father

Whatever their view of God, most people attribute it to the religious training they received in their youth. It is true that formal religious teachings—as well as pictorial images shown in religious art—have a powerful influence; however, the fact is that people who are exposed to identical religious teachings often end up conceptualizing God in very different ways.

Some of the difference can be accounted for by determining who it was who taught them about God. If a child was taught by rabbis, priests, ministers, or nuns who displayed certain characteristics—sternness and unmercifulness, for example, or gentleness and mercy—the child is likely to view God as having these characteristics, too.

But the most important factor in determining a child's view of God is what his parents are like. Generally speaking, *children select out from their religious training those beliefs about the nature of God that most closely match the personalities and behavior of their parents.*[4]

If a person had unforgiving, punishing and unpredictable parents, she probably would have accepted religious teachings depicting God as being like this. If, on the other hand, she had kind, even-tempered, and tolerant parents, she probably would have done one of two things: either she would have heard primarily the teachings about God as loving, forgiving, predictable, and so forth, and tuned out the rest; or she would have heard all the rest, but a discrepancy would have been created between what she was being taught about the world and what she knew to be true from her direct experience with her parents. To resolve this discrepancy, she either would have concluded that "something isn't right here" and rejected the teachings of organized religions; or she would have allowed them to enter her head but not to penetrate deeply enough into her inner self to have much impact on the formation of her conscience and ideal self.

The Change Process: Bob's Way

Bob's experience bears out the connection between the kind of parental treatment a child receives and the view of God that he embraces. Bob felt himself unworthy of God because his image of God in most important respects matched his image of his critical, perfectionist father. Just as Bob longed for his father's love but felt he'd never be good enough to merit it, he yearned to obtain a special closeness to God (hence his desire to become a minister), but was sure God found him unworthy.

Bob's first task in overcoming his "God's Love Isn't in the Cards for Me" block was to define his image of God, and to question how that image had been formed. This was very difficult for him. He felt guilty at the mere thought of it because, according to the viewpoint with which he was raised, "these are things that you're not supposed to question." When it was pointed out that all the great spiritual leaders throughout history experienced periods of profound doubt and questioning, Bob still could not let go of the idea that it was wrong to do so. What triggered a change for him was a discussion of "the agony in the garden" that Jesus went through before his crucifixion. If Jesus had questioned God, Bob concluded, then it couldn't be so wrong after all.

Bob's image of Jesus turned out to be the vehicle through which he was finally able to conceptualize God as more loving than not. Growing up, Bob had been taught about the Holy Trinity. Yet when he thought about God, his immediate association was with God the Father alone. Images of God the Son and God the Holy Spirit did not readily leap to mind. Bob's particular image of God the Father resembled his human father, but it turned out that Bob envisioned God the Son in a much more positive way. He saw Jesus as "warm, gentle, compassionate, openhearted, tender, forgiving, and effusively loving." This meant Bob did not have to create an entirely new image of God in his mind's eye, but could just move God the (Critical)

Father off center stage and put his already existing image of God the (Loving) Son in its place.

For Bob, this was a gradual transition that occurred only with a great deal of talking, questioning, lurching forward, then sliding back. He started to meditate daily, and this proved a very useful tool. At first, he used the mantra "Jesus is love." When that had become firmly implanted, he used the mantra "Jesus is God." Then he finally reached the point where he was ready to make a major conceptual leap to "God is Love."

When Bob would fall back into the habit of mentally running himself down, he also started to make an effort to replace his old self-criticisms ("You moron," "You klutz," "You good-for-nothing," etc.) with positive statements about his relationship with God, such as "You are only human, and if God didn't like that, He wouldn't have made you this way. After all, it's not as though He didn't know what He was doing." Since statements of this sort get Bob thinking about the nature of God and other questions of cosmic importance, they often get him off the track of judging himself altogether.

As Bob became more accustomed to associating Jesus with God, he then began to flesh out his image of Jesus. He visualized Him first as another man about his own age, holding his arms out to Bob in a welcoming embrace. He visualized Him doing carpentry work and asking Bob to lend a hand. He rented the *Oh, God!* movies and got a chuckle out of the image of George Burns as God. Throughout, his relationship with God was slowly changing. Although Bob had believed in God from earliest childhood, for the first time in his entire life he began to feel warmed by God's love.

The Change Process: Rosa's Way

Rosa's experience also bears out the link between a child's experience in her family and the way she will come to view God. Rosa, whose childhood is discussed in Chapter 4, based much of her image of God on her abusive older brother Raoul. Whenever she would feel depressed, sad, or tearful as an adult, she believed that God got angry at her and found her disgusting and unworthy, just as her brother had. So at these times, she experienced a loss of both self-love and

God's love. What's more, she would not permit herself to do what would have comforted and nourished her most at these times—pray, meditate, spend time alone in chapel, and attend liturgical services, especially Mass.

In therapy, Rosa became aware of the extent to which she had molded her picture of God in her bullying older brother's image. Very well versed in theology and especially in contemporary Christian and New Age spiritual thinking, Rosa had an intellectual view of God as "the essence of love, someone who's always there for us." However, her own personal and more visceral view was that God was a perfection-demanding tyrant who "only loves me as long as I'm doing and achieving, achieving at a high level." Rosa's real belief was that "God is only there for you when you're doing well. If you're tired or angry or making mistakes, He's nowhere to be found."

Rosa also became aware of the extent to which she had projected her own feelings onto God. She had always assumed God got angry with her for being depressed, for making mistakes, for not being perfect—for being human, in sum. But in therapy, Rosa began to realize that she was angry with God. She was furious that God had taken her father away when she was so young, then compounded her problems by forcing her to live under Raoul's rule. Rosa felt that God and her father had both abandoned her when she needed them most, and she was livid about it. In the process of overcoming her "I Don't Want to Deal with My Feelings" block, Rosa became more aware of her feelings and better about releasing them, including her feelings of anger at God. As this happened, she felt less and less that God was angry with her. Rosa began to understand what Sharon had learned—that human anger doesn't faze God; after all, He has heard and seen it all before.

Gradually Rosa began to see that by abandoning prayer and the other religious practices that she loved when she felt depressed, she was in effect reliving her early experience of being abandoned by her father and by God. Rather than retreating from God when she felt angry, depressed, and undeserving, she began to spend more and more time praying, meditating, and attending liturgical services. This helped diminish her depressions. It also helped to give her something she had always yearned for—a sense that "God is always there for me, no matter how much I've messed up, or how bad and unworthy I feel."

The question of whether there exists in the universe a higher power who connects and oversees us all has been debated since time immemorial. No one can prove there is a God, and in telling Sharon's story we haven't meant to suggest that people should or should not believe in God. And in pointing out some of the problems Bob, Rosa, and countless others have had because of the way they see God, we also haven't meant to suggest that everyone should reject organized religions, although for people who see God as punitive and unloving, this is often a very healthy thing to do. Decisions about faith, religion, and spirituality are very personal matters, best made on an individual basis. We have told of Sharon's, Bob's, and Rosa's spiritual struggles because they illustrate that a person's beliefs about God—whatever they may be—usually have a great deal to do with the way she sees herself and others, and also with her ability to both receive and give love.

Chapter 9
"I'll Never Get Another Chance"

All week, five-year-old Johnny has been looking forward to Saturday, when his parents have promised to take him to the new ice-cream store downtown and buy him a treat. Finally, Saturday comes, and Johnny orders a double-dip cone, chocolate fudge, his favorite flavor. Seeing that the huge mound of ice cream is perched rather precariously atop the cone, Johnny's parents warn him to be careful. "Push it down with your tongue so it doesn't fall out," they say. Johnny, however, is afraid the cone will crack, and he likes licking the ice cream into a peak. "It's going to fall out," his parents warn, "and if it does, we're not buying you another one." On the way to the car, Johnny trips on his shoelace, and his parents' prediction comes true: the ice cream lands on the sidewalk. Johnny wails, and his parents say, "See, we told you so." Although he begs them to get him another cone, they refuse. "We got you one, and you dropped it," they say. "It's your own fault for not listening."

Many people were taught to view love in much the same way that Johnny learned to see ice-cream cones. When you get a chance for love, they learned, you had better not be careless with it—and you sure had better not blow it. Because once you've used up your chances for love, that's it—you'll never get another shot.

As opposed to those with the "Love Just Isn't in the Cards for Me" block, those with the "I'll Never Get Another Chance" block don't see the world as a depriving place, but rather as a place where scarcity prevails. According to their world view, fate has arranged to give everyone opportunities for love—but only in limited numbers. They may vary as to just how many chances at love an individual gets: some believe it's only one, while others might believe it's several. Yet all agree that the number is limited, and that once they've used theirs up, that's it—they won't get any more.

In fact, none of us came into the world with a set number of chances for love. Although physical resources may indeed be in short supply, the world is so full of people that the possibilities for each of us to have meaningful, loving connections are vast. Nevertheless, the idea that chances for love come as rarely as Halley's Comet is continually promulgated in our culture, and it has an enormous impact on the way romantic love in particular is viewed. The myth of "one true love" is presented time and again in movies, TV shows, novels, and plays; and it's especially resonant in pop music, as songs like "My Only Love," "Nobody But You," and "I'll Never Smile Again" remind us.

Families, too, promote the myth of one true love, giving their children some version of the following messages:

"There's some*one* out there for you."

"Save yourself for that special some*one*."

"Someday you'll meet Mr. (or Miss) Right."

"One day, your chance will come."

The notion of one true love is so widespread and seductive because it recalls the time in our earliest infancy when our mother was our one and only love. And it's especially tenacious because it feeds an unconscious longing to find someone else who will love us the way Mother once did—or, rather, the way we *wish* she had.

Some people learned that the scarcity principle applies not only to romantic love, but to other kinds of love as well. Growing up, they may have gotten messages along these lines, too:

"You only get one best friend in a lifetime."

"Real friends are hard to come by."

"If you meet one other person in life you can really trust and talk to, you're lucky. Most people never even get that."

Still others learned to believe that life would give them hardly any chance for love outside their families at all. Growing up, they were given messages like these:

"We love you because we're your family, and we have to love you. People who don't have to love you won't."

"Do unto others *before* they do unto you."

"Blood ties are the only ties you can rely on. People outside the family will disappoint or hurt you."

"You'll be sorry when I die, because no one else will ever love you the way I do." (from mother or father)

The World as an Unforgiving Place

Some people who believe they'll never get another chance at love think they've simply used up their allotment. A classic example is the widow or widower who won't even consider dating, much less re-marrying, because it would be a betrayal of the deceased spouse's status as "my one true love." More often, however, people with this block feel they've *blown* or *ruined* their chances—or are at risk of doing so. To people with this view, the world isn't simply a place of scarcity, it's an unforgiving place as well.

People who believe they've already blown their chances for love generally think that failing to make a relationship (particularly mar-riage) work is a terrible crime warranting punishment. And what better punishment is there than to never get another chance and thus be doomed to perpetual loneliness? After a divorce, for example, many people berate themselves by reasoning, "Living out the rest of my life alone is the punishment I deserve for failing in my marriage."

Again, family influences play a big role. The world will probably seem a very unforgiving place to someone who grew up in a home where grudges were held and apologies unheard of, or the same accusations and hurts were trotted out again and again over the years. A person who grew up in a home where the pettiest of "crimes" (not making the bed, forgetting to empty the dish rack, dropping milk on the floor) were routinely met with threats of perpetual punishment ("I'll never speak to you again," "I'll give you something you'll never forget," "Go to your room and don't ever come out") probably will also have a hard time believing the world can be forgiving.

"You only get one chance and if you blow it, that's it" is the lesson of a classic childhood experience that even people from the most loving homes may have gone through. Most people can remember an episode when they lost a favorite object, broke it accidentally, or wrecked it in a tantrum. Instead of being consoled for the loss, they were scolded: "See what happens when you don't take care of your belongings? Well, if you expect us to buy you another [toy, dress, doll, etc.], you can forget it. You're the one who lost [broke, smashed, etc.] it, so it serves you right to go without."

People who grow up with a sense that the world is an unforgiving place end up in a terrible bind that is sure to limit self-love. Since there isn't a human being alive who will reach old age without at least occasionally hurting others and committing some other wrong-doings, knowing how to forgive one's own self is crucial to psychological well-being. But a person who doesn't believe in the possibility of forgiveness won't be able to, and as a result will be forced to embrace one of two distorted self-images: either he'll see himself as a bad person doomed to go through life stained by every wrong he has ever committed; or he'll see himself as having the special, exalted status of someone who cannot do any wrong and is therefore above the need for forgiveness. For someone with the first view, self-love is out of the question, and life is full of self-loathing and self-punishment. Someone with the second view will *appear* to have great self-love, but it will be a pseudo self-love based on an inaccurate self-concept and an equally inaccurate notion of his place in the world.

When people grow up viewing the world as an unforgiving place, they tend to be unforgiving with others, too. They respond to the hurts and disappointments they experience in relationships with an attitude of "That's it. You've blown all your chances with me, and I'm not giving you another chance to get close to me and do it again." Often, they become scorekeepers, feeling perpetually exploited and victimized, and lamenting "Why Do I Always Have to Give So Much to Get So Little?," the block discussed in Chapter 17.

A family's economic situation can also give a child the sense that the world is a place of scarcity. Many people who grew up in homes where there wasn't enough money continue to feel poor even after they have reached a state of financial stability or even abundance in their own adult lives. Beliefs such as "there won't be enough to go around" and "tomorrow it will all be taken away" are so firmly entrenched as to be unshakable. They often transfer their inner sense of scarcity from the financial realm to the personal realm, believing that if they have material abundance, fate will counterbalance the situation by making sure they get shortchanged in love.

Even those from well-off homes may have grown up feeling poor because of parental messages such as "money doesn't grow on trees," "your father breaks his back to keep this roof over your head," "you're going to eat us out of house and home," and "your school expenses are going to put us in the poorhouse." Since children are dependent on their parents for both love and material things, and money is often used as a means of expressing (or withholding) love, many grow up seeing money and love intertwined, and both always in danger of running out.

Today's AIDS crisis is making the "I'll Never Get Another Chance" block even more common, at least as it pertains to sexual or romantic love. Until recently, many gays and heterosexuals alike believed in the possibility of numerous different lovers over the course of a lifetime. AIDS, however, has forced people to alter this view and adopt more conservative sexual behavior. Whether one sees the new conservatism as a step forward or back, it clearly signifies a dramatic shift from a perception of the world as a place with plentiful opportunities for sexual love to a view of the world as a place where such opportunities are scarce indeed.

It's true, of course, that for most people each new day *doesn't* bring forth an endless supply of people with whom there's the possibility of a deep and lasting connection. At the same time, though, chances for love aren't as rare as many people think—they can and do come far more often than once in a lifetime. But people who believe that their chances are numbered don't realize this. Taught that love exists in very short supply, they've accepted this "fact" without question.

George

Ironically, it's often precisely because people view their chances for love as so limited that many relationships don't work out. When a person enters a relationship believing "this is it, my only chance," there is enormous pressure to make it work. At the same time, there is massive fear of the eternal loneliness they are sure will result if it doesn't. When it looms large, the fear that the relationship won't work out has the paradoxical effect of preventing the people involved from doing the one thing necessary to make an intimate relationship work—taking the risk of relating to each other honestly and authentically.

George, a state trooper and father of three, found this out through the collapse of his thirteen-year marriage. Tall and athletic in build, George has a boyish face and a friendly, gentle air. A closet intellectual and history buff, George was thirty-four when he started therapy. He had just moved out on his wife, Hillary, and their son and two daughters. At the time he and Hillary had not yet legally separated, and it was because of the conflict George felt over making the split a legal separation that he sought help.

Although both Hillary and George had been miserable in the marriage for years, the prospect of formally ending it filled George with so much fear, despair, and guilt that he was in torment. "My family has been the most important thing in the world to me," he explained in an early session. "Ending it means I've failed at the one thing in my life that has really mattered to me." Even as he began taking the legal steps towards divorce the following year, again and again he lamented that "if I let go of Hillary and the kids, I'll be losing the only chance I'm ever going to have."

George was one of three boys in a working-class home. His father, a mechanic, was an overbearing man whose main way of relating to others was by bullying them. His mother was a store clerk whom George described as "never standing up to my father or anyone else." Because both parents worked long hours, they were usually so tired when they arrived home that they didn't have much energy left over for any kind of interaction, whether talking or fighting. Instead, the whole family avoided interacting by watching TV. As George recalled, the TV "was always on in our house. We sat at the dinner table and watched TV as we ate, and when it was over we moved to the couch and watched it more, until it was time for bed." The kinds of shows the family most frequently watched were family shows—"Father Knows Best," "The Donna Reed Show," "Burns and Allen," and "Leave It to Beaver"—when George was young, and shows like "The Brady Bunch," "The Partridge Family," "Eight Is Enough," and "The Waltons" as he grew older.

These loving TV families seemed to George the antithesis of his own family, and watching them night after night he developed an ideal image of the kind of family he would have when he grew up. Although George spent a lot of his free time playing sports and working on cars, he also frequently sneaked off alone to the movies, where his favorite films were romantic ones. He was too embarrassed to tell anyone about this, but he kept going because there he could lose himself in increasingly vivid fantasies about someday finding the right girl, falling madly in love, getting married, and living happily ever after just the way all the happy people on screen did.

George was a senior in high school when he found "the right girl" in Hillary, a sophomore. They began going steady almost immediately, and two years later they got married, just one week after Hillary graduated. Within a year, their first child was born, followed by two others in the next three years. By this time, George had become a state trooper. Occasionally Hillary spoke about wanting to go back to school to become a hairstylist or computer operator, but she was too tied up with the children to do much outside the home.

While George remembers some very happy times with Hillary both before and shortly following their wedding, almost from the outset the marriage was a great disappointment to him. "I always thought that once I found the right girl, everything would fall into place," he said. "But it didn't happen that way." Instead of becoming like the Cleavers or the Waltons, George found that his life with Hillary much more resembled that with his own family. Although George spent a great deal of time playing with the children, taking them on outings, and helping them with school, he and Hillary rarely did anything together. "She was always too tired to go out. She was even too tired to talk," George recalled. "So at night, we'd just watch TV until we fell asleep." Hillary, as it turned out, watched TV almost constantly during the day, and eventually "we started to watch TV during dinner the way I had as a kid, too."

Throughout the course of their marriage George and Hillary remained virtual strangers to each other. They talked only about superficial subjects or practical matters concerning the raising of their children, and over time, "it got to a point where we hardly said much to each other at all," George recalled. When they experienced conflicts, as any couple does, they felt it was "better not to bring things up," and so avoided discussing their problems. In more than thirteen years, "we never once had a real fight or argument," George explained. Even George's departure did not generate any discussion or argument. "We never talked about why I was leaving, or what was going on," George said. "I just left, and Hillary just cried."

The Change Process: George Gains Awareness

For George, developing an awareness of what had happened in his marriage and why was the main task of his early therapy. This might seem like a small task, but in George's case it was anything but. It's probably obvious to many readers that the reason for George and Hillary's problems was a lack of communication. George, however, knew his marriage had been a bust almost from the start, but he had no idea why.

At the time he entered therapy, George had never discussed his problems and feelings with anyone, nor had he ever really been listened to. Thus, just the act of entering a relationship in which he would talk about his inner self made an enormous difference in his life, and marked a major step forward. For him to make an appointment with a therapist required great courage.

In George's initial sessions, the focus was on what had happened in his marriage. Gradually he came to see that lack of communication was the cause of its disintegration. But it was only later—after examining his and Hillary's behavior, and his own feelings and history—that George came to see that behind their failure to communicate was a mountain of fear.

George had resolved early in the relationship "not to bring things up" with Hillary because he was afraid that if he told her about anything that was bothering him, she would cry. In fact, on the few occasions that he had tried to broach difficult subjects, she did cry. In each instance, George felt so guilty that he immediately apologized, dropped the discussion, and reaffirmed his resolve never to bring things up.

When George was asked in therapy why he felt guilty when Hillary cried, he looked perplexed. "I hurt her feelings," he said in a tone of voice that indicated he considered the question extremely stupid.

"Anyone in that situation would feel guilty." That's not true, George was informed. Some people in that situation would see Hillary's tears as manipulative and would feel angry with her for using her vulnerability as a way of getting out of dealing with the issue under discussion. Other people would feel compassion for her, and regret that she was so easily upset, but would still not feel responsible for her tears, or see them as a reason to discontinue the discussion. Since George had never discussed his feelings with anyone, he had never learned that the way he felt in a given situation was not necessarily the way someone else would feel. He was genuinely shocked to learn that different people often have different responses to the same exact situation.

As George eventually discovered, he felt guilty when he saw Hillary cry not because everyone would naturally feel this way in a similar situation, but because her tears triggered responses that he had learned in childhood. Not surprisingly, George's mother was also easily given to tears. Whenever he would overhear his parents begin to have an argument, his mother would immediately begin crying, then turn to her children for consolation, telling them "see what your father has done to me. He's always criticizing me." In fact, George's father *was* an overly critical person. But instead of directly challenging him on this aspect of his behavior, George's mother would defend herself with tears, and then turn to her children to make her tears go away. George thus learned to feel that he was responsible for his mother's feelings and to feel guilty whenever another person, especially a woman, cried in his presence, particularly in response to anything he said or did.

George's sense of responsibility for his mother's feelings was reinforced by many episodes in which it was he rather than his father who was blamed for "making Mom cry." As a child, George often acted in ways that angered, disappointed, or annoyed his parents, just as all children do. But in these situations, his mother would not yell, tell him she was upset, or otherwise articulate her disappointment. Instead, she would dissolve into tears and say, "Can't you see how this hurts me? Why are you doing this to me?" And his father would say, "Look what you've done to your mother. Why do you always have to upset her?" Then he would banish George to his room. Time and again, the message was driven home: either George's father made his mother cry, and it was up to George to make her feel better; or it was George who made his mother cry, and his father had to make her feel better by putting the cause of her sorrow (George) out of sight and earshot. Only years later did it begin to dawn on George that his mother's frequent tears may have been caused by something rooted in her own history rather than by whatever she was supposedly responding to at the time.

Given his background, it makes a lot of sense that George would have approached his marriage with the belief that "it's better not to bring things up." First of all, he had no experience in talking about emotional issues and no models to draw on, either. Moreover, bringing things up would probably have meant seeing his wife cry, which was sure to summon up all the feelings of responsibility and guilt he had felt when his mother cried. Further, George believed that if he made his own wife cry, he would then be behaving exactly like his own father, whom he resented greatly for being so overbearing and critical, and whom he had decided he did not want to resemble in any way. In no way did George want to be guilty of "doing to my wife what my father did to my mother."

Also contributing to George's resolve "not to bring things up" with Hillary were a number of damaging stereotypes about women. His mother's pattern of never standing up for herself or expressing anger directly gave George the message that women are fragile and defenseless creatures who are incapable of fending for themselves. The TV shows and romantic movies he watched reinforced this view, as did the behavior of the girl he chose to marry. One of the reasons Hillary struck George as "the one for me," in fact, was that she seemed "so helpless," fitting both his image of femininity and bolstering his own sense of himself as a masculine protector. As he found out, though, the downside of this role was that he felt he had to protect Hillary from everything, including knowledge of any dissatisfactions, anxieties, or unhappiness he might be feeling.

But it wasn't just Hillary that George viewed as fragile. Since he thought it represented his one and only chance at love, George also considered the relationship itself too precious and delicate to withstand any stress. He thought that if he brought things up, it wouldn't just create some temporary problems, it would end the marriage altogether. Not only would this be awful in itself, but George would also be left to live out the rest of his life in desolate loneliness. No wonder he felt it was better not to bring things up; the stakes were simply too high.

As he became more aware of what had happened between him and Hillary and why, George slowly came to see that it was precisely because his desire to preserve his "one and only" chance for love was so strong that the marriage was bound to run into trouble. If George had brought things up, there's no guarantee that his and Hillary's relationship would have worked out. Perhaps Hillary would indeed "not have been able to cope," as George had feared. Perhaps if they had openly argued, they never would have found ways to resolve their differences. Then again, perhaps George and Hillary finally would have begun to establish a more meaningful relationship. As it was, after more than thirteen years of marriage, they separated, feeling, as George put it, "like we never took the chance of getting to know each other at all."

The Change Process: George Faces His Guilt

In the wake of the breakup of a marriage or other important relationship, anyone will inevitably feel full of loss, regret, and sadness and will probably worry about not being able to find someone else ever again. But since George looked at his marriage as his one and only chance for love, there was an utter hopelessness as well, which was compounded by an omnipresent sense of acute guilt. Some of George's guilt obviously came from his belief that he failed at his marriage and hurt his wife and children. But a lot came from his feeling that in leaving Hillary he had become "a worse ogre than my father. At least he didn't cut out and leave my mother." By all objective standards, George had remained a good father: he continued to spend a great deal of time with the children, spoke to them every night on the phone, was always available when they were sick, and took care of them financially. In many respects he had also remained a good husband: he took care of the house, offered to pay for Hillary to go back to school, and called her to see how she was doing every week. Nevertheless, in the first two years after he moved out, George considered his leaving an unforgivable, selfish act and himself a "total shit" deserving of scorn.

In the wake of the breakup, George's guilt and inability to forgive himself served to block his receptivity to love in several ways. He missed his children greatly, but he would not permit himself to see them as much as he wanted. This wasn't because Hillary didn't want him to come by (she had said he could come over any time) but because he felt he no longer deserved the joy and sense of being loved that his children have always brought to him. In withdrawing from his children in this way, George was reenacting his own child-hood experience of being banished to his room for making his mother cry, and he was punishing himself for being "a worse shit than my father ever was." While George was eventually able to recognize this, he had a much harder time seeing that by depriving himself of time with his children, he was virtually guaranteeing that his worst fear would come true—that his children, "the most important people in the world to me," would grow up "feeling their father wasn't really there for them."

Six months after his separation, George met a woman named Lau-rie, whom he later would describe as "the best friend I've ever had." She quickly fell in love with him, and over the course of the next year or so, George often had "the feeling that I'm falling in love with her." But he discounted this feeling, telling himself "it can't be real" because, he explained, "I had my chance [for romantic love] already, and I blew it." Also, since he felt so down on himself, George would wonder, "What could she see in me?" Rather than see his new re-lationship as holding out the potential for another chance, George believed "it won't last, so why get my hopes up?"

George also held back from letting Laurie's love penetrate to his inner self because he felt guilty about being involved with another woman. "After what I did to my wife and kids, I don't deserve to be loved by anyone," George explained. In fact, he felt he deserved to be punished, and harshly punished, for "getting from Laurie the kind of love I couldn't give to my family."

The Change Process: George Seems Stuck, Then Makes Progress

The process that people go through in therapy is often painstakingly slow, and so subtle as to be nearly imperceptible. As discussed in Chapter 3, people in the process of psychological change often go through periods during which nothing seems to be happening. Then one day something seems to snap. Suddenly all the pieces that they've been picking over for months or years fall into place and they experience the "click" of really "getting" what they've been seeking to understand. The next thing they know, they're making noticeable changes in the way they think, feel, and behave. This is what happened with George.

For more than two years, George tried to forgive himself for separating from his wife and children. He talked about the lack of models of forgiving behavior in his childhood. He realized that as a law-enforcement officer, he was in a profession where the idea of forgiveness was scoffed at. He explored the purposes his guilt served, how it was his way of punishing himself. He tried meditations, visualizations, cognitive exercises. He became more aware of, and attuned to, his feelings, and he poured them out. He raged. He cried. He laughed. And none of it appeared to have any impact. George was still spending less time with his children than he wanted. When they reached out to him with loving gestures, he tightened up inside. He felt that he was so terrible a human being that he did not deserve to let their love in. In his relationship with Laurie, George also remained blocked. Although he finally permitted himself to sleep with her, he still would not share any of his inner thoughts and feelings with her. She kept trying to deepen the relationship, and he kept rejecting her love.

After eighteen months Laurie told George she wanted to end the relationship. George noddingly acquiesced, saying "it's probably for the best." He felt nothing beyond a brief twinge of sadness and regret. Four days later he had a therapy session. He began by very calmly explaining that Laurie had called it quits. Asked how he felt about this, George sighed and said he wasn't too upset, "after all, it's probably for the best." These words had barely left George's mouth when suddenly he bolted upright in his chair, his hands gripping the armrests and a grimace of horrified disbelief appearing on his boyish face. "What's wrong with me?" he nearly yelled. "How can I let this woman who loves me leave my life? She's the best thing that ever happened to me. Yet to punish myself for my great crime of leaving my wife and our lousy marriage, I'm going to deny myself happiness. Bullshit! It's gone on long enough. I have my faults, but I'm not a bad person. It's okay for me to be happy. Enough of this bullshit self-punishment. I've served my time. I don't know if Laurie will have me after all I've put her through, but I'm going to do everything in my power to get her back."

The next session, George reported that he and Laurie had had several long talks and were back together. Although the threat of losing her had precipitated his apparent breakthrough, what really made it possible was all his plodding work on the issues of guilt and self-forgiveness. Without those months and months of effort, George would not have been able to open himself up to deeper involvement with Laurie. He would have remained enmeshed in his old pattern of believing "I had my chance and I blew it, and for that I deserve to live out the rest of my days unloved and alone."

The Change Process: George Continues

It would be nice to be able to say that after George's breakthrough, he and Laurie walked off into the sunset hand in hand and all his problems disappeared. It would be a lie, too. George was not a totally transformed man whose relationships all suddenly became trouble free. Although he finally did go through with official divorce proceedings and later began living with Laurie, George still had a good deal of lingering guilt about leaving his wife and kids. Although he eventually allowed himself to see his kids more often and became more open to taking in their love, he still felt horrible that they had been put through a divorce and would grow up in a "broken" home; and when he brooded about this, he felt that he didn't deserve their love and forgiveness. When the euphoria of finally making a notice-able leap forward faded, George found what anyone in his situation would have—that he still had work to do, work that would sometimes seem to be going nowhere and that he'd probably be engaged in for the rest of his life.

George still had a great deal of work to do on his fear of "bringing things up." Although he was far better at discussing his feelings with Laurie than he had been with his wife, just the idea of "bringing up" any anger, dissatisfaction, or ambivalence filled him with paralyzing anxiety and fear.

Many cultures have different legends to help people deal with anxiety and fear. George was helped by a parable about a dragon, which is similar to the Hindu story of Vishnu. The story goes like this: in medieval times, there was a village that was terrorized by a dragon which lived in a cave on the outskirts of town. Everyone in the village was terrified of the dragon, and as their fear grew, they moved their dwellings farther and farther from the cave. But the dragon kept growing. It grew from thirty feet to fifty feet to seventy feet long. It grew two heads in place of one. Great spikes grew out of its back. It began to breathe fire, and the more terrified the villagers became and the farther away they tried to get, the nearer the dragon came and the farther its fiery breath reached.

One day, a young villager who had grown up in terror of the dragon decided to go out to the dragon's cave to see if the beast was really as bad as everyone thought. His family and all the other villagers warned him not to go, but he was determined. Although his heart was racing with fear, he set off toward the dragon's cave. The closer he got, the more he felt his fear. His heart and head were pounding, sweat was pouring down his face, and his legs felt as though they might buckle out from under him. But he walked on.

Finally, the cave came into sight. The villager could hear the dragon inside and was terrified. He felt like he was going to throw up and wanted to run away. But he kept approaching the cave until he was finally able to peek inside. What he saw surprised him. The dragon was large and fierce, but not nearly as large and fierce as he had expected. It only had one head. It had no spikes. It breathed fire, but only in licks of flame that shot a mere three or four feet. Greatly relieved, the villager decided to sit down with the dragon in full view and take a rest. He fell asleep for several hours, and when he woke up he noticed something strange. The dragon seemed smaller and less fierce than it had before. He decided to spend the night. When he woke up the next morning, the dragon was still there but it was much smaller. He decided to go closer to the dragon and talk to it. As he did so, the dragon kept shrinking until it was no larger than an alligator.

The young villager returned home and told the other villagers about the dragon. At first, they didn't believe him, but eventually they began to go to the cave in twos and threes, then in larger groups, to see for themselves. The dragon was rather unpleasant and somewhat frightening at first, they found, but not nearly as ugly and fierce as they had thought. They still weren't thrilled about having a dragon living on the edge of their village, but now that they had faced the beast, they weren't particularly bothered by it either, and eventually they got used to it.

Everyone of us has his or her own dragons. One of George's dragons was his fear of "bringing things up." Like most people, he grew up believing that if only he could put his fears and anxieties out of his mind, they would go away. In fact, the more he tried to push them away, the larger and more disturbing his dragons became. Over time, George realized that since life is full of causes for fear and anxiety, it's wiser to learn to live with them than run from them, hoping that someday they'll disappear. George needed to stick his head in the cave and confront his dragons, otherwise they would continue to terrorize him. When he finally began facing his fear of bringing things up, he was still afraid but no longer paralyzed.

Significantly, when George began bringing things up with Laurie, her reaction was not at all what he expected. She did not dissolve into tears but listened calmly, said she could see many of his points, and revealed that she had many similar feelings herself. She also made some helpful suggestions of what they might do to resolve these problems. George was truly shocked. He had been so sure that Laurie would not be able to handle his bringing things up. His fears, he realized, had much more to do with who he was than who she was.

With Hillary, as well, George became better at bringing things up. There were important unresolved issues between them that they both had avoided dealing with for a long time. George finally confronted her, and she started to cry. But George found he felt less guilty and upset about her tears than he had thought. Something else unexpected happened: once Hillary had cried for a while, she regained her composure and was able to continue with the discussion. Now each time George has to bring things up with one of the women in his life, his fear of inducing tears and "feeling like a complete shit" lessens.

As George has become more forgiving of himself, another important relationship in his life has changed, too. For years, George was full of rage toward his father for the way he had treated his mother. He thought his father was "a bullying shit" and "a monster" who intentionally set out to cause his wife and children pain. But as George became more aware of his own dragons, he came to see that his father wasn't an ogre but a flawed human being who went through life bedeviled by his own dragons and never had sufficient resources or ability to face them. And as George started to forgive himself for "failing" at his marriage, he also began to forgive his father for failing to be the kind of father and husband George had wanted. Although George's father has not mellowed as he has aged, George is now able to spend time with him without getting as upset and enraged as in the past.

Chapter 10
"It's Too Late for Me; My Time Has Run Out"

"Time's up. Hand your papers up to the front of the class." To most people those are familiar words. To many, they're ominous words as well, recalling an occasion when the clock ran out before they had gotten the chance to finish an exam. Being told "time's up" when you hadn't yet finished a test was bound to have left you with a lot of unpleasant feelings, especially if you had studied hard. Perhaps you felt cheated, that the time frame was unfair. Perhaps you felt stupid and slow, and berated yourself for having dawdled in the beginning section. Inevitably you handed in the exam with regret, perhaps telling yourself, "If only I had had more time, I could have finished" or "If only I had been able to finish, I could have gotten an A."

For many people, "Time's up" is not just a phrase associated with school days: it's a phrase that sums up the way they feel about their chances for love as well. According to their world view, when fate doles out our chances for love, each chance is stamped with an expiration date that corresponds with a certain age in our lives. If we haven't used up our chances for love by that date, sorry, that's it—the opportunities all automatically expire.

At first glance, the "It's Too Late for Me; My Time Has Run Out" block might seem to be the same as the "I'll Never Get Another Chance" block of the preceding chapter. Sometimes these two blocks do go hand in hand. But, in fact, they are distinct blocks, and a person with one won't necessarily have the other. To people who believe they'll either use up or blow their only chances for love, the world is a place where the scarcity principle prevails and we each get only one or a few chances at love as a result. But to people who believe their time has run out, it's not that we each get a limited number of chances for love, it's that the time in which we have to use them is limited. Those with this block may believe they've been granted an *infinite* number of chances, but like game-show contestants who are given one minute to stuff as many groceries into a cart as they can, they believe that they have only a certain amount of time to use their chances, and that if they fail to do so before the buzzer rings, that's it—time's up, and the chances all disappear.

Given our cultural climate, it's inevitable that many people would be susceptible to believing "It's Too Late for Me; My Time Has Run Out." After all, American culture is one of overnight sensations, child stars, and fads and fashions that come in and go out with dizzying speed. It prizes the new and has little use or tolerance for the old, a word frequently equated with obsolescence. In many cultures, older people are revered, and aging is seen to bestow wisdom, but the American view is that older people accumulate only losses—the loss of their looks, vitality, sexuality, mental acuity, and aptitude for growth in both work and the personal realm.

The taboo against aging hits women especially hard. The conventional view is that men acquire dignity with age, while women just get decrepit. Moreover, there's a double standard that says women become "washed up" earlier than men. Many view a woman in her thirties as already over the hill, while viewing a man of the same age as in the prime of his life. Most of us have also learned to consider it quite normal for an older man to have a much younger girlfriend or wife, while at the same time learning that there's still something not quite right when an older woman is romantically involved with a much younger man. It's commonly assumed that an older man, particularly one with money and power, will always be able to find "sweet young things," but that even the most "well preserved" woman will be stuck with pretty slim pickings. Many people still respond to an older woman/younger man couple with such assumptions as "he must be doing her a favor," "he's probably got a mother complex," or "he might find her still attractive now, but he'll leave her when she starts to look really old."

Although the traditional taboos against aging have relaxed a bit in recent years, many women still feel additional insecurity because of the notion that a woman remains youthful and feminine only so long as she can bear children. Granted, since women do have a limited time in which to bear children, some of the current concern about biological clocks has a sound basis in physiology. But a lot of the anxious feeling that "my time is running out" that many women, particularly unattached heterosexual women, suffer from today has its roots in cultural attitudes. If women hadn't been taught from an early age that motherhood is the be-all and end-all experience of a woman's life, there would be far less worry about being "all washed up" once the prime reproductive years are past. Many women, in fact, would probably view the end of the childbearing years as Margaret Mead did—as a time of liberation, the beginning of a second youth.

In the late 1980s, a cultural backlash developed against independent women, causing many in their forties, thirties, and even twenties to feel a full-blown panic about their time running out. This was perhaps best demonstrated by the remarkable press response to a dubious 1986 study in which researchers associated with Yale and Harvard universities claimed college-educated women who ended their twenties and entered their thirties without marrying had only slim chances of ever marrying. Although the validity of the so-called Yale-Harvard study was immediately called into question by other researchers, the press treated the study as the gospel truth, with print and broadcast media alike touting it as one of the top stories of the decade. In the spring and summer of 1986, it was literally impossible to look at a newspaper or magazine or switch on the TV or radio without once again being informed that women who had the audacity to eschew early marriage were going to pay for their choice by living out the rest of their lives as lonely, forlorn spinsters. Newsweek went so far as to make the study its cover story, thus implicitly elevating it to major importance.[1] In the article itself, Newsweek said the study showed that an unmarried woman had as much chance of marrying as of "getting killed by a terrorist."[2] By lionizing a bogus study in this way, the ostensibly unbiased mass media was giving independent women an unmistakable message loud and clear. "You may think of yourselves as a new breed of women," the message said, "but you're really just a bunch of old maids."

Some gay men are particularly hard hit by cultural taboos against aging as well. In certain gay subcultures, there is an exaggerated emphasis on being young and an equally exaggerated horror of aging. Now with the specter of AIDS haunting the gay community, many also have a generalized sense that suddenly their time has run out—and it's not just their time to find new lovers, but also their time to be openly, joyfully gay, and to move through the world without constant fear of discrimination or attack.

Young in Age, Old at Heart

While extremely important, cultural factors alone do not account for the preponderance of the "It's Too Late for Me; My Time Has Run Out" love block. This is true because one of the most significant features of this block is that a person doesn't have to be beyond a certain age to have it. The fact is, there are people in their teens and twenties who already feel "It's Too Late for Me; My Time Has Run Out," and there are also many who have had this feeling with them as long as they can remember. This is well illustrated by Joyce, the woman discussed in the chapters on the "I Don't Need Anyone— I'm Strong" and "Love Just Isn't in the Cards for Me" blocks. As she put it, "already as a little girl, I felt like an old lady." And as another person we interviewed explained, "I felt that my time was up the moment I was born. The only time I could count on feeling safe and secure was in the womb. Once I was out, I was on my own."

As we explored the genesis of this love block, we discovered that those who developed it early tend to have had similar experiences in childhood. For some, the sense that their time for love has run out stems from an early experience of loss or abandonment. When they were young, a loved one died or they were abandoned by one or both parents. Others developed the sense that "It's Too Late for Me; My Time for Love Has Run Out" when they were displaced in their families because of the birth of a younger sibling, the catastrophic illness of a sibling or older relative, or an ailing grandparent moving in. With their parents' attention suddenly diverted from them to someone else, they came to believe that their time to be loved was now over.

Impatience

Still others developed this love block at an early age because they grew up in an atmosphere of impatience. Unfortunately, many parents don't understand that the enormous amount of learning children need to do in order to grow up takes a long, long time. They are extremely impatient with their children, berating them for being slow, criticizing them for not getting their shoelaces tied faster, and again and again telling them things like "Stop acting like a baby," "get a move on, we don't have all day," and "hurry and eat your eggs, they're getting cold." Virtually everyone has had the experience of seeing a small child walking hand in hand with a parent, struggling to keep up because the parent is walking at a pace that's just too fast for the child's short legs. For many people, that's what all of childhood was like. "Hurry up and grow up" was a message that was repeatedly conveyed in countless ways from the moment they left the womb.

People who grew up in an atmosphere of impatience usually go into adulthood with a great deal of unfinished emotional business. Children have built-in developmental clocks that dictate what stage they will naturally go through when, and in what order. In an ideal family, the child's inner clock will be respected. The child won't be forced to give up using a bottle when he still feels extremely needful of it, and he won't be expected to start forming sentences when he's just starting to utter his first words. In other words, he won't be forced or expected to behave like "a big boy" before he's had the time he needs to be a baby. In a home where parental impatience is the rule, the situation is very different. There the parents' needs dominate and it is their schedule, not the child's inner clock, that sets the pace for the child's development. Inevitably, children from impatient homes are forced to go through developmental phases at a speeded-up pace; before they've had adequate time to complete one stage, they're pushed on to the next.

These people often learn to take great pride in being "mature for their age" and "poised well beyond their years." Eventually, however, the unfinished business from childhood catches up with them, creating problems for them in adulthood, perhaps even leading to a major emotional crisis. If they want to move on, their only option is to go back and identify and finally complete the tasks so long left unfinished.

As adults, people who grew up in an atmosphere of impatience also tend to be very impatient with themselves and others. They do not allow themselves or others enough time to learn and grow. Nor do they give their relationships adequate time to develop. They have an urgent need to establish instant intimacy, as though they want to jump into the middle of a relationship at the very first meeting. A relationship that develops at a slower, healthier pace leaves them feeling frustrated and often infuriated; things just aren't happening fast enough and they can't stand it.

People who feel their time has run out often aren't interested in therapy. "It's too late in my life for me to start changing," they believe. "So why should I bother to try?" Or if they do start treatment, they tend to feel the same sense of urgency. They want to make dramatic changes and make them *now*. When that doesn't happen, they feel extreme frustration. Since the psyche integrates gradual change much more easily than sudden change, it is crucial for people with this block to learn to give themselves permission to go slowly and not let their sense that "my time is running out" so overwhelm them that they give up entirely.

The Infant View of Time

Not everyone who suffers from the "It's Too Late for Me; My Time Has Run Out" block experiences it constantly, or in such a way that it extends to their entire world view. Rather, the feeling that time is running out comes up occasionally, usually in the context of specific relationships, most often romantic ones, in which their primal needs are being aroused but not met. To a woman involved with an elusive or unreliable man, for example, the hours spent waiting for him to telephone will pass excruciatingly slowly, and she will feel that "if my need [to hear from him] does not get met in the next instant, I will literally die." If she is waiting to hear about whether she got a new job or promotion, she may feel anxious, but she probably won't get into the same frenzy of intense urgency, of needing to know *now*.

Why do so many otherwise patient people feel so much panic and urgency when waiting for a lover to call, show up, say "the right thing," or otherwise meet their needs? The panic arises because when a person's primal emotional needs are activated but then frustrated in a relationship, the experience stirs up an unconscious memory of what it was like to be a helpless infant whose parents had complete power. And when a person's memory of how it felt to be a tiny, helpless baby is triggered, there is usually an accompanying reversion to an infant sense of time.[3] Infants have no ability to distinguish between a minute or an hour or a week: the now moment is all they know. When a baby needs to be fed, he needs to be fed *now;* if he has to wait, he can't differentiate between waiting for ten minutes or an hour—however long he waits, it feels like forever. Moreover, he feels that if his needs don't get met *now,* they'll never get met, and if this happens, he knows he will die. Hence, the baby experiences a feeling of total panic following even a brief period of frustration and waiting.

Since intimate relationships, particularly sexual ones, bring back so many of the sensations and emotions of being a baby, it's very common and natural for adults to revert to an infant sense of time when they experience intimacy, especially when they fall in love. This can happen no matter what kind of childhood a person had. However, someone who grew up in a home where most of his needs were attended to will not feel as much panic and pain when it happens: he'll still feel pain and panic when his needs are frustrated in adult relationships, but he'll also have an accompanying sense that "I've felt this way before, and as bad as it felt, it turned out okay in the end." But a person whose needs in childhood got met sporadically or not at all won't be able to draw on past experience to put himself at ease. On the contrary, he'll be flooded by the sense that "I didn't get what I needed when I felt this way before, so I'm obviously not going to get it now. I'll have to live with this unbearable pain forever." Hence, when he experiences a lover's rebuff or other failure to meet his needs, it ignites a rage about being deprived that has built up over his entire life. Behind the rage is a wail, that says, "I've waited my whole life for my needs to get met, but they've never gotten met, and now it's obvious they never will be. What a fool I was for thinking for even a moment that maybe *this time* things would be different!"

Caroline

Caroline is a tall, slender woman with shoulder-length dark hair and a face so gracefully proportioned that she's often asked if she's ever modeled. She is also highly intelligent and successful. Although she is quick to laugh and has an unpretentious, easygoing air, under the surface there is a subtle tension and edginess about her. At the time she was first interviewed, Caroline was in her early thirties and had just received a major promotion to a very powerful position in the magazine industry.

At first glance, few people could be as different from George, the state trooper discussed in the previous chapter. Whereas George grew up with a conscious fantasy of finding his one true love, Caroline grew up with a sense that the possibilities for romantic involvement in her life were endless. Through high school, college, and her late twenties, she had dates and boyfriends galore. Many of her boyfriends wanted to marry her, but Caroline "always felt it was too soon. I wanted to get a solid career behind me before settling down. I wanted to take my time and play the field for a while, too."

In further contrast to George, Caroline was also not one to think "this is it" every time she became infatuated or sexually enthralled with someone. "There had always been boyfriends, so I was accustomed to thinking, 'If this doesn't work out, it won't be the end of the world. Soon enough, someone else will come along. Probably someone better, too,' " she explained. As a result, she felt great freedom to be herself in relationships. "A lot of women I know won't ever speak their minds in their relationships because they're afraid that if they do, the guy will leave and they'll never have another relationship again," she explained. "But with all my boyfriends, I was very straightforward about who I was and what I wanted. Some of them sometimes had a hard time with that, but most liked and respected me for it."

Although she described most of her past relationships as essentially good ones, none was ever so satisfying that Caroline felt she wanted to make a permanent commitment. In her early thirties, however, she began feeling that she was now ready to get married and have children. Yet at precisely the point in her life when she started to feel this way, she also began having the horrible feeling that "maybe it's too late for me, maybe I waited too long and my time has already come and gone." Fate seemed to have taken an ironic twist. "When I didn't want to settle down, men were always there," she explained. "But now that I want to settle down, I can hardly find decent guys to date. It's like fate is saying 'ha-ha on you: this is what you get for having squandered all those opportunities before.'"

When she was first interviewed, Caroline was aware that her ever-increasing sense that "It's Too Late for Me; My Time Has Run Out" was acting as a love block. Whereas once she had been very social, she was feeling too depressed to go out much. When she did marshal her energies and go out, she often behaved in ways unlikely to increase her appeal to men. "When I go to a party, I act like this is the last party I'll ever get invited to in my whole life, so I *have to* find someone there," she explained. "Or else I go already convinced I won't meet anyone interesting. Then I send out aloof, ice-queen vibes of 'who cares? what's the point?' and so, of course, I don't meet anyone." Either way, she would go home feeling even more convinced that her time was up.

Clearly, Caroline's sense of diminishing possibilities had some basis in objective reality. Many men her age and older prefer considerably younger women. Moreover, many men are intimidated by a woman's success, and even those who aren't intimidated often still become resentful if a woman isn't willing to curtail her involvement in work once they begin dating her. Finally, although Caroline still had plenty of time to have children, the end of her childbearing years was beginning to come into sight.

Although these facts contributed to Caroline's sense that her time was fast running out, they alone didn't explain it. Caroline knew a number of women many years older than she who seemed to have little problem finding suitable men to date. She also knew from her own experience that many younger men prefer older women. And she knew that while her childbearing years were not endless, they weren't going to be over tomorrow, either. Finally, Caroline further knew that "life is full of surprises," and that many people who once thought their time for romance was over found themselves meeting someone and falling in love anyway, even at the age of sixty-five and older. So the question remained: after so many years of believing that "the possibilities for love in my life are endless," why did Caroline suddenly shift her view and become susceptible to the sexist, pernicious, and fallacious belief that once a woman hits her thirties, that's it—her time for love is over?

When this question was posed to Caroline at the time of her first interview, she could not answer it. That changed when she was contacted a year and a half later. In the interim, she had gone into therapy and obtained a number of different insights that she thought explained why she had fallen prey to the "It's Too Late for Me; My Time Has Run Out" block. She also had made great headway in overcoming that block—enough headway that she was seriously and happily involved with a man and was considering marrying him.

The Change Process: Caroline Increases Her Awareness

Caroline was initially averse to the idea of psychotherapy. She feared she would be betraying her parents. "They did the best they could, and I had a pretty good childhood," she explained. "I'd feel terrible, really ungrateful, if someone started pushing me to look for ways they failed me. It would be disloyal." But after reading a number of self-help books and talking to friends who had been in therapy, Caroline decided to try it. Although still reluctant to view her childhood with even slight criticalness, she has stuck with the process because she feels it has helped her learn a great deal about "who I am and how I operate inside."

For Caroline, as for George in the preceding chapter, the major task of therapy was developing a heightened awareness of who she was, what she felt, how she behaved, and why. Although she had been brought up in a much happier, warmer home than George, and had many more material advantages—including an excellent education—than he, she, too, had gone through most of her life with only a limited awareness of her own psychology and its development. Never an introspective type to begin with, she had spent her school years focused on academics and having fun, and in her twenties had used her analytic skills mainly in her career. Although she gave the appearance of a woman who knew what she wanted and what she was about, in fact she had only a dim understanding of her own inner life.

One of the first things Caroline learned was that there was more synchronicity involved in her development of the "It's Too Late for Me; My Time Has Run Out" block than she had been aware of. It was no accident that she developed this block at the time in her life when her childbearing years no longer stretched ahead into the far, far future. Nor was it any accident that she developed it at precisely a time when there was a swelling of sentiment against women who had opted to stay single much longer than was traditional. These two developments helped make conditions right for Caroline to develop her block. But a third element of timing was equally important. Caroline developed this block at precisely the age when many people find that unresolved issues from childhood begin to catch up with them. There are many people who, like Caroline, appear to breeze through their twenties doing fine. Even if they came from very troubled homes, they often seem unaffected by the past. But when they get into their thirties, many start suffering from depression, dwindling self-esteem, and the general feeling that "things are falling apart." These feelings are usually signaling one of two things: either they *were* affected by the unhappy childhood experiences they thought hadn't affected them, or their childhoods weren't really as happy and trouble free as they had thought. Either way, they had better start dealing with their pasts, beginning with an honest look at what really happened.

In therapy Caroline realized that her underlying problem was guilt, just as it was for George. It was guilt resurfacing from her past that made Caroline susceptible to developing the "It's Too Late for Me; My Time Has Run Out" block at this point in her life. This block was, in effect, a form of self-punishment for Caroline. If she had not developed this particular block, her resurfacing guilt probably would have expressed itself in another way.

As Caroline took a closer look at what had happened in her life, she became aware that she felt guilty about three different things. First, she felt guilty about being "selfish and greedy." The youngest of four daughters, Caroline grew up in an upper-middle-class home where there seemed to be plenty of both love and money to go around. Her parents were responsible, generally kind people who did their best to provide their daughters with a loving, happy home. Yet there was always a faint air of resentment from the parents about how much they gave the children. As Caroline began to look below the surface of the happy scenes of home life she had preserved in her mind, she recalled that she and her sisters were often told they were spoiled and selfish, "that we were given everything in life and had things too easy." Her parents made it clear that their own childhoods had been much more difficult. "You've been given everying, it's been handed to you," Caroline's father would tell her. "But for me it was different. I grew up in the Depression, and either worked for what I got, or I did without." Caroline's mother also frequently made seemingly offhand references to the deprivations she suffered during her own childhood. In one incident, Caroline was having a birthday party (probably her fifth or sixth) and her mother became tearful as she watched Caroline open her presents. "My parents never gave me more than one present on my birthday," she said with a heavy sigh. "They couldn't afford to. You don't know how lucky you are." Another time, Caroline was making her father a pencil holder for Father's Day when her mother said wistfully, "It must be nice to have a father on Father's Day. I can hardly remember mine. He died when I was a little girl, just about your age, in fact."

During Caroline's childhood and adolescence, Caroline's father, a prominent lawyer, was rarely at home evenings. Years later, Caroline would discover that the main reason was that he had a mistress; at the time, though, the accepted line was that Dad was working late at the office or having dinner with clients. The children were told that they had no right to complain about his absences since he was out working to support them. "There was always the insinuation that Dad put in marathon hours because we were so greedy and expensive," Caroline recalled. "We were supposed to be grateful that he was out there earning money for our braces. We weren't supposed to want more."

Caroline's parents were not mean-spirited people. They did not set out to raise daughters who would feel guilty about how much they took or were given in life. But growing up in an atmosphere in which there was always a faint undercurrent of resentment in the air, the girls were bound to feel guilty about their good fortune.

Of all the daughters, Caroline may have had the greatest guilt, because she was the one whom fate seemed especially to favor. She was the one who got the most as far as brains, looks, and personality were concerned. Her guilt about having been given too much increased as she grew older and began to date. Although the youngest, Caroline quickly surpassed her sisters in terms of popularity with boys. "There were a lot of times when one of my sisters wouldn't have a date, and I'd get asked out by four different guys for the same night," Caroline explained. "No one came right out and accused me of stealing boys, but there was this general agreement in the family that I was hogging them, and that if I hadn't been around, my sisters' social lives would have been just fine."

But Caroline felt guilty not just about the number of boyfriends she had. The second thing she felt guilty about, she eventually realized, was that she'd been sexually active with a good number of these boyfriends over the years. Intellectually, Caroline was an emancipated woman who enjoyed her sexual freedom; emotionally, she was more conflicted. Consciously, she adamantly rejected such antiquated notions as "sex is dirty," and such sexist ones as "good girls don't," but these are the types of beliefs she was raised with, and somewhere in her unconscious they took root. Now that she was in her thirties, her long-buried guilt about having had "too many" boyfriends in the past was dovetailing with her buried guilt about having had sex with so many of them. Or, to put it in simpler terms, now her guilt about being "greedy" was combining with her guilt about being "dirty." As a way of punishing herself for having had a surfeit of sexual pleasure in the past, she was now telling herself, "You had more chances than you deserved, more than most people dream of getting. Well, now your time is up. You're just 'used goods,' and you're not getting any more!"

Caroline also realized that her guilt about having been so sexually active was further fueled by the moralizing that had arisen in the wake of the AIDS epidemic. Caroline has a number of male friends who are gay, and while she and they know that AIDS is *not* God's way of punishing the promiscuous, they have nevertheless been disquieted by the claim that AIDS is a curse that its victims brought on themselves by having too much sexual pleasure. Intellectually, Caroline has always rejected such charges as ridiculous and hateful. Emotionally, however, they have had an undercutting effect.

On top of all this, Caroline felt guilty for yet a third reason: because her life had turned out to be so different from her mother's. When Caroline was a child, no one in the family anticipated that any of the daughters would end up as an independent career woman who would enter her thirties neither married nor a mother. Each was raised with the expectation that she follow in her mother's footsteps, marrying early and defining herself primarily as a wife and mother. Now, even though Caroline was happy with her choices, she still was bound to experience pangs of guilt *because she had choices that her mother did not*—and had taken advantage of those choices. Once again, Caroline found herself in the position of having things—in this case choices—someone else didn't have, and that someone was her mother.

If Caroline had not been generally happy with her choices, she probably would not have felt so guilty. Her greatest source of guilt, in fact, was the satisfaction she had felt for most of her life. If she had been miserable, she and her mother would share at the least the same inner experience of being unfulfilled. As it is, Caroline's contentment means that not only has Caroline rejected her mother's way of life, she's also outdistancing her mother, showing her up.

In going beyond her mother, Caroline realized, she felt that somehow she had betrayed her mother. She knew in her head that this was not true, but unconsciously she viewed herself as disloyal. Moreover, she felt she had betrayed her entire gender. This, she eventually realized, was because she had grown up without any models of women who were at once independent, sexual, and happy. The only really happy women she was exposed to while growing up were mothers on TV family shows, and they were neither independent nor very sexual. In cultural depictions overtly sexual women were generally presented as miserable, Caroline realized: witness Hester Prynne and Anna Karenina from fiction, and Marilyn Monroe in real life. Moreover, if a woman was highly sexual, she couldn't be independent; if left without a man, she would fall apart or commit suicide.

Caroline's guilt about surpassing her mother and betraying the other members of her sex was enough to create problems in itself. But add to it her guilt about being "greedy" and her guilt about being "dirty," and it's inevitable that Caroline would have come to view herself at some level as a "bad girl" who deserved punishment. And given all the cultural messages she has been exposed to, it's no surprise that she would have ended up punishing herself by starting to buy the notion that a woman in her thirties with a history of affairs is "used goods" whose time for romance is long since gone.

The Change Process: Caroline Takes Concrete Action

As George's story in the preceding chapter illustrates, when a person has done something wrong or hurtful and suffers guilt as a result, the best antidote is self-forgiveness. But unlike George, who had done something that could objectively be considered hurtful—leaving his wife and children—Caroline had committed no "sin," only gone against some of the traditions and moral codes she was raised with. What Caroline needed, then, was not to forgive herself, but to understand and accept that she had done nothing that needed forgiving. She needed to give herself permission to be greedy.

Caroline's therapist, a woman in her late forties whom Caroline much admired, tried to get Caroline to do this but to no avail. Time and again, she asked Caroline to consider, "What's wrong with being greedy? What's wrong with getting a lot in life?" Caroline could never come up with a convincing answer, but still she could not let go of the notion that getting a lot from life was bad.

Knowing that Caroline respected and cared for her, the therapist said, "Caroline, I want to tell you something about myself. I'm a greedy pig. Whatever life offers me, I take. I am a selfish, spoiled, greedy pig. Do you think this makes me a bad person?" As the therapist said this, she grinned and held her head aloft in a show of exaggerated self-confidence. Caroline laughed. "I get the point," she told the therapist. "You want me to see that I don't condemn other people for getting a lot in life, only myself. I see that. I realize that I have a double standard. I think it's okay for you to be greedy and selfish, but it's not okay for me to. I realize all that, but still I can't get it out of my head. I don't think I'll ever feel there's nothing wrong with my being greedy."

After several months of being stalled on this issue, Caroline arrived for a session feeling very frustrated and angry. "I feel like I've gone around and around over the same territory over and over and I'm getting nowhere," she said. "I still feel guilty and I'm tired of talking about it! I want to get off my ass and do something about it!" Caroline's therapist sat forward in her chair and smiled. "Like what?" she asked. "I don't know," Caroline said in a lowered voice, "you tell me." "Okay," the therapist agreed. "There's an age-old way of getting rid of guilt that might help you. The Catholics call it penance, but I don't like that term, it's too punitive. I'd prefer to call it something like 'making amends.' Or, since your issue is guilt about supposedly having taken too much, it may be best to call it 'giving back.' Do you think there's anything you could do that would make you feel that you're evening things out, that you're giving back to the world in return for what you think you've taken? I'm not recommending that you actually do anything, just that you think about whether there might be some activity that would make you feel that you are giving to the world as much as you've taken from it."

Caroline and her therapist had many discussions about the notion of "giving back" in ensuing sessions. Caroline came to like the idea. She thought it might be a more feasible strategy in her particular case than giving up the notion that being greedy is bad—something Caroline believed she would never be able to do.

Caroline came up with several ideas of ways in which she could "give back" to the world—doing volunteer work caring for AIDS patients, working at a safe house for battered women, helping out at a soup kitchen for the homeless. Her therapist cautioned her, however, to consider whether these activities would really make her feel better; because they would bring her into such close contact with people far less fortunate than she, Caroline might actually end up feeling more guilt. The therapist suggested that, instead, she think more along the lines of helping someone with whom she had more in common. Finally, Caroline decided to volunteer as an aide in an after-school dance program for young children. The children came from a variety of schools, and thus a variety of socioeconomic backgrounds, so Caroline would not feel that she was being "one of the greedy helping out the needy." And while Caroline would be giving of herself, this work would be pleasurable enough to avoid the trap of "self-punishment through charitable acts" that her therapist warned her about.

Caroline's work with the children has had an impact on her life in several ways. First, she has felt a lessening of her guilt. Gradually, she is coming to feel that "it's okay for me to have gotten a lot out of life; after all, I give back." Second, by working closely with children, she has become more in touch with her own inner child, and aware of her neediness and sadness. She has come to realize that she did not, in fact, "get everything" when she was growing up; and as she has come to terms with the fact that she, like most people, suffered real emotional deprivation, she has become more compassionate toward herself. Third, the children Caroline works with have turned out to be an unexpected source of new love in her life. A boon in itself, this has also helped Caroline realize that as long as there are children on earth, there will always be opportunities for adults like herself to get love, no matter how "over the hill" they are.

Working with children has also helped Caroline develop more patience. She has grown more aware that learning and growth take time, and that children need to be allowed to proceed at their own pace. As she has become more sensitive to the danger of hurrying children to learn and grow, she has become more sensitive to her own inner clock, her own need to do things—including the task of "getting better" in therapy—at her own inner-directed pace. Whereas before she used to tell herself impatiently that she had to move faster, now she tells herself, "Easy does it. Go slow. Take your time."

Caroline's increased sense of patience has had a dramatic effect on her relationships with men. When her "It's Too Late for Me; My Time Has Run Out" block was at its peak, she nevertheless met several men in whom she was romantically interested. Yet her hopelessness caused her to approach them with too much desperation. "Every time I went on a date," she explained, "I had this anxious, panicked feeling that this guy has to be 'it' for me. The first time out I'd feel that if we weren't married and mortgaged and starting a family by next week, forget it—I'd never get another chance." With the pressure so high at the outset, it was inevitable that the men got scared early on and either let her down gently or just disappeared.

By the time she started seeing a man named Jeff, Caroline's earlier panic had been replaced by greater patience. As her therapist prodded her to look more closely at her past relationships, she had come to realize that in most cases she had never given them enough time to develop into something really serious and lasting. Although she had long viewed herself as someone who had already had numerous chances for love in her life, it dawned on her that, in fact, she had never given any of her prior relationships with men a chance. She had gone through her life like a woman running through a banquet hall, grabbing what she could off the tables and wolfing it down as though she were afraid that any second a buzzer would go off and her feeding time would be up. Now she decided that the time had come to try a seven-course, sit-down meal.

When she first met Jeff, she made a conscious choice to go slowly. In the past, she would jump into bed with a guy she felt attracted to, and be quick to pour out her innermost feelings to him, too. But this time they got to know each other slowly, as friends first. Only after three months of "friendly dating" did Caroline feel ready to return one of Jeff's kisses. And after they started kissing, they spent several weeks of kissing and petting before they finally slept together. At the time of Caroline's last interview, she and Jeff had been seriously involved for eight months and were beginning to talk about marriage. However, Caroline was "not interested in rushing things. We still need time to build a relationship before running up the aisle, and we're going to take that time."

Significantly, Jeff is six years younger than Caroline, but the age difference is something they hardly ever notice. "It's given me a real different perspective," Caroline said. "People place so much emphasis on the importance of chronological age, especially for women, but all that does is create a lot of unnecessary barriers for everyone." Moreover, Caroline has learned from Jeff that not all men are as interested in twenty-year-olds as is so often assumed. "Sometimes when we see a girl who is so young and untouched-looking, I'll ask Jeff if he wouldn't prefer someone like that—God knows, he could have his pick," Caroline explained. "But he always says, 'But someone my age or younger wouldn't have your wisdom, your depth, your experience. Besides, you're the one I love.' "

Guilt tends to linger in the psyche, no matter how much headway is made in overcoming it; and since Caroline had so much guilt about so many things, she of course has not eliminated guilt from her life entirely. Nor has she been completely "cured" of her "It's Too Late for Me; My Time Has Run Out" block. She still has vestiges of it, and there are days when she reverts to that panicked feeling of "uh-oh, my time's up. I'm over the hill." This happens particularly when she reads yet another magazine or newspaper article about the despair of single women in their thirties and forties, or hears another warning to women about their fast-ticking "biological clocks." Fed up, Caroline has devised new biological clock imagery for herself. "The image that used to come to mind was of a woman's ovaries and fallopian tubes running dry and shriveling up," she explained. "That was really depressing. Now when I hear the term 'biological clock,' I think of the Tin Man in *The Wizard of Oz,* and how we call the heart 'a ticker.' I've realized that your heart is the only biological clock that really matters. As long as you've got one ticking in your chest, love can still come into your life. Like they say in baseball, 'it ain't over until it's over.' "

Chapter 11
"I'll Inevitably Get Hurt"

Love and closeness always entail the risk of getting hurt. When you care about others and are open to receiving their love, you are then vulnerable to the vicissitudes of their individual personalities and the life events that affect them. Inevitably, there will be times when the people you care about criticize you, disappoint you, take you for granted, or in some other way cause you pain. And there is always the risk that someone you rely on for love will partially or completely withdraw from the relationship or will die, leaving you feeling abandoned and bereft, perhaps aching with loss.

For many people, these risks are worth taking because of the myriad pleasures and benefits that close involvements potentially could bring. Others, however, have a much harder time putting the risks of getting hurt in this sort of perspective. According to their inner view, love always leads to hurt, and to such enormous hurt that the pleasure is sure to be far outstripped by the pain.

When Being Loved Means Being Hurt

Some people equate being loved with being hurt because as children their primary contact with their parents was through violence or disinterest. Their parents related mostly by beating and punishing them; when not actively abusing them, the parents didn't pay much attention at all to the children, who then grew up believing being loved means being maltreated and ignored.

People who were beaten as children often say, "After a while, it didn't really hurt anymore" and "It was better to have been beaten than to have been ignored. Getting 'the silent treatment' was much worse than being hit." Similiar rationalizations are commonly used by victims of childhood sexual abuse, who say, "It wasn't so bad" and "At least I got some attention." Because children have such a great need for parental contact, even abusive, violent contact may seem better than none.

But even children who were not routinely abused may still learn to link being loved and being hurt. "I'm only doing this because I love you," "This hurts me more than it hurts you," and "If I didn't love you so much, I wouldn't be doing this" are all stock lines that have come out of many parents' mouths as they discipline their children. These words tell the children that what they're receiving is love, while the children's natural reaction is to feel fearful, angry, humiliated, victimized, and very much unloved. Children in this situation thus learn to invalidate their own feelings and, instead, to internalize the parental messages, telling themselves that "I got the punishment I deserved" and "they only did that to me because they loved me and wanted me to turn out all right."

Cultural Messages

The idea that love, particularly romantic love, inevitably leads to hurt enjoys widespread currency in popular culture, especially music. Again and again in country songs, singers lament the pain that love brings, as in the song "The Pain of Loving You." A main theme of jazz and blues is also the heartache and heartbreak that inevitably result from being in love, as the songs recorded by Billie Holliday illustrate so well. This is a time-honored theme in top-forty songs, too, with "Heartbreak Hotel," "I Heard It Through the Grapevine," "The Tracks of My Tears," "Tears on My Pillow" and "As Tears Go By" being just a few titles that quickly come to mind. That loving leads to hurting is a common theme in literature as well, from classics like *Romeo and Juliet*, *Anna Karenina*, and *Madame Bovary* to the

pulp romance novels known as "bodice rippers" to best-sellers like
Love Story.

Although everyone is exposed to the idea that love leads to pain,
males and females receive messages that are subtly, but significantly,
different. The common message relayed to males by parents and
peers, as well as the media, is that loving will lead to loss of power
and freedom. Boys and men are encouraged to sow their wild oats
by having sexual contact with the opposite sex, but they're also cautioned not to let themselves get emotionally involved. Once a man
gives his heart away, they learn, he becomes a "fool for love" who
has lost his autonomy and power and, like a draft animal, has been
"saddled" with burdensome, restricting responsibilities.

Girls and women learn that love brings pain of a very different
sort. The message they traditionally have received, often directly from
their parents, is that "boys are after only one thing" and if a girl
"gives it away" to a particular boy, he will inevitably lose respect for
her and discard her as "used goods." For girls and women, love
supposedly brings not only the private pain of heartache, it also carries
the risk of being branded a "bad" girl or "loose woman" and being
publicly humiliated and ostracized as a result. From that classic of
American literature *The Scarlet Letter* to the classic film *Back Street,*
carnal love has been commonly depicted as having particularly severe
consequences for girls and women who "give in" to it.

In recent years, this attitude has lost currency, yet it has not entirely
disappeared. This is clear from the punitive, shame-inducing beliefs
about women's sexuality adhered to by many fundamentalist Christians, Orthodox Jews, and Muslims. It's also apparent from the mainstream success of the 1987 box-office blockbuster *Fatal Attraction,*
in which assertive female sexuality is equated with lethal insanity,
and the 1986 best-seller *The Good Mother,* about a separated woman
whose newly blossoming sexuality causes her to become so addled
that she fails in her maternal duties and is duly punished by losing
custody of her young daughter.

Tragically, the notion that sexual intimacy leads to suffering has
been further fueled by the AIDS epidemic, which has devastated the
gay male community and taken the lives of thousands of others,
particularly among the nation's poorest. Given the grim statistics, it

makes sense that many people, especially those in high-risk groups, would now fear that sexual contact, even the most gentle and loving, could mean death. If someone in a high-risk group already had the "I'll Inevitably Get Hurt" block before the epidemic, his anxiety about AIDS would certainly reinforce it. However, if AIDS is a high-risk person's *sole* reason for fearing that physical intimacy could lead to harm, his anxiety would *not* fit our definition of a love block. A love block is a psychological pattern that can be overcome through emotional growth, whereas AIDS is a physical disease that as yet is incurable. The way to resolve anxiety about AIDS is to find a cure, and that requires a collective effort by the government and scientific community.

Pain Avoiders and Addicts

Those with the "I'll Inevitably Get Hurt" block usually fall into two general categories: pain avoiders and pain addicts. Pain avoiders are primarily motivated by their fear of the pain they're certain will follow if they allow themselves to love and be loved. Depending on the extent and exact nature of their fear, they either steer clear of intimate attachments altogether, or they get into relationships but then distance themselves or bolt as soon as genuine closeness begins to develop.

Although pain avoiders can be of either gender and any sexual orientation, this manifestation of the "I'll Inevitably Get Hurt" block is particularly common among heterosexual men. Many go from one romantic involvement to the next, retreating or disappearing when true intimacy begins to develop. If someone repeats the pattern of pain avoidance to the point where it becomes a way of life, he inevitably develops another major love block in the process. This block— "I Just Can't Make a Commitment"—and its relationship to the "I'll Inevitably Get Hurt" block are discussed in Chapter 13.

Pain addicts are also certain that pain will follow if they allow themselves to love and be loved. What sets them apart from pain avoiders is that they are more than willing to suffer incredible amounts of pain for the sake of love. In fact, like moths to a flame, they frequently are drawn to precisely those people who will hurt them most. To them, if a relationship does not entail a certain amount of pain, it's obviously not a real love relationship after all.

In recent years, pain addicts have begun to receive a good deal of attention in such books as Robin Norwood's *Women Who Love Too Much* and Susan Forward's *Men Who Hate Women and the Women Who Love Them*.[1] These books reflect the mushrooming interest over the past decade in the problems suffered by adult children of alcoholics, incest survivors, and others who grew up in so-called dysfunctional families. In this type of family, one or both of the parents have a severe problem—alcoholism, drug abuse, chronic gambling, incapacitating physical ailments, mental illness, frequent rage, or abusiveness, for example—that dominates family life to the point where the family's main focus becomes reacting to the troubled parent's sickness rather than taking care of the growing children's emotional and physical needs. The great majority of pain addicts come from this kind of family.

Although pain addicts can be either male or female, straight or gay, the most emblematic example has come to be the heterosexual woman who repeatedly gets involved with men who are as ridden with problems as were her parents. Be they alcoholics, drug addicts, womanizers, bullies, batterers, financial ne'er do-wells, or just emotionally withholding, these are men whose names spell trouble with a capital *T,* and who bring the women who love them enormous pain.

Yet these men also tend to have some very attractive qualities, and they have moments or go through periods when they can be extremely loving, which is usually true of even the "worst" parents. This crucial point is key to understanding why pain addicts behave as they do. Even the most egregiously maltreated children rarely grow up entirely without love. Parents who are generally unloving, distracted, or abusive to their children usually have moments when they can be kind, attentive, gentle, good-humored, and loving. It's the parental unpredictability that causes children to become "hooked" on painful relationships. When a parent is *always* unloving, his children may simply give up on him, turning their search for love to people who are more capable of giving it on a more sustained basis. When a parent is *occasionally* loving, however, the children will focus on trying to cause one of the loving occasions to occur; knowing that there's "good stuff" inside the parent, they'll do all they can to try to get some more of it to come out. Each time the generally unloving parent shows some kindness and affection, the children try to remember exactly what they said and did to make this happen; if they do those things again, they figure, more good stuff will come their way. When this doesn't happen, the children do not see that the parent's behavior has nothing to do with them; instead, they figure they haven't done the right thing, or done it in exactly the right way. Each failure to get the parent to show his loving side just further convinces the children that it's their own fault that the parent is unloving, that they must have done something wrong.[2]

Once hooked, pain addicts repeat this tragic pattern in their adult relationships, particularly the romantic ones. Again and again, they become involved with people who are as hard to get love out of as their problem-ridden parents were. Longing to finally get the parental love they never received, they are driven by a classic repetition compulsion, an unconscious urge to keep reexperiencing their early family relationships until they achieve mastery over the situation and can change the outcome. Unconsciously, pain addicts have decided, "I'm going to keep doing this over and over again until I get it right."

Some would charge that pain addicts, particularly female ones, are masochists—those who derive pleasure from pain. But pain addicts do not find being hurt in their relationships pleasurable at all; they often find the pain they experience excruciatingly hard to bear. Pain doesn't feel *good* to them, it feels *right*—because it's so familiar. It's easy to get frustrated with pain addicts, to say that if they're unhappy in their relationships, it's their own fault for continually choosing the wrong kind of people to get involved with. In fact, though, by replicating their early pain they're really trying to find a way to end their suffering. "If I go through this once more," they figure, "I'll finally be able to find the way out."

Elaine: Hooked on Pain

Elaine, a successful photographer with a dynamic personality, has been trying to find the way out for many of her thirty-two years.

Small-boned but buxom, Elaine has dark, exotic looks. While not conventionally pretty, there's something so alluring about her that she's frequently described as "a knockout." A great storyteller, she has a deep, husky voice that further adds to her magnetism.

Over the years, Elaine has had sexual relationships with both women and men, although the majority have been with men. Between the ages of fifteen and twenty-three, she was "very free spirited and daring, and slept with a lot of people." Since then, she's had a number of intense relationships. Two lasted more than a year, but most ended within six months or less. At the time of her first interview, she had been "passionately in love" for more than a year and a half with a married man named Roy, a powerful and wealthy executive in the entertainment industry who is twice her age. "I've known from the start that there's no future with Roy," Elaine said. "It's not just that he's married, it's also that he's not going to be around as long as I will." Then with a sigh that turned into a laugh, she added, "I sometimes wonder what's wrong with me that I can't have the same boyfriend for five years like everyone else."

The two longest affairs Elaine had in the past were with "men I thought could be committed at first, but who turned out to be noncommittal types." The other men she's gotten involved with have also been emotionally unavailable—either because they were married, gay, or incapable of being intimate and reliable within a romantic relationship. A generally assertive woman, Elaine wouldn't stand for it if a landlord, employer, or business associate treated her unfairly or exploited her. Yet in romantic relationships, it's as though she accepts pain as a given. "I've known some really nice guys, but I could never get very excited about them," she explained. "It's guys who are exciting and unpredictable and elusive that I seem really to go for. Whenever I fall in love, it's always with someone who can't fulfill my needs, or can't be bothered to try."

Elaine and her two older brothers grew up in an unconventional home. Her father, a painter and sculptor, stayed home and took care of the children while her mother, a union organizer, went off to work. Her parents were both children of Russian Jews who immigrated to the United States shortly before the Bolshevik revolution, and who held fast to the hope that a worldwide socialist revolution

would one day occur, ushering in a new age of progress and fulfillment for all humanity. Elaine's parents were actively involved in left-
wing politics themselves, but although this created some problems
for them during the McCarthy period, Elaine does not recall any
serious repercussions.

Elaine's mother "was a Marxist, but otherwise very conventional
and straitlaced and repressed." Her father, however, was "very flamboyant and passionate and sexy and hip." Although she was always
aware of her mother's strength and reliability, Elaine never felt much
warmth from her. Her father was "my real source of love and affection
and deep connection," Elaine explained. "He and I were kindred
spirits. He adored me, made me feel like a princess, like I was the
most special person in the world. I would run home every day from
school to meet him. We were together all the time."

Elaine's relationship with her father was also fraught with anxiety.
When she was four, her father had a major heart attack. Over the
next twelve years, he suffered others, and when Elaine was sixteen
he finally died. "He was everything in the world to me," Elaine
recalled. "And every day I woke up and went to sleep worrying that
he would die. I spent my childhood waiting for my whole world to
be taken away from me."

For Elaine, the feeling of being loved became inextricably linked
to the feeling that loss is imminent. In her relationship with her
father, "there was always the sense that I'm getting all this love and
attention now, but it's going to end soon, so I'd better get it while
I can." This is essentially the same scenario that she has replicated
with her lovers. When Elaine is involved in a romantic relationship,
she is by her own admission very demanding. She is forceful in
putting out her needs to her lovers and saying, in essence, "give me
what I want." But the lovers she chooses all have something about
them that virtually guarantees the relationships will be short-lived.
So while she gets a lot from her lovers when she is with them, it's
always within a context where she knows the lover will be leaving
within hours (often to go back to his wife or other lover), or that
the relationship is heading for a dead end.

The dynamic is illustrated by Elaine and Roy's relationship, which
revolves around passionate trysts at her apartment during the week
when he can steal away from his office. On occasion, they get to take

short trips together, but other than that they never spend the night together or see each other on weekends. When he is with Elaine, Roy showers her with gifts, flowers, champagne, and a good deal of money. He gives her his full attention, makes love to her with ardor, and tells her she is the most wonderful, beautiful creature on earth. Elaine believes Roy is sincere when he expresses his love for her, and when she is with him she says she feels "utterly, completely loved." All this occurs, however, in a situation wherein Elaine knows there is no possibility that this feeling of being completely loved will go on indefinitely. Roy has made it clear that he will never divorce his wife, and he is in his sixties besides. There is no chance, then, that Elaine's needs for love will continue to get met well into the future. With Roy, there is not even the chance that he will be there the next morning, much less ten years from now.

Elaine feels confident she has plenty of years left before her sexual attractiveness begins to wane. Nevertheless, there's an element of the "It's Too Late for Me; My Time Has Run Out" block at work in conjunction with her "I'll Inevitably Get Hurt" block. Within her relationships, she sees the time to get her needs met as definitely limited (which it is). Whenever she feels loved, there is always imminent loss looming in the background, framing the nature of the interactions and casting a shadow upon them. In this way, she replays her experience with her father.

One of the most significant aspects of Elaine's relationships with family members and friends as well as lovers is that they involve "a lot of dramatic ruptures." When she has a disagreement or argument with someone close to her, she explained, "often I sort of mentally blank out so I can't respond in a reasonable way. I freeze the other person out, refuse to budge from my position or even talk to them. I'll just slam the phone down with a big 'Fuck you! Get out of my life!' " But the last thing she really wants at these times is for the other person to take her at her word. "I really want the other person to come begging, to prove to me how much they care," she explained. "If they don't, then I feel abandoned and immediately my hurt turns to anger, and then to revenge. I imagine scenarios of the other person plotting against me, and then I concoct scenarios in which they have to suffer horribly for the hurt and suffering they've caused me."

Elaine is aware that this type of behavior is destructive and blocks her from receiving love, understanding, and sympathy from the people who are close to her. But she has a compulsion to bring on these "dramatic ruptures" for at least three reasons. First, in creating a situation of high drama, she reexperiences the same sense of being intensely alive that she had with her flamboyant, passionate father, and which was heightened even further by the way his illness put everyone constantly on edge. Second, in closing people out yet feeling that she is the one who has been abandoned, she reexperiences the pain of being left by her father while at the same time feeling she has some control over the situation. Unconsciously, Elaine is compelled to keep going through the experience of losing a loved one with the hope that one day she'll finally have mastered the situation and will be able to control—and change—the ending. Third, by creating a situation in which she feels hurt and becomes extremely angry as a result, she is giving herself an indirect but nonetheless effective way of letting out some of the rage she has toward her father for dying on her—rage that's boiled within for decades but has never been directly expressed.

Another significant aspect of Elaine's behavior is that she can be extremely tolerant of loved ones' failures and limitations in some contexts, but in others will suddenly become so impatient and intolerant that she again loses all semblance of reason. In her relationship with Roy, for example, Elaine accepts great limitations on the amount of time they can spend together. But when they are together, or have planned to be, Elaine cannot tolerate any of her needs being frustrated even in the slightest. If she and Roy are together and she wants to make love, Roy had better make love, and he'd better do it now. Or if she and Roy had plans to get together at four o'clock on a particular day, and he calls and says he can't get there until five, Elaine reacts with impatience, rage, and panic. She has to get what she wants now, this very instant. This is the same phenomenon discussed in Chapter 10, about the "It's Too Late for Me; My Time Has Run Out" block. What happens in these situations is that Elaine's primal emotional needs are activated, then frustrated, which causes her to feel like a small, needy, helpless baby again, and with that comes a reversion to an infant sense of time. Unable to distinguish between an hour or a day, the frustrated baby inside Elaine feels that if she has to wait any longer she'll die.

The Change Process: What Elaine Could Do

In the year between her first and last interview, Elaine broke up with Roy several times, each with a lot of loud fighting, dramatic scenes, and tearful, angry good-byes. Finally, however, they broke up for good. Since then, Elaine has become involved with another man with whom she's repeating many of the same patterns. However, through the process of talking about her childhood and adult relationships during the interviews for this book, Elaine started to gain some insights she thought were helpful, and she also started thinking "maybe I don't want to keep doing what I've been doing. I don't want to have to settle anymore. I want to be with someone I can spend a lot of time with, and I want more sex."

The fact that at this writing Elaine had not made any significant progress in overcoming her "I'll Inevitably Get Hurt" block does not mean that she won't eventually break free of this block. On the contrary, with a pain addict like Elaine there is enormous cause for optimism. Millions of people with very similar patterns have successfully broken them and moved on to more fulfilling relationships. What's more, never before in history have there been as many resources and as much information available for people like Elaine.

A whole book could be devoted to the problem of pain addiction. In fact, a book already has been—Norwood's *Women Who Love Too Much*.[3] If Elaine decided to start changing, getting a copy of that excellent book would be the most logical first step. Norwood's step-by-step advice is so comprehensive that it needs little elaboration, and it's so easily available that it makes no sense to try to reiterate it here. Suffice it to say that in the simple act of getting a copy, Elaine would be taking a giant step toward ultimately overcoming this love block.

The other major step would be for Elaine to find a caring, compassionate therapist who is not only familiar with the phenomenon of pain addiction, but also experienced in helping people deal with a loved one's death. One of the reasons Elaine keeps putting herself through experiences that replicate her loss of her father is that she has a never really dealt with her feelings about his death. Grief over the death of a parent or other close loved one, particularly one who died early, is not something that people work through in the few months or first year following the funeral. The sadness may become less constant and intense as time goes on, but most people never really "get over" a death. Instead they learn to live with the fact of their loss and the painful knowledge it brings, and the adjustment process continues for the rest of their lives, whether they consciously know it or not. However, people who have actively grieved and worked through the other feelings that death brings will be much more able to "get on" with their lives than someone who has not. If Elaine is to move on to relationships that will help her heal the wounds of the past instead of reliving them, she needs to do long-term work on a one-to-one basis with a compassionate, skilled, well-trained therapist or counselor who specializes in death-and-dying issues. Losing a beloved parent early in life causes such severe trauma and leaves scars so deep and lasting that it's virtually impossible to recover by self-help alone.

Patrick: A Pain Avoider

Patrick is a tall, lean former high-school basketball player who is a sports reporter for a daily newspaper. He started therapy when he was twenty-seven because he was having problems in his relationships with women. Bright, energetic, and a rapid-fire talker, Patrick had an edge of arrogance when he began treatment. He routinely referred to other people, especially men, as "assholes," and often came across as though his philosophy of life were "There's nothing anybody can teach me. I already know all I need to know about life." But behind this facade was actually a rather insecure young man who often felt intimidated by others, especially men, and who was eager to have relationships in which he could learn and grow. He also had a hidden curiosity about what makes human beings tick. These elements of his personality came more and more to the fore as his therapy progressed.

Patrick, one of two children from a working-class family, was a pain avoider. Whereas pain addicts like Elaine are driven to repeat past patterns again and again, pain avoiders are driven to make sure that the pain they suffered in the past is something they'll never go through again. "I took my chances once and got hurt," they in essence say. "And I'll be damned if I ever let that happen to me again."

When Patrick began therapy, he was still in pain over a relationship with a woman named Stephanie that had ended three years before, when he was twenty-four. After four years of steady dating, Stephanie told Patrick she no longer wanted to see him because she had met and fallen in love with another man. The news came as a "huge surprise" to Patrick, who had no idea she'd started to see someone else. It was also a crushing blow, because he loved Stephanie deeply and had begun having thoughts of marrying her. But he had never shared these thoughts with her. In fact, he had never once told her that he loved her.

Patrick was devastated. He started to drink a lot and had a series of one-night stands, but he still couldn't forget about Stephanie. He kept calling her, driving by her house, going by the place she worked, all in the hope that she would agree to come back to him. On several occasions he begged her to "say it's not over," but she told him emphatically that she wanted to remain with the other man. Although it was humiliating for Patrick to be doing these things, he explained that "I couldn't help myself. I couldn't bear the thought of not having her."

Six months after Stephanie dumped him, Patrick learned that the other man had left the area to pursue graduate studies and would not return until the summer. He seized the opportunity and badgered Stephanie until she finally agreed to go out with him again. They saw each other fairly steadily for a few months, and Patrick was convinced he had won her back. Then the other man unexpectedly came home one weekend and Stephanie canceled a date with Patrick to see him. This time Patrick knew that Stephanie was lost to him for good, but he kept pursuing her anyway. He wrote her love letters, sent flowers, and left scores of phone messages begging her to call back. But he never heard from her again.

Eventually, Patrick gave up and began dating other women. His post-Stephanie relationships all had a similar pattern. For a couple of months Patrick and the woman would enjoy seeing each other. Then the woman would tell Patrick she "really likes" or "really cares for" him and wants to see him more often, perhaps even exclusively.

Suddenly, Patrick's ardor and interest in the woman would vanish, and he would develop an infatuation with another. He'd tell the first woman that he's interested in someone else and therefore needed to end their relationship, which usually left the jilted one tearful, angry, and bewildered. The first time Patrick did this, a good friend of his said, "Are you crazy? She was terrific and she really liked you." In response, Patrick coolly remarked, "There are plenty of fish in the sea." After the pattern was repeated five or six more times, the same friend, Joe, told Patrick that he thought his behavior was destructive and irresponsible, and he suggested therapy. Conceding that his friend might have a point, Patrick eventually decided to give it a try.

The Change Process: Patrick Gains Awareness

Many people begin therapy acknowledging they might have a problem, but deep down they really don't believe it. Patrick gave lip service to the notion that he might need to do some looking at his life and behavior, and some changing, too, but basically he thought his way of relating to women wasn't really problematic. When his interest in a woman suddenly vanished, he really didn't think it had anything to do with any fears, insecurities, or unresolved psychological issues he might have. He believed that if he became instantaneously "turned off" to a woman he had started to feel strongly for, it simply meant that she wasn't "the right one for me." The first major task for Patrick was to become aware that things weren't so simple—that when a person repeats a destructive pattern in relationship after relationship, there's definitely something going on within that needs to be looked at and dealt with.

In his initial therapy sessions, Patrick talked almost exclusively about the emotional pain of being dumped by Stephanie, and repeatedly vowed, "I'm never going to allow myself to get hurt like that again." He spoke about his irreparable sense of loss and how utterly bereft her leaving had made him feel. The more he talked, the more he seemed to relax into his pain, to allow himself to feel it fully. This culminated in several sessions when he openly wept, tentatively at first, then in huge sobs that shook his whole body.

Working through his pain about being dumped by Stephanie

seemed to have opened Patrick up dramatically. When the links between his experience with her and what had happened since were pointed out, he did not express resistance or try to change the subject. He became animated, introspective, excited. He seemed to be experiencing the "click" of viscerally "getting it," understanding what his block was, where it came from, and how it worked. He said he realized that in each relationship since Stephanie his primary motivation had been to protect himself from reexperiencing the feeling of being dumped. He also said he realized that he was always overwhelmed with attraction to another woman at precisely the point when he began to feel really loved by the woman he was already seeing. He realized, he said, that he was afraid to take in this love and make himself vulnerable to the possibility that one day the woman might take her love away. And he said he realized that his sudden interest in another woman provided him with a convenient excuse to beat a hasty retreat.

As Patrick became more aware of his own motivations, he also became more sensitive to the fact that he had caused several women great pain. By playing a role of "hurt them before they hurt you" with the women in his life, Patrick had been doing to them precisely what Stephanie had done to him. But because Patrick still saw himself as a victim (of Stephanie's cruelty), it came as something of a shock for him to realize that in reality he had become an aggressor, one who had long since outdone Stephanie in racking up victims.

While Patrick did greatly increase his awareness of his behavior and the purposes it served, his awareness nevertheless only went so far. As discussed in Chapter 3, there's a big difference between "getting it" in your head and "getting it" in the gut way that's necessary for profound changes in perspective and behavior to take place. Although Patrick *talked* as if he had really "gotten it," the fact was that although he was staying in relationships a little longer, his pattern remained essentially the same. This suggested there was more behind his behavior than Stephanie's jilting, and that until he understood what it was, his "I'll Inevitably Get Hurt" block would prove intractable.

As he delved deeper into his past, Patrick was able to recall some incidents that indicated that his fear of getting hurt in intimate relationships had indeed been with him long before he met Stephanie. In one especially important session, he discussed the very strong friendship he had had with a boy named Henry when he was about ten, an age when a chum relationship with a friend of the same sex plays a crucial role in psychological development. For about a year, Patrick and Henry were inseparable. Then gradually Henry began to befriend some other boys who on several occasions had taunted Patrick and physically beaten him up. One day during recess at school, Henry joined in with his new friends in ridiculing and "ranking out" Patrick. In tears and feeling as though the wind had been knocked out of him, Patrick ran home. Both his parents were at work and his younger sister was out, so the apartment was empty. Patrick went to his room and sobbed into his pillow. That night he got sick to his stomach and had to stay home for almost a week. His parents were so absorbed in the daily struggle of their own lives that neither inquired in any depth about why Patrick wasn't playing with Henry anymore.

Another important and illuminating memory that eventually re-surfaced was of a time when Patrick was about five years old and there was a heavy snowstorm. The roads were impassable by car or bus, and most of the people in the city apartment building where Patrick's family lived waited out the bad weather indoors. Patrick's father, however, wouldn't let the storm immobilize him. Patrick remembers him taking off on foot very early in the morning, then returning several hours later with a brand-new sled. They went to a nearby park and spent the afternoon sledding, just the two of them. Patrick's face lit up as he began to recall this experience. "It didn't dawn on me until now," he said, "but my father must have trudged around in the snow for hours to find a store that wasn't closed that day." Then, as he described how special and loved his father had made him feel that day, Patrick suddenly felt a deep sadness well up in him, and he began to cry.

Patrick's tears were tears of grief over a loss he had never con-sciously acknowledged and never actively mourned. Just prior to recalling the time his father bought him the sled, Patrick had been talking about his sister, Pam, who is seven years younger than he. He had been saying that he had felt envious of her for as long as he could remember because she "was always the apple of my father's eye." Their father "adored" Pam and "they were always together laughing," Patrick explained. Also, he went on, "she could get away with things I couldn't get away with at all" and "she could do no wrong in my father's eyes."

Prior to this session, Patrick had paid little attention to his own relationship with his father, but as these memories unfolded he realized that he once had enjoyed special status with his father, and then promptly lost it when his sister came along. "After my sister was born, there was no more just having my father to myself," Patrick said in an understandably resentful tone. Nevertheless, when first asked whether he was upset about losing his father, Patrick persistently tried to downplay the impact that the loss had had on him. Only as he began to cry over his recollection of the sled incident did his true feelings start to surface. He felt nostalgic for his "paradise lost," angry at his father for emotionally abandoning him, and incredulous that his father could have been so insensitive to him. He also felt terribly sad. "How could he have just ignored me like that?" Patrick sobbed. "Didn't he know I still needed time for just him and me? Didn't he know how much he hurt me?"

One of the most important insights Patrick obtained in therapy was that his loss of special status with his father constituted his first experience of being dumped. The subsequent experiences with Henry at age ten and with Stephanie at age twenty-four devastated him because they were repetitions of his earlier experience with his father, who had compounded his "jilted" son's pain by replacing him with someone else. Fortunately, Patrick's mother, although not openly demonstrative, was a much more consistent and reliable source of love. Without her influence, Patrick might not merely have developed a problem sustaining relationships, he probably would have had trouble getting into them in the first place.

Another important insight Patrick reached in therapy was that whenever he had an experience of being dumped it was accompanied or followed by being in some way humiliated. When Stephanie dumped him, it was public knowledge among their mutual friends, and Patrick was mortified. His sense of shame grew with his desperate attempts to get her back. "I know I was making a fool out of myself, but I couldn't let her go," he later said. When Henry turned on Patrick and dumped him flat, that also involved the public humiliation of being "ranked out" and called names. And, finally, Patrick's relationship with his father occasioned feelings of humiliation as well. Patrick's father used a lot of put-downs and digs when dealing with his son. If Patrick had been more secure in his father's love, perhaps the boy would have experienced this treatment as teasing, but particularly after feeling he had lost that special place in his father's heart that he once had occupied, Patrick experienced it as hurtful and shame producing.

Tempting as it might be to condemn Patrick for being a heartless cad in his dealings with women, in fact he did not consciously decide to adopt a policy of "hurt them before they hurt me." It was simply that the pain Patrick experienced in being dumped by his father, then by Henry, and then by Stephanie was so great that his psyche automatically developed an unconscious means of self-protection. By ending a relationship as soon as a woman gave him signs that he was special in her eyes, Patrick was able to protect himself from the dumping he unconsciously "knew" would inevitably follow, just as it had in the past. Obviously, though, Patrick's protection came at great cost to others and to himself, and although he may have been largely unaware of what he was doing, he still was accountable. It was wrong for Patrick to use his own pain as an excuse to cause others pain, and as he became more aware of this, he went through a period of feeling ashamed and experiencing diminished self-esteem.

But Patrick also came to see that he had been hurting himself in two ways. First, by cutting off relationships with women as soon as he began to feel truly loved and loving, he was depriving himself of love that he very much needed and wished for. Second, by continually creating so much chaos in his relationships with women he was in essence throwing up a smokescreen that prevented him from recognizing a truth fundamental to his self-understanding and growth: that underlying his fear of getting hurt by women was an even greater fear of being hurt by men, and that in order to overcome his problems with women he would first have to deal directly with the pain he had experienced in his relationships with men, particularly his father.

Patrick further realized that he had been placing additional pressure on romantic relationships with women by expecting a woman to be his sole source of intimacy and love. Many people rely on one other person—spouse, lover, or "best friend"—to meet all their needs and think that one good relationship should supplant their need for additional sources of love. This is a major reason so many people are unhappy with their personal lives. The fact is, no one relationship, no matter how solid and loving, can meet all a person's emotional needs, just as no one food can meet all his nutritional needs. A person who looks to one relationship for all her sustenance may feel basically full, but she'll still have pangs or cravings for some other kind of emotional nourishment. Moreover, a person who leans so heavily on one relationship to meet all her needs maximizes her vulnerability. Since losing that relationship would mean losing her only real connection, the pain of the loss would be unbearable.

The Change Process: Patrick Makes Concrete Progress

Patrick's relationship with his friend Joe proved to be a principal vehicle for overcoming his fear of becoming close to men. At the time he met Joe, Patrick had a number of buddies he did things with, but no close male friends with whom he felt it was safe to open up emotionally. Patrick and Joe lived in the same apartment building but hadn't met until one Saturday morning when Patrick went out and saw Joe pushing his Volkswagen up the street, walking alongside it with one hand on the steering wheel, the other pushing against the door. "Need any help?" Patrick asked as he approached Joe. "No, it's okay," Joe said. "I'm just walking my car." Realizing the strangeness of what he just said, Joe burst out laughing and so did Patrick, who began helping Joe "walk his car." After a few minutes Patrick said, "I haven't laughed like that in a long time." This was the beginning of a friendship that involved a lot of humor and playfulness—and for Patrick, a good deal of the kind of affirmation he had not experienced in relationships with men before. Joe frequently said positive things about Patrick and made a point of telling him how much he enjoyed hanging out with him. Eventually, Patrick began to open up and reveal some of his deepest feelings and insecurities to Joe. When he did, he always found Joe accepting and

compassionate; he never made fun of Patrick, belittled his feelings, or tried to change the subject in the way that Patrick's experience with other men had caused him to expect. When Joe became
aware of Patrick's problems with women and recommended therapy,
Patrick wasn't put off. If anyone else had made this suggestion,
Patrick probably would have brushed it aside. Clearly, establishing
a close rapport with another man was healing for Patrick in and
of itself.

Patrick's experience with his father and then with his superiors at
work had caused him to expect men in positions of authority to be
either aloof or condescending, but Barry, the therapist he began
seeing, was not like this. He treated Patrick with warmth and acceptance and did not present himself as an ominiscient sage who had
all the answers. By allowing Patrick to go "his own way" and making
clear that he would stay by him no matter where that might lead,
Barry gave Patrick the unconditional acceptance that he had never
received from his father and that he had come to mistakenly believe
no man would ever provide.

Patrick's deepening relationships with both Joe and Barry resulted
in his feeling much more relaxed with women, for two reasons. First,
he felt he now had relationships with men that he could fall back on
for solace and love if and when he experienced pain in a relationship
with a woman. This enabled him to feel more confident about risking
intimacy with women. Second, he learned that loving and being loved
do not always result in pain. Not everyone in his life would dump
him the way Stephanie, Henry, and his father had. It was possible
to have sustained relationships, ones that lasted for years, and perhaps
could last his entire life. Knowing this permitted him to be more
trusting of the human race, God, and fate. As he put it, "What a
profound relief and joy it is to know that not everyone I get close
to will hurt me."

Patrick's breakthrough in his behavior toward women occurred
when he started seeing a teacher named Jeanne. From the start, he
had the sense that she was "someone really special," and that with
her there was the potential for a lifelong partnership. But early on,
he felt that "it's going to happen again, isn't it? I'm going to get
scared and lose all interest in her, aren't I?" Yes, Patrick was informed,

it probably would happen again. All those awful, scary, anxiety-producing feelings were going to come back. But, Patrick was also informed, those feelings do not have to lead to the same result as in the past. He made a pact with his therapist that, this time, he was going to handle his feelings differently. He was going to permit himself to experience them, he was going to express them (to Joe and his therapist), *but he wasn't going to act on them*. He'd just let them be and see what happened.

As Patrick's relationship with Jeanne became more intimate and pleasurable, sure enough, the time came when he began having thoughts of wanting to break up with her and see other women. He couldn't believe how many gorgeous women there seemed to be around; each day, he had "this free-floating horniness that makes me want practically every woman I see." He confided his feelings to Joe, and in therapy, and he recognized the old pattern. But this time he knew his sudden lack of interest in Jeanne and sudden desire to "screw every woman on earth" were signs that his fear of the inevitable hurt "I know is around the corner" was recurring. He also knew that as his lust signaled his fears, it disguised and distracted him from them as well. So instead of acting on his feelings as he had in the past, this time Patrick decided to just let his lust toward other women be, and to continue with Jeanne. As the ensuing weeks passed, his interest in other women waned, and his sexual attraction to Jeanne returned. Within a few months, Patrick reported that he was feeling "closer to Jeanne than I ever thought I would." He also commented, "I don't know what's happened, but we're having incredible sex. I thought for a while there that we'd reached a point where our sex life had settled down into sort of a sameness, that there was a level of passion we'd never feel again. And then, wow, something happened and it's really taken off again."

At the time of this writing, Patrick and Jeanne had been dating exclusively for ten months and were beginning to talk about living together and maybe getting married. This was reigniting Patrick's old fears, but they were not as intense as before. It's impossible to predict what will happen between Patrick and Jeanne in the future. Patrick has come to the conclusion that because of his history, "this fear of getting hurt will always be with me at some level of my consciousness." But he has also come to realize that "if I run away because of this fear, then it's certain that I'll be alone and without the love I need. I don't know if I can, but I have to take the risk, I have to try to hang in there. And that's what I hope I'm going to do."

Chapter 12
"I Feel Threatened When Another Person Gets Close"

Although legions of people today long for intimacy, for many the prospect of really getting close to another person, and letting the other person come close in turn, is extremely frightening. As much as they may want it, when closeness in a relationship actually begins to develop, they feel so threatened, anxious, and full of dread that they're overcome with a compelling urge to run away. To some, the "threat" of intimacy triggers a sense of being crowded, invaded, trapped, of not having enough air or room to breathe—and these feelings are often accompanied by physical symptoms such as shortness of breath, tightness in the chest, and stiffness and aches in the back, neck, and limbs. In more severe cases of this block, people respond to the "threat" of intimacy by feeling that their very survival is at stake: they fear that if they allow themselves to get close to another person, the price will be the annihilation of their separate sense of self. Or to use a business metaphor, they perceive potential intimate partners as huge conglomerates and themselves as tiny companies that are bound to lose their trademark identities when one of the conglomerates gobbles them up in a takeover. As much as they may want to let in love, deep within they fear that it will literally do them in.

Some people with the "I Feel Threatened When Another Person Gets Close" block have this pattern because they also have the "I'll Inevitably Get Hurt" block, the pattern discussed in the preceding chapter. But these two blocks do not necessarily accompany each other; and they need to be viewed as separate and distinct patterns. What frightens the people in the previous chapter is the eventual criticism, rejection, loss, or other pain they're certain will inevitably follow once they've become intimate. But it's not intimacy itself that frightens them; they desire closeness. By contrast, for those who feel threatened when another person gets close, it's intimacy itself that's unsettling. They fear, even dread the prospect of becoming close in the first place. Intimacy does not feel good to them, it feels threatening because it triggers their fear of loss of self. As one person with this block explained, "The idea that my lover will leave me is terrifying to me, but even more terrifying is the idea that he'll stay forever."

Why the Fear of Intimacy

At first glance, it might seem paradoxical that in an era when so many people are openly proclaiming a desire for intimacy (witness the burgeoning popularity of personal ads) many are at the same time so deeply frightened. Clearly, intimacy is an area fraught with ambivalence. People long for it, but then when they have a chance for closeness, many run away.

Many people fear intimacy because their earliest experiences of being loved led them to equate it with being overpowered and overprotected. As an example, take the classic situation of a father who, in the guise of "helping" his child with his homework, takes over and does the homework himself. If the father consistently overpowers the child in this way, the child's own sense of self will not fully develop; instead, he will feel tiny and inadequate in the ever-present shadow of his giant father. Or take the classic situation of the loving mother who stands guard at the window as her child plays outside and who runs to the rescue at any sign of distress. If a child is consistently overprotected, she will grow up lacking any sense that she can handle herself out in the world. In both cases the parents are loving and well-meaning, but their behavior hinders their children's development of a strong sense of themselves as autonomous beings. In adulthood, the children will remain psychologically overattached to their parents, and their sense of self will remain underdeveloped and fragile. When other people begin to get close to them, they will respond as if once again they are small children being taken over by all-powerful parents.

For many others, intimacy is scary because it's unfamiliar territory. Many people grew up never really experiencing any true connectedness to another human being. Since their parents did not connect with each other, they didn't learn much from example either. As adults, they may make stabs at intimacy in certain relationships, but with no sense of how to go about it these attempts result in disappointment, pain, and even disaster. This only adds to their fear of treading into unknown territory and reinforces their conviction that the safest course of action is to keep their defenses up and guard against anyone getting close.

Yet another reason fear of intimacy is so prevalent is that intimate relationships force people to discover, acknowledge, and deal with their deepest selves, including their darker, less attractive sides. This, too, is something many people are unable or unwilling to do. Many grew up cut off from whole parts of themselves—their deepest feelings, their real desires, their confusion, their anger, their ambivalence, their spiritual yearnings, for example—and were raised by people who had no connection to their own deepest selves, either. For many as well intimacy means forging into unfamiliar territory, the uncharted landscape of genuine self-knowledge. Also, some who seem willing to learn who they really are still often back out when a relationship forces them to confront parts of themselves they would prefer to disown or otherwise not face.

Sex-role conditioning can also cause people to feel threatened by closeness. Raised to believe that it is a woman's role to surrender her separate identity when she marries, and to go through the rest of her life defined as "Mrs. Somebody Else," many women understandably fear that heterosexual intimacy will mean the stifling, total loss or snuffing out of their individual selves. Women's training to be the emotional caretakers of men and children gives added reason for women to have such fears, as does the fact that most women are raised to feel they have no right to say no. For many women, being close to others translates into having to take care of their emotional needs around the clock. Such women don't simply feel threatened when another person gets close, they feel overwhelmed.

As with all love blocks, the "I Feel Threatened When Another

Person Gets Close" block can affect those who suffer from it to varying degrees and in different ways. Some people with this block will be so frightened of intimate attachments that they will form only the most superficial relationships, or go through life without many relationships outside of work ones at all. Others have numerous friends they feel comfortable pouring their hearts out to but feel threatened by the prospect of opening up in a similar way to people they are sexually involved with or interested in.

In sexual relationships, fear of intimacy is expressed in a variety of ways. Some people feel comfortable engaging in sexual gymnastics with their lovers and walking around naked in front of them, but they feel very uncomfortable about telling their lovers their deepest feelings. Others may be self-conscious about their bodies but feel entirely at home revealing their feelings.

Although it's a very common problem, caution should be exercised before deciding someone has the "I Feel Threatened When Another Person Gets Close" block. Wanting to run away from intimate involvement can sometimes be very healthy, in fact, because there are people in the world with invasive personalities. As soon as they meet someone, they rush in, wanting instantaneously to be best friends or lovers, or otherwise demanding intense involvement from the start. The person being rushed at will often respond by instinctively tightening up inside and pulling away, which in such a situation is a healthy, appropriate response, not evidence of a love block. The response is appropriate because the threat posed by the invasive person is a real one, not merely a perceived one. It's when a person *habitually* responds to intimacy by tightening up and pulling away, when he does so even when not involved with invasive personalities, that the "I Feel Threatened When Another Person Gets Close" block is at work.

Boundary Invasions

In order to be able to relate intimately in a healthy way, people have to have a clear sense of boundaries, a sense of where they end and where others begin. Clear and appropriate boundaries act as antennae that signal when someone else's behavior represents an encroachment or a threat. They also enable a person to set limits in relationships, to say "No, you can't treat me that way" or "No, I can't do what you want me to—it's asking too much." It is only when people have healthy boundaries that they are able to achieve successfully the delicate balance of closeness and separateness that intimacy requires—and to do so without feeling threatened by the closeness or the separation. Many people, however, grew up in homes where personal boundaries were constantly invaded, causing them to develop a skewed sense of boundaries. The only way they could protect their fragile inner selves from the invasions was by erecting a wall of impenetrable defenses.

Two different kinds of boundary invasions are common in families. First, there is physical boundary invasion. This occurs when there is little or no respect for privacy. Some people grew up in families where the children were not allowed to close the door to their bedrooms to read or study or just be by themselves. Any such attempt was interpreted by the parents as a hostile act, and the children would be accused of "trying to keep secrets," "being in a bad mood," or "acting like you're too good for us." Some parents took any desire for solitude on their offspring's part as a rejection, acting personally hurt any time a child expressed the wish to do something on his own.

Psychological boundary invasion is the second common kind. It occurs in families in which each individual member is not permitted to have his or her own separate feelings, thoughts, and opinions. Many people grew up in families in which it was considered impertinent or a heresy for a child to express a feeling, idea, or opinion differing from or contradictory to the parents'. The parents were so narcissistic that they were incapable of making distinctions between their own feelings and their children's. If they felt one way, they assumed their kids had to feel the same; if their kids tried to tell them otherwise, they reacted with denial. "Don't say that, you don't really feel that way," the parents might have said, or perhaps something like "What do you mean you hate lima beans? You can't hate lima beans. Why, I've always loved them!" Or perhaps they asked in disbelief, "How can you be afraid of the water? No one in this family has ever been afraid of the water. Everyone in this family loves to swim!" An even more subtle boundary invasion occurs when people say to each other, "Read this book, you'll love it" or "Don't go see that movie, you'll hate it" or "I bought this new coat, but I don't want to show it to you because I know you won't like it."

For children whose temperaments don't conform to parental expectations, this sort of psychological boundary invasion can lead to very low self-esteem. Take a child whose natural temperament is to be slow to warm up to others. In some families, the child's inner clock would be respected: he would be allowed to form relationships at his own speed, getting close to others and letting them in psychologically at the step-by-step pace that feels comfortable to him. In many families, however, his inner clock would not be respected because, as discussed in Chapter 10, parental impatience would be the rule. Rather than be seen as someone who needs time to open up, the child would be branded "shy," "standoffish," "a loner," perhaps even castigated for being impolite and "weird." He also would probably be forced into closeness before he was ready, which might cause the loner label to come true, and would almost certainly cause him to develop the "I Feel Threatened When Another Person Gets Close" block. Allowed to be himself, the child would still be slow to warm up in relationships, but he would not find them threatening.

James

Tall and broad shouldered, James has dark, brooding good looks that could easily have made him a movie star. Bright, intellectual, and always abreast of current events, he is strongly committed to a number of liberal political causes and is a staunch supporter of Israel. He started therapy in his mid-twenties, shortly after the death of his father. At that time, he was living at home with his mother and, having recently completed a master's in social work, was just beginning work as a caseworker at an employment and job-training center for Jewish immigrants.

James had established a pattern of quickly getting intensely involved with women, then losing interest and dumping them as soon as he started to feel emotionally close. This is essentially the same pattern displayed by Patrick, the pain avoider in the previous chapter, but the psychodynamics were very different. Patrick had the urge to extricate himself from relationships once closeness developed because he was afraid of the inevitable hurt intimacy would bring. In contrast, James bolted when he began to feel close because he was afraid that further intimacy would cause him to lose his separate sense of self.

James is a good example of someone who came from a home where there was no shortage of love but who developed love blocks anyway. He was the youngest of two boys in a middle-class family that lived in a modest but comfortable house in a suburban town. The general atmosphere in James's home was very calm, warm, and inviting. James's mother and father welcomed other children into the home, playing the role of surrogate parents, and other children envied James's home life. "You're lucky," they would tell him. "I wish my parents were like yours." James felt proud and fortunate to have such a loving home.

Yet there was something a little too insular about this loving home. James's parents did not actively discourage James and his brother from visiting other children's homes. But they would ask questions about the other children's parents and then act hurt and depressed if James or his brother said anything positive. Their mother became particularly upset when James said something nice about another child's mother.

James's older brother had a close relationship with their father, an insurance broker, and grew up to become his mirror image. James developed an especially close relationship with their mother, a house-wife. She adored James, dotingly treating him "like no child had ever existed before who was as wonderful as I was or could do what I could do." James's older brother was pushed to work hard and achieve in school, but James was treated as though he were a special case entitled to a different set of rules. During his elementary-school years, James would feign illness whenever he didn't feel like going to school. His father would already have gone to work by then, and his mother never questioned whether James was really sick, even when it was obvious he wasn't. She appeared to relish those days, in fact, and actually encouraged him to stay home for the slightest reason. James and his mother spent those days lolling and playing in bed together. She would cuddle and sing with him, tousle his hair, and spend hours confiding in him about her problems with his father.

James loved the attention he got from his mother, but always lingering on the very edge of his consciousness was a vague sense of uneasiness about their relationship. A major developmental task of the middle childhood years is to separate from the parents, to emotionally leave home and establish relationships with other children and adults (e.g., teachers), and develop an increasingly differentiated, independent sense of self. But James was not doing this; he was too bonded to his mother, and at one level of his psyche he knew that. At the same time, though, being with her in this special "the two of us against the world" way was very appealing and comforting.

In therapy, James recalled an incident that conveys the loving yet confining atmosphere of his childhood home. When James was about ten years old, he went up the street to play with some friends and was gone for about five hours. When he returned home, his mother acted hurt and upset, as though his absence were a rejection of her. "Why can't you play here where I know where you are?" she implored. "Isn't our house good enough for you?" Instead of seeing James's forays into the world as important steps in his growth and development, James's mother was aware only of her fear that something would happen to him and of her own needs for his companionship. This type of incident, repeated again and again, delivered a message that sank deep into James's psyche: that the price of intimacy with women is the loss of any separate sense of self.

When James was thirteen, he went to his first boy-girl party. His mother was against the idea, but his father thought it was time for James to be interested in girls, and she finally relented. While somewhat afraid of girls, James went anyway, hoping to have a good time. He danced with a few girls and was really starting to have fun when a very popular girl walked by him on the dance floor and loudly called him a "fag" and a "nerd." Everyone else heard and some giggled. Shaken and humiliated, James went home and told his mother what had happened. Rather than shore up his self-esteem by telling him that the girl was bad mannered and the world is full of much nicer girls who are certain to treat him more kindly, James's mother responded by enfolding him in her arms, saying, "I'll take care of you, honey. You're Momma's boy, Momma's precious. No girl will ever treat you as good as I do." Not only did this reinforce James's fear of being a "faggy, nerdy Momma's boy," it was also his mother's way of telling James that the outside world is a hostile place where he would be treated cruelly as a matter of course, and the only place he could be really sure of finding love was at home. Another even more powerful message came through as well: any time James attempted to go out into the world on his own, the family, especially his mother, would be there to pull him back in seductively and make him realize that it was a mistake even to try.

When it came time for James to think about going to college, his parents encouraged him to go to one near home, ostensibly so that he wouldn't have to pay the cost of room and board. But James wanted desperately to go out on his own, and so he worked out the financial arrangements that enabled him to go to a college several hundred miles away. Like many college freshman, James had a hard time adjusting that first year. His parents were aware that their son's unhappiness was normal, but instead of encouraging him to stick with school and work his problems out, they suggested that he come home. In his sophomore year James transferred to a college near home. He lived at home through his late twenties, even as he completed graduate studies in social work and found a job in the field.

James was so devastated by the humiliating experience at his first boy-girl dance that he did not date again throughout high school, something his parents never questioned. When he did begin dating, after returning to live at home, he very quickly became seriously involved with practically the first girl he went out with. She was a student at the same college, named Anat, and one of the reasons James was drawn to her was that she had grown up in Israel. Anat had a personality of stark contrasts: at times she was very needy and childlike, but there was also a powerhouse quality to her, and she could be quite controlling and domineering. Almost from the start, she and James had a hot-cold, on-again, off-again relationship in which they played a muted form of the classic distancer-pursuer game. They would go through a period when she would want commitment, but he wouldn't; then she would cool on the idea of commitment, and suddenly he would want it. They went back and forth like this for about three and a half years. Finally, Anat said she had had enough and was moving back to Israel.

One of the most significant aspects of James's relationship with

Anat was how his parents reacted to her. They loved her. Almost from the start, they pegged her as their future daughter-in-law and let both Anat and James know that she was everything they had always wanted for that role: smart, family oriented, politically liberal, desirous of children, and Jewish. Anat became so much a part of the family, in fact, that after she and James had been going out less than a year, she moved in with them. Asked about this in therapy, James could not recall how this decision had actually been made. "I guess I had a say in it, but I really don't remember any discussions," he said. "Suddenly she had just moved in, and everyone acted like this was the most natural development in the world."

After Anat broke up with James and moved back to Israel, he began a series of short-lived but rather intense involvements with a number of different women. The women were one of two types. Some were emotionally needy, rather depressed women who had low self-esteem and quickly became very dependent on James. With them, he took on the role of comforter and protector who would build up their confidence. The other women he went out with were mothering types, who wanted to take care of him and do everything together. With either kind of woman, James would very soon feel "crowded, suffocated, and panicked" and abruptly break things off.

Although still living at home while he had these affairs, James never brought any of his girlfriends home. He would not even tell his parents any of their names. Significantly, none of these women was Jewish.

What finally brought James to therapy was the totally unexpected death of his father of a heart attack at age fifty-eight. While James would have been in shock and grief under any circumstances, these feelings were exacerbated by enormous guilt because at the time his father died he had been seriously thinking about leaving home. Two days before, in fact, he had started actively looking into housing options. He had always felt guilty about wanting to be on his own, but now he was overwhelmed. How could he leave now? he wondered. Who would take care of his mother? Could it possibly be that his wanting to "abandon" his family had been intuited by his father and somehow contributed to his heart attack? It was with these questions on his mind that James intitiated treatment.

The Change Process: James's Way

As several other cases so far discussed have shown, when a person enters therapy to deal with one set of problems, he often ends up spending as much or more time on problems he was not initially aware of or concerned with. This happened with James. When he started therapy, he had no interest in discussing the affairs he was having. He wanted the focus to remain on the central people in his life so far—his family and Anat—and "not bother with the rest, because they're not important." It was only much later that James came to understand that it was because those major relationships had been so overwhelmingly, suffocatingly central that he was now having so many short-lived liaisons.

A number of the other people discussed in these pages had childhoods characterized by too much emotional aloneness, but for James, the issue was the exact opposite. He had a history of too much family togetherness. Feeling too "fused" with his parents, and then with Anat, who quickly became part of the family, James was now trying to protect his inadequately developed sense of separate self by getting into relationships that had no potential to last. However, even those relationships were bound to reach a point when James would start to feel "uh-oh, she's getting too close." So, in order to keep his fragile boundaries from further "invasion"—which was how James had begun to experience intimacy—he would have to get himself out of those relationships altogether.

James entered therapy at precisely the age when society says it's healthy for a man to be thinking of finding a mate and settling down. For James, however, this would not have been healthy. Whether male or female, straight or homosexual, each individual must go through the crucial developmental stage of building a separate sense of self before she will be ready to form an intimate pair-bond that can be fulfilling and lasting. If a person becomes part of a couple before the process of individuation has been completed, she well might experience the couple relationship as cramping, suffocating, or otherwise threatening to her inner self. Through his training as a social worker, James intellectually knew all this, but on a visceral level he did not believe it. He felt his desire for a separate sense of self was a betrayal of his family, an abandonment especially of his widowed mother. The first thing James needed was support—loud, repeated, insistent support—for his desire to develop his own self, his own interests, his own identity. He needed to learn that it was not only okay for him to get an apartment of his own, it was crucial.

It took James many months before he was able to give himself permission to break away from his childhood home and find a place of his own. He decided to share an apartment with a friend for a while, then take over on his own later on, if and when he felt ready. This was a wise tack. As discussed in greater length in the "It's Too Late for Me; My Time Has Run Out" chapter, people have a natural developmental clock and need adequate time to get through one developmental stage before going on to the next. When people realize, as James did, that they reached adulthood without having completed certain developmental tasks from childhood and adolescence, they often feel an urge to complete all their unfinished business fast, so that further time won't be lost. In most cases, however, this impatience diminishes self-love, with the person berating himself to "hurry up and get healthy" and wondering "what's wrong with me that I can't make progress any faster?" What's more, this impatience actually impedes progress on the developmental tasks that need to be completed. The fact is, the psyche incorporates gradual change much more easily than sudden change. For James, moving from his parents' home into a place shared with someone else was much less scary than moving directly into an apartment alone would have been. He found a roommate who would be moving away at the end of six months, at which point James could either try being on his own or get another roommate. He opted for going it alone, and while he felt "strange and lonely, and not exactly sure what to do with myself" at first, he eventually began to feel at home.

James also made a conscious effort to do things alone. All his life he had always done things with a family member, a friend, or a woman he was dating. If he didn't have someone to do something with, he did nothing. He had never traveled alone, gone to the movies alone, or even taken walks alone. Now James began attending professional workshops alone, purposely choosing ones where he was sure he wouldn't know anyone. He took himself to the movies alone. Eventually he even took a two-week vacation to Europe alone. Although he approached them anxiously, these ventures gave him a sense of exhilaration and freedom. For the first time in his life, he was beginning to experience himself as someone with the ability "to handle myself out in the world, and to keep myself company and make myself happy." People who grew up with a strong sense of self might look upon this as no great accomplishment, but for someone from James's background it was no small feat.

James's relationships with women also changed. He was increasingly attracted to women who valued their own career development and personal growth, who had a variety of interests, and who had numerous friends and professional relationships that were clearly important to them. These women respected and encouraged James's separateness. They were interested in his activities and wanted to spend time with him, but they did not feel a need to do everything together or talk to him every day. James dated some of these women and got to know others as friends and colleagues. These relationships felt "more grown-up" to him. He began to feel less afraid of losing himself when someone else began to get close. He slowly became hopeful that with the type of women he was getting to know, he could enjoy the kind of warmth and closeness he had once enjoyed with his mother, but not at the price of losing himself.

James's mother was very unhappy about his moving out. She sulked, acted depressed, and begged him not to leave her, and when he actually did move, she called him nearly every day. He visited her or took her out to dinner at least once a week, but this still was not enough for her. Then one day she shocked him by telling him she had decided to sell the house and move to Florida. James visits her there and calls often, but always comes away with the feeling that whatever he does, it's never sufficient. However, James's mother seems unexpectedly happy in Florida. She has joined a synagogue she's very involved with, taken up aerobics and jogging, made many new friends, and even started dating. Although he continues to feel guilty, James is aware that his feelings have more to do with the past than the present. He's also come to realize that "most people seem to feel guilty about their mothers. Maybe it's something you've just got to learn to live with, seeing it as part of life, but not letting it run your life."

James's first experience with therapy ended when he obtained a staff position with a prestigious social-work program in another city and started his own counseling practice. At the time, he was involved with a woman who loved him and whom he loved very deeply. They both wanted to get married, but James always resisted a formal engagement because he feared that making the commitment would mean losing his separate sense of self. After moving away, he started seeing another therapist and continued to make progress in dealing with his fears about getting married. When James read a first draft of this chapter, he had trouble identifying with the early sections—that's how much he had changed. More to the point, several months later James and his girlfriend sent an announcement of their recent marriage. For James, the "I Feel Threatened When Another Person Gets Close" block seems to be a thing of the past.

Linda

Linda is a raven-haired woman whose posture and dignified looks are best described by the phrase "she has presence." When she walks into the room, it's easy to imagine her as a leading lady in a stage play, or as a lecturer keeping an audience spellbound. She has a set-jawed, steely quality about her that belies an inner softness. Although she is quick to smile, there is a protective wall around her, and she likes to keep her distance. At the time she started therapy, she was approaching forty and had been married for more than twenty years. The mother of three children, she had worked as a secretary for the past twelve years.

Linda had the same "I Feel Threatened When Another Person Gets Close" block as James, but with more severe consequences. James allowed closeness, but only to a certain point. Except with her children, Linda could not tolerate any closeness at all. It was partly because this was preventing her from having good relationships with her colleagues at work that she began treatment.

Linda was the older of two daughters who grew up in a family where there was little privacy and a great deal of violence. Linda's father was a failed heavyweight boxer whose principal way of relating to others was through anger and force. He frequently flew into rages and beat Linda's mother, who suffered broken bones and cuts deep enough to need stitches.

Linda and her sister would try to distance themselves from the violence, but this proved impossible. Their father was unable to keep a job for very long and their mother could get only low-paying positions, so they could only afford a tiny apartment consisting of two rooms. One served as a combination kitchen, dining area, and living room, the other was used for sleeping and, in the girls' case, doing homework. The whole family slept in the bedroom, with only a flimsy room divider separating the two girls from their parents. This not only meant there was no privacy for the two girls, it also meant they were constantly exposed to everything that went on between their parents.

Unfortunately, sexual relations between Linda's parents were fraught with violence. After beating his wife, or in the course of it, Linda's father would frequently force himself on her sexually. On numerous occasions, Linda and her younger sister watched their father throw their mother down on the floor or kitchen table, or push her up against the wall, then rape her. Even "normal" sex between the parents tended to consist of the father using force or threats against his wife.

Growing up, Linda acted as surrogate mother to her younger sister. This relationship, in which Linda gave of herself but took little in return, was the only close relationship of her entire life, until her daughters were born. Linda was too afraid of her father even to imagine feeling close to him. Turning to her mother, who was chronically depressed, on edge, and critical, seemed out of the question as well.

Linda had no close relationships with anyone outside the home, either. She grew up never having a close "best friend" or chum type relationship with another girl, and thus missed what for most women is an important step in learning how to be intimate. Linda, in fact, was careful to guard against any hint of chumminess with other girls because she knew they'd want to share secrets, and she had been warned by both her parents "not to ever, ever let anyone know" the truth about what went on in their home. Linda was afraid that if she got close to any of the girls she knew, she'd "spill the beans," which would make her "a betrayer, a Benedict Arnold who gave away the family secrets."

In an attempt to put some distance between herself and what she was surrounded by at home, Linda would frequently get into bed and "go under the sheets." Curled into a fetal position, she would close her eyes and block her ears and "hide out there in the darkness for as long as I could." Some people who took similar refuge in childhood used their imaginations to escape into a rich fantasy world, but Linda simply "hid out" from the real world as if going into an empty cave. There, she felt "afraid and all alone."

As Linda neared the end of high school, her main goal was simply to get out of her parents' home. When she was eighteen she got out by marrying Ben, a twenty-year-old factory worker she had known since starting high school.

During the time they dated, Ben treated Linda well, and she felt lucky to have found a man who was so different from her cruel and abusive father. Shortly after they married, though, Ben's personality underwent what seemed to Linda a remarkable transformation. He would suddenly erupt into rages in which he would verbally abuse Linda and threaten to hit and maim her. Although he never actually hit her, he would grab, pinch and push her around enough that she became afraid of what he might do. He also started bringing home whips, handcuffs, leather costumes and other bondage gear, and the sexual practices he wanted Linda to engage in with him became "more and more on the edge of being violent and sadistic."

At first, Linda went along and did what Ben wanted. Over time, however, it became evident that Ben was sinking deeper and deeper into alcoholism, and the more often he got drunk, the less often he was able to perform sexually. Although he would still badger Linda and try to coerce her into having kinky and sadistic sex with him, as the years progressed they had less and less to do with each other. Eventually, it would become common for them to go through entire weeks with little in the way of direct interaction.

Linda started therapy after her husband tried to get her younger sister to have sadistic sex with him. She had been thinking about getting a divorce for several years, but it was only when her husband threatened to sully and harm the little sister she still felt duty-bound to protect that she began taking the idea seriously. She hoped therapy could help her "work up the nerve" to finally take some action.

For several years, Linda also had wanted to form better relationships with her co-workers. The women she worked with mistook her aloofness for snobbery instead of fear and disliked her as a result. Her boss also found many of her habits annoying, particularly her air of secretiveness and the way she whispered whenever she had to speak about anything more personal than today's headlines. But since getting help would necessitate letting another person (a therapist) get close, Linda had kept putting off actually making an appointment. For her, taking that step was an act of real courage.

The Change Process: Linda's Way

At the time Linda started therapy, she had been married to Ben for more than twenty years and had two sons and one daughter. With her daughter, Linda reenacted the protective relationship she had with her younger sister. With her older son, she had a comfortable relationship, although one that did not entail much confiding or closeness. With her younger son, she had a very close relationship that became more and more reciprocal and nourishing to her as he became older. These healthy intimate relationships stood as testimony to her inner strength and resilience, and as confidence-building models. One way Linda had always deprived herself of self-love was by labeling herself "someone who's just no good at relationships." A crucial step early in her treatment was to convince her to finally start giving herself credit for developing what were, in fact, some very good relationships.

After only about six months in therapy, Linda decided to divorce Ben and began the appropriate legal proceedings. Making progress on her other major issue—her inability to open up to other adults, particularly women—took much longer. Part of her problem, Linda discovered, was that never talking about what went on in her home allowed her to mistakenly believe that her family was the only one in the world to have such problems. This only fed Linda's sense of isolation. Some people who have difficulty being intimate nonetheless feel a sense of kinship with the world at large. But sure that no one else came from such a disturbed home, Linda felt utterly alone.

Of all the steps forward Linda made, perhaps the single most important one was to begin attending meetings of Al-Anon, the self-help organization for those who are or have been in some way involved with alcoholics or other addicts. In those meetings, there was no pressure for anyone to talk if they didn't want to, so Linda was able to sit back and learn to get comfortable listening to other people "reveal their family secrets" without having to reciprocate with disclosures of her own. Moreover, Al-Anon has shown her that millions of people come from families similar to hers, and have problems with intimacy as a result. This discovery in itself has done much to eliminate Linda's lifelong feeling of "being as alone in the world as I was when I had to go under the sheets."

Through her involvement with Al-Anon Linda became friendly with some other women who grew up fearing that if they allowed themselves to get close to other girls, they'd end up betraying their families' shameful secrets. None of these women had had much experience with healthy intimacy, and none had had extensive experience being close friends with other women, either. But together they started to learn, and with each awkward, slow advance each got a bit more comfortable in the context of an intimate friendship. Although Linda still often found herself wanting to "go under the sheets" and hide, bit by bit she began to feel less threatened.

Linda also joined a community theater group. She had always had a secret desire to act but had felt too afraid of "exposing myself in public." Acting, however, gave her an experience of "letting my hair down and letting other people see different sides of me." She not only received affirmation "that I'm really not so bad inside," but as she began to get to know the other people in the group she became further aware that "most other people aren't so bad, after all." Moreover, she learned that she could exert control over how quickly and in what way others got to know her. The one drawback of getting to know people through Al-Anon, she had found, was that such relationships were based on having a shared problem, and thus were "heavy," serious, and deeply personal right from the start. With the people she met through more frivolous theater activities, Linda could decide who she wanted to get to know, in what way, and how fast.

Two and a half years after her divorce, Linda began dating a widower with several children whom she had met at a cast party. She felt ready for a romantic and sexual relationship but found the reality of being with a man terrifying. They would begin to get closer, then Linda would get scared and not want to see him for a while. She explained to him what was going on with her, and he told her that he really cared for her, enough to go as slowly as she needed. They were still dating when this chapter was going through final revisions, and the outcome was unclear. Increasingly, Linda was becoming aware that the "I Feel Threatened When Another Person Gets Close" block, or vestiges of it, would always be with her to some degree. However, "I'm still not going back under the sheets," she vowed. "Each step towards closeness is scary, but it's getting easier. And my life is so much fuller now and I'm so much more alive."

Chapter 13
"I Just Can't Make a Commitment"

It is the nature of the human psyche to seek relationships that involve commitment and thus provide a sense of permanence and security. People need to know that no matter what happens, they have a home base they can always return to for love, acceptance, and care. Although some people have a greater need for security than others, everyone has some need for a person or persons to "be there" for them—and not just today or tomorrow, but also in the times ahead. The security of having a solid home base is what enables an individual to venture out into the world alone; without it, the world may seem more intimidating than exciting.

In a culture where heterosexual coupling is seen as the norm, the term "committed relationship" is often seen as synonymous with marriage. But this is a narrow view that overlooks the variety of human relationships. A committed relationship doesn't have to mean wedding bells—or sexual involvement at all. Deep commitment can exist between any two people, be they friends, lovers, spouses, work colleagues, or blood relatives of various types. Derived from the the Latin *committere,* meaning "to join, connect, entrust," the verb "to commit" means "to bind or obligate, as by a pledge." When a person makes a commitment to someone else, it is as if he has made a pledge that in essence says, "You can trust me, you can rely on me. I will be there for you in difficult times as well as in good times. The bond between us is important to me; I will do my best to keep it strong and make it last." Friends can be as devoted as the most ardent lovers, and homosexual lovers can be just as committed as heterosexual ones. By the same token, the fact that two people have entered into a marriage contract does not necessarily mean that they have made a deep emotional commitment to each other. There are countless marriages that in no way resemble the cozy, loving "safe harbors" that bridal magazines promise; nor do these unions provide the special sense of ease, security and joy that comes from having a stable, long-lasting bond of deep trust and intimacy.

Although the need for secure, committed relationships is central to the human psyche, there are legions of people who suffer from the "I Just Can't Make a Commitment" block. They tend to fall into two broad categories. The first group can be very loving and can also take in love from others—*but only on a short-term basis*. They may be able to connect very intimately with a partner, friend, or family member in the now, but they can't be counted on to be around six months or five years from now. Although they might want very much to promise loved ones that they'll be there for them always and forever, there's something operating within their psyches that makes it impossible or at least very difficult.

The second group of people with this block can stay in relationships for long periods of time, even their entire lives, yet they do so without giving their full emotional presence. Physically they're always around, but mentally and emotionally they've checked out, run away, retreated from the relationship, which causes others to complain that they're "not really there." Classic examples are: the man who rushes through dinner, then buries himself in the newspaper or glues his attention to the TV, tuning out his family in the process; the woman who is always so busy that she doesn't really notice what's happening with her children and other loved ones; and the man who responds to his wife or lover's expression of feelings by interrupting, switching the subject, offering a simplistic platitude, or acting as though he didn't hear. People with this subtle form of the "I Just Can't Make a Commitment" block often are not aware they have a problem. When a loved one complains that they're emotionally "not there," they usually respond with something along the lines of "What do you mean I'm 'not there' for you? I'm right here right now, aren't

I?" But those on the receiving end know the problem all too well. They know that the person who "isn't really there" is not fully committed to them; he may be willing to vow to stay in a relationship for all time, but at no time will he give it his emotional all.

Caution should be exercised in diagnosing an "I Just Can't Make a Commitment" block. Many people think they have a problem making commitments because in romantic relationships they continue to experience periods of doubt, ambivalence, and wanderlust. But most people have these sorts of feelings, even in the best of relationships, and they do not necessarily indicate the presence of the "I Just Can't Make a Commitment" block. Similarly, even the most committed, emotionally present people will go through periods where they are distracted, preoccupied, worried, or ill, and consequently can't be fully "there" for their loved ones. This, too, is entirely natural and shouldn't be taken as a sign of a suddenly developed block.

Who Has This Block

The picture that the "I Just Can't Make a Commitment" block most readily brings to mind is that of the stereotypical bachelor who goes from one romantic relationship to another, able to fall in love but not to stay in love long or fully enough to reach the point of being ready and willing to settle down for good. To be sure, there are legions with this block who more or less fit this description. However, the inability to make commitments and follow through on them is a pervasive problem for all kinds of people, and affects all kinds of relationships.

Some people have trouble making any kinds of commitments in the interpersonal realm. When Mark, a thirty-one-year-old designer, was approached for an interview for this book, he enthusiastically agreed. But when it came to setting up an exact date and time, he couldn't be pinned down. Later, he said he realized his noncommittal attitude toward the interview was indicative of the way he conducts nearly all his nonbusiness relationships. "Friends call up and want to make a date to get together, and I say I'll have to get back to them next week," he explained. "I constantly refuse to box myself in to any kind of commitment at all, even if it's just to having dinner or going to a movie. I even do this to my mother. She'll call and want to know whether I can come to dinner on a certain night, and I tell her I have to hang loose on that right now, I'll get back to her in a few days."

For other people, it's only within certain kinds of relationships that they have trouble making commitments. A person can be very committed to her friends, parents, and siblings but remain unable to commit herself to a lover. Or she may be able to commit herself to a lover but not be able to be there in a committed way for any of the other people in her life. Then again, she might be unwavering and utterly devoted to her children, but far less enthusiatic about being committed to their father.

Many people view marriage as the ultimate form of commitment, as well as an important passage into adulthood. As noted before, however, being married doesn't necessarily mean a person has no trouble making commitments. Many people marry simply because it's what is expected of them or they've reached what they consider "the marrying age." Their marriages are signs of how conventional they are, not how committed. Moreover, even married couples who started off feeling committed often can't carry through on their promises when the honeymoon period is over: witness the numbers of marriages that are either miserable or end in divorce, and the numbers of parents, particularly fathers, who routinely renege on agreements to pay child support after divorce. Although the common perception may be that married people are exempt from the "I Just Can't Make a Commitment" block, in fact, anyone—married or single, straight or gay—can suffer from one or more of its various permutations.

Cultural Influences

Part of the reason the "I Just Can't Make a Commitment" block is so common today can be found in the current cultural climate. There are a number of widely held beliefs about the nature of commitments, particularly those that marriage and having a family entail, which suggest that commitments should be avoided whenever possible.

One common belief is that making commitments is pointless because "nothing lasts." Given the nature of the times we live in, it's inevitable that some people would hold this view. In the past, when early death was so common and people were in much closer contact with nature, and vulnerable to it, they were also aware that life is impermanent and it is the natural condition of the world to be in constant change. At the same time, however, the ties that bound people together in the past were more permanent and stable than today. Prior to the industrial revolution, the norm was for people to spend their lives in one place, doing the same kind of work their parents and grandparents had done, and staying in close contact with the same people from birth to death. Today, people change jobs and move to new places with unprecedented frequency, couples are as likely break up as to survive the "test of time," and lifelong friendships are increasingly rare. In the modern world, in fact, *everything* seems impermanent: products are disposable, governments are constantly being overthrown, then toppled again, and the specter of nuclear war threatens every living thing. At a time when there's a pervasive sense that "nothing lasts," it's understandable that many would wonder "what's the point of seeking after permanence and security?"

Of course, personal experience plays a big role, too. Someone who grew up in an environment where relationships were stable and there were no deaths, divorces, or other disruptions will probably reject the notion that "nothing lasts" because it doesn't jibe with his inner view of the world as a place where security and permanence are the norm. But to someone whose early years were marred by divorce, the premature death of family members, or frequent moves, "nothing lasts" will seem a truism.

Another popular belief is that commitments, especially to a spouse and family, are burdensome. According to a view that gained currency in the 1960s and 1970s, marriage and sexual monogamy in general are stifling, particularly to men, who not only lose freedom when they marry, but also must give up control over their wallets and all chance for further personal growth. The language used in reference to marriage is especially telling: we speak of people "getting hitched," becoming "tied down," and "tying the knot," as if marriage were some sort of bondage. The idea that marriage is women's way of imprisoning men has led to additional colloquialisms: a betrothed woman is said to have "caught," "snared," or "landed" a man, perhaps by setting "a man trap"; and when a man is obviously enthralled with a woman he is said to be "pussy whipped," and she is said "to have him by the balls."

Many people understandably view marriage as a suffocating impediment to personal growth because that's the kind of marriages their parents had. Women in particular may have good reason to be wary of marriage, since so many are daughters of women for whom marriage meant perpetual confinement to the domestic sphere and loss of all autonomy. And men who saw their fathers' spirits crushed by the breadwinner's role have ample reason to be wary, too.

Being in a committed relationship over time is also viewed as boring and tiresome. There is a great deal of emphasis in American culture on the new and exciting—a way of thinking that has colored attitudes toward sexual relationships in particular. It's taken for granted that sex with the same person over a period of time is bound to get boring, while a popular myth has it that sex with someone new is sure to be exciting.

Another common belief is that it's better to keep your options open than make a commitment because something better might come along. What if a person accepts a dinner invitation and then gets invited to a gala ball for the very same night? What if a couple who have been living together companionably but without much passion for a number of years finally decide to marry, and the very next week one of them meets the partner of their dreams? The fear behind such rhetorical questions is that any commitment might involve settling for less than might have been gotten by holding out a bit longer.

Still another belief that has wide currency is that making commitments signifies the end of youth. Rather than seeing life as a continuum in which ongoing growth and increasing happiness are possible, many people see life as divided into two separate phases: gratifying childhood, when a person can be happy, have fun, feel free, and go on learning; and stultifying adulthood, a bland, gray, unbearably boring time when work and responsibilities occupy every waking moment and there's never any opportunity to have fun, to continue learning, or to just while away an afternoon. Understandably reluctant to leave childhood, they avoid the commitments they associate with adulthood—to a job, to a relationship, or to living in the same place and being an active member of the community, for example—with the hope that this will stop, or at least slow, the clock.

It's often hard to tell which came first—the negative beliefs about the nature of commitments just enumerated, or the aversion to commitment that characterizes the "I Just Can't Make a Commitment" block. Some people first acquire these beliefs, which then predisposes them to develop the block. In other instances the block is developed first, and then the beliefs serve as a way of rationalizing and reinforcing it. In these cases, the cultural messages are "taken to heart" because they jibe with a person's already ingrained inner views. But no matter which came first, the block and the beliefs about commitment commonly associated with it buttress each other; and overcoming the block means exploring and unlearning the beliefs.

The Underlying Blocks

It is easy to see the pain that people with the "I Just Can't Make a Commitment" block cause others, but the people who themselves have the block often appear enviably carefree. When people with this block are looked at more closely and a bit more compassionately, however, it becomes apparent that they too are in pain. This is because a closer examination always reveals that anyone with "I Just Can't Make a Commitment" block *always* has one or more other major love blocks. These entail considerable pain in themselves and serve as the foundation for the commitment block.

"I Don't Need Anyone—I'm Strong," "I'll Inevitably Get Hurt," and "I Feel Threatened When Another Person Gets Close" are the most common love blocks that precede and underlie the "I Can't Make a Commitment" block. Not everyone with one of these three blocks will develop problems with commitment, but almost everyone with the commitment block has one of the three. And in every case, overcoming the "I Just Can't Make a Commitment" block is impossible without first identifying and dealing with the block or blocks underneath it.

Elliot

If Patrick, the sportswriter in Chapter 11 with the "I'll Inevitably Get Hurt" block, and James, the social worker in Chapter 12 with the "I Feel Threatened When Another Person Gets Close" block, had not been able to break their "get close, then bolt" pattern in romantic relationships, they might have ended up like Elliot. Tall, thin, and handsome, Elliot was fifty-five when first interviewed but exuded a relaxed charm and openness that made him seem much younger. Once a highly successful business executive, Elliot had decided at age forty to "chuck it all" and direct his energies toward spiritual enlightenment, becoming an astrologer, teacher of meditation, and practitioner of various New Age therapies. Intelligent and intense, Elliot moves and speaks with a great deal of grace and refinement, and he listens intently. It's easy to see why women consider him extremely attractive.

Married for the first and only time at age twenty and divorced at thirty, Elliot has spent the more than twenty-five years since looking for the woman with whom he'll want to settle down for good. He's been involved romantically with a large number of women of different ages and types, entering each new relationship with the hope that "she'll be the one," he explained. But as time passes, he inevitably starts "getting signals that this woman is not the right one." At this point, "I start to feel trapped and to push her away, and finally I put an end to the relationship." As a result, most of Elliot's relationships have lasted only a matter of months; the longest lasted two years.

Each time he ends a romance, it's been Elliot's practice to tell the woman that he has trouble making commitments. While observing that "this is a line women today fall for and find reasonable," Elliot himself never really believed it. He's always been sure that with "the right woman," he'd have no difficulty remaining fully involved and faithful forever. Only in the months prior to his first interview had Elliot begun to question this view. It was slowly starting to dawn on him that when he says to a woman "I have trouble making commitments," he just might be telling her the truth.

Elliot's story illustrates the secondary nature of the "I Just Can't Make a Commitment" block. Although this may be Elliot's most obvious love block, his core block is "I'll Inevitably Get Hurt." At important junctures in Elliot's life, the people who were supposed to "be there" for him instead repeatedly abandoned him. It's because he equates closeness with abandonment that he developed such difficulty with commitments.

Elliot was the only child born to a financially struggling couple who were miserable together. Elliot remembers "a constant tension in the air" at home. His father abused his mother, and he also had a number of extramarital affairs. When Elliot was three, his parents finally separated; they divorced when he was four.

The divorce was only one of many disruptions in Elliot's childhood. The summer when he was four, he was sent to sleep-away camp. No one asked or told him about this ahead of time; he was simply picked up and taken off to camp one day. At age six, he was once again suddenly sent away with no word of preparation or explanation—this time to boarding school. At ten, more surprises were sprung on him. He was unexpectedly pulled out of school in the middle of a term, but instead of going home to his mother, who had custody, he was sent to his father's house, where he discovered that his father had remarried. A few weeks later he was sent to his mother's house, again without being told ahead of time, and found that his mother had a new spouse, too. From then on, Elliot "was shuttled back and forth" between his parents, seemingly at whim. He never felt comfortable or welcome in either home because neither stepparent liked him; instead, they treated him as an intrusive reminder of their respective spouses' former marriages.

These early-life experiences gave Elliot what he characterized as "a very confused sense of the world and who I was." To Elliot, the world was a chaotic, unpredictable place in which he had no control over what happened to him and no one to count on. Although his parents and stepparents were physically present, Elliot's emotional reality was that he was alone, abandoned, an "emotional orphan." He felt that he had been thrown out into "the cold, cruel world" and forced to fend for himself while he was still too young, needy, and defenseless. From earliest boyhood, Elliot carried within a sense of dread, convinced that he was doomed to go through life without ever finding a place where he'd truly belong.

Elliot's experiences in school reinforced his sense of never belonging. After first grade, Elliot's teachers and parents decided that because he was so smart they should "skip" him ahead two grades. As a result, Elliot went through school two years ahead of his peers, surrounded by children to whom he was intellectually equal but who were way ahead of him in every other way. "I had a tremendous identity problem," he recalled. "In neither my home world or the outer world was there any attention paid to my inner developmental clock. Repeatedly, I was put in situations that I was too young to handle emotionally; my parents and stepparents had no sense of how children grow up and what a child needs."

In junior high and high school, Elliot was "socially very insecure." From age eleven to fifteen, he was also overweight because of a glandular problem that was later rectified. "I always had friends because I had always wanted people to like me, but I still felt awkward and insecure." At around age fifteen, Elliot became thin again and grew more self-possessed and socially confident. He also became "slightly delinquent" at this time, "hanging out in pool halls, drinking, and associating with guys who were hoods."

When he was sixteen Elliot started college. He initially floundered, because he "had no idea of why I was there." Then two things happened that would change his life. First, he was having a conversation in his dormitory with some upper-class students whom he very much respected, when one turned to him and said, "You know, Elliot, you're intellectually sensitive." That night, Elliot stayed up reading *The Sun Also Rises* from cover to cover and "became an intellectual." Although he had been put two years ahead in school, never before had he had a sense of himself as someone with intellectual abilities that others might admire and be attracted to.

The second thing that changed Elliot's life was his discovery of sex. Shortly after arriving at college, he lost his virginity in an awkward one-night stand. A few months later, when he was seventeen, he began his first continuing sexual relationship, and became aware "that it was through sex and intimacy that I could really connect." Elliot also realized that he was "very sexually athletic," able to perform at a fever pitch for long periods, and that "girls really liked that."

When Elliot was nineteen, he got involved with a girl named Beth, whom he never really liked. He was planning to end the relationship when they found out she was pregnant, "another shocking event that seemed imposed from without." In the 1950s, Elliot and Beth didn't have many options; soon they married, and soon after that Beth gave birth to a boy.

Elliot very much liked Beth's parents, who "were exceptionally cultured. They gave me the kind of family and validation that I was looking for. In a way, I married *them*," he said. Beth, however, couldn't stand her parents, and for the ten years that they were married she and Elliot couldn't stand each other much, either. Their only blessing was their son. Elliot liked the experience of taking care of a small child, and watching and fostering his son's growth.

Throughout his marriage Elliot had affairs with other women, including two major ones, one with Beth's best friend, the other with the wife of his best friend. Never, however, did he consider leaving his marriage. "I was miserable but felt it was an acceptable misery because it was known, and leaving just never occurred to me," Elliot explained. "It was only after I went to therapy and my therapist asked, 'Why do you have to stay married?' that it dawned on me that I could leave. All the doors weren't closed as I had thought."

Elliot honestly feels that he has loved most of the women he's been involved with since his divorce. He has stayed in touch with most of them after ending the romance, and feels "very loyal" to them as a friend. "Even after I've started to pull back from a woman and the idea of a continuing romantic relationship, I still deeply care and am interested in her," he explained. Nevertheless, no matter how much Elliot still cares, the fact remains that for nearly a quarter of a century now he has gotten involved with woman after woman, then dumped each one.

Elliot's "I Just Can't Make a Commitment" block is really an outgrowth of the "I'll Inevitably Get Hurt" block, which he developed in response to his parents' early abandonments. Seeing himself as an emotional orphan, Elliot has gone from relationship to relationship as though each were a foster home. From the start, he has "known" none of his relationships will last, just as an orphan knows that each of his stays in various foster homes will be temporary. What Elliot needs is a relationship that would be to him what an adoptive home is to an orphan—a place where he could find permanent security and love, where he would really belong, where he wouldn't get thrown out or abandoned *no matter what*. But deep within, Elliot is so sure that closeness will inevitably lead to abandonment that he can't separate the two; as soon as he starts to feel close to a woman, it triggers the feeling that "uh-oh, abandonment and all its attendant pain is just around the corner." This in turn triggers a response of "I'd better get out of here fast" and causes him to quickly back away from deeper involvement.

To extend the emotional-orphan metaphor, as soon as Elliot starts to feel settled and secure in a foster home, he becomes scared that he'll be sent away, kicked out, or in some way forced to leave. So before that can happen, Elliot runs away from home. He knows that this will bring the pain of losing the closeness he was starting to feel "at home" with, but he believes this pain will hurt less than the pain of being thrown out once again. Moreover, Elliot can exercise control over *when* he'll experience this pain, whereas as a child he had no idea when he'd be sent away. As an adult, Elliot unconsciously assumes that although his life will continue to be one of constant leave-takings, at least he can determine how and when they occur.

Along with "I'll Inevitably Get Hurt" and "I Just Can't Make a Commitment," Elliot also has "I Want Love, But Only If It's a Certain Way," the block discussed in Chapter 16. As a way of protecting himself against the scary possibility of getting into a romantic relationship that he'll want to stay in permanently, Elliot has devised an idealized image of "the right woman" that no real woman could possibly live up to. His standards are so impossibly high that even the most promising candidates for the position of permanent mate inevitably turn out to be terrible disappointments. Consciously, Elliot wants to have a lasting relationship with a woman. Unconsciously, he would rather keep on looking for the perfect woman that he knows he'll never find than risk intimacy with a woman who realistically could offer him the love he desires. If he did get the love he longs for, there would always be the possibility that one day the woman would decide to take her love away. For someone who has suffered as many abandonments as Elliot, that is too great a risk.

Yet another love block that Elliot suffers from is "I Don't Deserve

Love," which dovetails with and reinforces the others. At his innermost core, Elliot feels that he is really "bad." Like all children who have been emotionally abandoned, he grew up convinced that there must be something terribly wrong with him to have caused the rejections. Afraid to let a woman see how bad a person he really is, Elliot gets involved with women whom he perceives as not smart enough to pick up on his badness right away—and just to stay on the safe side, he ends each relationship before even the least perceptive have enough time to start catching on. In this way, Elliot does indeed protect himself from being "found out" and dumped, but he also deprives himself of the chance to experience long-term love, and of the chance to be known and loved for his real self. Moreover, he deprives himself of the chance of being loved by an equal. At the time he was interviewed, Elliot was beginning to see this. "I choose women who will not abandon me the way I was abandoned as a child, but this means I choose women who are not independent enough, not challenging, not smart enough for me to stay with," he admitted. "I want to be validated by a woman who is my equal, but I am afraid that a woman who is my equal will find me unworthy the way my mother did, and then won't want me around."

The Change Process: What Elliot Could Do

Many people with this block take the approach long used by Elliot. They tell the people they're involved with, "I have a problem with commitments" and expect them to accept this, often adding, "It's just the way I am." They feel no compunction about their problem, no urge to resolve it, no sense that it might be their responsibility to do something about it. They think it's other people's duty to deal with it, in fact. For someone with this sort of attitude, the first major step toward overcoming the "I Just Can't Make a Commitment" block would be to finally admit, "It's arrogant for me to think that others should just accept my problem, especially when it has had such a negative impact on so many. I'm the one who has the problem, and it's up to me to do something about it."

At the time he was interviewed, Elliot was just starting to come to these conclusions, but had not yet made any noticeable changes in his pattern of relating to women. To really change, the next step would be for him to make a full commitment to his own emotional growth. The psychologist John Wellwood once observed that many people who have devoted themselves to becoming highly spiritually developed are nonetheless leading lives that are a mess as far as interpersonal relationships are concerned.[1] Elliot is a good example. He has committed himself to his own spiritual and emotional growth in many respects, but he has yet to make a commitment to overcoming the love blocks that prevent him from getting the sort of love he needs and wants from a woman. When Elliot was a child, no one ever said, "Your emotional health and security are of utmost importance. I will see to it that you get the love and sense of security every child needs." Elliot was being equally negligent with his adult self, and thus allowing his childhood state of inner deprivation to continue. To change, he needs to make the same sort of commitment to learning how to take in love as he made to learning how to meditate. Rather than tell others "I have trouble with commitments," he needs to tell himself "I have a problem that hurts me and others, and I need to work on it each and every day until I've overcome it. I have to give my emotional health the same attention and care I give to my bodily health and spiritual well-being."

Once he had made this commitment to his emotional well-being, probably the best thing for Elliot to do would be to find a psychotherapist he feels at home and safe with. Obviously, not everyone with the "I Just Can't Make a Commitment" block has it in such a pronounced form. Many with milder versions were not physically abandoned the way Elliot was; instead, they grew up in homes where the parents were physically on the scene but emotionally "not there." Such people don't necessarily need psychotherapy to overcome their difficulties with commitment. But someone who suffered the degree of trauma that Elliot did needs a caring, compassionate, reliable therapist who is willing to hang in there and "be there" fully for him until his childhood wounds have healed.

Many people with the "I Just Can't Make a Commitment" block are unaware of how much this block affects them. They're also unaware of what happened to them in childhood. But very often they display a pattern that is extremely telling: they fall in love instantly, seeing the newly beloved as the most perfect, wonderful creature on earth. When a person is prone to this sort of instant idealization, it's often an indication that early in life he suffered a traumatic disruption in a primal relationship, most often with his mother. As a young child, he probably adored his mother totally and saw her as perfect and all-loving. Then in some way she hurt him; in his pain and rage he mentally knocked her off her pedestal and saw her as flawed, human, even defiled. In his adult relationships, the woman (or man, if he's gay) he initially sees as utterly perfect is soon enough revealed to be all too human, so he rejects her with the justification that she's "not the right one." He feels guilty about doing to his once-beloved lover what his mother did to him, but his pain about what his mother did to him is so great that it outweighs the guilt. Moreover, unconsciously he is identifying with the aggressor by mimicking his mother's rejecting behavior, while at the same time he is getting revenge against her by causing a symbolic mother considerable self-doubt and pain. People who display this pattern very often protest, "But there was nothing wrong with my relationship with my mother (or father). My only problem is that I can't find the right woman (or man)." The pattern itself, however, suggests otherwise.

Psychotherapy does not need to be long-term to be successful. In the case of someone like Elliot, it would be important for both the client and therapist to begin their relationship by making a long-term commitment to it. People with the "I Just Can't Make a Commitment" block tend to start therapy, then stop after a while, then start again with another therapist (or method, program, or school), then stop with that one and later go on to another. Many do the same thing with spiritual leaders and approaches. Significantly, this usually replicates the pattern described above: at first, the new therapist, mentor or method is considered "the greatest," but eventually disillusionment sets in, and the person feels embittered about being once again betrayed and abandoned by a parent figure who has failed to live up to his expectations. In fact, this *is* happening: by never fully committing himself, the person with the "I Just Can't Make a Commitment" block is abandoning his own needy child within. He needs to commit himself to taking care of that child in a long-term therapeutic relationship. Flight from commitment may have enabled him to survive so far, but it has not nourished his growth in the way he hungers for it to be nourished.

Once a person like Elliot is engaged in an ongoing relationship with a therapist, he would then be in a position to enter the final stages of overcoming the "I Just Can't Make a Commitment" block. This would begin with doing what Patrick in Chapter 11 did: making a promise to stay with his current lover even as he felt the resurgence of feelings of dissatisfaction and itchiness, and making a commitment to examine those feelings and find out what they're really about. Although initially experienced as disappointment ("I thought she/he was the one, but I guess I was wrong") or outright revulsion ("How could I have ever seen anything in him/her? What a creep! I must have been blind"), fear is always what's behind the urge to get some "psychological space" or leave the relationship entirely. The fear may be of being hurt, of being dependent on another human being, of being psychologically invaded or overwhelmed, of being intimately known and thus "found out" as flawed and unlovable—or of all these things and others, too. Until these fears are confronted, a person with the "I Just Can't Make a Commitment" block will never find out if a relationship can conceivably provide the sustained, dependable, in-depth love he so very much wants.

Chapter 14
"Love Will Get in the Way of Success"

The photograph on the cover of the July 1987 issue of *Esquire* shows happy-looking tennis champ John McEnroe cozying up with his smiling wife, Tatum O'Neal, and their beaming first child. Superimposed over this classic "happy family" portrait is the ominous headline, HAS LOVE RUINED JOHN MCENROE? Underneath, a subhead says, "He Found Tatum and Became a Father, but Whatever Happened to the Fire?" The implication, obviously, is that McEnroe is a modern-day Sampson who has lost his ability to stay tops in his field because of his involvement with O'Neal, a twentieth-century Delilah.

Today most people would scoff at the once-popular notion that athletes shouldn't have sex prior to an important contest because it will sap them of their strength and stamina. Nevertheless, as the *Esquire* cover illustrates, it's still taken for granted in many quarters that intimate involvements threaten or at least interfere with an individual's chances of achieving worldly success. Many see life divided into two separate spheres—the love sphere and the achievement sphere—and believe it's possible to excel in only one. If a person becomes too entangled in intimate relationships, they also believe, his progress up the achievement ladder will inevitably be slowed or he might get sidetracked off the ladder altogether. This view implicitly assumes that a person has to choose between a rich and rewarding personal life and a rich and rewarding career; except in rare cases, it's not possible to have both.

Ways of Resolving the Split

People who see the world divided into two opposing spheres are faced with a dilemma they can resolve in one of two ways. One group puts all their energies into the achievement sphere, figuring that if they've got to make a choice, it's wisest to make success their first priority. The other group figures that if they have to make a choice between worldly success and successful personal relationships, they'd rather have the latter.

For people who make the first choice, the belief that "Love Will Get in the Way of Success" almost always functions as a love block. Some leave no room in their lives for personal relationships at all, while others may have any number of intimate relationships as long as those relationships don't get in the way of their ambitions. If someone they're involved with begins to express a desire for more time or consideration, they will likely respond that the other person is "too demanding" or "asking too much." If someone becomes seriously ill or gets into some kind of trouble, they might have every intention of being there to help, but somehow their workload will make it impossible for them to get away. To such people, the belief that "Love Will Get in the Way of Success" functions as a love block because it places strict limits on their emotional involvements or precludes them entirely.

For people who try to resolve the perceived split by rejecting achievement in favor of a more rewarding personal life, the belief that "Love Will Get in the Way of Success" doesn't necessarily serve as a love block. People who choose love over success may have very fulfilling personal lives; if they're blocked at all, it's in the achievement area. This does not mean, however, that they'll have no trouble with this particular love block. This is because many people who believe love and success are diametrically opposed also believe, paradoxically, that they must achieve success in order to earn love—and this remains the case regardless of how they've tried to resolve the love/success split in their lives.

Cultural Influences

As is the case with numerous other love blocks, the "Love Will Get in the Way of Success" block says as much about American culture in general as it does about the individuals who have it. In many parts of the world, the prevailing view is that while work may be necessary to sustain life, it's certainly not the main point of life: love, family, learning, enjoyment, spiritual development, and so forth, are seen as of more inherent value. In the United States, however, there's always been such a strong emphasis on achievement and material acquisition that many people have come to see work as the main reason for living. Work, such people believe, justifies a person's existence, making him worthy and whole. They so ardently believe this that they'd never think to question one well-known actress's assertion that "it's not what you feel that matters, it's the work you do."[1]

The 1960s and early 1970s brought a short but significant period when there was widespread questioning of the work ethic that has been so central to American culture since the country's beginnings. It was widely agreed that the traditional emphasis on doing, achieving, and getting rich made for narrow, unhealthy, and unhappy lives; people should spend more time relaxing, having fun, just plain being. And certainly, the argument continued, people should spend more time making love, less time making money. By the early 1980s, however, the laid-back flower children had given way to the dress-for-success crowd and the work ethic had come back into popularity with a vengeance. Suddenly, being rich and successful had become the baby boom generation's central concern, characterized by the money-obsessed yuppies who seemed to equate human worth with net worth.

With money worship and lust for success on the rise, there occurred an accompanying shift in popular perceptions and expectations of love. "Relationships? Who has the time?" became a popular cry. Suddenly, it was chic to be too booked up for personal involvements, unless they could be squeezed in between power lunch and aerobics class. Some people even began using the jargon of business management in the personal realm, substituting "falling in love" with "being in the merger mode" and "getting a divorce" with "going through divestiture."

Above all, however, the prevailing view among the success oriented in the 1980s was that relationships should be efficient and uncomplicated. If maintaining a relationship involves work, or if it looks as though there might be problems—forget it, it's not worth it. As an ambitious young woman told a reporter from *The New York Times* in early 1987, "I went with a guy last fall. He had a good job as a stockbroker. He was nice to me. But then he started telling me about his family. And there were problems. And I thought, 'What happens if I fall in love and we get married? What then?' "[2]

The Impact of Gender

At first glance, it's easy to get the impression that the "Love Will Get in the Way of Success" block is much more predominant among men than women. True, the socialization process that males go through in our culture encourages them to make achievement and success their priorities, and to place less importance on relationships, which are seen as women's main concern. For a man to devote himself singlemindedly to pursuing his worldly ambitions has traditionally been viewed not as problematic, but as normal and healthy—even if it has meant he neglected his family as a result.

Yet the cultural messages men have traditionally received are actually more complicated. Traditionally, men haven't been led to expect a conflict between love and success; they've taken it for granted that they could have both. This is because they've been taught that women are prospective "helpmates," and that marriage will therefore help further them in their careers; indeed, many a man has been taught that the single most important reason for marrying is that having a wife to provide emotional support, sex, and domestic services will better enable him to pursue his ambitions. At the same time, though, most men have learned that there are certain kinds of women who are *not* helpmates, and involvement with them surely *will* be a hindrance or liability. A woman who is highly sexual and alluring, for example, is a risky choice. Although such a woman might impress other men and serve as a status symbol, she also could very easily rob a man of his will, power, and drive, turning him into a "pussy-whipped" wimp; hence, men need to be very careful about not "falling prey" to this sort of woman and her "feminine wiles."

Also to be avoided are women who become burdens, whether because they get pregnant too often, have unreasonable financial expectations, let themselves "go to pot" physically, want intimacy and communication from their partners, develop health problems or mental illness, nag and complain too much, or generally make too many demands. Hooking up with such a woman will hurt rather than help a man's career (which makes it all the more unfortunate that many women who turn out to be burdens very often appear to be helpmates when a relationship or marriage begins). Finally, men have been taught to avoid women with their own ambitions, especially if they reject the notion that in a marriage the husband's ambitions should always come first. With this kind of woman, a man could feel a conflict between appeasing his mate and furthering his own career.

In essence, then, the lesson that men in our culture receive is not so much that love will get in the way of success; it's more that the love of the right kind of woman will foster success, while the love of the wrong kind of woman will hinder it. Even with the right kind of woman, though, smart men learn not to get too deeply or passionately involved, for a man who wants to scale the peaks of success can't afford to "lose his head."

Since women traditionally were not allowed to entertain dreams of worldly success and achievement, and love was designated their primary concern, most experienced no overt conflict. As women have moved into the paid labor force in greater numbers and with higher aspirations, however, more and more have developed the "Love Will Get in the Way of Success" block. In fact, a case could be made that today women are more susceptible than men. This is because for women the conflict between intimate relationships and work success is a real conflict of enormous proportions, not simply a perceived one. Not only does a woman still have to work harder to achieve success, but she most likely also doesn't have a devoted helpmate standing behind her the way many men do. Whether she's straight or gay, her partner probably won't be willing to put fostering her career first—if she has a partner at all, that is. In many cases, the demands of time and energy placed upon ambitious career women are so great that they are unable to sustain or even begin a one-on-one relationship of great intimacy.

An additional reason so many women are susceptible to this block is that they've not had a loving sponsor or mentor to encourage them in their career and give emotional and practical help. Most successful people can point to one or two, usually older, people in their field who smoothed the way for them. A person being sponsored learns that loving relationships can facilitate success, and might even be necessary for it. But many women have had to try to make their way without this critical form of support. Worse, like Carole in Chapter 2, many have been actively discouraged from seeking to excel by parents, teachers, work superiors, and colleagues. Large numbers of women have been told time and again, in a variety of ways, that they don't have what it takes to make it in a man's world, and that even if they do, they still should eschew a career because it would interfere with their "real" job—taking care of men and children.

The kinds of role models a person had in childhood can also affect susceptibility to this block, and this is true for men as well as women. Individuals who believe love will get in the way of success very likely grew up without much close contact with adults who were able to balance their work with personal relationships. Those from conventional middle-class homes probably saw having a job, making money, and being successful in the outside world as Dad's role, while Mom's role was making sure everyone was fed and happy. Those from working-class homes where both parents held jobs, or from homes headed by single parents who were employed outside, probably grew up with people whose work left them so depleted that they had little left over to put into relationships.

Addiction to Work

Many of the people who have made success their highest priority are workaholics—people addicted to work as others are addicted to drugs or booze. Workaholics are so obsessed with doing well and getting ahead that they are driven to work relentlessly. They are very conscious of their belief that "Love Will Get in the Way of Success," and often cite it as the reason their lives are so lacking in the area of personal relationships. "I'd love to have an intimate relationship," a single workaholic will say. "But I'm so beat at the end of the day and on weekends that socializing is out of the question. Plus, going out on weeknights would leave me so tired, and I can't afford to be tired at work." Similarly, a success-oriented workaholic who has a relationship that's supposed to be intimate but really isn't might say, "I'd love to spend more time with my partner, but my work requires that I put in long hours. Then when I get home, I'm too exhausted to do anything but watch a little TV and then go to sleep. I don't like this situation, but that's how it is; there's nothing I can do about it."

Of course, and this is an important point, not everyone who works long and hard does so for unhealthy reasons. In an economy with so many low-paying jobs and such high prices, a large percentage of the population must spend the bulk of its time working just to make ends meet. But these members of the working class are not the people with the "Love Will Get in the Way of Success" block. Most people who must work hard and long to make ends meet are doing so in order to support their families; given the choice they would prefer to spend more time relaxing and being with loved ones, and less time working. But workaholics who fear that "Love Will Get in the Way of Success" tend to be very different. Usually middle class or with middle-class aspirations, they think about work in terms of careers rather than jobs. More important, people with this block don't really *have to* work as hard and long as many of them do in order to make ends meet; on the contrary, many make far more money than they really need. And while they may claim it's on account of their families that they work so hard and long, this usually isn't entirely true—or true at all. They use work as a way of limiting or avoiding the kind of relationships—close, time-consuming ones—that could hinder their efforts to fulfill their own career ambitions. If they have somehow found enough time during their career building to marry and have children, it's very likely that their families would be far happier if they spent more time at home, even if this meant a cut in income.

Fear of Intimacy

The rationalizations that workaholics use sound so reasonable that many people simply take them at face value. But in nine cases out of ten, workaholics are not telling the whole story when they say, "I would spare more time for relationships if I could, but I can't." This is not to say that they are intentionally lying; on a conscious level they may sincerely believe they have no other choice. Somewhere in their unconscious, though, lurks a fear of intimacy, and it is this fear as much as anything else that causes their devotion to work.

In a number of different fields, particularly such demanding ones as medicine, investment banking, corporate law, and journalism, a person really does have to give his all to make it to the top. However, there are usually compelling psychological reasons why certain individuals choose such demanding careers, and why they put up with the ridiculous hours and enormous personal costs these careers entail. If some are motivated purely by the desire for money and prestige, many others are also driven by the fear of intimacy. As much as they may complain about the "rat race," they've chosen demanding, time-consuming work for two reasons: it provides a socially acceptable way of avoiding or constraining intimate involvements and it keeps them so busy that they don't have a moment to experience their loneliness fully.

Why do success-seeking workaholics fear intimacy? The main reason is that those with the "Love Will Get in the Way of Success" block inevitably have other, underlying blocks, and among these underlying blocks there's always one that's most central—"I Don't Deserve Love." Deep down, they believe they are inadequate and unlovable, and they're afraid of letting others get close and finding this out.

At first glance, it might be hard to believe that success-seeking workaholics are really suffering from low self-esteem. After all, so many are extremely accomplished and appear so confident and pleased with themselves. But regardless of their accomplishments, they harbor within the belief that they're really not quite good enough, not worthy enough, not whole enough. They see worldly achievement as a way to justify their existence and make themselves worthy of love.

Most workaholics are perfectionists who see the world in black-and-white, all-or-nothing terms. To them, life is a success-failure dichotomy. If they're not succeeding, then they must be failing; when it comes to their own performance, there's no middle ground, no doing "passably" or "okay."

Moreover, most workaholic/perfectionists apply these harsh and rigid standards not just to their work performance but to nearly everything they do. Activities that are supposed to be fun and relaxing are approached with the same drive to succeed that they bring to work. They must be excellent tennis players, great golfers, ace squash players; if they run or ride bikes, they must enter marathons or participate in grueling hill climbs. Lovemaking is also approached as if performance rather than union or pleasure is what matters most. After sex, "How was it?" and other similar questions are veiled ways of asking "How did I do?" If their lover happens to be sexually experienced, there's usually an additional concern: "How am I in comparison to other lovers you've had?" Even if this question is not asked aloud, its presence in the achiever's mind has the effect of distancing him from both his partner and his own inner experience.

Although they appear to be seeking success, most workaholic-perfectionists are primarily concerned with something more subtle— *not experiencing failure*. When they achieve success, they tend not to enjoy it, for it is not really what they're after. What they really want is to avoid the feelings of shame, humiliation, and regret they know failure will bring. In such cases, intimacy represents another area in which they could very well fail, so they steer clear.

While they often do achieve great success, workaholics generally feel that no matter what they've accomplished, it's not enough. They never reach a point where they say, "I've done pretty well. I'm going to give myself a break and rest on my laurels for a while." Either they feel their successes have been flukes, and therefore are not indicative of their true talent and worth; or they feel their successes are legitimate but fleeting, and that tomorrow they're bound to fall flat on their faces and lose everything achieved so far.

Success-obsessed workaholics also usually don't realize that while their achievements may make them more admirable, they don't necessarily make them any more lovable. They don't see the distinction between love and admiration at all, in fact. They've gone through their entire lives thinking "If I am really successful, then I will be lovable and worthy." But in truth, the only way they'll ever be able to feel loved by themselves and others is to give up the belief that the more success and worldly achievement a person piles up, the greater his or her lovability and inherent human worth. Overcoming their block means seeing that being successful and being a worthy, lovable human being have nothing to do with each other; it's only in cultures that emphasize work and wealth as ours does that people learn to mistakenly equate the two.

Sara

Sara is a TV producer in her late thirties with dark, curly hair and large brown eyes that appear to miss nothing. Although her freckles and comical facial expressions give the impression of innocence, after talking with her for a few minutes, it's evident that she's savvy, sophisticated, and impossible to shock. A heavy smoker, she has a deep voice and a quizzical way of tilting her head as she speaks.

Sara was the only girl in a family of three children, and much younger than her older brothers, who were close in age. Her parents were both children of immigrants who had fled the persecution of Jews in Poland around the turn of the century. Although a small chain of furniture stores they'd started and owned made Sara's parents very well-off, they did not have the opportunity to get the kinds of educations they dreamed of. Sara's father went to a public college but had to drop out after one year when his father died, and illness in her family had prevented Sara's mother from going to college at all. They vowed that their children would be able to attend any of the nation's most elite universities, achieving what they themselves could not.

Sara's parents' marriage "consisted of them bickering and picking at each other," she explained. "They never showed any affection towards each other, but you could tell they really needed each other. They were dependent on having each other to pick on." Of the two, the father was the more passive. "He was very noncommunicative, and when you were with him you'd get the feeling that he was there in his body but not there in mind or spirit. Every night after dinner he'd bury his face in a book, then fall asleep."

Sara's mother was much more vocal. She could be very loving but was also very demanding and critical. When she gave the children love and affection, she did not give it unconditionally; the children had to earn it. And the best way the children could earn it was to be successful. As children, this meant excelling in academic subjects and also in extracurricular activities like debating and working on the school newspaper. As adults, it meant being successful in a career that was both lucrative and prestigious.

One of Sara's older brothers responded to their parents' concern with success by becoming involved with drugs and dropping out of high school. Eventually he would turn his life around and become a very conventional young man who married, had children, and joined his father's business. But the years of turmoil he caused left their mark on the family, particularly on Sara. Sara's parents, especially her mother, "acted as though my brother developed his problems intentionally, for the single purpose of making them upset and embarrassing them in the eyes of their friends," Sara explained. "My mother would go on for hours and hours, weeping and complaining, 'how can he do this to me? What kind of son have I raised? Why is he so set on breaking his mother's heart?' "

Sara's mother repeatedly made her daughter promise that she would not break her heart the way her brother had. This was a promise Sara wanted very much to keep. She longed for love and affection from her mother and knew that the only way she'd ever have a chance of getting it was to become a superachiever. This way, she thought, "maybe I could get my father to wake up and pay some attention to me, too."

Sara eventually "did my parents proud" by being valedictorian of her high school class and being accepted into a number of prestigious colleges. In devoting herself so single-mindedly to her schoolwork, however, Sara never developed much of a social life. She felt awkward in social situations, "not really knowing what to do or say." She also felt competitive with both girls and boys. "I felt with the girls that they were much prettier and had better social skills than I did," Sara explained. "With the boys I felt it was important to outdo them, to prove how much smarter or better at math I was. I could only compete. I didn't know how to have fun or flirt or just hang out."

In college and the years afterwards, Sara had a few affairs with men, but "each time we started to get close, one of us pulled away." Afraid that she was a failure at romance, she avoided later involvements so she wouldn't have to go through the unpleasant experience of failing and feeling humiliated, stupid, and full of self-loathing again. After college, Sara began work in the television industry, and as she went through her late twenties and early thirties, she focused single-mindedly on getting ahead, which struck her as the most sensible thing to do. After all, not only is TV a very competitive industry, but work is something she's always felt confident about being very good at; besides, in work, unlike in love, she has control.

Sara's devotion to professional success has paid off handsomely. Beginning as a news-writing intern at a TV station in the Southwest, she eventually worked her way up to a powerful position as a news producer at one of the major networks. By her mid-thirties, she was making a six-figure income, had won several awards, and was highly respected by her peers.

Sara's devotion to her career didn't mean she had gone through adulthood without forming strong attachments. Like many workaholics, she made the people she worked with the center of her social and emotional life and was thus able to enjoy relationships that offered her intimacy but didn't entail all of the usual risks. In a "work family," the various members may have strong feelings for one another, but they have been brought together and stay bound together for reasons other than, and apart from, their feelings. In an intimate relationship outside work, if either person's feelings begin to wane, the relationship could end, but a work relationship will continue because it wasn't based only on feelings to begin with. Thus work families can help a person like Sara mediate between the fear of closeness and the desire for it.

The Change Process: Sara's Way

Although work families often are very rewarding, they sometimes break down unexpectedly. A person who has relied on her work family as her primary means of emotional sustenance is then left stranded. This is what happened to Sara. After many years of stability, suddenly there were major cutbacks and a lot of reshuffling at her network. Many of the people she had been closest to lost their jobs, while others were transferred to other divisions. Sara ended up working with an entirely new group of people, many far younger than she, and quite cutthroat as well. Suddenly, the safe, secure work family she had so long relied on had disappeared.

Also, even when things at work were fine, Sara sometimes found herself feeling lonely, and as she grew older, her bouts of loneliness had grown deeper and more frequent. More and more, she said, "I found myself thinking that what I really wanted to do was find someone and fall in love and get married." She became increasingly aware that if her intimacy needs were going to get met, she'd have to begin making some changes in her life, and shortly after her thirty-seventh birthday she sought out help.

Sara discovered her ambivalence about intimate involvement with a man runs deep. On the one hand, she has a romantic fantasy of one day meeting "that special someone who will sweep me off my feet," and she thinks "it would be really wonderful to have a partner I could be best friends with and grow old with," and who would "stand by me as I'd stand by him." At the same time, though, neither her parents' partnership, the only one she's observed up close, nor her own limited experience with men gave her much reason to think her romantic fantasies could ever come true. "I never once went out with a guy who I think would really, truly put his wife's career or fulfillment on level with his own," she explained, adding that among her peers she hasn't seen many heterosexual relationships that suggest otherwise.

Yet none of this went to the root of Sara's block. Eventually she learned that in her case, as in ninety-nine out of a hundred cases, there's another block underneath the "Love Will Get in the Way of Success" block—and it's almost always "I Don't Deserve Love." As discussed in Chapters 3 and 5, building self-esteem is not an overnight or one-step process. Nevertheless, it can be broken down into some concrete tasks, which Sara started tackling one by one.

Like most people with low self-esteem, Sara has always tended to discount her strengths and successes while focusing on—and magnifying—her weaknesses and failings. One of her main foci—in fact, *the* main one—has been her weight. Of course, the cultural emphasis on female thinness makes it hard for any girl or woman to feel good about herself if she is not extremely slender. For Sara, however, it was especially difficult because she was always a bit plump while both her parents were "obsessed with being thin," she explained. "They were mortified by my not being skinny like they are. It was like I planned it to embarrass them. It was my one failing, and I was never allowed to forget it. Every time something good would happen, like my winning a National Merit Scholarship or aceing an exam, my mother would say, 'That's wonderful. Now if only you lost fifteen pounds . . .' " To this day, Sara says, the first thing her mother does when she visits is to visually inspect Sara from head to toe and then comment on her weight.

In the past, Sara dieted constantly. Although she lost weight numerous times, she's always gained it back eventually. This made her feel like an utter failure, which only lessened her self-esteem. Moreover, even at her thinnest, Sara remained preoccupied with her weight and still felt fat. She had always believed, "If only I were thin, I'd feel good about myself," but, in fact, this never proved true.

An important step for Sara in building self-esteem has been to stop focusing on her weight, making the whole issue less central to her self-esteem. She used to say to herself, "Yes, I'm smart, successful, energetic, talented, organized, efficient, et cetera . . . *but I'm also fat*," allowing that last statement to totally discount all that came before. Now she recites a slightly altered script: "I'm smart, successful, funny, energetic, talented, organized, efficient, et cetera," she tells herself, "and I'm also a bit fat. So big deal! That's not the most important thing about me, and it doesn't nullify or overshadow all my other qualities, not at all."

Sara has also worked on her habit of all-or-nothing thinking. In the past, whenever she made a mistake, she would mentally berate herself for being "a complete idiot," "a total mess," and "entirely worthless." Now she tells herself, "Oops, you really screwed up there, didn't you? But that doesn't mean you're an idiot or a mess or worthless. It means you're human." By changing the way she habitually talks to herself in these types of way, she has liberated herself from constant self-inflicted assaults on her self-esteem.

As Sara has looked more closely at her childhood, she's become more aware of how terribly afraid she is to fail. Growing up, she learned that if she failed, she would be "breaking my mother's heart." With such an onerous potential consequence, no wonder she feared it so much. In therapy, she was prodded to consider what would happen to her now if she failed. Would she break her mother's heart? No, Sara acknowledged, that was no longer something she thought would happen. Would she be laughed at? Humiliated? Thrown out of her apartment? What exactly would happen? As Sara considered this, she realized there wasn't anything specific she was afraid of. "If I lost my job, I'd be miserable for a while, but I'd get another," she said. After a moment's pause she added, "I've never really thought this out before, but I think that if I failed, I wouldn't even feel that embarrassed. Oh, maybe a little, but not that much. I think I may be afraid more out of habit, because failure is something I've *always* feared and avoided."

As a way of further exploring this fear, Sara decided to take up an activity that she was pretty sure she would fail at, in this case tennis. As a child, Sara never received any athletic instruction or encouragement. She tried a couple of sports a few times, but soon gave up, deciding that she was a klutz. As she expected, Sara did turn out to be a pretty poor tennis player, at least at first, but the strange thing was, she had fun doing it anyway. She took lessons with a group of other adults who had just taken up the sport; no one cared about impressing anyone, and everyone had a great time just getting out there and hitting the ball around.

For Sara, tennis opened up new social worlds, for she met many people she became friendly with, and they in turn introduced her to friends of theirs. It opened up new worlds for her internally, as well. All her life she had lived by the motto "If something's not worth doing well, it's not worth doing at all—and my worth is dependent on doing well." Now, however, she had given herself permission to not do well—and had found that it was not only fun, it helped her self-worth. For the first time in her life, Sara was learning how to play (to really play, not to work at play), and for the first time she was learning that "I can be myself at my least competent and not feel like I'm worthless as a result."

As she has become less afraid of failing, Sara has begun to work toward a new realization—that the notions of success and failure really don't apply to human relationships. One of the reasons Sara has shied away from deep intimacy in the past is that she believed "I don't know how to do it." She thought that getting close to someone was like learning to ride a bicycle—there's really only one way to do it, and if you can't get it right, then you can't ride. But she learned that to understand relationships, it's better to think in terms of flowers. Flowers not only come in all different varieties, but also have many different kinds of unfolding. It's the same with people, who differ in appearance, personality, and the ways they naturally open up to intimacy and love. Some are like crocuses—they just pop out and are open to closeness and the exchange of love. Others are like roses—they start out very tight and closed up, then gradually unfold and open. Realizing she'd never condemn a rose for "failing" to flower in the same way that a crocus would, Sara has begun trying to stop thinking of relationships in terms of success and failure. The fact that she has gotten to her late thirties without a romantic relationship working out does not mean she is a failure in the intimacy sphere. It means she's more like a rose than a crocus—a late bloomer when it comes to love.

Another key realization that Sara has been working toward is that for everyone who was raised to see love and success in opposition the key word is *balance*. It is generally true that when people feel genuinely loved, they don't have the same obsessive hunger for or preoccupation with success that workaholics display. At the same time, though, most people find love does not eliminate the need for other kinds of fulfillment, whether through work, athletics, politics, hobbies, or some other creative activity. To be healthy and live life to its fullest, most people need a balance of both love and work or a similar endeavor.[3] That's been said so many times as to perhaps seem trite by now. But in an era when so many people are living lives that are so heavily tilted toward the success side, it can stand being stated once again.

Chapter 15

"I Don't Want to Have to Ask for What I Need" (Or "Why Can't You Read My Mind?")

Imagine you're in an ice-cream store, one that serves dozens of different flavors. After the counterman fills your order, he asks the couple standing next to you what he can get them. You think this is a reasonable question, but the couple reacts as though they've been insulted. This is because they think that just by looking at them the counterman should know what they want. They expect him to read their minds and, without their saying anything, ascertain which of the fifty different flavors they want, and how they want it—whether in a cone, a cup, a sundae, or a banana split, and whether with nuts, sprinkles, and/or a cherry on top. When the counterman asks what they want again, they respond with hurt and anger. "Oh, never mind," they say in a put-upon tone as they huffily storm out the door. "We're really hungry for ice cream, but if we have to tell you what kind we want and how we want it, that spoils it."

Most reasonable people would never go into a store expecting the salesclerk to intuit what they want. Yet large numbers approach their intimate relationships with precisely this expectation. They believe that they shouldn't have to tell their loved ones what they need in order to feel loved and appreciated; somehow the loved ones are just supposed to know, and if they don't, then obviously the loved ones don't really love them after all. For example, a man with this block might say of his wife, "If she really loved me, she'd just know what

I want, I wouldn't have to tell her." Or a woman might say, "If I have to tell my lover what I want, then what good is it?"

The "I Don't Want to Have to Ask for What I Need (or Why Can't You Read My Mind?)" block almost always sits atop another love block. Some people have the "I Don't Deserve Love" block, and consequently believe that even if they did ask for what they need they still wouldn't get it because they're not worthy enough. People with the "Love Just Isn't in the Cards for Me" block see the world as such a depriving place that they, too, figure that asking for what they need is pointless. "Why should I bother?" they reason. "I'm not going to get what I ask for, anyway." For people with the "I Don't Need Anyone—I'm Strong" block, asking for what they need is out of the question because it would entail acknowledging that they have needs in the first place. And for people whose love blocks rest on a view of the world as a punishing place, there is always the fear that if they say those supposedly selfish words "I need" or "I want," a terrible punishment will befall them.

Many people believe it's simply bad manners to ask for what they need. When an individual is going through a crisis, friends, neighbors, and relatives will say time and time again, "Let me know if you need anything" or "Let me know what I can do." But how many can respond, "Well, since you offered, there *are* some things I need . . ." without feeling awkward and as though they're imposing? Although many will agree in theory that it's best to be direct, most people learned as children that coming out and saying "this is what I need" or "this is not what I want" is impolite, pushy, and greedy. Rather than risk being viewed this way, many understandably stay silent, hoping others will "just know."

A central premise underlying the "I Don't Want to Have to Ask for What I Need" block is that *if you have to tell someone what to do in order to show his or her love for you, then the love becomes somehow tainted*. A gourmet meal does not lose any flavor or nutritional value because the waiter asked and had to be told what to bring. But in many people's view, a loving gesture that is made in response to a request ("Would you please . . . ?") or instructions ("This is how I like to be touched" or "It makes me feel good when you . . .") hardly counts at all when compared to a loving gesture that's performed spontaneously and with no instruction. They don't realize that by taking a stance of "if I have to ask for what I need, then it's no good," they're ensuring that they will go through their days with many of their needs unsatisfied. For in effect they're saying, "Only love that I don't have to ask for will be accepted," which translates into, "I would rather live entirely without love than receive some by telling others what I need."

If a person is severely affected by this block, she'll have difficulty expressing even the simplest of needs and desires, such as what she wants in a restaurant or how she wants her hair done in the beauty salon. Others will experience difficulty only in certain types of situations. Some people who are generally assertive in expressing their needs and wants, for example, may have trouble doing so in relationships in which they feel the other person has more power—in a relationship with a lover who is elusive, say, or an authority figure.

Some people have trouble expressing only certain kinds of needs. For instance, many people who know it's foolish to expect others to read their minds still bring this expectation to bed. They believe that "if it's right" their sexual partners will somehow "just know" what they want. It's easy to get this idea from the way sexual relations are portrayed in movies and on TV. Rarely, if ever, do love scenes show the two people telling each other what they like; they hardly talk at all, in fact. Although in reality there is usually considerable awkwardness the first time two people make love, when it happens on screen the lovers always seem magically to know exactly what to do for each other from the start.

The Desire to Be Babied

What's probably most significant about the "I Don't Want to Have to Ask for What I Need" block is that even the most psychologically healthy people have at least a small touch of it. This is because this block is an extension or extreme manifestation of a strong, albeit often unconscious, desire shared by virtually all of us—the desire to be transported to an idealized infant state in which our every need would be fulfilled without our having to ask. For those who actually did experience this in childhood, the wish is *to return* to the time when their parents really could read their minds. For those who weren't so fortunate, the wish is *finally to experience* the babying they missed out on as infants.

The desire to be babied by a mother figure who has eyes for no one else is a natural desire that is most commonly activated in—and helps to explain—the process of falling "in love." One of the powerful attractions of being "in love" is that it re-creates—or creates for the first time—the blissful feeling of being an adored baby. To many people the more mature, reality-based love that follows the honeymoon stage of falling "in love" is by comparison a big letdown. As a result, they either break off romantic relationships once the initial ecstasy fades, or they stay with their partners but spend the rest of their time together trying to recapture that early state.

As long as it's recognized as just so much wishful thinking, there's no harm in harboring the wish to be a baby whose every need is intuited and instantly satisfied. It's when people expect this wish to be fulfilled in real life that problems arise and the wish begins to serve as a love block. Unfortunately, too few people realize that while the dream of someone who "just knows" is entirely normal, it's not fair or reasonable to approach real-life relationships with "read my mind" as an implicit demand.

Princes, Princesses, and Mind Readers

Although most people have this love block to at least a small degree, two groups are especially susceptible to it and tend to manifest it in extreme form. First are the princes and princesses who grew up in homes where their parents anticipated and indulged all their needs. Princes and princesses have an enormous sense of entitlement. They believe others owe them love and that it should come their way without any effort on their part. When this doesn't happen, they whine, fall into self-pity, and become enraged.

The other group of people who are particularly prone to this block are themselves mind readers. From an early age, they were taught that it is their duty to anticipate and meet other people's needs, and as a result they developed special skills that enabled them to be adept at doing so. Many women, in particular, have developed a special radar that enables them to tune in to other people's feelings and determine what they need without being told. Although often called "women's intuition" and regarded as an innate trait, the ability to pick up on nonverbal cues and seemingly read minds is, in fact, a learned skill.

Children of alcoholics and others who grew up with unpredictable, mercurial parents also tend to become adept at mind reading at an early age. Since the family's primary focus is on the addictive parent's needs rather than the children's needs, the children spend every waking hour in the home alert to subtle cues about how the addictive parent is feeling and what he or she is going to do next. The children from such families often reach adulthood knowing far more about what is going on inside their parents' psyches and bodies than inside their own.

Because they are so adept at intuiting what others need, mind readers typically expect others to be adept at it, too. A mind reader will figure that since she just knows how to make her loved ones feel appreciated and cared for, they should automatically know how to make her feel special and loved in turn. When others fail to do this, the mind reader feels frustrated, angry, unappreciated, and unloved. Very likely, she will feel some condescension toward those who fail to read her mind as well. For example, a mind reader might say of her husband, "Why is he so dense that I have to spell everything out for him? He doesn't have to tell me what he needs from me—*I know*."

Larry the Prince

The owner of an extremely successful real-estate company, Larry has a bright smile and the confident air of a man who believes he deserves the best from life and expects to get it. Short and stocky, he is a flashy dresser whose clothes, cars, and jewelry obviously cost a lot of money. He doesn't walk into a room, he struts. At the time he started therapy, he was in his mid-thirties and had been married for nearly ten years. He was also the father of two children, aged five and seven.

Larry began therapy because of long-standing dissatisfactions with his marriage. His major complaint was that his wife, Sue, didn't make him feel loved. This is a common reason for entering therapy, as many of the cases in preceding chapters illustrate. Very often, it's a valid complaint, as many spouses can give numerous specific examples of inconsiderate or cruel behavior on the part of their mates.

But Larry's situation was different. As he went down the list of the ways in which Sue failed to make him feel loved, it quickly became apparent that Sue was not the ogre Larry made her out to be. If Larry's list proved anything, in fact, it was only that he was a petty, demanding, and narcissistic man who was very difficult to be married to. One of Larry's major gripes was that sometimes Sue would make a comment about a movie or TV star being good-looking or intelligent. This, Larry explained, made him feel angry, distant, and unappreciated. Larry also often heard Sue praising or "cooing at" one of their children, and this really irritated and enraged him, too. Frequently Larry would come home from work and tell her about some terrific achievement he had pulled off that day. But more often than not, Sue would fail to react with proper enthusiasm, which in turn would leave Larry feeling angry and "empty inside." Periodically, Larry also explained, he would stop off at the local pool room or health club on his way home, spend a few hours there, and then arrive home late. Each time he was surprised and "ticked off" that his wife was upset and angry that he hadn't called. "Why wouldn't she just be very glad to see me?" he asked aloud in one early session. "If she really cared about me, she wouldn't be so damned critical."

Many readers will take an immediate dislike to Larry and feel sorry for his wife. But Larry didn't choose to have such a self-centered personality. He developed it in response to how he was treated in childhood. Although this may not make Larry any more likable, it should make his arrogance and demandingness easier to understand.

The youngest of three children, two boys and a girl, from an upper-middle-class home, Larry was by far his mother's favorite. She acted as though "the sun set and rose around me," Larry explained in therapy. "She made me feel like the Second Coming, the Messiah." Throughout his childhood, Larry's mother lavished attention on him, constantly cuddling him, kissing him, and catering to him. Over and over she told him how wonderful he was, and she listened to every word he uttered as though each one were a "pearl."

Larry's older brother and sister were hardworking students who did very well in school, yet it was Larry, and Larry alone, whom their mother saw as "destined for greatness." She did not expect him to work hard in school, and he didn't. He saw himself as special and assumed everything would somehow just work out for him without any exertion on his part. His siblings' significant achievements received little attention in the family, while every little thing that Larry did was heralded as a major feat, and a miraculous one at that. As Larry summed the situation up years later, "All I had to do was move my bowels and it was treated like a great event. The way my mother acted, you would've thought my shit was made of gold."

Larry had very little interaction with his father, and doesn't recall him ever objecting to the adoration his mother lavished on her favorite son. "The thing I remember most about my father was his coolness, his distance," Larry later explained. Larry did recall several instances in which he tried to get his father to show him some paternal interest and warmth, but each time his father responded with more coolness and distance, which in turn caused Larry to seek out his mother's affection even more. And her total devotion seemed to more than compensate for the lack of fatherly attention. "As a child I didn't feel like I was lacking for love," Larry later said. He felt more than loved, in fact. He felt adored.

Around adolescence, however, Larry started to lose status in his mother's eyes. Larry's fall from grace happened bit by bit over time, and there was no one incident to mark it. But Larry distinctly got the message that although his mother still loved him and always would, she had found him most wonderful and worthy as a small child. In Larry's adult years, she would often talk about how "precious" and "adorable" he had been as a child, punctuating her comments with faraway looks and nostalgic sighs.

After Larry grew up and left home, his mother also kept childhood pictures of him centrally located in her house, proudly displaying them to guests as if Larry had been a boy wonder. These photo arrangements, which included photos of Larry and no one else in the family, were like shrines. Whenever Larry saw them, his feeling of being special was enhanced, while at the same time he felt a wistful longing to recapture the exalted status he once enjoyed.

In his late teens, Larry began to date. The girls he went after didn't have to be particularly pretty or smart or fun to be with, only willing to fawn over him and massage his ego the way his mother had. When he was twenty-three he met Sue, a nineteen-year-old who had come to work as a receptionist and file clerk at the real-estate agency where Larry was then employed. After two years of dating, Larry felt sufficiently adored that he asked Sue to marry him. Three years later, Sue gave birth to their first child, a son.

In another era, Sue might have gone through her entire marriage struggling to fulfill her husband's expectations. After all, generations of women were raised to believe a husband should be treated like God, and a wife should constantly bolster her mate's "fragile male ego," even if it meant tolerating a lot of grandstanding and domineering on his part. In the first years of Sue and Larry's marriage, in fact, building up Larry's inflated image of himself and catering to all his needs is precisely what Sue did. After Sue became pregnant with their first child, however, her focus turned more inward, and once the baby came she was consumed with his needs. Larry felt abandoned and enraged, and it was then that he began to keep count of all the various ways that Sue failed to make him feel loved.

The Change Process: Larry's Way

Although it was Larry who sought help, when he started therapy he was convinced that Sue was the one who had the problem, and he wanted to be told what he could do to get her to change. When informed that he might need to do some changing himself, Larry was surprised and indignant. It is testimony to his maturity that he was finally able to swallow his wounded pride and see that his sense of being insufficiently loved by his wife had more to do with his own past than her current behavior.

Larry came to realize that his principal problem was twofold. First, he expected total adoration from his wife. His mother had raised him to believe that he was entitled to no less, regardless of how he behaved. Second, Larry expected his wife to be able to read his mind, to automatically know precisely what the special treatment he expected entailed. When it was suggested that Larry actually come out and tell his wife what he wanted and needed from her, Larry responded with incredulity. "She's supposed to know what I need, it's part of being a wife," he asserted. With resentment in his voice he added, "I never had to ask before, and after all these years of marriage I sure as hell shouldn't have to now."

Many readers will feel compassion for Larry's wife, Sue, but not have much sympathy for Larry. Think for a few minutes, however, what life has been like for him. For a number of idyllic years as a child, he was treated like a prince. His mother made him feel that he was the center of the universe. Then he started growing up and his mother no longer found him so wonderful. She stopped adoring him and treating him like a prince. What a huge loss this must have been for Larry. And what a rude awakening he must have gotten when he gradually became aware that not only was he *not* the center of the universe, he wasn't even very exceptional.

For Larry, the kind of love he received from his mother in childhood became his model of "real love," and he entered his marriage expecting his wife to reenact it. When Sue inevitably failed, once again Larry experienced the mournful sense of "paradise lost" he had felt when he reached puberty and his mother's adoration started to noticeably wane.

As Larry became more aware of his feelings, it also began to emerge that being adored by his mother was not as entirely wonderful as he originally had thought. As much as he longed to reexperience it, in the deepest part of himself Larry had never fully trusted his mother's love. Larry's mother saw him in idealized, exalted terms, and thus never loved him for his true self and human qualities. Unconsciously, Larry had always been aware of this, and so intermingled with his sense of self-importance and specialness were fears that his real self was unlovable. Paradoxically, it was precisely when Larry's doubts about his lovability were most intense that he was most insistent that Sue exalt him as his mother once had.

Larry and Sue agreed that their marital troubles began when she became pregnant with their first child. However, after Larry had been in therapy for several months, he let it slip that Sue had not in fact suddenly turned her attention from her husband at that time, as he had earlier indicated. *It was Larry who had retreated first.* In an almost offhand manner, Larry explained one day that "after Sue got pregnant, I got very busy at work so I couldn't be there a lot of times when she needed me." Sighing and raising his eyes to heaven as if to say "aren't women impossible?" Larry then continued: "It wasn't my fault, but work was so hectic that I couldn't get to the hospital until the day after the baby was born. It was a difficult birth. She feels I wasn't there for her at a crucial time. She's been mad about it for years."

What was most significant about this admission was how blithe Larry was about it. On a surface level, he knew that when it came time for some of Sue's needs to take precedence, he had abandoned her, giving her valid reason to be angry. But deep down, he really didn't believe he had been in the wrong, and he was enraged at Sue for not being more tolerant and understanding. In fact, Larry felt *he* was the one who had been most grievously wronged, for at the most visceral level Larry was convinced that he hadn't really deserted Sue, rather that she had deserted him through the act of becoming pregnant. "From the time she first got pregnant, I knew I was going to be pushed aside and left out," Larry said. "Everything would go to the baby, and there'd be nothing left for me."

This admission turned out to be a crucial moment in Larry's therapy, leading him to some important insights: First, his experience as a child had left him unable to imagine that Sue could make room in her heart for a new love (the baby) while continuing to keep her old love (Larry) centrally located, in her heart. Since his mother had focused her love on only one particular family member—Larry—and closed everyone else out, Larry assumed that if his wife loved their child he'd inevitably be "shut out," too.

Larry's second important insight was his recognition of how he created a self-fulfilling prophecy for himself by making his worst fears come true. Afraid that Sue's pregnancy meant he was soon going to be displaced, Larry retreated from her, saying through his behavior "I'll leave you before you leave me." In response, Sue did indeed turn energy that once would have gone to him to their child, just as Larry always "knew" would happen.

In therapy, Larry also realized that his parents' hot-and-cold behavior had caused him to view love in all-or-nothing terms: other people would either love you totally and exclusively as his mother had, or they wouldn't have much to do with you at all, as had been the case with his father. Larry's unconscious belief that he'd either get all of someone's love or none of it dovetailed with, and further fueled, his fear that once a child arrived, he'd go from being the central figure in Sue's life to being "nothing to her."

If Larry had been able to express his fears to Sue when she became pregnant, their relationship might have turned out very differently. But at the time, Larry could not discuss his feelings because he really didn't know what he was feeling; he had neither enough awareness of what was going on inside nor the skills to understand it. Besides, Larry thought, it was his wife's job to figure out his feelings, to understand exactly what he was experiencing inside even when he had no idea himself. After all, his mother had always seemed to know, so why couldn't his wife?

In therapy Larry long resisted the idea that identifying and expressing his feelings was his job, no one else's. Like most people who expect others to read their minds, Larry did not want to take responsibility for his own self-awareness and self-definition; knowing who you are and what you feel takes hard work, and Larry wanted someone else to do it for him. First it was his mother, then his wife, and then his therapist. Initially in his treatment, in fact, Larry was often angry at his therapist for not knowing what he felt, even when Larry hadn't a clue himself. Only gradually did Larry become aware that by leaving his feelings for others to figure out, he was putting himself in an infantlike position that any adult would find enraging. Once he saw this, he then slowly began the painstaking process of identifying and expressing his own feelings, using the methods outlined in Chapter 20.

Interestingly, as Larry became more introspective he became less self-centered, not more. When he realized how little he knew himself, he also realized how little he knew about others, which caused him to become more curious about them than ever before. Speaking of his wife in therapy one day, he remarked, "It's dawned on me that I really have no idea how Sue feels and thinks about anything. I've never asked her, and whenever she's tried to tell me, I've just let it go in one ear and out the other. It was always my attitude that her only concern should be with how I felt, so I actually got pissed if she tried to tell me how she felt." For the first time in more than ten years of marriage, Larry made a conscious effort to ask Sue what she thought about various issues, how she felt about their relationship. Just as important, he forced himself to listen attentively to her replies.

One of the first things Larry discovered was that Sue had always hated the gifts he gave her. On her birthday, Channukah, Valentine's Day, and all other special occasions Larry always bought Sue sexy, flamboyant clothes for her to wear to social events with him. Going out, Larry would experience his sexy wife as an extension of himself, so when others complimented Sue's sexy outfits, Larry felt a "huge ego rush." Although for years Sue had told Larry that she felt like "a Fredericks' of Hollywood freak" in these outfits, and often resisted wearing them, Larry had never really heard her before. Now when he wanted to get Sue a gift, Larry began getting her something *she* wanted—flowers, which for years, she had told him she would have far preferred.

Larry also began hearing how angry—and justifiably so—Sue was about his habit of not calling to say he would be coming home late. When she had complained about this in the past, Larry always felt abused and henpecked, as though she was "trying to deprive me of the release I need at the end of the workday." Now he began calling her to inform her of his plans ahead of time, often telling her, "Don't wait dinner for me. I'll pick up a sandwich or some pizza for myself."

To some people, these might seem like trivial changes, but they marked a profound difference in the way Larry related to Sue. For ten years, he had treated her like a servant and had behaved as if he were a baby on a demand-feeding schedule. For the first time, Sue started to feel "like the woman in his life, not his galley slave." And as Sue started to feel respected, appreciated, and loved by her husband, she then began to feel some of the inner warmth and expansiveness that made her want to show him love and appreciation in return.

Larry also began to change how he related to his friends. Over the years, he had alienated a number of friends through his "take me as I am or you're not a friend worth having" attitude. For example, at parties Larry thought nothing of turning on the TV or going off to watch sports events on TV for several hours, and when someone objected, he took offense. Another obnoxious habit of his was monopolizing conversations. He'd say what he had to say, then abruptly change the subject, as if his were the only opinion that mattered.

One night when Larry left a birthday party to go upstairs and watch TV, Sue followed him and finally said, "Maybe *you* don't care, but we're losing too many friends because of your bad manners, and *I* care about it." Previously, he wouldn't have listened, but now he realized that he had been raised to believe "the rules of social behavior are different for me because I'm a prince, and princes can do whatever they want." He returned to the party, and was gratified that several of the people there said they were glad to have him back.

The more Larry has dropped his princely way of behaving, the more others have warmed up to him, and the more loved he has felt. For the first time in his entire life, he said, "I'm starting to feel that I'm a grown-up man and that people like me for that, that people actually like the real me, not the hot-stuff guy I always felt I had to pretend to be."

Maura the Mind Reader

Maura is an example of the second group of people who commonly have this block—mind readers. Attractive, with rosy cheeks, sparkling eyes, and a plump build, Maura has a warm, earthy personality. At the same time, she is self-doubting and quick to apologize, even when she's done nothing wrong. When she started therapy, she was thirty-two, had been married for twelve years, and had two children.

When Maura married at age twenty, she postponed her own education so that her husband, Tim, could complete his undergraduate work and go on to get a master's degree in business. However, after the children were born, Maura began to work in a bank, and because of her "good business head" she had unexpectedly received a number of promotions. At the time she started treatment, she was a branch manager and was also working toward her bachelor's degree on a part-time basis, hoping eventually to work with "kids with problems." Within the next seven years she completed her B.A., earned an M.S.W., and entered a training program for family therapists.

Maura began therapy because she and her husband, Tim, were having great difficulty getting along. She tried to get him to go with her to marriage counseling, but he wanted no part of that, so she decided to get help for herself anyway. Many married women enter therapy believing their domestic problems must be their own fault, but Maura was of a very different opinion. She believed that if anyone was responsible for the problems in the marriage, that person was definitely Tim.

When she started treatment, Maura had been carrying around a great deal of anger at Tim for years. She had many complaints about his numerous failings, but what irked her the most was that he no longer made her feel loved. He never knew what to do or when to do it, Maura explained, and consequently "he was always doing the wrong thing." He approached her or tried to hug her when she wanted to be alone, but backed off and gave her room when she wanted to be held. He tried to cheer her up when she wanted to be allowed to have a good cry. He tried to make love to her when she was so tired that all she wanted to do was sleep, but fell asleep when she wanted to make love. . . . And on and on it went. As Maura recited this litany, her voice was full of disdain. "What's wrong with him?" she asked. "After all these years of marriage, is it asking too much to expect a grown man to have figured out what works with me and what doesn't?"

To Maura, these were rhetorical questions, so she was quite surprised to be told that yes, it was asking too much. No matter how long two people have been together, no matter how long and intimately they've known each other, it simply is not fair for either party to expect the other one to read his or her mind. Sure, it's wonderful to be given love in exactly the right way at the right time, and it's particularly wonderful when this happens without having to make requests or demands, supply instructions, or drop hints. But to expect this to happen all the time is unfair and unrealistic, particularly in long-term relationships since both parties' needs and wants will probably change over time.

Maura found Tim's failure to read her mind particularly aggravating after she had an especially rough day at work. Asked what she would like him to do on those occasions, she answered that "I want him to hold me in his arms for a moment and then make me a drink and rub my feet while I sit in an easy chair." But, she quickly added, "that's not what Tim does. When he sees that I've had a real hard day and am particularly tense, he just clears out and stays out of my way." Asked if she had ever told Tim what she'd really like, Maura said, "No, of course not. If I had to ask him, it wouldn't be the same. It would spoil it. Anyway, he should know. After all these years, I shouldn't have to ask him to treat me right."

Maura did not grow up doted upon like Larry, yet in her marriage she ended up taking a very similar position. It was a position that in essence said, "I would rather continue through life without getting my needs met than ask someone to meet them."

Maura was the younger of two children. Her brother, David, had learning disabilities and emotional problems that caused him to have trouble in school and in the neighborhood. He frequently came home crying or very irritable. Maura's parents, understandably concerned, devoted the bulk of their time and energy to David. They reasoned that Maura, who did well in school and was by all standards a "perfect little girl," had far less need of attention. Years later, Maura could still vividly remember being a little girl and approaching her mother with a confusing homework assignment or a problem she needed help with. Each time, her mother dismissed Maura's request for help, telling her, "You're smart enough (or strong enough, or old enough) to take care of that on your own; you don't need me." When she approached her father, she got the same reaction. Maura responded as any child would: she didn't conclude that her parents were wrong in brushing their daughter's natural, entirely normal needs aside; she concluded that "there must be something wrong with me for having these needs."

Over time, Maura finally stopped seeking out advice, help, and comfort from her parents. While her brother continued to be incompetent and obviously needy, Maura increasingly became the responsible "darling of a girl" whom her parents could always count on to do well in school and handle her own problems. Unable to get her parents' love by showing them who she really was—a child with a child's needs—she settled instead for getting their respect and gratitude by showing off how mature and adult she could be.

But Maura's need and longing for more nurturing from her parents did not disappear. Her needs and desires only became more and more suppressed. As this happened, they also became transformed or sublimated. Like many people in similar situations, Maura responded to not being taken care of by becoming someone who takes care of others. She was very envious of the treatment David received, but she suppressed this too, allowing only her concern for him to be openly expressed. She literally became her brother's keeper, doing whatever she could for him. Eventually she developed such sensitivity to his inner emotional state that she could tell how he was feeling and what he needed from his facial expressions, body language, and "vibes" alone.

As Maura grew up, she extended the caretaking to others. Wherever she went, others quickly learned she was a responsible, caring, supportive person who could always be counted on for advice, sympathy, and help. She took great pride in the fact that her friends would readily call on her whenever they had any problems. She played a mother role in her marriage, too, taking it upon herself to tend to all her husband's emotional needs. In fact, Maura thought of her husband as "one of the kids," and when asked about her family she would actually say, "I have three kids."

Maura's mind-reading skills improved along with her caretaking ones. This was partly a result of having two babies. After all, there's only one way to know what infants want, and that's to "read" their minds via their cries, facial expressions, and body movements. And it was partly the result of the sex-role conditioning that taught her a feminine woman is always alert to subtle cues about how others around her are feeling. Although Maura broke with the traditional model of femininity in that she had a successful career, she conformed to it by assuming responsibility for keeping tabs on everyone's feelings in her family—everyone's except her own, that is. Like many other women, Maura was so attuned to other people's feelings that she was out of touch with her own.

The Change Process: Maura's Way

Although it was unhappiness with her marriage that brought her to therapy, as her story unfolded it became clear that Maura had a number of different love blocks operating all at once. Like Larry, she had the "I Don't Want to Deal with My Feelings" block, which she had to begin overcoming before she could make significant headway on her "I Don't Want to Have to Ask for What I Need" block. But perhaps Maura's most deeply rooted and troublesome one of all was "I Don't Need Anyone—I'm Strong." As she discovered in therapy, she would not be able to let go of her expectation that Tim intuit her needs until she had begun to understand for herself what those needs were and why she felt so compelled to hide and disavow them.

Although Maura presented herself to the world as a mature adult with few emotional needs, in fact she had a hungry child within who was just waiting for the day when some parent figure would finally notice her and give her the kind of care she gave others. Unconsciously, Maura wanted to get what her brother had gotten; she wanted someone to intuit her needs and attend to them the way her parents, and she herself, had done for David. The longer Maura's needy inner child went unnoticed and uncared for, the more attentive and giving she would be to the other people in her life—her husband, her kids, her still-troubled brother, her parents, her friends. Although she was not consciously aware of it, she was modeling the kind of caretaking she wanted and needed in the hope that "what goes 'round will come 'round." Unconsciously, she was showing others what they could do for her. But no one, not even Maura, ever picked up that this is what was happening. So Maura continued to give out, but without the unconsciously desired results. Meanwhile, her resentment about always giving so much grew, as did her anger at others for not seeing how much she needed or figuring out how they could help her.

Most people feel some reluctance about coming out and telling loved ones what they need from them, but Maura had more than the usual hesitancy. One reason, she realized, is that she grew up in a house where lying and being indirect were the norm. Throughout her childhood, Maura's father had a number of affairs. Her mother knew, but pretended she didn't. She made her hurt and displeasure known through veiled remarks, subtle jabs, and stony silences. At the time Maura knew nothing of the affairs, only that something was going on that no one was talking about. She also knew that her mother was secretly squirreling away money from the household budget. Her mother had told her, though, "never tell your father or brother about this." Looking back on her childhood home life, Maura said, "Everybody was always lying, doing something behind someone else's back. No one was ever direct or up front. It was all innuendo, hints, lies, pretense." So it wasn't just that Maura had trouble expressing her needs, it was that she had never learned to express herself straightforwardly about anything. The techniques in Chapter 20 helped her change this.

Another reason Maura had such difficulty expressing herself was that she feared she wouldn't be able to do it "in exactly the right way." When Maura finally got to the point in therapy where she began trying to tell Tim what she needed from him, she had several experiences that caused her to want to abandon the whole endeavor. She'd decide to tell him about a need, but she'd get so nervous that she'd speak too quickly and in a flustered, not entirely clear manner. Then she'd ask, "Do you know what I mean?" and he'd respond, "Not exactly" or "I'm not sure." Rather than try to explain what she meant again, in a clearer fashion, Maura would immediately conclude she was wrong to have tried the first time. "Oh, never mind," she'd tell Tim. "I knew I never should have brought this up. Just forget it." When she arrived for her next therapy session, she would recount the experience and say, "See? I told you it would never work. It's a pointless waste of time."

Why did Maura act this way? At first, it seemed that she was simply angry at Tim for once again not being able to read her mind. But as she became more aware of the genesis and depth of her "I Don't Want to Have to Ask for What I Need" block, it emerged that something more complex was going on. Whenever Tim did not immediately understand what Maura meant when she tried to express a need or desire, she interpreted his not "getting it" not as a sign of stupidity on his part, but as a criticism of her. Although in her anger she portrayed him as inferior to her in many respects, Tim had always had a much better way with words than Maura did, and she felt he was mocking her relative inarticulateness when he said he didn't understand exactly what she meant. Equally important, Maura also thought he was criticizing her needs as not having validity, as wrong. Maura had so long felt that her needs were shameful and selfish, she was sure anyone who got wind of them would recoil in disgust and condemnation. In fact, as Maura eventually discovered, Tim thought nothing of the kind. He did not perceive her as "a bumbler with words," and he did not see her needs as wrong or lacking legitimacy. These were Maura's own judgments against herself that she had projected onto him. Acknowledging this forced Maura to recognize an important truth: although she often was correct in intuiting her husband's true thoughts and feelings, sometimes she was wrong, dead wrong.

After she had recovered from the shock of discovering that her mind-reading skills were not always infallible, Maura suddenly started to become aware that she made mind-reading mistakes rather often. On several occasions, she went to the video store and brought home movies she "just knew" everyone in the family would love. But her children either expressed no interest in watching them or walked out of the room after twenty minutes. After this had happened several times, Maura angrily stormed into their bedroom and demanded, "What's going on?" They told her, "Your taste in movies is terrible. The movies you get are boring. Why don't you ever ask us what we want to see?"

On another occasion, Maura purchased tickets to a Eugene O'Neill play for herself and Tim and two other couples. She excitedly called the other couples to tell them "what a wonderful time we're going to have." To her great chagrin, she learned that one couple had no interest in the play; they liked light musicals and comedies, but had no taste for serious drama. The other couple didn't want to see the play because it dealt with O'Neill's alcoholic parents, and thus cut too close to the husband's own family. Through embarrassing experiences like these, it dawned on Maura that because she assumed she "knew" what the other people in her life liked, she had never bothered to ask them.

As Maura became increasingly aware of how often she was wrong, she realized it was unrealistic to expect others to read her mind "like I could do for them." She resolved to inquire about what was on other people's minds, and to be more direct and vocal about letting people know what was on hers. Her own mind reading decreased considerably, as did her expectation of it from others.

In admitting that she didn't always "just know" what her family and friends thought and felt, Maura had to give up a long-held belief that had always been the source of self-esteem for her: the belief that her ability to "just know" what others need made her a superior person. It was humbling for Maura finally to come to the realization that if she really wanted to know how her loved ones thought and felt, the best way to find out was to come out and ask them. But it was freeing as well, because when she was released of the burden of always trying to intuit what others wanted and needed, she was finally able to start focusing on figuring out what *she* wanted and needed and how to effectively go about getting it. She was finally liberated from a belief that for most of her life had guaranteed that no matter how much she got from others, she'd continue to feel deprived.

Chapter 16
"I Want Love, But Only If It's a Certain Way"

Tracy, a teacher, is short and dark with frizzy hair, wire-rimmed glasses, and an electric smile. Marie, a restaurant manager, is tall and porcelain skinned with long, straight straw-colored hair and a reserved air. They have been lovers for more than eight years, and have lived together for six. Although they generally get along well, there are certain issues they've fought about again and again. One argument they've had repeatedly concerns the way food is put on their table at mealtimes. Marie feels very strongly that food should never be put on the table in the dish it was cooked in; everything—even stew or scrambled eggs—must be transferred to a serving dish. This is the way it was done in the house she grew up in, and it's the way she wants it done now. Tracy, however, grew up in a very different kind of home. She couldn't care less whether food is placed in a serving dish or served directly from the cooking pot, and she thinks Marie is ridiculous for being so rigid in her requirements. Whenever Tracy cooks, which is frequently, she either asks Marie in an exasperated tone whether she has to use serving dishes, or she just goes ahead and places the food on the table in the pots it was cooked in. Inevitably, this leads to anger and hurt feelings for them both. "If you really loved me, you'd put the food out the way I want it," Marie says. "Why is it so hard for you to accept that this is important to me?" But Tracy is equally adamant. "If *you* really loved *me,* you'd loosen up and stop trying to get me to be as prissy about this sort of thing as you are," she retorts. "You'd just be grateful that I cooked."

Someone observing these mealtime spats might want to jump up and say, "Stop it! This is such a trivial issue, it's not worth fighting over." In fact, though, Tracy and Marie are not really fighting over a trivial issue, they just appear to be. As is often the case with repeated arguments over seemingly small issues, this argument needs to be interpreted symbolically in order to be fully understood. When Tracy and Marie fight about the way food is served they are actually fighting about a much bigger issue: the way love is given, or rather, the "proper" way to give love. Tracy and Marie both love each other, and each wants to feel loved in return. But each also has specific ideas about the correct way to express love, ideas that unfortunately clash.

According to Marie's view, being loved means having all her habits and foibles accepted and indulged. By demanding that Tracy put the food on the table *her* way, Marie is in essence saying, "If you really loved me, you'd give me unconditional acceptance of my total self, even those aspects that are annoying, demanding, unreasonable, and hard to put up with."

But Tracy has her own beliefs about how love should be demonstrated. In her view, two people who love each other will accept their differences, with neither one trying to get the other to do things her way. She believes a loving person is above all flexible, and thus interprets Marie's rigidity as evidence of Marie's lack of love for her. By her resistance to serving food the way Marie wants it, Tracy is saying, "If you really loved *me,* you'd stop trying to change me to be more like you. You'd be less picky—like me."

Universal Expectations

Tracy and Marie are not unusual in believing that "love has to be a certain way." Most people grew up with rigid ideas about what love is and how it should be expressed. But unfortunately, it's rare for two people's ideas about this to completely coincide. One thinks the correct way to show love is through lots of physical contact, while the other thinks that a lot of physical contact, especially sexual contact, means they're just using each other for libidinal release. Or one takes the attitude that it's important to say "I love you" often, but the other feels uncomfortable with that and believes it's better to express love more indirectly. The possibilities for disagreement about the proper way to show love are so great, in fact, that at one time or another, most of us have been upset with loved ones for not showing their love in "the right way" or "the way I want it." And most of us have also thought or said those immortal words, "If you really loved me, you'd . . ."

Unfortunately, a lot of people go through life without ever examining, questioning, or revising their ideas about how love should be expressed. When someone offers them love in a way that doesn't conform to their preconceived notions of how it should be shown, they reject it, telling themselves that what they're being offered can't be real love because it falls outside their definition of the "correct" way. It simply doesn't occur to them that they might feel much happier and more fulfilled if instead of always asking "Does this fit my definition of love?" they asked, "Where did my definition of love come from, and how does it limit my ability to love and be loved?"

People with the "I Want Love, But Only If It's a Certain Way" block are often fortunate enough to have many people in their lives offering them love. But they can't fully take it in because "it's not the way I want it." They are much like the man who goes to a banquet looking for frog legs. He spends the whole night searching but can't find any because frog legs aren't among the dozens of different kinds of foods offered at this particular fête. The man is encouraged to try some of the other delicious foods, but he is adamant: it's frog legs for him, and only frog legs—nothing else will do. He leaves the banquet hungry, angry, and feeling deeply deprived. People with the "I Want Love, But Only If It's a Certain Way" block have this same sense of deprivation with them very often; many, in fact, feel it their entire lives.

People with the "I Want Love, But Only If It's a Certain Way" block frequently also have the block discussed in the preceding chapter, "I Don't Want to Have to Ask for What I Want and Need (or Why Can't You Read My Mind?)." In fact, one of the most common ways—perhaps *the* most common—for people to complete the phrase "If you really loved me" is with the words "you'd just *know* what I need and want." While most people who want love to be "a certain way" have numerous criteria according to which they define "real" love, nearly everyone with this block would agree that one sure way to tell the "right" kind of love is that it doesn't have to be asked for.

"Real Love Means Romantic Love"

For many with this block, real or "true" love equals romantic love, and this is the only kind of love that really counts. The love of friends, although perhaps deeper and more sustaining over the long run, is seen as of lesser value than the more exciting sort of love a sexual relationship promises (or *seems* to promise). Witness the way people say "we're just friends," as if friendship were a lower order of relationship.

What's more, those who equate true love with romantic love usually won't settle for just any version of romantic love. They'll be satisfied only if certain requirements are met. First, potential partners must have the correct personal qualities; if someone doesn't have the right kind of job, background, looks, age, skin color, religion, ambitions, and so forth, he or she will automatically be rejected. Second, even when partners do meet these personal specifications and a relationship develops, they'll keep having to pass test after test. For people with this block tend to have equally rigid and specific requirements for how partners should show their love and generally behave in an ongoing relationship, too.

We don't mean to suggest here that there's something wrong with having preferences and expectations in relationships. These are only a problem when they narrow a person's chances of feeling loved. If a person only "goes" for a certain physical type, that's fine, so long as she can find someone of that type to love her. But what if someone who doesn't fit her "specs" offers her love? If she rejects that love simply because "it's not the way I want it" or "it's not the way I always dreamed it would be," she may be doing herself real damage.

Unconscious Beliefs

Some of the ideas people have about what love is and how love should be expressed exist in the conscious mind and can be verbally expressed. For example, if asked to complete the sentence "When two people love each other, they . . ." most people will quickly come up with responses like these:

—try not to hurt each other.
—show concern for each other's feelings.
—want the best for each other.
—are honest with each other.
—can trust each other.
—don't take advantage of each other.
—give each other unwavering support and comfort in times of crisis.
—are happy when the other person is happy.
—listen to each other's problems.
—are always "there" for each other.
—don't feel envious when the other person has good fortune.
—don't talk behind the other person's back.
—are willing to make compromises to keep the relationship satisfying for both.
—don't make promises they can't keep.
—don't always expect to get their own way.

Some of these responses will strike some people as stupid, or just plain wrong. Other readers will find the list incomplete and will want to add their own responses. But both reactions are further proof that most of us do have strong and varied ideas about what love is and how it should be shown.

Although many of these ideas can be put into words, this is certainly not always the case. Often, in fact, a person's most fundamental beliefs about what love is and how it should be expressed remain unconscious. As a result, people often have only the vaguest conscious notion of what exactly they mean when they say they want love to be "a certain way." Pressed, they usually end up saying something to the effect of "I can't tell you what it is exactly that I want. All I know is that this [what I'm getting now, or have gotten so far] isn't it."

Beliefs that are buried in the unconscious exert the most powerful influence. Overcoming the "I Want Love, But Only If It's a Certain Way" block requires that a person gain conscious awareness of just what this "certain way" means in his particular case. Often, people are very surprised when they discover just what this "it" is that they've been looking for all along.

When people begin obtaining more conscious awareness of what they mean when they say they want love in a certain way, two things usually become apparent. First, many people want a kind of love they'll never realistically get. Second, most people have very different standards for the kind of love they want versus the kind of love they are willing to give. For example, many people want others to give them what Marie wants from Tracy—unconditional acceptance of the totality of her being, annoying traits and all. At the same time, though, most people who want this kind of unconditional love are entirely unwilling to give it—not even to those they want it from. Marie, for example, wants Tracy to accept her feelings about the way food is served but can't accept that Tracy's feelings about this count, too.

Brian

For some people, the "I Want Love, But Only If It's a Certain Way" block has its roots in a long-standing secret wish, developed in childhood, for a special love that will make up for—and magically whisk away—their inner sense of deprivation. Brian, a married businessman with three children, harbored this type of wish in his unconscious for nearly all his life. As a result, he was blocked from taking in much of the real or "regular" love that others, especially his wife, tried to give him.

Of medium height and build, Brian has graying hair and a bushy mustache. He speaks in a loud, booming voice and has a distinctive laugh that seems to come from deep in his belly. While most people would not initially describe him as handsome, there's something so earnest and pleasant about him that people find him very appealing.

When he was thirty-eight Brian and his wife, Tanya, a musician, went to a couples' counselor because of long-standing problems in their relationship. After a few sessions, the counselor suggested that they each begin individual treatment, which they did.

Brian's initial focus was his dissatisfaction with his marriage. Since he and Tanya first got together, he had felt that "this is not what I want," yet he had been unable to pinpoint or articulate exactly what he was unhappy with. "Something's missing, something's not right in our relationship," he said. "I don't know if it's her or me, or maybe we're just not right for each other." He described his wife as a down-to-earth, friendly, and vivacious person whom most people warm up to quickly. "Yet," he said, "with me she never does or says the right thing at the right time. Like she hardly ever says the words 'I love you.' I need to hear them. I often have the feeling that she doesn't love me, because if she did then she'd say so." Asked if his wife showed him affection in other ways, Brian spoke of numerous instances in which she had bought him little presents, surprised him with his favorite meal, approached him with hugs and gentle caresses, and signed birthday and holiday cards "with love" or "love ya, honey." But these types of gestures had no impact, and Brian continued to feel deprived, that "there's something I need and want to get from Tanya that she's not giving me."

Brian's chronic dissatisfaction had left Tanya feeling hurt and confused. She worried that there was something wrong with her and was very frustrated. She also sometimes felt overwhelmed by futility, fearing she would never be able to meet Brian's needs.

Although Brian was most aware of his inability to feel sufficiently loved by his wife, early on in treatment it became clear that he had great difficulty taking in love of any kind, and from anyone. If a friend, colleague, or client praised him, Brian would smile awkwardly for a moment, then mentally dismiss the compliment, never allowing it to penetrate below the surface to his inner self. Much of Brian's general difficulty taking in love could be traced to two love blocks working in tandem—the "I Don't Deserve Love" block, and the "I Don't Need Anyone—I'm Strong" block. His "I Want Love, But Only If It's a Certain Way" block sat on top of these more fundamental blocks, making it especially difficult for him to take in love from his wife specifically.

When Brian started therapy, he did not project the sense of emotional distance often seen in people with the "I Don't Need Anyone—I'm Strong" block. He came across as a warm, open person. However, his own view of himself was as a person with a great deal of "quiet inner strength." Generally, "I don't need much from people," he said. "It's only from my wife that I need more." As Brian gradually became aware, he was splitting up his emotional life into two separate areas—outside the house and inside the house. He had difficulty taking in affection and affirmation from people outside the house because he believed all his emotional needs should be met at home. At the same time, his expectation that his wife should meet all his emotional needs only increased his sense of frustration and dissatisfaction with the marriage.

The Change Process: Brian Gains Awareness

In fact, Brian entered his marriage with needs that no one person inside or outside the house could meet. But this was too painful and humiliating for him to admit, even to himself. It was several months before he was willing to stop simply reiterating his complaints about Tanya and begin looking at the true source of his chronic dissatisfaction.

As Brian began to look back on his childhood home life, he first got angry with himself and felt ashamed "for wallowing in self-pity." He had always felt contempt for people "who complained about their rotten childhoods and felt sorry for themselves." Only gradually did he open up and begin to feel some compassion for his younger self.

Brian was the oldest of four children. Financial necessity dictated that both his parents work outside the home. When his parents got home at night they were too physically and emotionally depleted to give much to the children. At dinner, conversations were short and limited; after dinner, the most common activity was watching TV. The weekends were devoted to errands, shopping, and household chores. Only rarely on a Saturday or Sunday did the parents have any extra time or energy for Brian and his siblings.

Brian's father was an alcoholic, which created additional problems. Every night as the children and their mother waited for his return from work, each felt rising fear and dread. They never knew whether he would enter the house drunk or sober, and if he was drunk they never knew what kind of drunk he'd be—a happy, boisterous drunk; an angry and violent drunk; a slobbering, about-to-pass-out drunk; or a silent, sullen, glare-eyed drunk. A palpable tension always hovered over the household.

Until he started treatment, Brian had always maintained that the difficult circumstances of his childhood hadn't affected him. But one night he had a dream in which "there was a young boy in tattered clothes standing on a street corner with a tin cup in his hand begging for money. People would walk by, stop, put some money in the cup, smile at him, and tousle his hair." As soon as he woke up, Brian recognized the boy as "the little boy inside me who is begging for love and understanding." Until then, Brian had spent most of his life maintaining an image of himself as someone who didn't need much from others because he could not bear the pain of confronting his own neediness. As he gradually came to acknowledge and accept his feelings of deprivation and neediness, he slowly became better at opening himself up to others and letting in their love and concern. He and Tanya grew closer, and he slowly became more satisfied with their relationship, too.

Nevertheless, Brian still felt "there's something wrong, something missing" from his marriage. After being in therapy a while, "I know now that she loves me," Brian explained. "But it's still not enough. She doesn't do it in the right way." When pressed to explain more precisely what he meant, Brian still could not define what he wanted and became very frustrated. Of course, Brian's vagueness was most frustrating for his wife, Tanya. Think of the difficulty of being married to a man who can't say what he wants, only "this isn't it."

But finally, a clearer picture began to emerge. Asked to describe whatever visual images popped into his mind when he thought of the kind of love he longed for, he spoke about watching couples walking hand in hand on the beach or in the park. What he noticed most about each of these couples was the adoring way the woman looked up at the man, as though he were the most handsome man she had ever seen. As he described the woman's look, another image flashed into his consciousness, from a scene in a movie he once saw. This was an image of a woman caressing and kissing a man, telling him he is the most wonderful man in the world. The man, with a dreamy, contented look on his face is just lying there, basking in the woman's rapt attention and soaking up her love.

Brian finally realized that what he wanted from his wife was adoration; as he put it, "I want her to love me in a special way, to see me as the most special person in the world." He also realized that he wanted his wife to love him exclusively. It turned out that whenever she spent time with a friend or talked and laughed with friends on the telephone, Brian felt slighted and jealous. In fact, any time Tanya showed affection for anyone else, even their children, Brian felt "angry and put out, as though something had been taken from me." Brian was very embarrassed to make these admissions; "I feel so childish," he said again and again. But they were important admissions because they revealed how he unconsciously defined "the right way" for his wife to love him. Anything short of total adoration from Tanya was insufficient and unacceptable to Brian, who couldn't take in any of her "lesser love."

As Brian brought his "secret wish" to his conscious awareness, he began to have some recollections that helped to explain how this secret wish originated. One memory that kept coming back to him was of being called "a mistake" by his parents. On several occasions as a child he overheard conversations in which his mother casually referred to Brian as "a mistake." He also recalled his parents telling him he was "a mistake" when they were angry at him. Since his parents were strict Catholics whose only form of birth control was the rhythm method, perhaps what they meant was that Brian was unplanned. Brian, however, took the word to mean that he was unwanted, and this "fact" became central to his self-concept. If Brian had been asked to describe himself, the word "unwanted" would have been one of the first to come out of his mouth.

It's excruciatingly painful for a child to believe his parents don't want him. Brian found comfort and relief by fantasizing that some day someone would come along who would want him, really want him, want him more than anyone else in the world. In Brian's fantasy, he would know who that someone was by the special look in her eyes, when she gazed at him. It was the look of utter adoration, of awe, of maternal love in its most perfect form. Indeed, as Brian later became aware with some embarrassment, it was the look that the Virgin Mary had for her infant son, Jesus, in all the religious paintings Brian had seen throughout his boyhood. As Brian gradually discovered, his secret wish wasn't simply that his wife adore him and have no feelings for anyone else. He wanted to be his wife's baby, and to be allowed to be as dependent and helpless as a baby. At the very same time, though, he wanted to be God in his wife's eyes, and for her to see him as having the omnipotence and perfection only God can have. With this being "the right way," it's no wonder Brian's wife kept getting it wrong.

The Change Process: Brian Acts on His New Awareness

Once Brian became consciously aware of what he had wanted from his wife, he realized how unrealistic and unfair an expectation it was. He also realized that he had to give this wish up. This was not easy; lifelong wishes do not disappear overnight, and as Brian allowed his to slowly die, he found that he mourned it. However, Brian was also able to see the humor in the situation—wanting to be both his wife's baby and her God is pretty funny, after all. He was also quickly able to see a positive difference in his marriage. The more he let go of his wish for the impossible, the more he could take in the love that his wife did offer, and had been trying to give to him all along.

Whether it's human nature or not, the fact is that most people are a lot more vocal about what they're unhappy about in a relationship than what pleases them. This had certainly been the case with Brian, particularly in regard to Tanya. Now Brian began to write down all the loving things Tanya did for him. For years, she had been in the habit of going to the library once a week, usually bringing home one or two books she thought might interest Brian. Her guesses were almost always on target; he did enjoy the books. But he had never appreciated Tanya's thoughtfulness and efforts in this regard. Although sometimes mouthing a cursory "thanks," his inner view was that "she goes to the library to get books for herself anyway, so it's not like she's making a special effort for me." He was similarly oblivious to all the love and effort Tanya put into feeding him. Often she went out of her way to prepare his favorite meals and frequently came home from work with special desserts for him. In the past, his response to these gestures had been a cursory "thanks," or maybe a "nice meal, honey" or "good dessert." Now he began to savor the food Tanya gave him and to appreciate all the planning, shopping, and cooking it involved. For years he had moaned and groaned about all the ways in which she failed to make him feel loved, but now he took time each week to reflect on all she did for him. Frequently this would bring tears to his eyes. "I never felt it before, but actually she is very loving to me in her own special way," he explained. "What a fool I've been not to have seen it before."

Many people fail to sufficiently appreciate their close relationships. Time spent with loved ones is often not experienced in the moment. Although they might be physically in the same room, mentally and emotionally they're elsewhere—thinking about what happened at work today, or what they're going to do tomorrow, or where they'd rather be right now. Brian became aware that this was how he usually spent his time with Tanya and his other friends as well. He began to make a special effort to savor the time he spent with his loved ones, trying to focus on being with them in the moment and on appreciating their unique qualities. He started taking walks with Tanya in the evening and keeping his attention on her, rather than looking around at everything else. Each day he tried to take a few minutes to just hold her, focusing all his awareness on the warmth, feel, and smell of her skin, the way she felt in his arms. With his male buddies, he began to make an effort to be emotionally and mentally present rather than just watching sports on TV and not really interacting whenever they got together. The more he was able to experience himself as really with others in the present moment, the more he felt warmed by their love.

Brian's also started paying closer attention to his breathing. An athletic man, he was aware of how he breathed during exercise; he also had some experience using deep breathing as a relaxation technique. Now when he felt Tanya and others being loving to him in their own special way, he would spend a few moments doing deep breathing exercises. With each intake of air, he would imagine himself as taking in the love that the world holds for him. With each expulsion of air, he would imagine himself returning that love to others. This way, the love that he was taking in seemed to be able to penetrate to deeper levels.

As Brian has become more aware and appreciative of the love others give him, it has been a natural progression for him to become more expressive of his gratitude. He now tells Tanya how much her efforts mean to him. He has started doing little things for her, like leaving her affectionate notes before he leaves for work in the morning and bringing her flowers. When he goes out with his male buddies and has a good time, he now calls them the next day to tell them how much he enjoyed their company. Whereas he used to assume that "you shouldn't have to do things like this because your friends and family know you love them," his own experience with being unable to take in Tanya's love taught him otherwise. Interestingly, these efforts have had an unexpected effect. The more Brian has expressed his gratitude, the more appreciated Tanya and his other loved ones have felt, and the more they have given him. Paradoxically, the less he wants the more he gets.

Chapter 17

"Why Do I Always Have to Give So Much to Get So Little?"

Deidre, an artist with two daughters, is a pretty blonde of medium height with a nervous smile and an infectious laugh. She started therapy in her mid-thirties because she could not decide whether to divorce Ed, her husband of fifteen years. "I'm not sure if I love my husband anymore," she explained in her first session. "But I'm definite he doesn't love me." As she continued, her chief laments were that "my husband has never really made me feel loved," and that most of the work of maintaining their relationship was hers. "He's so loving towards our daughters, I can't understand why he can't be that way with me," she said. "But with me he never goes out of his way to show any affection. I'm the one who always has to initiate, and I'm tired of it. I'm tired of being the one who makes sacrifices—and for what? This isn't the kind of marriage I always dreamed of. I give and give and get so little in return, and I'm sick of it!"

If Deidre's complaints sound familiar, it's because she is only one of a multitude of people who keep score in relationships. Scorekeepers approach relationships armed with mental ledgers in which they're constantly—if often unconsciously—adding up all that they've given to the other person and tallying the total to see who's been getting more. They also keep a running inventory of all the mean, rotten, insensitive things the other person has done to them since the beginning of their relationship. The most salient feature of a scorekeeper's ledger is that regardless of the reality of each particular relationship, things *always* add up so that the scorekeeper comes out way ahead in giving and way behind in getting. As a result, scorekeepers experience a sense of being continually deprived, topped off with a great deal of bitterness about having to give so much to get so little.

Of course, a certain amount of scorekeeping is bound to go on any time two people are involved. It can even be healthy periodically to step back from a relationship and take stock of the give and take; for people who "love too much" and have a tendency to allow themselves to be exploited in relationships, this type of exercise is crucial, in fact. But scorekeeping is unhealthy and harmful to relationships when it's something a person does constantly, and always with the same results. The people we're referring to as scorekeepers are *always* keeping tabs, and *always* feel they're giving more.

There's another group of people who keep careful watch of the give and take in relationships, but they do so for different reasons and with different results. This group consists of people who have low self-esteem. Believing that they don't deserve much in life, they're vigilant about making sure they don't get or take more than their fair share in relationships. Their perceptions of relationships might be just as skewed as those of the people we're calling scorekeepers, but in the opposite direction. Whereas a person with the "Why Do I Always Have to Give So Much to Get So Little?" block sees himself as getting less than his due, a person with the "I Don't Deserve Love" block sees himself as getting more.

Kinds of Scorekeepers

Some people who believe they give more in relationships aren't bothered by the imbalance. Being extremely giving is part of their basic makeup; they do it because it comes naturally to them, not because they hope to be paid back in kind. But scorekeepers *are* bothered by the imbalances they perceive. Although it may be in their nature to be giving, they don't like being the more giving one in a relationship. They feel that the other people they're involved with should give as much as they have given themselves, and when the others fail to do this, they feel angry, resentful, cheated, and exploited.

Some scorekeepers adopt the stance of martyrhood. When the other person they're involved with seems to be ahead in taking, the martyr scorekeeper just keeps on giving and giving, all the while keeping mental count of how much she's done for the selfish, ungrateful other. When the martyr finally reaches a point where she can't give any more, she explodes, taking everything she's tallied on her mental ledger and throwing it in the other person's face. "I've done everything for you, and you've done nothing for me," the martyr says, often in those very words.

Other scorekeepers respond to the perceived imbalance by deciding to be withholding until the other person acts to even up the score. For example, a person who feels one of his friends has not been giving enough might resolve, "I'm not going to call him. I'll wait until he calls me. It's about time he did some initiating for a change." Sometimes this strategy works, but more often than not it backfires. This is because people who wonder "Why Do I Always Have to Give So Much to Get So Little?" are typically not only givers by nature, but initiators, too, whereas the people they end up in relationships with often are not. Right from the start of a relationship, the pattern is for the initiator to be the one who makes contact (by calling the other, or walking across the room to him), gives the first kiss or hug, makes the first moves toward lovemaking, comes up with the first suggestions of things to do (like going to a movie or playing tennis), and first asks, "So how *are* you? What's been going on?" When the initiator decides to break this pattern and wait until the other person initiates for a change, it often happens that nothing gets initiated. For a variety of reasons, the other person just doesn't have the same need or urge to "take charge and get the ball rolling." So the scorekeeper/initiator ends up suffering the pain of having his own strong needs go unmet as he waits for the other person to make a move. And all the while his resentment mounts.

Scorekeepers' Common Traits

Although their styles may differ, one thing scorekeepers have in common is selective memory. They usually have no trouble recalling what they've done for others and what horrible things others have done to them. But when it comes to all the kind, helpful, loving acts they've been recipients of, their memories often fail them. Thus, when someone responds to a scorekeeper's attack by saying "It's not true that I've done nothing for you. What about when I did such-and-such . . . ?" the scorekeeper often will be flustered at first, then will try to deny that the other person might have a point.

Most scorekeepers also don't believe a statute of limitations should apply to personal relationships, or at least not to the horrible wrongs they've suffered in such relationships. No matter how long ago a scorekeeper was hurt or mistreated, he can't let it be forgotten or at least forgiven. He keeps it in the ledger as a permanent part of the case he's building against the person who hurt or angered him. Even years after a particular wrong was committed, the scorekeeper feels free to bring it up and throw it in the other person's face once again.

Scorekeepers usually suffer from other love blocks as well. Many, for example, have the block discussed in Chapter 15, " 'I Don't Want to Have to Ask for What I Need' (or 'Why Can't You Read My Mind?')." Because of their belief that others should "just know" what they need or want, they never just come out and say they feel there's an imbalance in a relationship, and they're unhappy about it. Besides, if a scorekeeper simply came out and said "I feel I give more than I get, and I don't like it," he'd also run the risk of learning that his perception of the relationship isn't entirely accurate—that when he made entries in his ledger, he somehow overlooked a lot of the kind, loving, and giving things the other person has done. Moreover, if a scorekeeper were to tell a friend that he's unhappy with the friendship, the friend would then have the chance to remedy the situation. To some scorekeepers this would be a frightening prospect, because the only role they know how to play in life is the role of an aggrieved, exploited, unappreciated party.

Another love block scorekeepers frequently have is the one discussed in the previous chapter, "I Want Love, But Only If It's a Certain Way." Since this block causes people to discount or reject much of the love that others try to give them because it hasn't been given "in the right way" or "the way I wanted it," it inevitably screens out a lot of evidence that could refute or challenge a scorekeeper's claim of how little others give to him.

If there's any one love block that *always* underlies the scorekeeper's block, it's "Love Just Isn't in the Cards for Me," discussed in Chapter 7. People with this block see the world as a depriving place because as children they received so little love, affection, and comforting that they grew up literally starving for it. Although not all such people become scorekeepers, all scorekeepers learned early in life to see the world as a depriving place.

Starved for love in their early years, scorekeepers go through life looking for someone to provide the emotional sustenance they didn't receive in childhood. They bring to their adult relationships the hungry, needy child they've kept buried within, and it's with the sensibility of this inner child that they judge their current relationships. The hungry inner child thinks the world owes him the love and affection he's been deprived of, and he feels he's waited long enough to get paid his due. As with any long-overdue debt, it's not just the original principal he wants to collect, but also all the interest and penalties that have accrued. The longer the inner child has to wait to get paid the love and affection he sees as his due, the larger the total debt becomes. And as the amount "owed" him mounts, so does his rage and impatience about having to wait so long. Typically, then, the scorekeeping block is also accompanied by "Anger Keeps Getting in the Way," the block discussed in Chapter 18, and a form of "It's Too Late for Me; My Time Has Run Out," which was examined in Chapter 10.

Unfortunately, the inner child's growing neediness, rage, and impatience add up to big trouble in adult relationships. Any love that is offered now is bound to seem like too little, too late. So he disregards, dismisses, discounts, rejects, or otherwise blocks the love that others try to give him in adulthood. Of course, the people who become involved with this type of individual usually have no idea what's going on. They haven't been told that they're expected to make up for his lousy childhood, providing all the love, affection, and comfort he never got as a kid—and then some. All they know is that whatever love they give is devalued as insufficient, and that their efforts to make the other person feel valued and loved are as effective as using a toy sand shovel to try to fill a bottomless pit.

Deidre

Deidre, the artist mentioned at the beginning of this chapter, came to therapy very angry at her husband. "He never initiates anything," she complained. "Whenever we do anything, it's because I had the idea and went ahead and carried out the plans. Whenever we have a problem, it's up to me to bring it up. It's up to me to take care of keeping up our social life, to get the car inspected, to remind him that it's his mother's birthday. I do everything in this relationship, and what for? I've got my two girls at least, but that's about it. I get hardly anything else."

Deidre's biggest complaint was that she wanted to buy a home, but Ed didn't want to, and they couldn't afford to besides. Deidre had wanted to own a home for as long as she could remember, and through the fifteen years she and Ed rented this remained her most passionate desire. Ed, however, had moral qualms about property ownership; he felt owning a home was too materialistic, and that in a world where so many people have so little, it's wrong to acquire much in the way of personal possessions.

As the years went on, Deidre wanted a home more and more, while Ed wanted one less and less. She would religiously scout the real estate listings and express interest in hokey "no money down" real estate schemes, while he put more and more of his energy into social and political activism on behalf of the homeless. An excellent carpenter, Ed actually helped build a house for the homeless in their community, which Deidre very much resented.

Deidre felt that she would have longed for her own house regardless of her background because "it's the normal American dream," but her particular family played a key role, too. Deidre's mother often said, "No woman can be happy until she has her own house," and she nagged Deidre's father until they finally bought one. Deidre's sister, Victoria, her only sibling, also believed this, and as the result of having married a millionaire, she had a magnificent home and two vacation houses, too.

At this point, puzzled readers probably want to ask, "If Deidre wanted a home so much, why on earth did she marry a man who had such different feelings about the issue?" The answer is simple: Deidre grew up thinking she could read minds, so when she and Ed first met and then married, she simply assumed that Ed shared her feelings and thus never bothered to ask. When she did finally discover his attitude, she felt shocked and betrayed, as though his differing from her on such an important issue was evidence of disloyalty.

Early on in Deidre's therapy, it became evident that she had several love blocks working together. First, she had the "Love Just Isn't in the Cards for Me" block, which manifested itself in her marriage as a nagging sense that "no matter how much Ed and I improve things between us, I'll still never get what I want." Second, she had the "Why Do I Always Have to Give So Much to Get So Little?" block, which caused her to keep score on Ed in a way that guaranteed this premise would be proven true. Third, Deidre suffered from the "I Don't Want to Have to Ask for What I Need" block. As long as the third block remained in place, it was certain Deidre would remain blocked by the first two, feeling perpetually deprived and full of smoldering rage.

Many of Deidre's complaints were legitimate. She was not exaggerating Ed's passivity, and it wasn't unreasonable for her to desire a more fulfilling life and a more balanced marriage; on the contrary, these were healthy desires that needed encouragement. But it was unreasonable for Deidre to see herself as so victimized and put upon. The fact is, in all the years when her dissatisfaction and sense of deprivation were mounting, she had never actually told her husband how upset she was and why. She assumed Ed should have been able to figure out how angry she was and why, and when he failed to do this, she grew even angrier, placing the blame on his faulty comprehension skills ("he's so dense he needs everything spelled out") rather than on her poor communication skills. As often happens with many people who expect others to read their minds, it had simply never occurred to Deidre to sit down with Ed and in a calm, nonaccusatory fashion say, "I am unhappy in this relationship; here are the reasons, and I want us to start making some concrete efforts to change things."

The Change Process: Deidre's Way

Deidre's first major task in therapy was to let go of her expectation that Ed read her mind, and to give up her anger at him for not being able to do so. She had to accept that it was her responsibility to express her feelings directly and clearly. She also had to learn how to do this in a manner that was effective and felt comfortable to her. She accomplished this by using many of the techniques detailed in Part Three, especially Chapter 20.

As Deidre became more comfortable articulating her feelings, she discovered that Ed wasn't so dense after all. He not only was able to understand and handle her feelings, he actually sympathized with some of them because he had been feeling dissatisfied and frustrated himself. In fact, when she began to voice her dismay and resentment about the imbalances she saw in their relationship, Deidre discovered that Ed also thought there were imbalances and he was upset about them, too.

However, not everything Ed said was easy for Deidre to hear. He agreed that Deidre often gave and did more than her fair share in their marriage, and that one of the reasons was that in many areas he was too passive and lacking in initiative. But Ed didn't think this was the entire explanation. He believed another reason Deidre ended up doing more than her fair share was that she had a tendency to be bossy and controlling, to go ahead and take on tasks all by herself without even consulting him. At first, Deidre was shocked and upset to learn Ed saw her this way. But as she thought about it, she finally had to admit that there was some validity to what he was saying. Because she assumed that Ed would postpone or never get to any task assigned to him, Deidre had gradually taken over all the responsibilities of running their household. Her exhaustion, anger, and resentment told her that this was unfair to her; however, it was only when she looked at how this setup insulted and infantilized Ed that she became aware of how unfair it was to him, too.

It wasn't easy, but after they finally started communicating with each other, Deidre and Ed were able to make progress toward rectifying the imbalance between them. Aided by some counseling sessions together, they outlined areas of their lives they were unhappy with, and both agreed to change their behavior in specific ways. For example, in response to Deidre's complaint that Ed never initiated activities, he agreed to take it upon himself to propose one outing or activity a week, and to make whatever necessary plans it entailed. In response to Ed's complaint that Deidre "took over everything and treated me like a child," Deidre agreed to sit down with Ed, jointly make a list of all the household chores that needed to be done in a given week, and then to decide jointly who would do which chore and when.

One aspect of their marriage that Deidre and Ed had both been particularly unhappy about was sex. In this area, it was Dierdre who played the more passive role, while Ed was the initiator who customarily felt he gave so much to get so little. After fifteen years of marriage, Ed had become extremely angry and resentful about Deidre's passivity in bed. He felt it was his "job" to turn her on, and he increasingly felt like an observer watching his own performance. His anger and resentment eventually deadened his sexual desires, resulting in periods of impotence. Deidre, meanwhile, was unaware of Ed's resentment because they never talked about their sex life. When they finally did, she revealed that she felt resentful as well, because her perception was that "as soon as I get into bed, Ed starts pawing me." She explained that she needed time to unwind and free her mind of the day's concerns before she could begin to feel sexual. Until she spoke about it in counseling, however, Deidre had been unaware that this was what she needed. Once they began to verbally express their feelings and desires, Deidre and Ed found themselves much more interested in being sexual with each other than they had been for years.

The Change Process: Deidre Digs Deeper

For Deidre and Ed, better communication led to more closeness. And for Deidre in particular, it led to feeling satisfied enough that she stopped seriously considering divorce. Still, it was apparent in her individual therapy sessions that she continued to feel she wasn't getting enough to fully eradicate her feeling of being deprived. "Things have gotten really better, and that's real nice," Deidre would say, and then immediately she would let out a long sigh. Asked what was happening inside her to cause the sigh, Deidre looked ashamed. "I know I should be grateful things have gotten better," she said. "But I keep thinking I want my own home probably more than anything else in the world, and as long as I'm with Ed I'm not going to get it. I resent that." Over time, in fact, Deidre seemed to be growing more resentful about not having a home rather than less so.

When Deidre's marriage had improved in so many ways, why would she focus on the one area in which she still wasn't getting what she wanted? Part of the reason, obviously, is that for a married couple the issue of whether or not they'll buy a home is a major issue, and disagreements about it are of greater consequence than differences over less fundamental issues such as whether to get a new TV. And for Deidre in particular, the issue was loaded with symbolic meaning. In part because of her mother's influence, Deidre's sense of self-worth and security was directly related to whether she owned her home. Owning her own home, Deidre believed, would anchor her, make her more adult, provide her with a sense of safety, solidify her identity, increase her significance, and generally make her a better person.

But there were other less obvious elements at work, too. In therapy Deidre discovered she clung to her desire to own a home also because it served a very important function—ensuring that regardless of how Ed's behavior changed, she would continue to feel unloved and unhappy in the marriage. It was as if Deidre had a secret ledger with the left-hand page showing a big picture of the home she always wanted, and the right-hand page showing a list of the relatively small ways her husband could show her he cared. No matter how hard Ed tried to show Deidre that he loved her, whatever he did would look paltry when entered into the ledger and compared to the house she had always wanted but never gotten. Put simply, Deidre was blocking herself from receiving the love that Ed could offer by saying, in essence, "As long as my big desire for a home remains unsatisfied, nothing else you do for me will count."

One of the clearest-cut examples was Deidre's refusal to allow Ed to use his carpentry skills to make improvements in their rental home. Contrary to Deidre's claims, Ed did *not* "put all his energy into building a house for the homeless while not giving a damn about the kind of home his own family lived in." Ed frequently came up with ideas for fixing up their rental home, and he spent his days off puttering around the house, making repairs, working in the yard, and so forth. But Deidre always nixed Ed's major home improvement plans and belittled the smaller things he did. "Why bother fixing up a place that isn't ours?" she would ask.

As Deidre became aware of how she was using scorekeeping to block herself from taking in her husband's love, she was struck by the feeling that her behavior pattern was familiar. "Who do you know that acts this way?" Deidre was asked. "I'm not sure," she replied. She thought for a moment, looking genuinely perplexed, when suddenly a flash of recognition brightened her face. "Of course I know who acts this way—it's my mother," she said. "It's so obvious, how could I not have seen it right away?"

In fact, Deidre's mother was not only a scorekeeper, she was a scorekeeper *par excellence*. From the time Deidre was a little girl, she had the sense that her mother wanted something from her and was keeping tabs on Deidre's failure to give it to her—whatever it was. When Deidre was small, her mother constantly pointed out how good and helpful other children were to their mothers, implying that Deidre was a great disappointment by comparison. Now as a full-grown adult Diedre could not see or speak to her mother without the older woman saying something along the lines of, "Isn't it wonderful how much Jack does for his mother," "Aunt Joan is so lucky to have a daughter like Liz. Did you know Liz and her husband just bought Joan a brand-new VCR?" Deidre's mother could always be relied on to work accolades about Deidre's sister into the conversation, too, raving about how much Victoria has done for her recently and how generous Victoria is with her money. Whenever Deidre would offer to help her mother, however, her mother always turned her down, saying "No, I'll do it myself." And whenever Deidre would go ahead and actually try to do something helpful, her mother inevitably would find fault. If Deidre set the table, her mother would tell her she's done it wrong; if she bought her mother a gift, her mother would say, "You shouldn't have," and then go on to remark that it's the wrong size or color, or that the material would probably either cause a skin rash or be very difficult and expensive to clean.

By the time Deidre started therapy, this lifelong pattern of mother-daughter interaction had left her with a pervasive sense of failure and frustration, as well as feelings of rage and guilt. Her mother made it clear time and again how much she had given Deidre over the years, and how much she *gave up* for her as well. Yet she never acknowledged or even hinted that Deidre had ever given anything back. Deidre's mother was like an accountant whose books were strangely unbalanced. There were endless columns listing each and every thing her mother had done for Deidre over the years, but where there should've been a list of what Deidre had done for her mother, the page was entirely blank. No matter what Deidre did or tried to do, it was impossible for her to get anything recorded on *her* side of the ledger.

Why couldn't Deidre get anything on her side of the ledger? What has been standing in her way? These questions started Deidre talking about her lifelong sense that her mother had always wanted something from her that she could never give her. Although Deidre had never been able to identify what it was that her mother wanted, in fact she had unconsciously known it all her life: her mother wanted Deidre to be a boy. Time and again throughout Deidre's childhood, her mother let Deidre know how much happier she would have been if she had been "lucky enough to have a son," and these misogynist messages continued well into Deidre's adulthood. For example, Deidre's mother always took pride in her ability to do "man's work" like heavy digging, but she kept her growing daughter away from it, explaining "you'd do it wrong, just like a girl." As she began to age, she lost her ability to do heavy work and would frequently complain about having no one to help her. But on the numerous occasions that Deidre offered to pitch in and do heavy chores for her mother, the older woman has always rejected her, saying "no, you shouldn't do that kind of work. If I had a son, he could do that for me." And always her mother's words would be followed by a wistful sigh, much like the wistful sigh Deidre gave each time she spoke of waiting to own a home.

An important part of Deidre's therapy has been exploring her mother's history, and trying to figure out why her mother was so fixated on having a son. However, it isn't necessary to go into her mother's background and motivations to understand the origins of Deidre's love block. What's most important to recognize here is that Deidre's desire for her own home has played the same role in her marriage to Ed that her mother's desire for a son has played in the mother-daughter relationship. In Deidre's mother's mental ledger, Deidre's not being a boy is the bottom line, and no matter what else Deidre might do to win her mother's love, it will be measured against the bottom line and deemed inadequate. In the mental ledger Deidre was using to keep score in her marriage, the bottom line was her unfulfilled desire to own a home. After fifteen years, it was evident that the chance of Ed's doing a turnaround and making Deidre's dream of home ownership come true was as remote as the chance of Deidre's getting a sex-change operation to make her mother's dream come true. Yet Deidre persisted in holding on to her impossible dream, just as her mother has always persisted in holding on to *her* impossible dream. It was thus guaranteed that no matter how much love and affection the two women received, they'd feel deeply unsatisfied, even cheated.

The Change Process: Deidre Continues

Scorekeeping in relationships is a difficult habit to break. So far, Deidre hasn't been able to beat it entirely, but she has developed enough awareness of her history and motivations that she is now able to catch herself when she uses scorekeeping to perpetuate her lifelong sense of not being loved enough. When she finds herself running through her mental ledger and thinking "Ed doesn't really love me," she now stops herself. Instead of automatically reiterating her old lament, "Why do I have to give so much to get so little?" she now asks herself some other questions: "Am I really seeing things accurately? Am I forgetting the things he has done, the ways in which he does make it clear he loves me? Does my feeling that I'm not getting enough have basis in the reality of this relationship as it is now, or is the feeling left over from another time or even another relationship, like the one with my mother?" Deidre sometimes realizes she is being unfair, while other times she decides her feelings are justified. But just by going through the questioning process she almost always learns something that helps her break a bit more free of the old patterns that block her receptivity to love.

One major step Deidre has taken is to change how she deals with her mother. She realized that each time she visited her mother, she inevitably returned home with a heightened sense that she did more for Ed than he did for her, accompanied by strong feelings of resentment toward him. In fact, what Deidre was really resentful of was the way her mother treated her during these visits, particularly her refusal to allow anything Deidre did to please her. Unable to vent her anger at her mother, she would go home and take it out on Ed by doing to him what her mother had done to her.

Although she feels guilty about this, Deidre has stopped visiting her mother so frequently; she has cut down on the length of each visit, too. This way, "my mother doesn't have as much time to drive me nuts," she explained. "Now I leave before I'm at the end of my rope." During her visits, Deidre has also stopped trying to please her mother, accepting that "since it's a hopeless case, whatever I do for her is a waste of energy." When she visits with her mother now, she curbs the impulse to be useful and just talks to her. This not only saves Deidre a lot of wasted effort, it also means her mother can't criticize her for doing things the wrong way. Now Deidre is able to get through these previously draining, frustrating visits with her self-esteem and good spirits intact. And when she returns to her own house, she feels emotionally lighter and more appreciative of the positive aspects of her relationship with Ed.

Deidre also treats Ed's home-improvement plans differently. She began to see that by not letting him use his carpentry skills to make their rental house more of a home, she was blocking concrete attempts on Ed's part to demonstrate his love. She also began to see that she was devaluing him while at the same time depriving herself of the chance to live in an environment that came closer to her dream. Realizing that her attitude of "what you have to offer is insufficient" was hurting them both as individuals and as a couple, Deidre decided to try taking what Ed had to offer. She asked him to fix up the house, which he did. Later, he began making beautiful handcrafted furniture for their bedroom. Ed did not magically become the ideal husband, nor did their marriage suddenly turn into a wholly satisfying union. But Deidre realized that Ed was indeed demonstrating love in his own special way, and when she allowed herself to dwell on this for a moment, she felt "warm all over and real good."

Deidre has also put her own time and energy into developing a more secure and stronger sense of self. Gradually, she has come to see herself as an adult woman who is entitled to, and capable of, expressing her needs—not a helpless little child who must settle for what few crumbs are offered and isn't allowed to ask for more. She has also come to see that while there's no guarantee she'll get everything she wants in life, it might be possible for her to get some of what she wants—as long as she's willing to ask. So while she doesn't see the world as a place of infinite plenty, Deidre no longer views it as an utterly depriving place the way she once did.

Not coincidentally, as Deidre has begun to feel more "at home" with herself and in the world, her desire to purchase a home has lessened considerably. She'd still like to have her own home, but she no longer needs a physical place to give her a sense of being emotionally and spiritually grounded. That's something she is beginning to carry within.

Chapter 18
"Anger Keeps Getting in the Way"

Sybil is a small, pretty woman with a stocky build and very expressive manner. A flamboyant dresser whose style of clothing changes dramatically from day to day depending on her moods, she makes people sit up and take notice when she walks into a room. The sharp impression she leaves is heightened by the fact that the color and style of her hair tend to change from week to week, too. High-energy to the point of often seeming wired, Sybil is an entertaining raconteur who speaks quickly but with an excellent sense of comic timing.

Sybil began therapy when she was twenty-nine and in the process of putting her life back together following an acrimonious divorce the year before. At the time of the divorce, she and her small son had moved from Denver, where the family had lived throughout the three-year marriage, and returned to New York, where Sybil grew up and was now working as a buyer for a department store. Since returning East, she had periodically gone with friends to singles bars. As she is an attractive and vivacious woman, men would often approach her and ask her to dance or try to strike up a conversation, and whenever this happened, Sybil would smile and make a conscious effort to appear friendly. But at the same time she would feel "a wall" going up inside her. As this "wall" went up inside, her body would stiffen and she would feel herself sending the man nonverbal signals or "vibes" that said, in essence, "bug off, jerk. Go away."

After a number of therapy sessions, Sybil was asked if she could be more specific about what she meant when she spoke about "a wall" going up. Immediately she clutched at her throat and said, "It's getting warm in here, I'm having trouble breathing." Looking panicked, she began to squirm about in her chair, her chest heaving and her hands still grabbing at her throat. Asked to describe exactly what she was feeling, Sybil suddenly released a flood of feelings she had been expending enormous energy trying to contain. "Those bastards," she said in a voice quaking with anger. "Men are such bastards, I'm never going to let any of them hurt me again. Never. I hate men for what they've done to me. I don't trust them and I don't want any of them near me ever again. I hate it when they come near me. I hate them. I'm so angry I feel like I'm going to explode."

As will become evident from the details of her story, Sybil had ample reason for her anger toward men. In fact, what was remarkable about Sybil when she started treatment was not how angry she was, but that she had any openness toward men at all. But valid and understandable as it was, Sybil's anger had the effect of blocking her from receiving love from half the human race.

Anger is a normal human emotion that everyone is bound to experience in life. In fact, to become angry, even outraged, is a totally appropriate and healthy response to many of the injustices, cruelties, and frustrations people inevitably go through in an imperfect and often very unfair world. There's nothing wrong with anger, and the feeling in and of itself does not create problems or serve as a love block. It is when anger is not given direct, full, and responsible expression or release that it becomes a love block. Typically, what happens is that anger is handled in one of two ineffective ways, and it's the manner of handling anger—not the feeling itself—that creates so many problems in relationships and causes people to be blocked from receiving and giving love.

Swallowers and Venters

The first way anger is typically handled is through swallowing or suppression. When anger is kept "bottled up" and "held in," it stays there within a person and makes it very difficult for him to receive love. One therapy client described his anger as "like a cement block in my chest." This "cement block" was very effective in preventing any anger from flowing outward. But it was equally effective in preventing the flow of any emotions inward, including the kindness and affection he wanted to receive.

The second troublesome, but common, way of handling anger is to go ahead and vent it, with no or little thought as to how blowing up might affect others. As opposed to suppressors, who can walk around with bottled-up anger for years before finally letting it out, venters tend to have hair triggers. If something angers them, they'll be sure to let others know, and right away, too.

Venters' tendencies always to be fuming—or on the verge of fuming—blocks them from receiving love in two ways. First, if someone is always cranky, obstinate, and hostile, others will be too scared or put off to even try approaching with an offering of love. Often, they'll be driven away completely. When this happens, it inadvertantly reinforces the venter's belief that "it doesn't matter how I treat others because no one cares about me anyway." Second, if others do have the temerity to approach a venter with an offering of love, the anger that's so constantly flowing outward will prevent the love from flowing in. In fact, venters very frequently respond to soothing words, caresses, and other signs of love by getting even angrier.

Childhood Lessons

One obvious reason so many people have trouble handling anger is that growing up they were never taught how. Adults often have great difficulty accepting and respecting anger in children. So rather than teach their children how to express anger effectively and responsibly, many parents instead deny the reality and validity of the children's feelings, telling them "you don't really feel that way," "you shouldn't feel that way," or "it's stupid [babyish, immature, silly, etc.] to feel that way." Some children have been taunted or teased when they tried to release anger, told "bet you can't smile" over and over, or warned that "if you don't get that expression off your face, it's going to freeze that way." Sadly, many children have also been punished for having anger. Whether they've been hit, sent to their rooms, given "the silent treatment," denied food, or deprived of love, the message they got was that anger was a bad feeling and they must be bad for having it.

Most people didn't learn much about healthy ways of handling anger from watching the behavior of their parents and other adult figures, either. Growing up, many people were shown only two ways of handling anger. Either they saw adults suppressing their anger outright, perhaps relying on alcohol, drugs, cigarettes, compulsive eating, or verbal denial to help. Or they saw adults exploding with anger, "flying off the handle" and going berserk with rage, usually leaving a lot of hurt feelings in their wake—and perhaps physically damaging people and things in the process, too. With no constructive model to draw on, it's no wonder so many people grow up to have such difficulty finding a middle ground between swallowing anger completely and coming out swinging.

Often, the lessons learned at home are reinforced by a child's contact with the larger world. From a newspaper or the nightly news, a child learns that the world is full of angry adults who are barely able to contain their explosive rage. The inadvertent message is that if you're angry, the only option is to use violence and force, or at least to threaten to do so. Even the "soft" news, with all the reports about the most recent move in the latest nasty celebrity divorce, conveys the message that when there's anger between two adults, it's a given that they'll go for each other's throats and seek revenge rather than seek to resolve their differences amicably.

Unfortunately, the entertainment media, particularly TV and movies, also teach that violence is the answer. Many TV shows and films aimed at young audiences show that if there's a dispute, the way to resolve it is to blow the other person's head off, or at least beat the crap out of him. The enormous amount of screen violence the average American child witnesses is bound to affect his sense of behavior by sheer volume alone.

The gender roles children are taught also don't help them learn to handle anger in a healthy, responsible way. Boys learn, first of all, that anger is one of the few emotions it's okay for males to feel; and they also learn that when a male feels anger, the manly thing for him to do is to let it out—by having a fistfight or, if he's older, by letting his wife "have it," or, if he's a head of state, by engaging in some military action. Girls, by contrast, learn that anger is not appropriate if a girl or woman feels angry, she'll lose her femininity and be transformed into an ugly, castrating bitch or a hideous, monstrous witch. Hence, while boys are learning to take their anger out on someone else, girls are learning to hold their anger in and to deny that they have any anger at all. Despite two decades of upheaval in relations between the sexes, these differences were as strong as ever in 1988, according to reports presented at the annual meeting of the American Psychological Association.[1] This might help account for the fact that the vast majority of people in prison for crimes of violence are male, while the majority of psychotherapy clients and sufferers of depression are female.

Regardless of gender, people with the "Anger Keeps Getting in the Way" block nearly always are suffering from one or several other love blocks as well. In fact, it's because of their other love blocks that they feel anger. A person who believes "I Don't Deserve Love" may be very angry with himself for not being a better, more worthy person. A person who believes "I Don't Need Anyone—I'm Strong" may be angry about always having to keep such a stiff upper lip; or he might be angry at other people for trying to get him to take love and help he swears he doesn't need. Someone who believes that "Love Just Isn't in the Cards for Me" may be full of rage at the entire world for giving her a lousy deal. A person who believes "God's Love Isn't in the Cards for Me" may be very angry at God for failing to be loving enough or failing to exist at all. Someone who believes "I'll Inevitably Get Hurt" in an intimate relationship is probably still angry at those who hurt him in the past, and may also be angry with God or fate for giving him a life so full of heartbreak and hurt to begin with.

The Messages Behind Anger

Whenever there is anger, it usually is in reaction to another, deeper, feeling and serves as a way of covering that feeling up. This is particularly evident among people whose anger is expressed readily and in an obvious way. Generally, a person who gets angry often and easily is trying to convey another message through his anger, such as "I am hurting," "I feel vulnerable," "I'm afraid," "I am ashamed," or "I am tired." Even a person who believes anger is a bad feeling that shouldn't be felt at all might find it easier to admit to anger than to one of these other feelings. Moreover, he may have become so habituated to the inner experience of anger that it feels more comfortable and tolerable to him than other less familiar feelings.

The most common messages behind a stance of "I am angry," are "I am hurting," "I am depleted and in need of love and affection," and "I feel unappreciated and unloved." But when anger is expressed in lieu of these underlying feelings, it has precisely the opposite of the desired effect. The anger drives other people away when their presence and concern is most needed. And it blocks receptivity to love when letting in love is the only way to really assuage the anger and the other feelings underlying it.

For example, Alan, the attorney with the "I Don't Need Anyone—I'm Strong" block discussed in Chapter 6, had a reputation for losing his temper and striking out angrily at his staff and family when he got upset. For years, he had been aware that this had the effect of hurting others and driving them away from him. But he still did not see that behind his anger lay years of buried pain and neediness. Only gradually did he realize that by getting angry, he was really trying to say what he felt it wasn't permissable for a man to say— "Help me! I need love and affection and tenderness!" As he became more comfortable with accepting his own emotional needs and straightforwardly asking for help, his inner store of anger diminished and his outbursts became less frequent and less vitriolic.

Sharon, the filmmaker with the "God's Love Isn't in the Cards for Me" block discussed in Chapter 8, was in the habit of expressing anger in a different way. Sharon had a history of getting involved with men whom she "made into God," and whom she expected to meet all her emotional needs—and give her a sense of spiritual peace, too. When the men turned out to be incapable of doing this, she was disappointed and angry. But taught that anger is unfeminine, she didn't openly take her anger out on others—she turned most of it on herself, transforming it into depression, and released the rest through whining. It's been said that a whine is anger forced to come out through a tiny opening,[2] and in Sharon's case that certainly seemed true. Although less destructive to others than throwing things at them, whining is nonetheless quite aggravating; and in Sharon's case, it had the same effect that Alan's angry outbursts had on him— it drove others away. As Sharon learned that it was unrealistic and self-destructive to expect a romantic relationship to take the place of her own spiritual development, she felt less anger at the men in her life, and she was able to cut down on her whining.

Anger at Self

"I hate myself" is another common message behind anger. As anger is often a signal that a person doesn't feel adequately loved and appreciated by others, it can be a sign that self-love is in short supply, too. Often, in fact, people who come across as very angry and hostile to others have within them an enormous amount of anger toward themselves. Their anger toward others is a way of distracting themselves from their own self-hatred.

When a person feels anger directed at herself, she really might be angry at someone or something else—at her parents, or at the government, or at the world in general. But for a variety of possible reasons—shame about feeling anger, fear of expressing it, confusion about what she's really feeling and why—she cannot direct her anger at its true source. So she turns the anger inward, against herself instead. Just as anger toward others can be displaced anger at the self, anger at the self is very often displaced anger at someone or something external.

Women in particular tend to transform anger at others and the world at large into anger at themselves. Although women's second-class status has given them ample cause to be angry at the outside world, women for the most part have not been given any support for feeling or expressing their anger. Women who *do* attempt to articulate their anger about their treatment in a man's world are routinely criticized as unbalanced, told in essence, "the problem isn't with the way the world is run but with the way you react. If anything's wrong, it's you for being angry."

Other times, when a person has anger at the self, it's not displaced anger—it really *is* anger that originated against the self. Sometimes people are angry with themselves for valid reasons—they did something truly hurtful or wrong, for example. But many people who feel a great deal of anger toward themselves really have not done anything wrong. These are people who have low self-esteem and set perfectionistic standards for themselves. Unable to live up to their internal notions of who they should be, they experience themselves as always failing or falling short—and they are angry at themselves for being such failures.

Rosa, the political activist, magazine writer, and nun with the "I Don't Want to Deal with My Feelings" block discussed in Chapter 4, had a problem with self-anger. She had a history of depression, and considering the losses she had experienced in her life, chronic depression was an understandable reaction. But because she was suffering from the "I Don't Want to Deal with My Feelings" block, Rosa could not accept this and instead felt angry at herself for being depressed. She saw her depression as "weak," "soft," "wrong" and constantly berated herself for "wallowing in self-pity" and "not being strong enough." As she gradually became more self-accepting and self-loving, she slowly let go of the anger at herself with which she had tortured herself since childhood.

When Anger Is Suppressed

Many people were taught that if they just push their anger out of their consciousness, it will simply go away. But there is only one way to make anger go away—and that's to let it out. When people suppress anger instead of expressing it, the anger gets buried in the unconscious, and as time wears on keeping it buried takes up more and more psychic energy. But no matter how much energy goes into suppressing anger—or how many drinks, drugs, cigarettes, cookies, or pints of ice cream are consumed in the attempt—the anger will eventually force itself out. When this happens, the anger usually comes out in a way that can do major and lasting harm to personal relationships.

Suppressed anger sometimes forces its way out in an unintentional, explosive burst. Everyone has either had or witnessed the experience

of flying off the handle and exploding in rage over something relatively trivial—an offhand remark a friend has made, a minor traffic
tie-up, a child's crying, a foul-up at the bank, a spouse's forgetting
to pick up the laundry at the dry cleaner as promised . . . In these
situations, the relatively trivial incident is not the real cause of the
anger. The anger is old, pent-up anger about something else that
occurred in the past, and the relatively trivial incident has only triggered its release—a release the anger has been seeking since the
moment it was first felt and suppressed. When the conscious mind
will not permit the anger to be expressed directly, the unconscious
displaces the anger onto something else and obtains release in a
roundabout way.

Anger that is not given overt, direct expression, may also be expressed covertly. Covert anger is aimed at the correct target, but in
a very subtle, sly way. As an example, consider the case of Bob and
Sue, a long-married couple. Sue has been angry with Bob over a
variety of things for a long time, but she would never just come out
and tell him so. Instead, she keeps the anger bottled up; she would
deny that she feels any anger at all, in fact. But the anger leaks out
in little ways. Yesterday, for example, she was supposed to meet Bob
at noon so they could begin shopping for furniture they're thinking
of buying for their living room. Somehow, however, a morning
meeting Sue had at work "went on longer than expected," and Sue
"couldn't help being late" by about a half hour. And the other day
when their daughter asked if she could have a slumber party next
Friday, Sue said yes, conveniently "forgetting" that was the night
Bob had planned to have some of his buddies over to watch the
NCAA basketball finals on TV. "I just don't know what I was thinking," Sue would later tell him. "The basketball game completely
slipped my mind." Incidents like this can corrode a relationship over
time.

When anger is not directly expressed, it also may be transformed
into physical symptoms. Skin rashes, neck and back problems, ulcers,
chronic digestive problems, insomnia—all can result from keeping
anger bottled up inside. Anger at the self is particularly likely to be
transformed into physical symptoms, with some people experiencing
it as sharp pains in the chest. As one woman who was harboring a

lot of angry feelings toward herself decribed it, "It's as if I'm stabbing myself in the heart." But regardless of where a person hurts, it almost goes without saying that when physical pain is being felt, interest in relationships tends to wane, and there's less energy left to put into them.

Sibyl

Sibyl, the woman who was so angry at men that she psychologically walled herself off from them, was the oldest of three daughters. As a young child, she had a strong and close relationship with each of her parents. Her father, however, is the parent she remembers as being the special one; he was handsome, calming, protective, playful, and "really there for me." Obviously understanding the importance of time alone with each of his children, he often would take Sybil and her sisters on separate, individual outings. Well into adulthood, Sybil still remembered these outings vividly. She could describe in detail the sights, sounds, and smells of going to the amusement park with him and riding the carousel, of going to matinees of Walt Disney films and eating popcorn with him, and of strolling in the park and eating ice cream with her cone in one hand and his hand in the other. At these times, Sybil felt "like there was no one else in the world. There was just the two of us, together and happy."

When Sybil was nine, her mother took her and her two sisters to Australia, where they lived with her mother's mother for six months. The children were not told of the trip ahead of time, nor were they ever informed of its reason. "It all happened very suddenly, there was no warning," Sybil recalled. She and her sisters hated living with their grandmother, a proper and very formal woman whom Sybil characterizes as "an old witch." They missed their father terribly and longed to return home. But almost immediately after they got back to New York, their father packed his bags and moved to New Mexico. Again, the children were given no warning or explanation.

Devastated, Sybil and her sisters longed for their father's return, but they rarely heard from him at all. Meanwhile, their mother had to work several jobs to support them, and Sybil took on the role of surrogate mother to the two younger girls. At age ten, she was pretty much running the household, doing the bulk of the cleaning, cooking, and shopping. Increasingly, she also became her mother's confidante and closest friend. "Sometimes it was hard to know who was the mother and who was the daughter," Sybil would later say.

As she grew older, Sybil grew angrier and angrier at her father for leaving. "Things were never the same after he went, and I hate him for that" she explained in therapy. "He robbed me of my childhood. I don't think I can ever forgive him for that. Never ever."

When Sybil was twenty, she went to see her father in New Mexico, where he had remarried and settled for good. She went there "to tell him off, to let him have a piece of my mind about what he did." Her father reacted by allowing her to express her rage, telling her he understood, and offering belated but heartfelt apologies. Afterward, they shared an experience that made Sybil feel as if she were a little girl and with her "old" father again. They went to an amusement park. For Sybil this rekindled many fond memories, but as it heightened her awareness of how much she had lost when her father left, it also rekindled her anger.

As Sybil went through her teenage and early adult years, her relationship with her mother became increasingly close, so much so that Sybil felt she and her mother had become nearly fused. "I had her shadow always over me," she explained in therapy. "I tried to become a carbon copy of her. That's what she wanted." As for herself, Sybil wanted to get away, although at the time she wasn't consciously aware of how much. She felt so guilty about abandoning her mother as her father had that it would be years before she could admit to herself that she wanted to have a life of her own apart from her mother.

When she was in her late teens and early twenties, Sybil had her first real boyfriend. Andy was gentle, easygoing, caring, and fun to be with. Later, Sybil would look back on this relationship and realize how much Andy had loved her and had helped her to feel loved. At the time, however, Sybil thought Andy was "too nice." From her late-teens perspective, Andy's kindness and gentleness looked like evidence of wimpishness. Sibyl dated Andy for several years but because he was "too nice" she did not find him attractive enough to have sexual intercourse with. Andy's respect for Sybil's expressed desire to wait ironically reinforced her conviction that Andy was wimpy, and thus made her even less interested in having sex with him.

One night when she was twenty-four, Sybil went to a party with some girlfriends and met Howard, "a Clint Eastwood type" who was visiting the New York area after finishing engineering school out West. "He swept me off my feet," Sybil said later. "Right from the moment we met, I was crazy about him." Sybil had sexual intercourse with Howard the night they met, and then began seeing him exclusively and steadily. Less than six months later, she quit her job, married Howard, and moved with him to Denver, where he had landed a job.

As is usually the case in whirlwind romances, the instant intimacy that Sybil and Howard shared at first turned out to be a false intimacy. At first they had felt as if they had known each other all their lives, but once the first glow of infatuation wore off, Sybil and Howard woke up to find they were virtual strangers. Worse, as they got to know each other it became apparent that they didn't have much in common at all. "It was a disaster almost from the start," Sybil would later say. "We fought all the time. The only thing that kept us together was that we still had good sex. Then I got pregnant, and that seemed like another reason to try to make it work out."

After two years of marriage, Sybil gave birth to a son and for a time, she and Howard got along better. Then, about a year later, Sybil found out that Howard had been having an affair with another man. As Howard would eventually reveal, he had always been actively bisexual, and during his marriage his desire for men had become stronger and stronger. Sybil, who had always enjoyed the sexual power she felt she had over her husband, was shocked and disbelieving when he told her that during their sexual encounters he had been fantasizing about men. She felt used and violated. It made her sick to her stomach to think that during their moments of greatest intimacy her husband had been with her physically but emotionally was elsewhere. Within a few weeks of finding out about her husband's other life, she decided to end the marriage and return East with her son.

By this time, Sybil had built up a great deal of rage, and a growing distrust of men. First her father had abandoned her, and now her husband had turned out to be "a lying bastard," too. Then, a few months after returning to New York, she had another bad experience with a man. As she was preparing to leave from a singles bar, a man with whom she had danced several times that night offered to drive her home. He "seemed like a nice guy," so she accepted. He drove in the general direction of her neighborhood for a while, then pulled into a dark parking lot behind a supermarket. He shut off the engine, reached under the seat, pulled out a switchblade, and put it to Sybil's throat while grabbing her hair with his other hand so that her head jolted back. "You suck me off, or I'll cut you into pieces," he hissed. Her mind racing, Sybil protested and tried to fight him off. This only enraged him further. Realizing that "if I don't do what he wants, this nut really will kill me," Sybil submitted, and performed fellatio on him as he wanted. He drove her home, and the next day she went to the police and reported the crime.

The Change Process: Sybil's Way

It was about nine months later that Sybil started psychotherapy. The rape had added to the anger and mistrust she had felt toward her father and then her husband. Now it wasn't just these specific men she felt rage toward, it was beginning to be all men. Since the legal process worked so slowly and so inefficiently, even the eventual arrest of the man who raped her didn't provide much sense of satisfaction. (Although charged with a number of similar crimes, as of this writing Sybil's attacker had not been tried.) As time wore on, Sybil's sense of both victimization and powerlessness further fueled her anger.

Given Sybil's ample justification for her feelings toward men, it was remarkable that she was trusting and open enough to turn to a male therapist for help. Without her early positive experiences with her father and with Andy, and her own willingness to acknowledge them, she might have truly believed it when she said "all men are bastards. I hate them all."

Perhaps the most troublesome aspect of Sybil's rage was that it had no place to go. She could not direct it against the men who were its source and force them to rectify the wrongs they had committed against her. For a while, she tried to "just not feel" her anger, to pretend it didn't exist. But eventually she found this didn't work. "I was irritable all the time, my stomach was constantly in knots, and I would wake up in the middle of the night with my jaw aching from grinding my teeth," she explained. "And I was starting to take it out on my son. He'd do the slightest thing and I'd lose my temper. My nerves were shot, I had no patience, no peace." She turned to therapy as seemingly her only resort.

In a just world, the men who hurt Sybil would have to apologize and somehow make amends. But as Sybil was aware, this is not a just world. Given that sad reality, it was up to her to find a way to somehow work through her anger and move beyond it. Otherwise, she would have gone through the rest of her life with anger eating up her energies and causing her to discount half of the human race.

One of the most important things Sybil has gained from therapy is validation for her anger. She has been told—and by a man—that it makes perfect sense for her to feel rage toward men. Men have hurt and violated her. And in a society that favors men, they've been able to get away with it. Sybil's anger is entirely appropriate, understandable, and normal. If she didn't feel great anger, *that* would be cause for worry.

In therapy, Sybil has also been given permission to vent her anger. In fact, she's been encouraged to vent it—by talking about it, shouting and swearing, and punching pillows. Although venting her rage directly at those who provoked it might be more satisfying, she's nevertheless discovered that just having *someone* to vent it at feels pretty good.

Like many people, women in particular, Sybil has been reluctant to actively express her anger. When encouraged to shout and punch pillows, she says she feels stupid and awkward. Such behavior goes against all her training. Therefore, it's been crucial to continually prod Sybil to experience her anger and express it. When someone has as much anger as Sybil and is as reluctant to release it, a few sessions dealing with it is not enough. Anger needs to be a topic continually addressed in therapy, and time for venting it must be set aside on a routine basis.

For Sybil, revenge fantasies have been another useful tool. Raised to believe that turning the other cheek is the noble and ladylike thing to do, she would never permit herself to wish ill on anyone else, no matter how much pain he had caused her. So she was shocked when it was first suggested that she think up punishments for those who had hurt her. The whole idea of a revenge fantasy was taboo to her. However, with encouragement she eventually came up with some ideas of specific, and rather gory, things she'd like to see happen to those men. She found that allowing herself to imagine those scenes, and to share them with someone else who nodded in agreement, felt pretty good.

Of course, if Sybil had a serious mental illness that left her unable to distinguish between fantasy and reality, encouraging her to entertain revenge fantasies would have been irresponsible. But Sybil knows the difference between the two full well. In her case, entertaining revenge fantasies has been a harmless way of mitigating some of the pain, anger, and frustration she felt because of the reality of what she has been put through.

Although Sybil was still in the middle of treatment at the time this was written, there were signs that her efforts to work out her anger had begun to pay off. Some of the resiliency, warmth, and humor that are her nature were beginning to return. She had made a decision not to date for a while, but was starting to open to the possibility of meeting some nice, loving men and perhaps letting one in. She was also thinking about channeling some of her remaining anger and outrage into some constructive political work—volunteering with an organization that helps rape victims or battered women, for example, or another organization that more generally works for the advancement of women's rights, which would help her feel empowered rather than victimized.

The Change Process: Bernice's Way

Another person who has made great strides in overcoming the "Anger Keeps Getting in the Way" block is Bernice, the bookkeeper discussed in Chapter 4 who had the "I Don't Want to Deal with My Feelings" block. While Bernice had a hard time accepting any of her emotions, the emotion she had the hardest time of all with was anger. Whenever she became angry, she immediately got angry with herself for it; in other words, she became angry at herself for feeling angry. She looked upon anger as a bad feeling she was wrong to feel, and each time she experienced anger her self-loathing became a little stronger.

Not surprisingly, Bernice married a man who reinforced her negative view of her emotional self, particularly her capacity for anger. Because of his own upbringing, Bernice's husband, Will, feared confrontations and was especially put off by anger in women. Whenever Bernice became angry, Will would either withdraw or become critical. He'd make comments sure to fuel both her anger and her shame over it—comments like "What are you getting so upset about?," "It's not necessary to raise your voice," "There's no reason to get angry," and "When you get that way, you're just like a Nazi."

After being in couples' counseling for several months, Bernice and Will had a breakthrough experience that helped her to become more accepting of her anger, and that strengthened their relationship, too. For months, Bernice had been having a number of problems with a new car. When the car broke down once again, she got very upset. In the past, she would never have even thought about calling the car dealership and registering a complaint; she knew she'd probably start crying on the phone, and then the dealer would have dismissed what she said as the hysterical rantings of an "emotional woman." On this occasion, however, Bernice allowed herself to get very angry. Crying, she slammed doors, banged things around her kitchen, and threw pots and pans against the wall. Will, who usually would have reacted with "What the hell is the matter with you?" quietly allowed her to vent her feelings. Much to her surprise, after "having a conniption" Bernice was able to call the car dealership and very calmly but firmly voice her complaint, thereby initiating a process that eventually led to the car being fixed at the dealer's expense.

Although seemingly small, this incident marked a dramatic shift in both the way Bernice relates to her own self and the way her husband relates to her. She has begun to free up her emotional self, to let out her feelings, including her anger, and not feel guilty about it. This is a signal that her self-love is increasing, and the process itself is causing her self-love to increase even more. Her husband's acceptance of her feelings has also caused her to feel more loved by him, and to believe that she and her feelings were being valued, respected and affirmed.

Interestingly, as time went on Bernice discovered that the more valued and loved she felt, the less often she found herself feeling angry. Her experience illustrates an important truth: when people feel loved and appreciated, they generally feel much less angry. They still have the capacity to feel anger and certainly do feel it at times, but they tend to be angry less often and then about specific things. A person who feels loved and appreciated may have very strong, righteous anger over the injustice in the world or a particular wrong committed against him. But he will be freed of the terrible burden of feeling the kind of free-floating anger that can cast a poisonous sort of pall over everything, and that for so many makes daily life seem so unpleasant and onerous.

Part Three

Letting Go
of Love Blocks:
A Step-by-Step Guide

By this point, perhaps much sooner, you're probably saying to yourself something along the lines of, "Okay, okay, I've heard plenty about how various people developed and dealt with their love blocks. But what about my own situation? Where do *I* go from here?" In this section we offer a number of different exercises and suggestions to help you understand and overcome your own particular love blocks. Since this is not an overnight or simple process, we can't offer fast and facile solutions. We *can* say with complete confidence, though, that the exercises and suggestions we offer do work, and if they won't make your love blocks magically disappear, they'll certainly get you going in the right direction.

The first two chapters in this section are applicable to persons with love blocks of any kind, so we recommend them for everyone. The third chapter contains more specialized exercises, and we suggest that you select those that fit your particular situation. For those interested in further sources of help, the fourth and final chapter offers advice on finding a psychotherapist and provides a list of other books related to love blocks.

Before you begin, a word of caution: many of the exercises we suggest might initially strike you as stupid. You might feel foolish when you try them, or even refuse to do so. But they are in fact effective methods that really can help you understand and overcome your love blocks, and as such they definitely are worth trying.

Chapter 19
Exercises to Help You Understand the Origins of Your Love Blocks

The first step in overcoming love blocks is understanding where they came from. This means going back and looking at what happened to us when we were children, for it was in our early years that we first developed the defenses that are now affecting our lives as love blocks. Most of us spent childhood as members of a family, or in foster homes, orphanages, boarding schools, or other family substitutes. It was then that we had our first and most powerful intimate relationships. These shaped our most basic ideas about what love and closeness are all about and gave us our first experiences of acceptance, security, and joy—and of rejection, loss, and emotional pain. It was within our childhood family or family substitute that we also developed our most fundamental ideas of who *we* are. And it was from our family that we learned our basic values, along with our ideas about how the world in general operates, and what life is all about.

The exercises in this chapter are designed to help you recall more of your early years and to understand better how your early experiences influenced you. We suggest initially reading them over in the sequence in which they're given so that you don't feel overwhelmed by the tasks involved. However, when you actually do then, it's not necessary to stay in strict numerical order. Since many of the exercises complement one another, you'll probably find yourself doing them in tandem.

It's also not necessary to "finish" one exercise before moving on to the next. In fact, we advise you to forget about the whole idea of finishing them. The information-gathering process the exercises in this chapter are designed to facilitate is a lifelong process, one that is never fully completed. You'll very likely find yourself going back to the different exercises as you acquire more information about your past and more memories return to you.

When you do these exercises, go at your own pace. Some people will want to try tackling all of them in a day or weekend, while others might want to focus on one a month for several months. But once you've begun the process of obtaining information about your past, we recommend that you try making it a part of your ordinary, every-day life. Make it a habit to seek information about your family history, to recall what happened when you were a child, to find answers to some of the unanswered questions you may have grown up with. Remember, the more you know about your past, the better you'll understand the problems that you're having in the present, and the greater your chances for overcoming them and enjoying a more emotionally satisfying life in the future.

1. Finding Your Place in Your Family History

We are all products of our individual family histories, but many people are vague about the details of the families they come from. And even those who are well acquainted with their family histories often have blank spots—periods of time, particular events, or certain relatives who remain a mystery.

To get a clearer picture of the family you came from, it would be helpful to draw a genogram, or family tree. Get a large piece of paper, big enough for a poster or a drawing. If it's rectangular, turn it so that the width exceeds the length. Choose a spot in the middle of the page, an inch or so from the bottom. Draw a dime-sized circle representing yourself, and underneath label it with your name and year of birth. Now make circles representing your siblings, placing them at one-inch intervals to the left or right of your circle so that the arrangement corresponds with the order of birth, and label them appropriately. The circles should go across the page in a row, and above them you should draw a horizontal line, connecting each circle to it with a vertical line. Siblings who have died should be included, with a slanted line put through their circle, and the year of death included.

Now go several inches above the row representing you and your siblings and draw two separate horizontal lines parallel to the first, two or three inches apart. On the left-hand line place your mother and her siblings in their order of birth, including names and dates. The right-hand line represents your father's family, and he and his siblings should be placed on it in the same way. Once the information has been filled in, draw angled lines connecting your mother and father, mark the intersection with the year of their marriage, then draw a vertical line that connects with the line on which you and your siblings are located.

Now for your grandparents' generation: Above the two lines representing your parents and their siblings, draw four horizontal lines, two on the left-hand side for your mother's mother and father, and two on the right for your father's. Fill in the information as before.

Continue in this manner as many generations back as you can go. Include approximate dates of death for those who are deceased. Include unions that ended in divorce, signifying them by using a dotted line. The diagram will look something like the one on page 343.

2. Understanding the Content and Context of Your Family History

Once you've completed your family tree, look at each generation, one by one. What do you know about the era that generation grew up in? What was going on in the world then? Wars? An economic depression? Massive migrations? What were the social mores at that point in history? What constraints were placed on people because of gender roles?

Now consider what was going on within your specific family at this time. Imagine, for example, you are considering how your maternal grandmother grew up. You've come to realize that she grew up in an era that encompassed World War I, the Roaring Twenties, and the Great Depression. These were clearly turbulent—and anxiety-producing—times. They were times of great social upheaval and confusion, characterized by women's struggle for the vote, rapid industrialization and urbanization, massive immigration, and the contradictory reality of Prohibition on the one hand and speakeasies

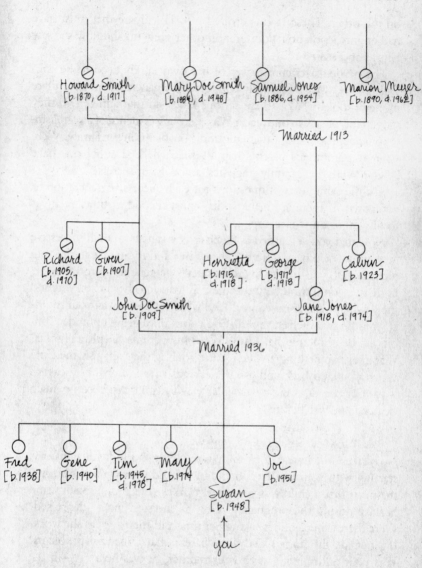

on the other. These factors created a social climate that must have had an impact on how your grandmother grew up and how she saw herself and the world.

The particular circumstances of her own family need to be considered, too. Was her family comfortable financially, or were there money problems? Was there serious illness in the family? Did they move a lot, or stay in one place? Was there any evidence of alcoholism, chronic depression, or other emotional problems in the family? Were your grandmother's parents happily married? Did either one have affairs? Were there family tragedies, scandals, or secrets?

Ask the same sorts of questions for each successive generation to your own. If there are blank spots, enlist the aid of other relatives to fill you in on what happened.

Now that you've learned as much as you can about each successive generation, step back from the family tree and try to take in the "big picture." Do you see any patterns from one generation to the next? Is there a connection between the way your mother raised you and the way her mother raised her? And what about the way your mother's mother was herself raised? Did your father grow up under conditions of economic hardship? Were his parents deeply religious? Was there something in their backgrounds they felt ashamed of? When you step back and ask these kinds of questions, the reasons why your parents were a particular way to you often become much clearer than ever before.

3. The Major Events of Your Childhood

Now take some time to look more carefully at *your* individual history, starting with your conception and birth. Did your parents welcome the news that a child was on the way? Was your mother happy and healthy during the pregnancy? Or was she sick and/or depressed? Were there other siblings taxing her time and energy? Was she working outside the home? Did your parents have financial problems? Was your father living with your mother, or was he away—in the service, perhaps, or working a job in another state? Was your birth itself easy or difficult? Did you need special medical attention? What kind of baby were you—happy and easygoing or cranky and difficult? Where did you and your family live at the time? What else was going on in your parents' lives at the time? Was one of their parents sick or dying? Were there work troubles, marital problems, health worries . . . ?

Go through your life year by year in this way. Write down events that you remember yourself and events others told you about. Are there any periods that you can't remember, or that seem vague? Ask different family members what they remember of that time. Be careful, however, not to get into fights about what really happened. Each family member will remember different events, and the same events in different ways.

As you go through the major events of your life, keep in mind that speed is *not* of the essence. Some people might want to sit down and pour out their life story in one session; others might need years to jog their memories and put all the different pieces together. For most people, assembling and interpreting the facts of childhood are on-going processes that take considerable time.

4. Gaining Access to Childhood Memories Through Meditation

Some people are baffled when others talk about their childhoods because they really don't remember anything of their own. Others can remember certain periods and episodes, but for large parts of their early years they have only dim memories—or draw a complete blank. This is normal and nothing to get upset about. If you give yourself permission to remember and you put time and effort into unburying your childhood memories, they will eventually start returning to you.

To gain access to childhood memories, you need to gain access to deeper levels of your psyche, to get in touch with your inner emotional core. Meditation is one of the most effective means. If you are not already familiar with ways to meditate, we suggest that you try this simple technique. At first it will take about thirty minutes, but once you've gotten the technique down, you'll be able to use it to meditate effectively for shorter periods.

This general meditation technique can also be used to do some of the more specialized exercises that we'll be recommending in forthcoming pages. When we introduce those other exercises, we'll provide specific instructions for adapting this technique. Readers who already meditate according to their own methods can use whatever techniques they feel most comfortable with.

First, choose a place, inside or outdoors, where there's relative quiet and you can remain comfortable, relaxed, and undisturbed for twenty minutes to half an hour. You should also choose a time of day when you feel alert, fresh, and the least preoccupied and worried.

Once you've chosen your place and time, get in a comfortable position. Depending on your physical capabilities, this should be either sitting cross-legged on the floor or ground, or sitting in a chair with your legs bent at the knees but not crossed, and your feet resting flat on the floor. If in a chair, it should be one with a firm seat, not a soft cushion. In either case, your back should be straight and your head and shoulders should be upright.

Now that you're comfortable, close your eyes and begin concentrating on your breathing. Do not force your breaths out, rather focus your conscious awareness on the breathing process as it naturally occurs. Find and focus your attention on your diaphragm, the part of your body between your lower chest and rib cage. Notice that when you take in a breath, it begins with your diaphragm moving up. This allows air to be taken into your lungs. Notice that when you let out a breath, the diaphragm moves down, allowing the outgoing air to leave the lungs and exit through your nose (and/or mouth). Follow your breathing, in and out, in and out. Sometimes it will be deep, sometimes shallow. That's fine. This is not a deep-breathing exercise, but an exercise to help you focus your attention.

After getting focused on the in-out of your breathing, now start to count each breath-in/breath-out cycle one by one. Feel the breath come into you, feel it go out, then count "one." After the next full cycle, count "two." Do this up to "ten." Then start again at "one" and go up to "ten" again.

Most likely, other thoughts will keep coming into your mind, making it difficult to complete a sequence up to ten. This is to be expected. Do not fight the distracting thoughts. Each time you notice that you've gone off into some other thought process and have lost count, simply refocus on your breathing and start again, counting from "one." Keep going until you've repeated the ten-breaths cycle three times. You may find this impossible to do at first. You may not be able to get to "ten" even once. That's okay. In time, and with practice, it will come.

In upcoming pages we'll be giving instructions for affirmations and visualizations that utilize meditation. It's here—at the point when you've done the ten breaths three times and are relaxed and focused—that you'll go on to the additional instructions given for those specific exercises.

The meditation method we've given may seem simplistic, but it's not. It's an ancient technique that can help you get away from the everyday "clutter" of your conscious mind and bring you in touch with deeper levels of your being. Since it's at those deeper levels that your childhood memories are stored, gaining access to those levels will make it much easier for you to recall what happened in your childhood.

Meditation is always helpful, even if it's done only sporadically. However, to get the best possible results, we recommend that you try to work in a half-hour meditation session at least once a week. Some people meditate once each day, others twice. If it is possible for you to make meditation a part of your daily routine, we highly recommend it. But if this is unrealistic for you—and we realize it may be—don't think that you must pass up the benefits of meditating altogether. Even if you can squeeze it in only once a week, it still is worth doing.

5. From What Happened to How You Felt About It— Using Photos to Reconnect with Your Inner Child

As you develop a clearer picture of what happened when you were growing up, you also need to find out how you felt about those events. You may have recalled, for example, that when you were three your tonsils were taken out, and when you were five the family moved. How did you feel when those things happened? Happy? Sad? Scared? Anxious? Special? Lucky? Unlucky? Don't worry if your feelings seem to contradict one another, or seem to make no sense. Often we feel two entirely different ways about the same thing; this is normal. The goal here isn't to judge the *appropriateness* of what you felt, it's to simply identify *how* you felt at the time.

If you find it difficult to recall what happened during your childhood and how you felt then, photos can help jog your memory. Most people reading this book grew up long after the advent of the snapshot, so it's likely that you had photos taken of you and your family when you were a child. Get ahold of some of those photos. They contain important clues about what happened and how you felt when you were growing up. They can also help you get in touch with the child still within you.

You might find it helpful to go over your childhood photos with a friend who shares your interest in learning more about his/her childhood. Ask him/her to go get some photos from his/her child-hood and then do this exercise with you.

You should each choose a few photographs of yourself at a young age, three or four or so. Study your photographs for a few minutes, then introduce the child in the pictures to your friend. Describe what the child is like—general disposition, interests, fears, likes, and dis-likes . . . Describe how she is feeling in each particular picture. Your friend should feel free to ask questions about the child, and to share his/her reaction to the child and photos as well. When you're finished with your photos, go over your friend's photos in the same way.

Two things will probably happen. First, your friend is going to point out things that you hadn't noticed—that the child is cute, or looks scared, or is very tiny and vulnerable, for example. Second, it's very likely that your friend will have a much more positive, com-passionate, loving reaction to the child you once were than you do. Seeing your childhood self through someone else's eyes can not only yield more information about your earlier self, it can help you become more accepting of that earlier self, too. And the more accepting you become of your childhood self, the easier it's going to be for you to remember what happened to you as a child and how you felt at the time.

6. Gaining Further Access to Your Childhood Self Through Visualization

This exercise is for those of you who want further access to the childhood self at your inner core. It's a simple visualization exercise that builds on the basic meditation technique already given.

Begin by by doing the ten-breaths technique described on pages 346–47. Once you've become relaxed and focused, form a picture in your mind of yourself as a small child. This may take a few minutes. If you get distracted by other thoughts, as you doubtless will, focus on your breathing again. Then return to picturing yourself as a small child in your mind.

Now picture your present-day self approaching your childhood self. Have your adult self introduce him/herself, then take the smaller self's hand and assure the smaller self that he/she is loved and perfectly safe. Picture them both smiling and happy together.

Now visualize your adult self and childhood self walking hand in hand into the house or apartment you lived in as a child—or one of the homes, if you moved often. As you watch them enter, focus on the childhood self. How is he/she feeling? Is your childhood self happy to be home? Anxious? Scared? Sad? "Whatever you're feeling, it's okay. I understand," the adult self should tell the younger one. If the child is scared or upset, your adult self should offer reassurances: "Don't worry. I'm going to stay with you. I'm not going to let anything bad happen."

Now picture your childhood slowly leading your adult self through the rest of the house, room by room. In each room, focus on what the child feels in that particular place. Keep concentrating on what the room looks like and what the child is experiencing, but don't fight other associations that come into your mind. Very likely, you'll start remembering events that occurred in those rooms long ago, but that you previously had no recollection of. When you feel ready, move on to the next room. All the while, make sure your adult self is holding the hand of your younger self and asking him/her what he/she is feeling now.

As you do this visualization, don't worry if other images intrude. Just concentrate on being with your young self, experiencing the world and your childhood home through his/her eyes, and understanding what he/she is feeling. You might see colors, lights, shapes, objects, structures (buildings other than the house you're "visiting," say). Or you might not "see" anything; instead, you might have a heightened sense or awareness of a particular part of you, a warm feeling, or a "liquidy" feeling, or an anxious feeling. Whatever you feel, relax and go with it, continuing to concentrate on the inner experience of your childhood self.

When you no longer can keep concentrating inwards, open your eyes. Stay relaxed and focused by resuming conscious concentration on your breathing. Let the air in, then let it out. After a few minutes, take a pen or pencil and a sheet of paper and write the words, "When I was a child," and allow whatever words that naturally come to mind to flow out. You might find yourself writing "When I was a child, I felt lost" or "When I was a child, sometimes I was lonely," or "When I was a child, my parents fought a lot and that made me scared." The words that come might surprise you; you might find that your experience as a child was a lot different and more complex than you thought.

Many people will have trouble with this exercise. It may take several attempts before you can visualize your childhood self. You may not be able to picture your childhood home or to go farther than the entryway or into one or two particular rooms. This is okay. The goal of this exercise is not to reconstruct a floorplan of your childhood home, it's to get you more in touch with what happened in your home and how you felt about it when you were growing up. If you have trouble with the exercise, don't push yourself. Try it for twenty minutes to a half hour, then let it go. A few days or a week later, you can do it again. Each time it will get easier and you'll remember more.

7. Predominant Memories of Childhood

As you recall more clearly and extensively the events of your childhood, certain memories will probably stand out much more vividly than the rest. In fact, even without actively trying to recount the events of your childhood, you may be able to describe one or two things that happened to you, things you've always remembered more strongly than anything else. Very likely, one or two memories from childhood have repeatedly played back in your mind throughout your adult life with no prompting or other conscious effort on your part. Predominant memories like these should be given special attention. Often they are memories of events that seem insignificant, or that we think we shouldn't have been affected by. But memories from childhood, especially early childhood, that are particularly vivid or come back to us again and again are, in fact, encapsulations of our early emotional life. Take, as an example, a man whose strongest memory from childhood is of being alone in a room playing with wooden soldiers. Hearing about this memory, you might react, "So what?" or "Big deal, all kids do that." But in this particular instance, the memory sums up the man's childhood experience as an isolated child whose most meaningful interactions were with wooden figures.

Although you may think the predominant memories from your childhood are silly or insignificant, they contain information that can be a great help in understanding the origins of your love blocks. Don't dismiss your memories. Examine them and explore what they may be trying to tell you.

Chapter 20
Exercises for "I Don't Want to Deal with My Feelings" and Related Blocks

The more attuned you are to your feelings, and the more at home you are with them, the more you'll be able to enjoy a sense of emotional connection with others. The exercises in this chapter are designed to help you become more aware of your emotions, and more accepting of them, too. They're also designed to help you find healthier, more constructive ways of expressing your emotions. They are crucial steps in the process of overcoming your love blocks.

People who recognize themselves as having the "I Don't Want to Deal with My Feelings" block will find these exercises especially helpful. However, even if you don't identify with that block, we strongly recommend that you go over this chapter. The fact is that in our culture virtually everyone has problems dealing with some aspect of his or her emotional life. Although you may think you don't have the "I Don't Want to Deal with My Feelings" block, chances are good you have at least a mild form of it—and that you could benefit from these exercises.

These exercises should also be of special interest to those whose most apparent block is "Anger Keeps Getting in the Way," "I Don't Need Anyone—I'm Strong," or "I Don't Want To Have to Ask for What I Need," which are all extensions or particularized manifestations of the "I Don't Want to Deal with My Feelings" block. Because these blocks are all interrelated, exercises that help overcome one inevitably help with the others, too.

These exercises are also recommended for those with the "I Don't Deserve Love" block, which very frequently goes hand in hand with the "I Don't Want to Deal with My Feelings" block. People with low self-esteem often condemn themselves for being "too emotional," or having "bad" feelings. These "bad" feelings, they believe, mean they're "bad" people; and since they're "bad" people, they reason, then obviously they don't deserve love. In many cases, overcoming the "I Don't Deserve Love" block thus requires unlearning the patterns and beliefs that underlie the "I Don't Want to Deal with My Feelings" block.

The following exercises are not at all complex. Nevertheless, you may find them difficult to do. You may resist them with all your will, in fact. But try to get beyond your resistance and give them a shot, so you'll be able to share a sense of emotional connection with others.

1. Identifying What You Feel

Many people have trouble identifying what they feel. They experience a wide variety of feelings and they're aware that they have these different feelings, but they can't describe, differentiate, or name those feelings except in the vaguest of terms. Since they can't *identify* what it is that they feel, they have trouble deciding on the appropriate response to their feelings. Since they can't *say* what they're feeling, they also have trouble sharing their feelings with others. Because the ability to share innermost feelings is the cornerstone of intimacy, this makes it impossible for them to achieve the sort of closeness that most people seek in relationships.

To become more adept at identifying your feelings, begin by making a list of all the human emotional states you can think of. It might be helpful to do this alphabetically. Under "A," for example, you might list angry, annoyed, anxious, afraid, and apologetic. "B" could include bitter, bereft, bored, bitchy, bold, brave, and bawdy. Don't worry about leaving certain feelings out; you can always add more.

Once you've familiarized yourself with the wide variety of human emotions, take a few minutes each evening to look at your list, picking out those that applied to you on that particular day. Write in a notebook, "Today, November 12, I felt ———, ———, and ———," using as many of the descriptive words as apply. Try to do this every night, until knowing exactly what you feel is something that comes to you automatically, with no special effort. This might take months, or longer. But stay with it until knowing what you feel has become a matter of habit.

2. Feeling in Your Body, Not Just in Your Head

As you get into the habit of identifying your various emotions, start paying close attention to how specific emotions actually feel to you. Write down the physical sensations that accompany different feelings. When you're angry, for example, you might experience a "hollow feeling" in the pit of your stomach or a desire to throw up, and your back, neck, and facial muscles might tense. Anxiety might cause your heart to race, irritate your bowels, or give you an inner feeling of crawling dread. Joy might make you feel buoyant, light-headed, or energetic. Note also what you usually do when you feel these symptoms. For example, you might respond to the physical sensations of anger by eating or drinking, lighting a cigarette, chewing gum, biting your lip, or kicking something.

Pay particular attention to anxiety. Often anxiety is a cover for a feeling we're blocked from experiencing directly—like anger, fear, or jealousy.

Also pay attention to physical pains and ailments that seem to have no cause. Sometimes we are so completely unaware that we have a certain feeling that our psyche has to try to alert us via physical pain. Chronic backaches and neck aches, stomachaches, skin rashes, and so forth sometimes serve as ways of signaling that "hey, something's going on here that you're overlooking. You need to pay attention to what you're feeling, and you'd better find some healthier way of dealing with it."

3. Determining Your Discomfort Zones

Which of the feelings you've learned to identify make you uncomfortable? Anger? Jealousy? Lust? Selfishness? Where did you get the idea that some emotions are wrong or inappropriate? Who taught you that you shouldn't feel certain things? Think about the different emotions you censor one by one; what images, associations or people come to mind?

Now think about the ways you stop or dull the sensations of the emotions you believe you shouldn't feel. When you have a feeling that makes you uncomfortable, does your breathing become faster or shallower? Do you feel a knot in your stomach? Get dizzy? Clench your teeth? Fidget and pace? Suddenly get hungry? Lose your appetite entirely? Usually, we don't do these things by conscious choice. They're ways of drowning out and blocking our feelings that occur automatically.

4. Gaining Greater Access to Your Inner Life

Some people will be unable to do the preceding exercises because they have learned to so thoroughly repress their feelings that they are completely out of touch with their inner life. They are cut off from their own emotional center. Others have only partial access to their inner life. They are not as attuned to their emotions as they could be.

If either of these descriptions fits you, you'll need to make a conscious effort to gain more access to your inner life. One of the best ways is through meditation. The simple meditation technique given in the preceding chapter (pages 346–47) can help you. If you feel you could benefit further, we strongly advise making a twenty-to-thirty-minute meditation session a part of your daily routine.

Dreams can also be a vital means of obtaining greater access to your inner life. For thousands of years, people knowledgeable about the human psyche have stressed the importance of dreams. Dreams can be viewed as the means by which the unconscious part of the psyche communicates with the conscious part. Dreams are the unconscious's way of letting our waking selves know what's really going on inside of us. When a person becomes engaged in the process of psychological discovery and growth, it often happens that she dreams more.

Unfortunately, it's not always easy to decipher a dream, to figure out exactly what message—or messages—the unconscious is trying to communicate through a particular dream. You will probably need the help of someone who is both skilled at interpreting dreams *and* sufficiently familiar with your particular psychological issues to help you figure out what various dreams might mean. This usually means a psychotherapist you have been working with for a time. Generally, it's not a good idea to take your dreams to a friend, partner or other loved one for interpretation. Even if your loved ones are skilled at interpreting dreams, they're too close to you; very likely, they will unconsciously project their own fantasies and desires onto your dream. If you want to "mine" your dreams, we strongly suggest getting into therapy.

5. Learning to "Ride" Your Feelings

By now, you probably have dramatically increased your awareness of what you feel, how your various feelings actually feel in your body, and what you do in order to tune out, suppress or get rid of those particular feelings that make you uncomfortable. The next step is learning to relax and feel your feelings—all of them—without trying to quiet, dull, or stop them. This sounds simple, but it's not. You are probably afraid that if you let yourself fully feel your feelings, you'll get "out of control." You might also fear that certain feelings—anger, say, or grief, or hurt—could kill you. Once you have learned to "ride" your feelings, you'll find out that this won't happen, and your fear of your own feelings should dissipate.

This concept of "riding" your feelings comes from the Tibetan practice of "riding the wild horse." The horse is our feelings. Most of us learned that we have to "break" the horse, that we have to get it under control and show it who is master. The Tibetans teach that it's wiser to get on top of the horse and see where it takes you. If the horse senses that you are trying to break it, chances are good it will fight you and try to throw you. Your energy will then be consumed in an ongoing battle for control which might hurt or even cripple you. If the horse senses you are simply riding it, it won't try to throw you; it will take you for a ride, then it will eventually get tired and come to a stop. The same thing happens with feelings: if you allow yourself to ride them without trying to rein them in, they'll carry you away for a while, but soon enough they'll wear themselves out and come to a stop.

The next time you have a feeling that makes you mildly uncomfortable—anxiety or sadness, for example—try this: Do the ten-breaths meditation exercise on pages 346–47 until you are in a focused state. Now name the feeling you are having ("I am anxious," "I am sad," etc.). Let yourself really *feel* it, immersing yourself in the physical sensations. Don't fight the feeling, just let it be, allowing it to take you wherever it wants to. Notice that you may be calling yourself names you learned to punish yourself with whenever you had this feeling ("weak," "babyish," "stupid," "emotional," "basket case," etc.). Tell yourself, "These labels aren't accurate. My [name feeling] is not bad. I am not a bad person for feeling it." All the while stay with the feeling. Keep riding it. Be aware of your breathing. Continue with one breath in, one breath out. Stay with the feeling until it stops.

After the ride is over, ask yourself how you feel. Was the ride as scary as you thought? Are you surprised that you "gave in" to your feeling and it didn't overcome or kill you? Do you feel calmer? More whole? Slightly less afraid?

After you have become experienced taking "pony rides" on mildly disturbing feelings (annoyance, mild anxiety, or mild sadness) gradually ride bigger horses (rage, panic, grief). Don't force yourself into experiencing these feelings so that you can ride them; wait instead until these feelings naturally arise in the course of your life, then do the exercise.

As you take on more powerful emotions, the rides will be longer and scarier. But remember, the horse will stop. And if you make it a habit, you'll eventually find that it takes less and less time to deal with particular feelings. It's fighting our feelings that takes up so much of our time and energy; the feelings themselves come and go rather quickly.

6. Expressing Your Feelings

As you become more aware of, and comfortable with, your own feelings, you may want to find better ways of expressing them. Do not pour out your feelings to anyone and everyone. Be selective. Choose one or a few people who seem emotionally alive and comfortable with feelings. If someone is the type who is always telling others what they should and should not feel, this is *not* a person to open up to.

Choose your words carefully, too. Use "I feel . . ." statements, not "you" statements such as "You make me feel . . ." and "You always get me [angry, upset, etc.]." Do not ask other people to tell you that your feelings are right or valid. No one can do this for you. Your feelings are neither bad nor good; they are simply your feelings.

In verbally expressing your feelings, acknowledge that they probably stem as much from past experiences as from present ones. Don't downplay the impact of present-day events on your feelings, but don't present your feelings as though they stem solely from present-day occurrences, either. Don't say: "It makes me feel like dirt when you make fun of me like that. How could you be so insensitive?" Instead, say: "When I was little, my family used to make fun of me a lot, and I feel that same humiliation when someone makes fun of me today. There's no way you could have known how sensitive I am about this, but now that you do, I'd appreciate it if you'd lay off."

As you learn to verbally express your feelings, try to get into the habit of expressing loving feelings as much as the ones that upset you. We usually spend more time talking about what makes us unhappy in life than about what makes us happy. Tell your loved ones "I love you," "I am so glad I know you," "I think you're a very considerate person, and I appreciate that," "I admire how diligent you are," etc. Don't make up nice things to say, just articulate the loving feelings you really do have within. But be careful not to go overboard, expressing only "nice" feelings. This may seem like a way to help relationships, but in fact it's sure to doom them. In any relationship, all kinds of feelings can come up and need to be expressed.

Not all emotions need to be expressed in every situation, however. Sometimes, it's not in your best interest to express certain feelings to a specific individual. If you want to tell your boss to go to hell, for example, it's best to confide this to a friend or therapist; informing your boss is not recommended. If you're feeling ambivalent about your spouse, it might be a good idea to hash out your feelings with a trusted friend or therapist before deciding whether they are significant enough to tell your spouse, or whether they're fleeting feelings that really have more to do with other issues in your life than with your marriage.

Sometimes, verbal expression of feelings isn't sufficient. Especially in the case of very powerful emotions, some form of physical release is usually needed. Pounding pillows, getting a good physical workout, doing something creative like painting or playing piano are all good ways of releasing strong feelings like anger, frustration, grief, and anxiety. Keep in mind, however, that it's important to have outlets not just for feelings of anger, frustration, grief, and anxiety but also for feelings of joy, pride, optimism, and sexual desire.

7. Expressing Anger in Particular

As discussed in the chapter on the "Anger Keeps Getting in the Way" block, anger is an emotion that many people find extremely troublesome. People who have difficulty with anger tend to fall into two broad camps. First, there are the venters—people who express anger so quickly, vehemently, and frequently that they end up driving others away. Second are the swallowers—people whose inability to express their anger causes them to turn it inward, which leads to emotional numbing and depression, thereby leaving them without the emotional aliveness necessary to connect deeply with others.

If you're a venter, you need to find a more responsible and less destructive way of dealing with your anger. You may excuse your explosions by telling yourself that you'd be doing yourself psychological damage if you kept your anger bottled up. While there's truth to that theory, it's not the whole truth, at least not in your case. On the contrary, over the long run taking out anger on others is just as harmful to your own psychological well-being as holding it in. Your venting may feel good at the moment but may ultimately cause you to end up disliked and without meaningful human relationships—and what could be more unhealthy than that?

The key task for a venter is to identify what feelings lie behind your anger. Venters are usually so quick to announce "I'm angry" and let the world know it that they don't say, "Wait a second—what's happening here? Am I really feeling angry right now, or is something else going on inside me? Could it be that underneath my anger is some other feeling that I'm using my anger to hide?" Venters need to get into the habit of asking questions to help identify which other feelings precede their anger and are masked by it. Very likely, they'll find that much of the time their anger is a cover for another feeling they want to avoid—fear, hurt, sadness, loneliness, for example.

The next step is to express that underlying feeling, not the anger. Venters usually find that this strategy yields a much more constructive result than throwing temper tantrums ever did. If you scream at your spouse, "You thoughtless jerk! I'm so sick of your insults that I could kill you," your spouse will probably get angry in response. More effective would be something like "I felt really hurt by some of the things you said before. I thought you were insulting me, and because you're so important to me, I felt really wounded." This sort of statement is much more likely to be met with a comforting, loving, apologetic response. And that's the kind of response you need in this type of situation, for it directly addresses and can assuage the hurt that gave rise to your anger in the first place.

If you're a swallower, the key is learning to give your anger some form of outward expression. This does not mean adopting the irresponsible ranting and raving characteristic of venters. You can still discharge your anger without being abusive and insensitive to others. You can, for instance, write out your anger in a journal or letter that's never sent, or you can kick and punch pillows, or you can play tennis or racquetball and pretend that each time you hit the ball you're smashing the face of the person you're angry with. You can get a photograph of the person you're angry with and throw darts at it. You can also tell an uninvolved third party about your anger, asking him or her to help you decide whether your anger is entirely justified and what action—if any—to take. While some may seem silly, these are effective methods that are not destructive to you or to anyone else, and they're much healthier than holding anger in and hoping it will somehow just go away.

For swallowers who are learning to let anger out, some words of caution are in order. If you decide to express your anger to the source—your boss or spouse, for example—please keep in mind that this could have negative consequences. Consult other people first. Confrontations can backfire, particularly if the person you confront has power over you or violent tendencies. If after careful consideration, you do decide to confront the person you're angry with, think carefully about what you're going to do and say. Plan it all out beforehand and *rehearse* it with someone else—a friend, a counselor, or therapist. Also decide ahead of time what you'll do if the confrontation does indeed backfire. Remember, although assertiveness is generally a good policy, in a world with so much emotional and physical violence each situation needs to be assessed and approached individually.

8. A Graduated Way to Express Needs

If it's difficult for many of us to constructively express anger, it's just as difficult for others of us to say we have needs. Many people are so uncomfortable with saying the words "I need," and so unaccustomed to saying them, that they literally can't force them out of their mouths. They completely deny that they have needs, as is the case with those who have the "I Don't Need Anyone—I'm Strong" block. Or they acknowledge to themselves that they have needs but refuse to tell anyone else, instead insisting that others should be able to read their minds. This is the tack taken by those with the "I Don't Want to Have to Ask for What I Need" block.

If you have a problem voicing your needs, a gradual, step-by-step approach is best. First, in a notebook practice writing the words "I, [*your name*], need," followed by specific things that you need. Write down as many "I need" statements as you can think of. These might include, for example, "I, Jane Doe, need air and water," "I, Jane Doe, need love," "I, Jane Doe, need a raise," "I, Jane Doe, need a haircut," "I, Jane Doe, need privacy." Write out various "I need" statements every day for a couple of weeks.

The next step is to say your "I need" statements to yourself but *aloud*. Go into the bathroom, face the mirror, and voice your "I need" statements. Pay attention to how you look when the words "I need" come out of your mouth. Many people think that if they were to let their neediness out, it would make them unattractive, perhaps even disfigured- or monstrous-looking. But when you say the words "I need," does your face really get all distorted? If you look, you'll discover the answer is no.

Once you've gotten more comfortable with uttering the once-dreaded words "I need" in the privacy of your own solitary presence, start considering who in your life might be receptive to hearing about and responding to your various needs. If you needed to borrow a car, who of your friends/family would be most likely to help? If you needed advice about home repairs or finding a new job, who would be the best person to ask? If you needed a shoulder to cry on, or someone to indulge you while you whined, who would be most sympathetic to your request? Not everyone in your life is going to be good at meeting all your needs, and some won't be good at meeting any. But if you understand this ahead of time, you can escape the self-destructive trap of taking a need to a person who is incapable of meeting it. You'll also then avoid the old habit of thinking "If this person can't meet my needs, it must mean there's something wrong with my needs—and with me for having them." When you start taking your needs to those who *can* and will meet them, you'll further learn that it isn't your neediness that's been the problem, it's been your choice of people.

As you begin identifying who in your life is going to be most receptive to hearing about and meeting which of your various needs, try out different ways of expressing your needs—ways that are at once straightforward and polite. Don't beat around the bush. Don't be either overly obsequious or demanding and manipulative. There's a significant difference between saying something like "I need a night out this week. Would you be willing to take care of the kids yourself one night? Next week, I'll give you a night out" and "Why can't you see that I'm at my wit's end? What do I have to do to get you to offer to spell me for a night?" There's also a big difference between stating your needs and asking for them to be met, and saying "These are my needs. Meet 'em, or else."

When you need something very much, asking for it can be extremely intimidating and anxiety producing; the risk of disappointment and humiliation if the answer is "no" is just too high. So as you begin voicing your needs to other people in your life, start with items that really aren't that important to you and gradually work your way up to what you *really* want and need. For example, you might call up a friend who lives close by and say, "I'm cooking dinner and realize I need garlic. Do you have any you can spare?" Or you can call the local library and say, "I need to get some information on [pick a topic]. I was wondering if you could please help me." Or you might tell your spouse or partner, "I need a hand hanging this new potted plant. When you've got a moment, would you please help me with it?" If the answer in any of these situations is "no," you won't be devastated, and you'll still have gotten practice in asking. Remember, the point of making these types of requests is not solely to get the need met (although that would be nice), but to get you accustomed to saying that you have needs and asking others for help.

Eventually you'll build up enough confidence to ask for things that are more important to you, such as more attention or affection from a loved one, more respect from your kids, more privacy at home, for example. A good way to get going is to say to your closest loved ones, "I have trouble saying what I need, and I want to change that. You can help by humoring me when I ask for small things. Will you?"

Chapter 21
Exercises for Overcoming Other Specific Blocks

Most people have more than one love block, and their different blocks are usually interconnected. Thus, we would caution against viewing your different love blocks in isolation from one another, and we'd also warn against trying to overcome one without dealing with the others you have. If you're serious about letting go of your love blocks, you've got to be willing to work on all of them.

This does not mean, however, that you need to work on all your love blocks at once. That would be a daunting and overwhelming task. To facilitate the process of working on your blocks, we've divided the exercises in this chapter into three general categories. The first group contains exercises for those blocks that primarily affect your view of yourself. The second includes exercises for those blocks that primarily affect your view of the world. In the third group are exercises for those blocks that primarily affect your views and expectations of others. Of course, since some blocks affect your view of yourself, the world, and others simultaneously, these categories are not mutually exclusive. We've found, however, that organizing the exercises in this way is an extremely effective conceptual and therapeutic tool. The three categories make it easier to conceptualize the different blocks and their interconnections, and make working on them easier, too.

For Blocks Primarily Affecting Your View of Yourself

Although most love blocks have some effect on how you view your self, those that most obviously and directly affect your self-image are "I Don't Deserve Love" and "I Don't Need Anyone—I'm Strong." But several other blocks are primarily linked, albeit in less immediately obvious ways, to self-image problems, too. These include "I Just Can't Make a Commitment" and "Love Will Get in the Way of Success." Although these two blocks appear very different at first glance, they are usually extensions of "I Don't Deserve Love," and the underlying issue for virtually everyone with them is low self-esteem. Similarly, "I Don't Want to Have to Ask for What I Need" often goes hand in hand with "I Don't Need Anyone—I'm Strong," and one can't be overcome without dealing with the other.

1. Identifying and Understanding How You See Yourself

If you have at least one of the blocks just mentioned, you need a better understanding of exactly how your self-image has been affected. Write down on a piece of paper all the adjectives and labels you think describe you. You might want to make four categories, starting with "I am" statements, then going to "I'm not" statements, followed by plain "I" and "I don't" statements. Your list might include such things as: I am honest, I am kind, I am fat, I am no good, I am bad at math; I'm not good with machines, I'm not very funny, I'm not interested in politics, I'm not aggressive and energetic enough; I love cats, I worry a lot, I often feel depressed; I don't tell lies, I don't like to cook, I don't have many close friends.

As you make your list, include whatever comes to mind, even if you don't consciously believe it's true. For example, in writing your "I am" statements, something like "I am a worthless piece of shit" or "I am a loser" might spring to mind. Even if you know in your head that this is not true, write it down anyway, because in another equally powerful part of your being you might not be so sure.

Once you've made your list, circle those statements and labels that you think are most representative of you, that are most central to your personality. For example, you may have written down "I'm not mechanical" and "I love cats," but your not being mechanical may be far less important to you and your self-image than your love of cats. The statements and labels you circle add up to form your core self-image.

When we get down on ourselves, certain labels and statements tend to go through our heads again and again. Pay attention to these, too. For example, when you fail to live up to your own expectations, you may silently tell yourself something like "you jerk, you always screw things up" or "you asshole, why can't you ever do anything right?" Whenever any self-berating comments like this cross your mind, write them down. Better yet, add them to a running log called "Words I Beat Myself Up With." In your more self-loving moments, you might know for certain that the self-denigrating labels and statements you make to yourself aren't true. Therefore, you might not see them as being central to your self-image. But any label or statement about yourself that frequently flits through your thoughts seemingly of its own volition does indeed play a central role in determining how you see and feel about yourself.

The next task is to learn where your central beliefs about yourself come from. Most of us assume that if we believe that we're worthless, or pretty, or smart, or klutzy, it must be because we really are that way—and we also assume we were born believing these things to be true. Yet the fact is, we see ourselves the way we do because we've been taught to, because we *learned* to see ourselves that way. And a lot of our perceptions are either inaccurate or completely untrue.

Look at the various beliefs you have about yourself one by one. In each case, ask yourself where that belief came from. If you think, for example, that you're "no good," who taught you to see yourself that way? What images and associations spring to mind? Do you remember anyone ever actually telling you that, or was the message communicated more indirectly? For example, perhaps your mother frequently complained that your father was "no good," and she and other family members sometimes commented that "you're just like your father." In that sort of situation, you will have gotten the message loud and clear, even though no one ever spelled it out for you.

This exercise can be painful, and it is not meant to be done in a day or even a few months. Identifying your central beliefs about yourself and learning where they came from is a long-term process.

Do not try to get it all "done" in a short period. Go slowly, at a pace that feels comfortable to you. If you find that too many painful memories are being stirred up and you begin to feel overwhelmed, we strongly advise seeking the help of a caring professional therapist.

2. Revising Your Self-Image Through Affirmations and Meditation

Your list of beliefs about yourself probably contains many negatives, ranging from the mildly critical, such as "I am slow to get things done" to the *really* negative, such as "I am a complete mess," "I am worthless," and "I don't deserve love—I deserve nothing good, in fact." Considering these beliefs can be depressing, but the good news is that what's been learned can be *un*learned. Even if you have lived with certain negative beliefs about yourself for as long as you can remember, you don't have to live with them forever, or even much longer. You can begin unlearning them—and replacing them with more accurate and self-loving beliefs—today, starting *now*.

One of the best ways is by using affirmations. Although commonly used and recommended by numerous sources, the affirmations we'll be doing have been largely inspired by Sondra Ray's book, *I Deserve Love*.[1] Since most people reading this book probably have the "I Don't Deserve Love" block to some extent, the simple "I deserve love" affirmation referred to in her title is a good one to start with.

But a few words about affirmations are in order first. An affirmation is a simple, positive statement that you write or recite over and over, like a chant or a mantra. "I deserve love," "I am growing happier and healthier day by day," and "I am at peace" are all common affirmations. Many people scoff at the notion of affirmations, and we understand the impulse to dismiss them, saying "Oh, come on now, they can't possibly make a difference." But we can assure you in no uncertain terms that affirmations really do make a difference. Think how often in your life you've called yourself names, mentally beat up on yourself with self-denigrating, depressing, negative thoughts. You know those negative thoughts work. They can make you feel utterly miserable in a matter of minutes. Doesn't it make sense, then, that spending some time reciting positive thoughts might work equally well? If you try just the first affirmation exercise we suggest here, we promise you'll feel better within days.

Begin by going out and buying a lined notebook with 8½ × 11 paper. Pick a color you like. This will be your affirmations book. It will only cost a dollar or two, and improving your self-image is definitely worth the small expense.

When you can set aside about twenty minutes to concentrate, turn to the first page of your book. Draw a line down the middle, dividing it in half. Now write in the left-hand column "I, [your name], deserve love." As you write this, a negative response will probably come immediately to mind. For example, you'll write "I, Janet Brown, deserve love," and immediately you'll hear in your head something like "No you don't" or "Only if you pay for it later." Whatever negative response comes to mind, write it in the right-hand column. Keep writing "I, [your name], deserve love" in the left column and the negative responses in the right until you run out of negative responses. The page will look something like this, only in your own handwriting:

I, Janet Brown, deserve love.	Oh no I don't.
I, Janet Brown, deserve love.	But who would ever love me?
I, Janet Brown, deserve love.	If I'm a good girl.
I, Janet Brown, deserve love.	But only if I pay for it somehow.
I, Janet Brown, deserve love.	If I were thin, that is.
I, Janet Brown, deserve love.	But I'll be punished for it.
I, Janet Brown, deserve love.	What a crock!
I, Janet Brown, deserve love.	But if I get it, it won't last.

It may take half a page or two pages before you run out of negative responses, but however long it takes, keep going until you've run out. Then keep writing "I, [your name], deserve love" in the left-hand column, thirty more times before you stop.

For this exercise to be most effective, we suggest you do it once a day to start. If you can spare the time, doing it in the morning and evening would be great. Eventually—it may be a week or two for some, considerably longer for others—the negative responses that you've been putting in the right-hand column will stop coming so quickly and forcefully. Ideally, there will come a point when they stop coming to mind at all. If and when this happens, keep writing "I, [your name], deserve love" thirty times in your book each day anyway. It's not enough simply to get out of the habit of rejecting the notion that you deserve love; you have to start really believing it, too—and you need to drill that belief into deeper and deeper levels of your being.

Depending on how extensive your "I Don't Deserve Love" block is, the length of time you'll need to practice this particular affirmation will vary. Some people write out the "I deserve love" affirmation 30 times a day for a month, then feel ready to move on to another affirmation. Some people stick with it forever, making writing it down thirty times a part of their daily routine. Some people do this affirmation daily but wind down to writing it ten or twenty times, and eventually add other ones to their routine. Other people do the "I Deserve Love" affirmation for a while, then drop affirmations entirely and go back to them when their self-esteem starts feeling shaky. There is no one "right" way to do it. Do what feels best to you.

When you feel ready, move on to another affirmation that can help undo another of your major love blocks. For "I Don't Need Anyone—I'm Strong," a good affirmation is "I, [your name], have many needs, and that's okay." For "Love Will Get in the Way of Success," effective affirmations are "I, [your name], don't have to be successful (or hardworking) to be worthy," and "I, [your name], am worthy and lovable regardless of the work I do." In later exercises we'll give additional affirmations for other blocks.

Some people find it helpful to write down on index cards the affirmations they're working on, and then carry the cards around for reference during the day. If you frequently spend time riding a bus or train, cooling your heels in waiting rooms, or with nothing to do at home or work, index cards would be a good idea. You can pull them out and silently recite your affirmations during those free moments when your mind tends to wander and fill up with self-denigrating thoughts. Even without cards, it's a good idea to make an effort to silently recite your affirmations whenever you've got free time—when you're walking home from work or standing in the checkout line in the supermarket, for example.

Many people find it remarkably helpful to meditate using an affirmation as a mantra, too. To do this, follow the instructions for the ten-breaths meditation on pages 346–47. After you've relaxed and gotten focused on your breathing, repeat the particular affirmation you've selected—"I, [your name], deserve love," say, or, "I, [your name], am worthy and whole and at peace"—slowly and carefully. You can do this aloud or silently, in your head. Do it for as long as you can—five or ten minutes would be good—then open your eyes and stop. It would be most helpful to do this on a daily basis, but even sporadically will still help.

When you start with a new affirmation in your affirmations book, always follow the same format used for "I deserve love." Always personalize it by using your own name. "I, Janet Brown, deserve love" will have a much more powerful impact on your psyche than an anonymous "I deserve love" will. Equally important, always start out by writing down the negative responses that come to mind. Keep doing that day after day until those negative responses fade away and start disappearing entirely. If you try to insert the positive belief into your psyche without identifying and allowing out the corresponding negative ones, the affirmations will be much less effective. Remember, learning new beliefs is only part of the job; you've got to unlearn the old ones, too.

3. Understanding Your "Should-Be" Self

The goal of the preceding two exercises was to get a better understanding of the self you think you are, or your perceived self, and to replace those beliefs about yourself that are destructive and inaccurate with beliefs that are positive and more truthful. The goal of this exercise and the next one is to increase your understanding of the self you think you should be, or your ideal self, and to develop an ideal self that is more realistic and conducive to self-love.

In addition to learning beliefs about ourselves such as "I am smart" and "I am shy," we also learned a variety of beliefs like "I should be good," "I should be outgoing," "I should always work hard." These beliefs about how we should be add up to form our ideal self. Generally, we're constantly, if unconsciously, comparing our perceived self to our ideal self. The closer the match between the way we think we are and the way we think we should be, the higher our self-esteem; the bigger the gap, the lower our self-esteem.

Make a list of all the things you think you should be, should have, should be doing. This might include: I should be thin, I should eat right, I shouldn't yell at my children, I should be out getting some exercise instead of sitting here reading, I should be successful, I shouldn't be needy, I should be polite, for example. Also make a list of "you should" statements in which "you" means "any person." This might include statements along the line of: you should be punctual, you shouldn't speak too loudly, you should always keep your emotions under control, you should avoid talking about unpleasant or upsetting subjects. Whatever "you should" beliefs you adhere to, chances are that you expect yourself—and others—to live up to them, and many of your problems accepting both yourself and others in your life probably stem from your and their failure to behave as you think everyone should.

Once you've obtained a clearer picture of your shoulds, go through them one by one, asking where they came from. Where did you learn, for example, that you shouldn't be shy or that you should always work hard? What images and associations come to mind when you think of each should? Did a particular person, or persons, teach or tell you? Or did you pick up this specific should from books, advertising, the mass media?

4. Revising Your "Should-Be" Self Through Affirmations and Meditation

With a clearer understanding of what your shoulds are and where they come from, you're ready to start getting rid of your unrealistic, self-punishing standards and expectations. This doesn't mean giving up the positive standards and goals that give you something to strive for, it means eliminating the impossible ones that make you miserable and undercut your self-esteem.

Select one of your shoulds that is a constant or frequent source of trouble for you. This may be something like "I should always be a nice person," "I should be thin," or "I should work harder." Now compose an affirmation that counteracts it. This might be, "I, [your name], don't always have to be a nice person to be worthy and lovable," "I, [your name], don't have to be thin. I'm okay the way I am," or "I, [your name], don't have to work harder. My worth is not dependent on how hard I work." When you've chosen an appropriate affirmation, write it in your book the way you did with "I deserve love." Follow all the same steps. When you feel that you've made headway getting rid of this particular should, pick another one and work on that. Keep going until you've covered all the ones that tyrannize you.

You also might want to try some general affirmations that can be used no matter what your own individual shoulds are. "I, [your name], am lovable and worthy just the way I am at this moment" is an effective general affirmation. Another is "I, [your name], don't have to change to be lovable and worthy."

Both your own individualized affirmations and these general ones can also be used very successfully with the ten-breaths meditation technique given on pages 346–47. Once you've relaxed and become focused, repeat the affirmation aloud or to yourself over and over for five or ten minutes.

It can also be helpful to meditate while repeating "I, [your name], am more than either my accomplishments or my failures." It is equally effective while meditating to go through your positive and negative traits saying, "I am intelligent, but I am not my intelligence. There is a core me that's separate. I have an ugly nose, but I am not my ugly nose. There's a core me that's separate. I have a short temper, but I am not my short temper. There's a core me that's separate . . ." Continue listing as many traits in this fashion as you want. This will help you become more self-accepting and less tyrannized by perfectionistic notions of how you should be.

Exercises for Blocks Primarily Affecting Your View of the World

"Love Just Isn't in the Cards for Me," "I'll Never Get Another Chance," and "It's Too Late for Me; My Time Has Run Out" are all predicated on a view of the world as a depriving, punishing place where scarcity prevails. People with "God's Love Isn't in the Cards for Me" either view the world as a cold, chaotic place characterized by emptiness and absence of purpose, or as a place ruled by a creator who is cruel, judgmental, capricious—certainly not warm and loving. Overcoming these blocks ultimately means learning to see the world and God in a very different way.

5. Understanding the Origins of Your World View

If you see the world as a punishing, depriving place where scarcity prevails, it's because you learned to see it this way. Where did you pick up your world view? From parents? Teachers? Religious instructors? Books, comics, TV and movies? Take some time to think about what these various sources conveyed to you about the nature of the world and how it works. Pay special attention to your parents. How did/do your parents view the world? How was that conveyed to you through both what they told you and the way they behaved?

Many families have shared beliefs about the way the world works, and these beliefs are communicated to the children overtly and covertly. Were there any accepted beliefs in your family or neighborhood—beliefs such as "It's a dog-eat-dog world," "It's a jungle out there," "Eat first or be eaten," "Do unto others before they do unto you," "Get what you can now, because tomorrow everything will be gone," "The world is going to end any day now," "Life is brutish, nasty, and short," "Life's a bitch, and then you marry one," et cetera? If you think about it, some will probably come to mind.

Go back over your memories of childhood discussed in Chapter 19 and think about how your early experiences in life might have shaped your world view. If you grew up in a home where there was constant worry about money, you probably learned to see the world as a place where scarcity prevails. If you were frequently punished as a child, or you witnessed a lot of physical or emotional abuse, you probably came to see the world as a harsh, punishing place where bad things were bound to happen to you, and humiliation is the norm. If you are one of the twenty-eight million adult children of alcoholics in the U.S. today, or one of your parents was unstable or mentally ill, you probably came to see the world as an unpredictable place where something bad and crazy could happen at any minute.

The experiences that shaped your basic world view often won't be obvious to you. One woman we interviewed recalls her childhood home as a "very loving one" and her parents as "wonderful and tremendously giving." Yet she, the youngest child, grew up sharing a bedroom with her brother, who decorated it with military para- phernalia, while their two older sisters each had her own frilly lavishly done room. This situation existed until the children grew up and left home, but no one in the family ever questioned it. Of course, the younger sister grew up unconsciously convinced that her older sisters were destined to get the best from life, while she was fated to get by with very little. If you examine your own childhood, you may become aware of occurrences that have shaped your own view in subtle but lasting ways, too.

6. Understanding Your Image of God (Even If You Think You Don't Have One)

Even if you feel you don't have the "God's Love Isn't in the Cards for Me" block, we strongly advise taking some time to reflect on your personal image of God, where it came from, and how it has affected you. We all have our own image of God, which has been shaped by our life experience, the religious teachings we've been exposed to, images gleaned from ecclesiastical art and pop culture (*The Greatest Story Ever Told, Jesus Christ Superstar,* etc.), and the manner in which adult authority figures have treated us. Although you may not believe in God, it's probably true that these influences have nevertheless left you with a pretty clear picture in your head of the God you don't believe in, and this picture can still be a factor in your view of the world and life.

We tend to talk about God as if each of us were talking about the same being, but this is not so. These questions can help you get a clearer idea of who your God is:

Do you see God as a physical being having human or animal form, or as an etherlike presence in the cosmos?

Is your God a He or a She, or both?

Does God love us humans? Does God love *you*?

Does God in your view expect us humans to act a certain way and live up to certain rules? If yes, what are those rules and why is it so important to God that we follow them?

If God does expect us to live up to certain rules, how does He/ She react when we fail to do this? Does God get angry with us?

Become critical? Withdraw love? Feel personally hurt? Condemn us to suffering forever? If we die at a time when God is displeased with us, what happens to us?

Does your God forgive easily? Or does He/She hold grudges?

Does your God laugh easily? Laugh at all?

Is God always there for us? If not, is it because we've done something to make God withdraw, or it is because God is unpredictable and has other things on His/Her mind?

Once you've more clearly defined your image of God, think for a few moments about your mother and father. Think about the kind of people they were/are, and how they treated you when you were growing up. Think of the general atmosphere in your childhood home. Can you see any connections between the way your parents were when you were a child and the image of God you developed? Most likely, there will be many.

Go through the same process for other important adults from your childhood—uncles, aunts, neighbors, teachers, and so forth. Pay special attention to those who served as conduits for religious beliefs—Sunday school teachers, rabbis, ministers, priests, nuns, for example. You'll probably see connections between some of these people and your image of God, too.

7. Using Affirmations and Meditation to Revise Your View of God and the World

Just as we can learn to see our individual selves in a more positive and accurate way, we can also learn to see the world and God in ways that are more realistic and will make us better able to let love into our lives. First, identify your predominant beliefs about the world. These may include things like "The world is a scary place," "The world is a punishing place," "The world is a snake pit," "There's love in the world for other people, but not for me." Starting with the one that's most predominant for you, compose an affirmation to counteract it. Following the same steps you used for the "I don't deserve love" affirmation (pages 367–70), work on this affirmation for at least several weeks, or until you feel it's having a positive affect and changing your world view. Then go to your other beliefs one by one in the same fashion.

Depending on what your particular love blocks are, you should feel free to compose and use whatever affirmations you feel are best for you. But these are some of the ones that people with a negative world view generally find helpful:

The world is a good place to be.
The world is a place of bounty and beauty.
There's plenty of love in the world for everyone.
It's okay if I, [name], make mistakes or fail, because the world is a forgiving place.

Equally helpful are:

I, [name], am attracting wonderful, loving people into my life.
I, [name], belong in the world and deserve all the good things that are coming to me.
I, [name], am drawing more love and joy into my life each moment of each day.
I, [name], feel safe, at home, and at peace in the world.

For those who despair that a certain kind of love will never come their way, these kinds of affirmations are also very effective:

I, [name], am attracting wonderful, loving men/women into my life.
I, [name], will soon have a lover who is perfect for me in every way.
I, [name], am drawing the kind of love I want into my life.
I, [name], am going to be blessed by all the [familial or romantic love, or friendship, or loving children] that I want.

Again, these sorts of affirmations—indeed the whole idea of affirmations—might strike you as silly. But if you work on them in the way we've suggested, they really will have a positive impact on your life.

Try meditating on whatever affirmations you're using, too. Even if you can do this only sporadically, it will help. Use the ten-breaths meditation discussed on pages 346–47 in the same way that it's used with the other affirmations discussed in Exercises 2 and 4 in this chapter.

Since your view of God shapes your view of the world and yourself, we recommend that you do some work in this area, too. You can change your view of God as you change your world view, or you can work on these two areas sequentially. In either case, start by asking yourself why you must go on for the rest of your life with the image of God that you developed in childhood. Don't you know a lot more than you did as a kid, and have better judgment, too? Are you still completely convinced that your image of God really represents the "true" God? Or could it be that there are other ways of conceptualizing God that might be equally valid—and less self-punishing?

Now start looking for images of God that make more emotional sense. What kind of God would you like to have? What kind of God do you feel the world needs? You might envision God as a woman rather than a man, the epitome of gentleness rather than sternness, a being who is quicker to crack a joke than crack the whip. You might abandon the idea of God as a being altogether, envisioning God as an invisible presence, a light, a color, a flower, or the sky.

When you've found an image that appeals to you, do the ten-breaths meditation on pages 346–47, and when you're in the meditative state, try visualizing God in this new way. Stay with your new image of God for several minutes, then come out of the meditation. How does the new image of God make you feel? Do you like this God? Do you feel loved, warmed, and at ease in this God's presence? Do you feel close to this image of God? You might find your new image of God doesn't feel right to you. Don't worry; this is normal. Keep trying out different images of God, using visualization, until you find one—or some—that "click" for you, that feel right at the deepest, most visceral and spiritual levels of your being. Don't rush the process, but keep at it steadily, trying new images of God periodically—whether once a week or once a month. Over time, you should find one that works for you.

Some affirmations about God and your relationship to Him/Her can be very helpful in your search. Here are a few samples:

God is love.

God is loving, kind, and gentle.

God is watching over me, [name], every moment, with love.

I, [name], am a child of God, and God loves me.

God made me, [name], the way I am and loves me the way I am.

God and I, [name], will always be together.

God wants the best for me, [name].

8. Opening Up to the Natural World

Many people who view the world as a depriving place have such a deep and pervasive sense of emotional emptiness that the love of other humans, even if available, is not enough to counteract it. When there's this much inner emptiness, filling it requires learning to recognize and take in all kinds of emotional nourishment. This often means becoming more spiritual. It also means becoming more open to the world in the broadest sense.

One of the best ways to become more open to the good things the world offers is to learn to allow yourself to be more nurtured by nature. In nature, people feel more connected to the cosmos, more in touch with primitive spiritual forces, more whole, calmer, and more at peace. In what natural settings do you feel best? The beach? The mountains? The woods? The desert? Underneath the water near the ocean floor? Floating through the air in a hang glider? If you don't already know, find out. Explore the world around you a bit more. This doesn't mean expensive trips around the globe; it could mean simply taking an afternoon off and driving to the beach, hopping a train to the country, or walking to a nearby park.

How often do you go to the natural environment where you feel best? How much time do you spend there letting the natural surroundings nourish and replenish you? Chances are, not nearly enough. Identify where it is in nature that you feel best and make an effort to begin spending more time there, on as regular a basis as possible.

Many people find they become more open to the good things the world can offer by reaching out to members of the animal world. This might mean getting a pet, taking riding lessons, going birdwatching, or visiting the zoo. All these are effective, but getting a pet is often the easiest and the most immediately rewarding. Pets give many people their first taste of sustained, dependable, consistent love. Especially for people who have grown up unaccustomed to much love, it can be far less threatening to let in the love of an animal than the love of another human. Having a pet can also be very reassuring. No matter what happens in other relationships, each time you go home to a loved and loving pet, you'll be confronted with living, breathing proof that there is love in the world for you, after all.

9. Increasing Your Sense of Connectedness

This exercise has two purposes: to help you feel a greater sense of connectedness to other living and nonliving things in the cosmos; and to help you let go of the idea that you're unworthy and God loves you only if you are trying to live up to impossible standards of supposed perfection.

Think for a few minutes about the kind of person you are. Make a list of adjectives describing your central characteristics. This could include, for example, reliable, vulnerable, sweet, bitchy, stubborn, shy, clever, inarticulate. Be honest, including aspects of yourself that you both like and dislike.

Now turn your attention to the natural and animal world. Take one of your characteristics and visualize what part of nature or animal could represent it. For example, your reliability could be symbolized by a sturdy oak tree, your stubbornness by a granite boulder or a mule, your sweetness by a honey-producing flower, your cleverness by a fox or cat. Write down the possible connections. Let your mind "go" and allow others you've not thought of yet to enter your mind.

Now select one of the symbols you feel represents an aspect of your personality especially well. Close your eyes and picture it. For our purposes, let's assume that you're picturing a mule, which represents your stubbornness. Most of us tend to look upon stubbornness as a negative quality or flaw. We also tend to look upon mules as being rather inferior animals. But as you picture the mule in your mind, think of how God views it. God does not look at the mule and say, "What's wrong with you that you're so slow and stubborn and mulish? Why can't you be more like a horse?" God looks at the mule and sees precisely the animal He/She created, stubbornness and all. God does not condemn the mule for not being something else but accepts and loves the mule as it is. As you picture the mule in your mind, imagine God looking at the mule and accepting and loving it. Relax and let a clear image of God accepting and loving the mule come into your mind. Stay with the image. Believe it. Enjoy it. Now imagine God seeing the mule in you and accepting and loving that part of you, too. Often we think "God would love me if only I weren't so ———." But God is the one who made you the way you are, and chances are good that God accepts and loves you that way too.

10. Special Exercises for Those with "I'll Never Get Another Chance" and "It's Too Late for Me; My Time Has Run Out"

Related to our view of the world is our sense of time. This is very much apparent when we look at those with the "I'll Never Get Another Chance" and "It's Too Late for Me; My Time Has Run Out" blocks. People with these blocks not only see the world as a place where chances for love are limited, they also believe that if they haven't used their chances by a certain time, the opportunities expire. According to their view of the world what little love exists out there is getting scarcer by the minute.

A. *Understanding the Origins:* If you have one or both of these blocks, you most likely grew up in an atmosphere of impatience. You were probably expected to grow and develop according to other people's schedules—your parents', the school system's, the potty-training timetable in a child-rearing book, for example—rather than at the natural pace set by your own developmental clock. Very likely, your own natural pace was slower than the adults around you could tolerate; *hurry up and grow up* was the constant message. (See Chapter 10.)

Go back to the exercises dealing with childhood memories in Chapter 19 and take some time—as much time as you need—to think about how your early experiences may have shaped your sense of time. Do you remember being hurried to do and learn things? Were your parents frenetic people, always in a rush? Did they have a problem with punctuality? Did your parents blame you for making them late? Can you remember ever arriving somewhere late with negative consequences? For example, did you miss a bus or a test because you were late leaving for school, get to a birthday party so late that the cake was all gone, arrive so late for a movie that you couldn't catch up and figure out what was happening? Were you told things like "grow up," "stop acting like a baby," "act your age," and so on? (Very likely when you were told to act your age, you *were* acting your age. What your parents or whoever else said that really meant was "Act older than your age, because your appropriately childish ways are too much for me/us to handle.") Were you skipped a grade in school, or encouraged to perform beyond the normal expectations of your age group? Did adults often praise you for being "so poised for your age," "mature beyond your years," "like a little grown-up"? If you have either the "I'll Never Get Another Chance" or "It's Too Late for Me; My Time Has Run Out" blocks, you'll find some of the clues as to why by examining your early years with these sorts of questions in mind.

B. *Models:* If you have either or both of these blocks, there are probably a number of important people in your life whose emotional development seemed to end some time in their twenties. Perhaps they got into an unhappy relationship then and have stayed stuck in it since. Perhaps they reached a certain level in their career or job, and stopped caring about advancing or learning new skills. Perhaps they started drinking heavily then, and seem to have gone only downhill since. Whatever has actually happened to them, it's as though they got to a certain age and suddenly their lives were effectively over.

If you're to be able to continue your own growth throughout your own life, you have to become aware of who you know fits this description, and how their model has affected you. We're not recommending dropping such people from your life, just becoming aware of them. Remind yourself that they do not represent the only way; *you* can continue to grow and develop with each passing year. Actively seek out as role models individuals who have continued to grow throughout life, especially those who have developed new and healthy relationships and found satisfying work at late ages. You may meet such people personally or learn about them through the media, especially autobiographies, biographies, and novels.

C. Awareness and Respect for Your Own Inner Clock: Since you never learned to respect your own inner clock as a child, chances are good that you're still operating without respect for it. In fact, you may be unaware of your own inner rhythms and pace. Fortunately, it's not too late to do this. Start by paying close attention to how you feel at various times of the day, the month and year. If left to your own schedule, what time would you go to bed and get up? What times during the day do you feel most like eating? When you wake up each day, do you get going immediately, or do you enter the day very slowly? Does it take you a while to fall asleep at night, or do you go out as soon as you're in bed? When during the day, and month (this is especially important for women), do you feel most tired and most energetic? Become familiar with your own natural patterns and try to be more tolerant and accepting of them. You probably berate yourself because your internal rhythms don't match the rhythms of the external world, which diminishes your self-love and sense of feeling at home in the world. Whatever your particular patterns are, there are millions of people who have similar ones.

As you try to become more aware and accepting of your inner clock, pay special attention to how and when you naturally wake up and go to sleep. The periods of entry into and exit from wakefulness are critical times because they set the emotional tone for the day or sleeptime that follows. When you were a child, your parents may have been critical of you because your waking and going-to-sleep patterns did not fit their schedule. You probably have continued this pattern, perhaps berating yourself for not being a morning person, or for never being able to get to bed early enough. Isn't it time that you finally started accepting yourself for who you really are?

D. Patience: Those with the "I'll Never Get Another Chance" and/or the "It's Too Late for Me; My Time Has Run Out" block usually have a great deal of difficulty being patient. They're impatient with themselves, which diminishes their self-love. They're impatient with others, which creates problems in their relationships. If they have children, they're probably especially impatient with them, which will leave the kids with problems of their own.

If you tend to be impatient, you first need to identify when it is that you get most impatient. When you're waiting for a check in the mail? When you're waiting for someone you're dating, or your partner, to call? When you're trying to learn something and it's going slowly? When you're teaching your child something and he's slow to get the hang of it? When you're stuck in a traffic jam? Waiting in the checkout line at the supermarket?

Once you're aware of when you feel most impatient, now become aware of what happens inside you when you feel that way. Does your chest tighten? Do your pulse and heartbeat speed up? Do you clench your jaw? Does your breathing become rapid and shallow? Do your hands sweat? Do you feel dizzy? Do you talk very fast—and loudly? Since impatience leads to anxiety and panic, and anxiety and panic feed on themselves, learning to control these symptoms is key.

Begin by doing the ten-breaths meditation on pages 346–47. Practice this technique on a regular basis so that you really have it down. Then the next time you feel impatient and experience the inner racing that goes with it, immediately use the ten-breaths technique to slow and deepen your breathing. The other symptoms of anxiety and panic will disappear. Make it a habit to do this whenever you feel impatience and the anxiety and panic that go with it.

Very likely, you'll feel you're not learning how to be patient fast enough. As you make your first attempts to calm yourself down through the ten-breaths meditation, you may find yourself silently berating yourself with such comments as "Hurry up," "Let's get a move on, you haven't got all day," and "What's taking so long?" If this happens, counteract these statements with something like "Take your time, there's plenty of time," "Easy does it," or "Time is my friend, not my enemy." Then get the focus back on your breathing.

E. *Approaching New Relationships Slowly:* If you have either or both of the blocks we've been discussing, you probably have a tendency to want to rush headlong into new relationships, particularly romantic ones. You feel so much panic that each new relationship represents your last chance for love that you may come across as desperate and overly invested in the relationship from the start. You very likely have unreasonable expectations on the first few dates, and you may make demands that strike the other person as premature. In your rush to get love from this new person in your life, and get it *now,* you may end up scaring him or her away. This reinforces your inner belief that you'll never find love, which in turn causes you to approach the next new relationship with even more anxiety, desperation, and hurriedness. To break out of this self-destructive cycle, follow the instructions for going slowly in Exercise 14, pages 389–390. It wouldn't hurt to read Exercise 13 on pages 387–89, either.

For Blocks Primarily Affecting Your View of Others

Some love blocks have their most obvious impact on the way we view others, and the expectations we have of them. In this category are "I'll Inevitably Get Hurt," which is tied to the belief that others are sure to do us emotional harm; "I Feel Threatened When Another Person Gets Close," which stems from the notion that others will emotionally suffocate us; "I Just Can't Make a Commitment," which is based on the fear that others will abandon us once they really get to know us; "I Don't Want to Have to Ask for What I Need," which partly comes from the belief that others have a duty to read our minds; "I Want Love, But Only If It's a Certain Way," which is in part based on the idea that others should have to live up to our impossible standards of perfection; and "Why Do I Always Have to Give So Much to Get So Little?," which arises from a belief that the world is unfair, and other people will always take more from us than they give. It's also possible to include in this category "Anger Keeps Getting in the Way." While this block is really an extension of "I Don't Want to Deal with My Feelings," a key component is often the belief that most other people in the world are rotten jerks out to do us harm.

Although we'll be giving specific exercises for these blocks, if you've gotten this far and done the bulk of the exercises that have appeared so far, you may find that you don't need these new exercises as much as when you began reading this book. The fact is, whenever we have trouble in our relationships with other individuals, it's almost always because we're having more fundamental problems in our relationship with ourselves and the world at large—and often with God, too. Although they may be the ones we're most aware of, the blocks just listed are always ancillary blocks. Look underneath them, and you're sure to find a more basic block or two—such as "I Don't Want to Deal with My Feelings," "I Don't Deserve Love," "I Don't Need Anyone—I'm Strong," "Love Just Isn't in the Cards for Me," "God's Love Isn't in the Cards for Me," "I'll Never Get Another Chance," and "It's Too Late for Me; My Time Has Run Out." What usually happens is that when you work on overcoming these more fundamental blocks, your secondary blocks diminish automatically. If you're having particular trouble with one of the ancillary blocks, what you need to do first is figure out what other more fundamental block is behind it, and begin directly working on it.

11. Understanding Your Beliefs About Others and Relationships

Your susceptibility to the love blocks that are linked to a skewed view of others has a great deal to do with the kinds of ideas you were brought up with. What are your beliefs about other people? About human nature? What do you think motivates most people? Do you think humans are by nature kind and loving, or cruel and competitive? Do you believe that people are naturally warlike, or peaceful? Do you think most people are honest? Trustworthy? Interesting? Boring? Out only for themselves? Or concerned about others? Do you think some people are inherently evil, or "born bad"? Or do you think people are shaped by their environment and upbringing?

Also reflect on your beliefs about particular groups of people. Do you think men are superior to women? Or that women are better than men? Do you believe that all men are jerks, liars, or children? That all women are predators, nitwits, or incompetents? That all WASPs are conservative snobs, all Jews smart in school, all Hispanics hot tempered, all lesbians man haters? That people of a certain race or ethnic group are all criminals, cheats, cheapskates, and so on? That homosexuals are sick and depraved? That all heterosexuals are ho-mophobic "breeders"?

Identify the beliefs you have about particular sorts of relationships, too. Do you believe marriage or any other long-term relationship is akin to prison? Do you believe that love never lasts? That intimacy ultimately brings heartache, disappointment, and loss? That being close means giving up independence and privacy? That having a good relationship means never fighting? That after a couple goes through a marriage ceremony, something magical happens that allows them to just know how to live happily ever after? That having a child is the most emotionally fulfilling experience in the world? Or that parenthood is one big trial?

Once you've started to identify what your beliefs are, take some time to think about where they came from. From your parents and other family members, teachers, books, TV and movies, for example? From what other people have told you? How they treated you? The ways you've seen them behave?

Now go over the important relationships in your life and consider how they might have been affected by these beliefs. Have you had problems being trusting in romantic relationships because you believe things like "Men [women] can't be trusted," "Men will screw anything given the chance," or "All women want from men is their money"? Have you not let people get close, or pulled out of potentially close relationships, because you believe "people will just hurt you in the end"? Have you cut off potentially close relationships because of your belief that "once you let others close, you can kiss independence and privacy good-bye"? Have you ever created unnecessary havoc in a relationship by flying into a rage when someone failed to live up to your belief that "if another person loves you, then he/she should just know what's on your mind"? Do you get angry with people in your life and feel put upon and taken advantage of by them because regardless of what's really going on in your relationships, you believe "I'm the only one in the world who gives, others just take, take, take"?

Also consider whether some of your beliefs have caused you to write certain people off from the start. Love can come from a number of different sources, but many people reduce their chances for loving relationships because they'll only permit themselves involvements with a narrow range of people. Have you ever thought something like "I can't be friends with—or date—that person, because he/she's too old, too young, from the wrong class, a different religion, the wrong color," . . . ? Have you ever decided, "Well, I like so-and-so, but I can't become friends with him, because he's a Republican (or a Democrat), or Chinese (or German), or gay (or straight)"? Very likely, you have some prejudicial beliefs that are vastly reducing your chances for finding more love and having more fulfilling, interesting, and growth-inspiring relationships.

12. Using Affirmations to Change Your Beliefs About Others, Human Nature, and Relationships

You've probably come across several beliefs that are especially problematic for you. To help get rid of them, compose affirmations that directly refute them. For example, for "People are rotten," try "Most people are good," for "Marriage is hell," try "Some marriages are wonderful," and for "People with [color] skin are inferior," try "People with [color] skin are God's children, just like me." Then follow the directions for affirmations given earlier in this chapter.

It will be helpful to try to find some models to support these affirmations. People familiar to you in your own life are always best, but media figures work, too. For example, if you're trying to replace "All men are philanderers" with "Many men are faithful," it will be doubly effective if you can think of a specific man—or men—who have been faithful. (Paul Newman is always a good choice for this one.)

13. Finding New Relationships

As you become aware of the ways in which your beliefs have limited your chances for love in your life, you might want to form new relationships. This is a good idea so long as you think seriously about the kinds of people you want to be involved with. Most people who go "shopping" for friends, and especially for lovers and potential mates, come up with a very narrow checklist of criteria that they want the potential friend or mate to meet. Generally, the criteria focus on such traits as intelligence, looks, money, education, class, and so on. But typically, the checklist overlooks criteria that are actually far more important—such as emotional maturity, kindness, and the capacity for love.

We suggest that if you are looking for new relationships, keep two simple questions foremost in your mind: is this person a kind, caring individual who is capable of intimacy and love? And is this person capable of and interested in loving *me*? If you can answer both these questions with yes, it's fine to consider pursuing a personal relationship with this person. But if the answer to one or both is no, *do not* under any circumstance pursue an intimate relationship with this person. Even if this person meets every other specification you can ever imagine having, if he/she is not capable of love and not capable of or interested in loving you in particular, this is *not* someone you should be personally involved with.

But how can you tell if a person you're just getting to know is capable of love, and capable of loving you specifically? Of course, there's no surefire way to be completely certain, but getting a good sense is a lot easier than you might think. The key is to keep your focus on the quality of your inner experience when you are with this person. Do you feel really good, calm, and warm when with him/her? Or do you experience a tension, an anxious feeling, or a twinge of worry and despair? To get closer in touch with how you feel in this person's presence, spend twenty minutes meditating after you've spent time with him/her. Follow the instructions on pages 346–47, and when you are relaxed and in the focused, meditative state, visualize the person, then visualize him/her with you. What feelings come up for you then? Is it particularly hard for you to keep a picture of this person in your mind? When you visualize you and him/her together, does the picture make you happy and seem "right," or do you get a feeling of "uh-oh, there's something wrong with this picture"?

For most people who have been in a destructive or unhappy relationship, there was a time very early on when they had a sense that "this isn't right." Whether you use the meditation or not, pay attention to the innermost feelings you have at the beginning of a new relationship. Trust them. Very likely, they will guide you in the right direction.

A word of caution, however: if you have a history of getting into relationships with people who have obviously been bad for you, you may need actively to ignore your old "go ahead" signals. Especially if you suffered a great deal of hurt, deprivation, or loss as a child, it may be that there's a problem with your inner emotional wiring system; the wires for "love" and "pain" may have gotten crossed, perhaps inextricably intertwined, particularly when it comes to sexual or romantic love. As result, when you meet someone who is sure to cause you pain, the deepest part of your being picks this up but sends the wrong signal to your conscious mind. Your innermost self is screaming "Danger! Pain and hurt sure to follow! Run away!" but the message your conscious mind receives is "Love! Happiness to be found here! Pursue with all your might!" If this seems to be the case for you, you're going to have to understand that the feelings you usually associate with sexual excitement and falling in love are really danger signals. When you feel them, do not follow them, ignore them. This is not easy, and you may find you need professional help.

14. Forming New Relationships—Going Slowly

Once you've found someone in whose presence you feel warm and at ease, how do you go about establishing a relationship without getting either threatened by the closeness or overly invested too soon? The answer is simple: go slowly. In an era of instant intimacy, this is advice that everyone could benefit from, but it will be especially helpful to those who suffer from "I'll Inevitably Get Hurt," "I Feel Threatened When Another Person Gets Close," and related blocks. It's also advice that those with the "It's Too Late for Me; My Time Has Run Out" block would do well to heed.

Before diving headfirst into a swimming pool, you'd probably take a look to see how deep the water is, and you'd probably stick your toe in to check the temperature. But many people dive into relationships headfirst, only to find out too late that they're either in freezing water way over their head, or there's no water in the pool whatsoever. If this has been your experience, we suggest that when you start your next relationship, you take your time and allow closeness to develop in graduated steps:

In the earliest stages of a relationship, particularly a romantic one, focus a lot of the time you spend together on an activity—tennis or another sport, dancing, a concert, going to a museum or a movie. Pick an activity that you enjoy and feel comfortable doing, and that does not involve sitting for long hours over a table staring at each other and talking. That can come later. For now you just want to spend time in each other's presence, seeing what that feels like, without getting into revealing all the intimate details of your lives. This will help keep your anxiety in check.

In the next stage, increase the amount of talking, but try to keep half the focus on impersonal topics—politics, art, books you've read, and so forth. Share some information about yourself, but do not focus an entire evening on pouring out everything. Go slowly. Allow yourself to open up at a gradual pace, and allow the other person to do the same. If you find yourself with the impulse to blurt out everything at once, calmly tell yourself "Stop. That's enough for now. There's plenty of time." If you open up gradually, you'll feel far less anxiety.

As you begin to get into deeper and deeper levels of emotional disclosure, don't stop the shared activities. If you begin to do nothing but reveal your innermost selves each time you get together, you both might begin to feel frightened and overwhelmed, and one of you might pull back. So continue to go slowly, interspersing the "heavy" tête-à-têtes with lighter activities, like sports or museum visits.

But what about physical contact? Our advice is to go particularly slowly in this regard. Become friends before you become lovers. And when and if you get to the stage where you're both ready for sexual contact, don't jump in and do everything at once. Gradually introduce touching, kissing, caressing, holding into the relationship. Gradually get to undressing and genital sex. This will eliminate anxiety about having gone too far too fast. Savoring each stage will also make the sexual relationship more exciting.

This is not particularly sophisticated advice, but it's amazing how many people ignore it. And it's sad how much pain results. If you give yourself permission to go slowly and build relationships at a gradual, easy pace, there's no guarantee you'll find love that lasts, but you'll surely increase your chances.

15. Becoming More Open to the Love Already in Your Life

Many people who feel insufficiently loved really don't need to go out and find new relationships. There's no lack of love in their lives, it's just that they're not fully open to it.

Some simply can't see how much love is in their lives. They take what others give them completely for granted, not noticing when they're being given to. Are there people *you* depend and rely on without really being aware of how much they do for you?

Before saying no, take a few minutes to mentally review a typical day of yours, taking care to notice all the people you depend on and connect with, and who give to you in some way, as the day progresses. Include everyone, from your family, neighbors, and work colleagues to the kid who delivers the paper, the dry cleaner, and the bus driver. Try to develop an appreciation for all that others do for and give to you, even if these are only small things (like someone opening a door or saying "good morning" on the street). When people do things for you—even if it's part of their job, you're accustomed to their doing it for you, or it's something small—take notice and say "thanks," instead of acting oblivious.

Now look at those relationships that you realize you get a lot out of. Make a list of the people already in your life in whose presence you feel uplifted and nourished. How much time do you spend with those individuals? How often do you initiate activities with them? How often do you make a point of spending one-on-one time with them, rather than as part of a group? Do you ever plan special activities and outings with them—a hiking trip, museum visit, a play?—or do you always do the same thing, like getting together for a fast meal and a movie? Make an effort to spend more time with these people, and in such a way that will permit a real connection and continued deepening of your relationship.

In all your personal relationships, make an effort to really be there with the other person. So often we spend time in the presence of those we love and want to feel loved by—a friend, lover, partner, relative, or child—but we're not really with them. We're distracted, thinking about other things, not paying attention, only half listening, only partly there. When you are with loved ones, try to be fully present with them in the moment. Before, during, and after the time you're with them, pay attention to your breathing. Imagine yourself taking in their love as you breathe in, letting go of your love blocks as you breathe out.

Chapter 22

Continuing the Growth Process: A Guide to Further Help

The exercises and suggestions we've given so far are a constructive start for anyone wanting to overcome love blocks, but they don't represent all you can do—not by a long shot. Many readers will find they want further help. If this is your inclination, we strongly encourage you to pursue it, and hope some words of wisdom on psychotherapists, self-help groups, and other books to read will be of use.

Finding a Psychotherapist

You've probably heard that a lot of people who have become psychotherapists chose the profession because they had emotional problems of their own they wanted to work out. This is true, and for many the choice has turned out to be a fortuitous one. In the process of their professional training, they've confronted and overcome their own problems, and as a result have turned into excellent therapists with a great deal of empathy and insight. Unfortunately, not all therapists fit this category. Despite their training and degrees, some therapists have not confronted and overcome their problems, and remain emotionally unhealthy or disturbed. "Treatment" with this sort of therapist can be damaging, even disastrous. Since your own psychological well-being is at stake, we urge you to choose a therapist with utmost care.

But how can you find a therapist who can really help you with your particular problem and history? Some people simply look in the Yellow Pages and randomly select someone whose office is conveniently located or whose name strikes their fancy. This is not a smart approach. If you were told by your family physician that you had a brain tumor, would you select a brain surgeon that way? Of course not. Treat your psyche with the same care with which you'd treat your brain. Finding the right therapist is an act of self-love. It's also a wise investment, because the better the fit between you and your therapist, the more you'll get out of the process.

Start by taking some time to clarify why you're interested in therapy. What are the primary issues or problems you want to work on? Romantic relationships? Family and childhood? A vague sense of depression? Developing more self-esteem? Feeling less guilty? Of course, once you get into therapy, you'll probably end up delving into areas you hadn't considered in advance, but still, a general idea of what you want to work on will make finding the right therapist much easier. For example, if you want to work on intimacy and relationship issues, a therapist who specializes in eating disorders, phobias, or addiction may be a great therapist, but not the one great for you.

Think about the kind of person you'd feel most comfortable with, too. Would you feel more at ease with a woman or a man? Someone your age, older, or younger? Does it matter to you if the therapist is of a different race or comes from a different religious, ethnic, class and/or cultural background, or would you prefer someone you know has shared your own experiences? If spirituality or politics are a big part of your life, you might want a therapist who shares your own views. Similarly, if you're gay, you might want a therapist who shares your sexual orientation; you'll at least want one who is not homophobic and who is familiar with and sympathetic to your particular issues. Of course, you might not find a therapist who meets all your criteria, but if you have a better idea of what issues are important to you and what you're looking for, you'll be more likely to find someone close, and you'll be able to talk to him/her about your concerns in your early sessions.

The next step is to consider professional training. There are three main groups who qualify as professional psychotherapists today. Some therapists are psychiatrists. They've had full training as medical doctors, and they're the only ones who can prescribe drugs. Some psychiatrists are very pharmacologically oriented; in other words, their preferred method of treatment is medication. Some people wouldn't go to anyone but a psychiatrist for treatment because they think they give the best and most professional care, while others are of the opinion that psychiatrists make the worst therapists. It's a very individual choice.

The second group of therapists is psychologists. They've completed doctorates in psychology, and usually postdoctoral training as well. The third group is social workers, who have completed at least a two-year master's program. The training that psychologists and social workers have received can vary greatly. Having a Ph.D. does not necessarily make a person a better therapist than someone with an M.S.W. Ideally, both psychologists and social workers will have a broad-based training, have gotten advanced training, and be licensed by the appropriate state bodies.

As you consider professional training, you'll also want to think about an equally important topic—how much therapy costs, and how you'll pay for it. Psychiatrists are usually the most expensive, but therapists' fees vary widely, not necessarily according to training or ability. If you're planning to use health insurance to help pay for therapy, you'll want to find a therapist who meets the specifications set forth in your policy. If you're living on a budget, as most of us are, you'll want to find a therapist who is sensitive to your financial situation. Many therapists will adjust their fees on a sliding scale according to your income, and others are willing to barter.

Once you've clarified these issues, ask around for names. If you have a friend, relative, or acquaintance who has been in therapy, ask him/her to suggest some. It's entirely appropriate to ask someone you know to briefly fill in his/her therapist on who you are and what you're looking for and to ask the therapist for recommendations. This is an excellent method, in fact.

If you don't have friends, relatives, or acquaintances who have experience with therapy, or you don't wish to reveal that you want help, you can ask another professional whose judgment and discretion you respect. This might be your physician, minister, priest, rabbi, or even your attorney. Usually people in these professions have been asked for recommendations before and know some psychotherapists. They might even know some who have been quite helpful to people with problems very much like yours.

If there's no one you feel you can approach, probably the wisest tack is to look in the phone book for the name of your local mental health association. Call and request a list of names. There's probably a community mental health center in your area. Usually, these types of centers have numerous therapists associated with them, and these therapists have different training and different specialities. Often, such organizations will have a careful screening process to match you up with a therapist well suited for you. There are also local—city, county, or state, depending on where you live—associations of psychiatrists, psychologists, and social workers that you can call and ask to send the names of therapists and their specialties. These associations should also be able to direct you to therapists who see clients with minimal financial resources.

Once you've found a therapist—or several—who sounds as if he or she might be what you're looking for, the next step is to call and make an appointment. The goal of the first few appointments is for you and the therapist to assess whether you could develop a productive relationship. Use the first meetings—it might take several— to find out about who this person is, what his/her background is, and whether you feel comfortable working with him/her. Ask questions, not personal ones like where the therapist lives, but ones that would have a bearing on your working relationship: What kind of training does the therapist have? What kinds of clients does he/she mostly have? Does the therapist adhere to any one particular school of thought—is he/she a behaviorist, a Jungian, a cognitive therapist, or eclectic in his/her approach? Is he/she a feminist, or one who adheres to a traditional view of women? Does the therapist have strong views on religion, politics, moral issues, and so forth? Does the therapist rely on another therapist to supervise his/her work? In other words, will the therapist be checking out his/her reactions and insights regarding you with another competent professional to make sure he/she's giving you proper guidance?

Also pay close attention to the therapist's manner. Is he/she warm and relaxed or cold and stiff? Does he/she seem compassionate and reassuring? Does he/she seem to have a sense of humor? Does he/she seem vibrant and alive? Do you feel at ease in this person's presence? It's crucial that you feel the therapist is a kind, caring, trustworthy human being with a loving heart and a healthy attitude toward life. Remember, this person is going to be your guide on a journey into your innermost, most private self. Taking this journey with someone you don't like or feel at home with is not advised. You might want to do the meditation on finding new relationships in Exercise 13 of the last chapter, pages 387–89.

If you have the sense that this therapist is not right for you, tell him or her. A competent therapist will be interested in your reactions. He/she may learn from your comments, and decide to adjust his/her way of relating to you and others. A competent therapist will probably also pursue the subject with you, turning it into an opportunity for you both to learn more about each other. If the therapist reacts to your comments or questions in a defensive manner, refuses to deal with them, or criticizes you, *find another therapist*.

Also find another therapist if the one you see starts giving advice in the first few sessions. A therapist's task is to help you determine what your love blocks and other psychological problems are, why and how these developed, and then to guide you in finding ways to overcoming your problems in a manner that suits your individual personality and history. This is a process that takes time, a lot of time. A therapist who starts giving diagnoses and advice early on is being simplistic.

Once you're in therapy, make it a point to periodically review your progress and your satisfaction with the relationship. A competent therapist will not be averse to this; on the contrary, he/she will see it as an integral part of the process. A helpful resource to use is *Making Therapy Work: Your Guide to Choosing, Using, and Ending Therapy,* by Fredda Bruckner-Gordon, Barbara Kuerer Gangi and Geraldine Urbach Wallman (Harper & Row, 1988), which is available in paperback.

Finding a Self-Help Group

Many of the people whose stories we've told in *Love Blocks* have been helped enormously by participating in various self-help groups. Currently, there's a profusion of such groups in the country, many based on the twelve-step model developed by Alcoholics Anonymous and Al-Anon. If you feel a self-help group could be beneficial for you, by all means seek one out. It really can make a great difference in your life.

However, a few words of caution are in order. Although self-help groups can facilitate the growth process, they should not be regarded as a substitute for individual therapy. They can greatly aid you in your efforts to deal with specific problems—for example, addictions, compulsive spending and gambling, "co-dependency" in relationships, overeating. But if you have more general problems with love blocks, you'd be wise also to seek treatment that's tailored to your individual needs. In fact, because self-help groups often stir up repressed memories and a lot of buried emotional pain—this seems especially true of Adult Children of Alcoholics groups—having a therapist to turn to might be not just advisable, but necessary.

If you do get involved in a self-help program, beware of the tendency toward oversimplification that occurs in many programs. A favorite saying of ours is "When all you have is a hammer, the whole world looks like a nail." Sometimes people heavily involved in self-help programs fall into a similar trap, believing that every problem they experience in life can be explained by the fact that they're children of alcoholics, or incest survivors, or abuse victims . . . Sometimes they become convinced that every problem everyone else experiences can be explained by this one cause, too. The danger is that when problems are viewed in overly simplistic terms, it's impossible to find the appropriate solutions. Helpful as self-help programs are, remember they're based on broad generalities; each individual's case is usually a bit different and more complicated.

Just as we've cautioned you to find a therapist who is right for you, we strongly suggest that if you're looking for a self-help group you shop around and find one you feel comfortable in. Many people who have gone to various meetings say, "I don't feel that I belong here. These people are so different from me, so much more messed up." Often, this sort of reaction is symptomatic of denial: the person just can't face that he/she is as troubled as the people at the meeting. But sometimes people have this type of reaction because it really is not right for them. It may be that the entire program is wrong for them, or that they've found the right program but stumbled into the wrong meeting. Within the same program—AA, OA, ACOA, Compassionate Friends, and so forth—there's often a great variety in the meetings. Different people go to different meetings, and each has its own feel, tenor, and makeup. Don't dismiss a program on the basis of a meeting or two. Rather than conclude something like "AA isn't for me," consider that it might just be that a particular meeting that isn't for you.

SUGGESTED FURTHER READING

There are a number of other books pertaining to subjects we've covered in this one. These are some you might find helpful:

Buscaglia, Leo F. *Loving Each Other: The Challenge of Human Relationships*. New York: Ballantine Books, 1984.

Eichenbaum, Luise, and Susie Orbach. *What Do Women Want: Exploding the Myth of Dependency*. New York: Berkley Publishing Group, 1987; and *Between Women: Love, Envy, and Competition in Women's Friendships*. New York: Viking Penguin, Inc., 1989.

Fromm, Erich. *The Art of Loving*. New York: Harper & Row, Publishers, Inc., 1956.

Grant, Joan. *The Monster That Grew Small*. New York: Lothrop, Lee & Shepard Books, 1987.

Halpern, Howard M. *Cutting Loose: An Adult Guide to Coming to Terms With Your Parents*. New York: Bantam Books, 1976; and *How to Break Your Addiction to a Person*. New York: Bantam Books, 1982.

Lerner, Harriet Goldhor. *The Dance of Anger*. New York: Harper & Row, Publishers, Inc., 1985.

Katz, Stan J. and Aimee E. Lin. *False Love and Other Romantic Illusions*. New York: Ticknor & Fields, 1988.

Le Shan, Lawrence. *How to Meditate*. New York: Bantam Books, 1974.

Levine, Stephen. *Healing Into Life and Death*. Garden City, NY: Anchor Press/Doubleday, 1987.

May, Rollo. *Love and Will*. New York: W.W. Norton & Co., Inc. 1969.

Middleton-Moz, Jane, and Lorie Dwinell. *After the Tears: Reclaiming the Personal Losses of Childhood*. Deerfield Beach, FL: Health Communications, Inc., 1986.

Miller, Alice. *The Drama of the Gifted Child: The Search for the True Self*. Originally published in the U.S. as *Prisoners of Childhood*. New York: Basic Books, 1981; and *For Your Own Good: Hidden Cruelty in Child-Rearing and the Roots of Violence*. New York: Farrar, Straus & Giroux, Inc., 1983.

Napier, Augustus Y. *The Fragile Bond: In Search of an Equal, Intimate and Enduring Marriage*. New York: Harper & Row, Publishers, Inc., 1988.

Paul, Jordan, and Margaret Paul. *Do I Have to Give Up Me to Be Loved By You?* Minneapolis, MN: CompCare Publishers, 1983.

Peck, M. Scott. *The Road Less Traveled*. New York: Simon & Schuster, Inc. 1978.

Ray, Sondra. *I Deserve Love*. Berkeley, CA: Celestial Arts, 1976.

Rubin, Lillian. *Just Friends: The Role of Friendship in Our Lives*. New York: Harper & Row, Publishers, Inc. 1985.

Sanford, Linda Tschirhart, and Mary Ellen Donovan. *Women and Self-Esteem: Understanding and Improving the Way We Think and Feel About Ourselves*. New York: Viking Penguin, Inc., 1985.

Scarf, Maggie. *Intimate Partners: Patterns in Love and Marriage*. New York: Ballantine Books, 1987.

Trungpa, Chogyam. *Shambhala: The Sacred Path of the Warrior*. Boulder, CO: Shambhala Publications, 1984.

Wile, Daniel B. *After the Honeymoon: How Conflict Can Improve Your Relationship*. New York: John Wiley & Sons, Inc., 1988.

Notes

Preface
1. Louise Bernikow uses the term "intimacy crisis" in *Alone in America: The Search for Companionship* (New York: Harper & Row, Publishers, Inc. 1986).

Chapter 1
1. For examples of books of this kind, see especially Leo Buscaglia, *Loving Each Other: The Challenge of Human Relationships* (New York: Ballantine Books, 1984) and Erich Fromm, *The Art of Loving* (New York: Harper & Row, Publishers, Inc. 1956).

2. Sigmund Freud, *A General Introduction to Psychoanalysis* (New York: Liveright Publishing Corp., 1924).

Chapter 2
1. Sigmund Freud, *The Unconscious* (London: The Hogarth Press, 1915).

Chapter 3
1. Chogyam Trungpa, *Shambhala: The Sacred Path of the Warrior* (Boulder, Colo.: Shambhala Publications, 1984).

Chapter 4
1. Some of the ideas in this chapter were developed by Mary Ellen Donovan with Linda Tschirhart Sanford in *Women and Self-Esteem* (New York: Penguin Books, 1986), and further developed by Mary Ellen in "Emotional Rescue," an article published in *Ladies' Home Journal* (June 1986).

2. Philip Slater, *The Pursuit of Loneliness* (Boston: Beacon Press), p. 4.

3. The ideas in this paragraph are a condensation of those in "This is Definitely What I Want—I Think," by Mary Ellen Donovan in *New Woman* (March 1987), pp. 36–39.

4. Alice Miller, *For Your Own Good: Hidden Cruelty in Childrearing and the Roots of Violence* (New York: Farrar, Strauss & Giroux, Inc., 1983), p. 261.

5. Daniel Goleman, "Strong Emotional Response to Disease May Bolster Patient's Immune System," *The New York Times* (October 22, 1985), pp. C1, C3.

Chapter 5
1. Some of the ideas in this chapter are extensions of those first developed in *Women and Self-Esteem* and in a chapter written by Mary Ellen Donovan and Linda Tschirhart Sanford for *Everywoman's Emotional Well-Being*, Carol Tavris, ed. (New York: Doubleday & Co., 1986).

2. For further discussion of the inability to accept compliments, see Part Four, Chapter 7 of *Women and Self-Esteem*.

3. The concept of "shame-based" or "shame-bound" families comes from Merle A. Fossum and Marilyn Mason, *Facing Shame: Families in Recovery* (New York: W.W. Norton & Co., Inc. 1986).

4. William Masters and Virginia Johnson, *Human Sexual Inadequacy* (Boston: Little, Brown & Company, Inc., 1970).

Chapter 6
1. Nancy Chodorow, *The Reproduction of Mothering: Psychoanalysis and the Sociology of Gender* (Berkeley: University of California Press, 1978); Carol Gilligan, *In a Different Voice: Psychological Theory and Women's Development* (Cambridge, Mass.: Harvard University Press, 1982).

Chapter 8
1. Howard M. Halpern, *How to Break Your Addiction to a Person* (New York: Bantam Books, 1982), p. 224.

2. Ibid., p. 226.

3. C. Alan Anderson, *The Problem is God: The Selection and Care of Your Personal God* (Walpole, N.H.: Stillpoint Publishing, 1984).

4. For an interesting discussion of the way children perceive God, see David Heller, "The Children's God," *Psychology Today* (December 1985), pp. 22–27.

Chapter 10
1. *Newsweek* (June 2, 1986).

2. Ibid., p. 54.

3. The concept of infant time is developed in Halpern, op. cit., pp. 25–34.

Chapter 11
1. Robin Norwood, *Women Who Love Too Much* (New York: Pocket Books, 1986); Susan Forward, *Men Who Hate Women and the Women Who Love Them: When Loving Hurts and You Don't Know Why* (New York: Bantam Books, 1986).

2. A good discussion of this pattern can be found in Janet Woititz, *Adult Children of Alcoholics* (Deerfield Beach, Fla.: Health Communications, 1983).

3. Norwood, op. cit.

Chapter 13
1. John Wellwood made this observation in a workshop he gave at the Omega Institute in Rhinebeck, N.Y., in August 1985.

Chapter 14
1. Glenda Jackson as quoted by Madonna Kolbenschlag in *Kiss Sleeping Beauty Goodbye* (Garden City, N.Y.: Doubleday & Co., 1979), p. 74.

2. Bruce Weber, "Alone Together: The Unromantic Generation," *The New York Times Magazine* (April 5, 1987), p. 26.

3. Rollo May, *Love and Will,* (New York: W. W. Norton & Co., Inc., 1969).

Chapter 18

1. Daniel Goleman, "Sex Roles Reign as Powerful as Ever in the Emotions," *The New York Times* (August 23, 1988), pp. C1, C12.

2. Rokelle Lerner gave this definition in a workshop on adult children of alcoholics and intimacy in Boston, Mass., in February 1986.

Chapter 21

1. Sondra Ray, *I Deserve Love* (Berkeley, Calif.: Celestial Arts, 1976).

Index

FOR THE BEST IN PAPERBACKS, LOOK FOR THE

In every corner of the world, on every subject under the sun, Penguin represents quality and variety—the very best in publishing today.

For complete information about books available from Penguin—including Pelicans, Puffins, Peregrines, and Penguin Classics—and how to order them, write to us at the appropriate address below. Please note that for copyright reasons the selection of books varies from country to country.

In the United Kingdom: For a complete list of books available from Penguin in the U.K., please write to *Dept E.P., Penguin Books Ltd, Harmondsworth, Middlesex, UB7 0DA.*

In the United States: For a complete list of books available from Penguin in the U.S., please write to *Dept BA, Penguin, Box 120, Bergenfield, New Jersey 07621-0120.*

In Canada: For a complete list of books available from Penguin in Canada, please write to *Penguin Books Ltd, 2801 John Street, Markham, Ontario L3R 1B4.*

In Australia: For a complete list of books available from Penguin in Australia, please write to the *Marketing Department, Penguin Books Ltd, P.O. Box 257, Ringwood, Victoria 3134.*

In New Zealand: For a complete list of books available from Penguin in New Zealand, please write to the *Marketing Department, Penguin Books (NZ) Ltd, Private Bag, Takapuna, Auckland 9.*

In India: For a complete list of books available from Penguin, please write to *Penguin Overseas Ltd, 706 Eros Apartments, 56 Nehru Place, New Delhi, 110019.*

In Holland: For a complete list of books available from Penguin in Holland, please write to *Penguin Books Nederland B.V., Postbus 195, NL-1380AD Weesp, Netherlands.*

In Germany: For a complete list of books available from Penguin, please write to *Penguin Books Ltd, Friedrichstrasse 10-12, D-6000 Frankfurt Main I, Federal Republic of Germany.*

In Spain: For a complete list of books available from Penguin in Spain, please write to *Longman, Penguin España, Calle San Nicolas 15, E-28013 Madrid, Spain.*

In Japan: For a complete list of books available from Penguin in Japan, please write to *Longman Penguin Japan Co Ltd, Yamaguchi Building, 2-12-9 Kanda Jimbocho, Chiyoda-Ku, Tokyo 101, Japan.*